THEOLOGICAL
INVESTIGATIONS

Volume X

Also in this series

THEOLOGICAL INVESTIGATIONS

Vol. I
God, Christ, Mary and Grace

Vol. II
Man in the Church

Vol. III
Theology of the Spiritual Life

Vol. IV
More Recent Writings

Vol. V
Later Writings

Vol. VI
Concerning Vatican Council II

Vol. VII
Further Theology of the Spiritual Life 1

Vol. VIII
Further Theology of the Spiritual Life 2

Vol. IX
Writings of 1965–67 1

Still to be published
Vol. XI
Confrontations

THEOLOGICAL INVESTIGATIONS

VOLUME X
WRITINGS OF 1965-67 2

by
KARL RAHNER

Translated by
DAVID BOURKE

LONDON
DARTON, LONGMAN & TODD

DARTON, LONGMAN & TODD LTD
85 Gloucester Road, London, S.W.7 4SU

A Translation of the second part of
SCHRIFTEN ZUR THEOLOGIE, VIII
published by Verlagsanstalt Benziger & Co. A.G., Einsiedeln

This translation
© Darton, Longman & Todd Ltd. 1973
First published 1973
ISBN 0 232 51187 X

Printed in Great Britain by Western Printing Services Ltd. Bristol.
Nihil Obstat J. M. T. Barton, *Censor*
Imprimatur David Norris, V.G.
Westminster, 24th October 1972

CONTENTS

PART ONE *Ecclesiology*

PART TWO *Sacraments*

PART THREE *Eschatology*

PART FOUR *Church and World*

PART ONE

Ecclesiology

I

THE NEW IMAGE OF THE CHURCH

ON an accurate view of the findings of the Second Vatican Council one finds that in all of its sixteen constitutions, decrees and explanations it has been concerned with the *Church*. Thus in the ecclesiastical constitution *Lumen gentium* and in the Decree on the Church's Missionary Activity it has been concerned with the Church's basic understanding of herself. In the Constitution on Divine Revelation and in the Explanation on Christian Education it has been concerned with the teaching office of the Church. In the Constitution on the Sacred Liturgy it has been concerned with the function of the Church as conferring salvation through the sacraments. In the Decree on the Pastoral Office of the Bishops it has been concerned with the government of the Church. In the Decrees on the official functions of priests, the life and formation of priests, the religious orders and the apostolate of the laity it has been concerned with the various ranks in the Church's hierarchy. In the Decree on Oecumenism and in the Decree on the Oriental Churches the Council has stated its position with regard to the relationship of the Catholic Church to the other Christian Churches and communities, while in the Explanation Regarding Non-Christian Religions it has defined the Church's relationship to these. In the Pastoral Constitution on the Church in the Modern World and in the Decree on Mass Media of Communication the Council has defined the Church's attitude towards the secular cultures of the modern world, and in the Explanation concerning Religious Freedom it has stated her position with regard to a society that is pluralistic in character.[1]

[1] In this article the author attempts to sum up the more important ecclesiological findings of the Council insofar as these have theological and pastoral implications which are important for a wide circle of interested parties. It must be admitted that this attempt is subject to numerous limitations. For this reason the author may be permitted to refer to the fuller studies on conciliar theology which he has published in *Theological Investigations* VI, as well as in the present volume. In addition to these see below p. 7 n. 2.

3

I

This Council, then, was a Council of the Church about the Church, a Council in which all the themes discussed were ecclesiological ones; which concentrated upon ecclesiology as no previous Council had ever done. For even the First Vatican Council, with its definition of the primatial power of the pope, treated of other themes apart from this question and quite different from it, as for example the question of God and his relationship to the world. When we say that the Second Vatican Council is the Council of ecclesiology this is, of course, neither to deny nor to overlook the fact that within the general ambience of this subject-matter a whole range of different truths come to be expressed, truths which, indeed, when their place in the total 'hierarchy of truths' is adverted to, are of more decisive importance *in themselves* than they are precisely in their bearing on the question of the Church. But still, this does not in the least alter the fact that in this Council the Church was not only the author but the subject too of the conciliar statements, that this Council was the Council in which the Church reflected upon her own under-standing of herself.

This conclusion may at first sound harmless enough. Yet it is startling enough in itself to bring us up short; startling enough to raise in our minds the disconcerting question of whether in that case the Church of today, faced as she is with a future that is vast and unknown, and that presses in upon her (upon us) so urgently and so menacingly, has nothing more important to say than how she understands her own nature – she who, nevertheless, exists *not* for *herself* but for *God*, for her Lord, for *mankind* and for their future. Of course we might reply to this question that in speaking of herself and her own nature the Church is, in fact, speaking also of all these more fundamental realities and truths. Admit-tedly it is also possible to say that the 'Church' was chosen as the central theme because of the fortuitous circumstance that this subject had been embarked upon in the First Vatican Council and then interrupted when that Council was prematurely broken off; and also because, as things are today, everywhere and in all the Churches and all the systems of theology belonging to them ecclesiology has come to be one of the most immediately relevant subjects of discussion, if not actually the primary subject. But in fact the first reply simply opens the way to the further question of why the Church should choose to discuss these themes, more important as they are in themselves, merely indirectly in the context of ecclesiology, when all the time it is so necessary to speak in quite new terms of God, of

Christ his anointed one, of man and of his future. As for the second rejoinder, this still leaves the question unanswered of whether a Council is *ipso facto* taking the right course in its choice of subject-matter merely because this subject-matter happens to be precisely that with which contemporary theology is engaged. It could perfectly well be the case that by concentrating its interest so much on ecclesiological questions theology itself has created a tendency to neglect the more difficult and more urgent questions. This is a startling question, and one which cannot be answered adequately merely by pointing out that ecclesiology has in fact an objective importance in its own right. Nevertheless in the last analysis only two observations can be made in reply to this question. First, man is subject to the conditions of history, and this means that the topics with which he finds himself engaged are decided for him rather than by him. And this also applies to the Church. The very inevitability with which this theme of ecclesiology became, so to say, spontaneously and without much conscious reflection, *the* theme of the Council shows the extent to which man and Church, for all the responsibility they have to reflect and decide upon such matters, continue to be those who are guided and controlled by factors outside themselves. This is something that is both alarming and consoling at the same time. Alarming because it raises the question of *who* or what is really guiding the course of events in all this. Consoling because we sinners – yes and even the devil himself – continue to be those who are guided by God. Secondly, every recognition of truth – including those which the Church arrives at – comes about not because the subject has voluntarily raised the question for himself, but because of the pressure of factors outside his control and arising from the particular place allotted to him in history. And because of this such realisations of truth always remain open to further modifications in the future. The history of the Church's faith is still in process of development, and every statement of faith posited in the here and now, and truly posited at that, can be modified and transformed by factors belonging to a future that is still unknown. Thus such a statement may be changed once more into a question, the question namely of whether and in what way it can, while still retaining its essential identity, acquire a quite different form in different historical situations, and when viewed in different perspectives. With regard to a whole number of theological statements, therefore, the question is how will they be initially constructed and how will they be applied in practice. Certainly even a genuine truth can fail to be realised at the time appropriate to it, its *kairos*. Obviously this applies primarily to the process by which truths come to be recognised as such in the life of the individual. But we may presume that it is not so certain that this could not also take place in the history of the Church's developing realisation of truth. How otherwise could the Catholic Church, prior to a definition, and abstracting from her solicitude for the truth, raise the distinct question of whether the time is 'opportune' for defining the truth concerned and quite manifestly consider that to recognise a proposition as true is not *ipso facto* to decide that it is opportune to define it. So long, therefore, as history endures there remains also a truth that is still unexpressed in the present. The only proviso here is that there is a truth of this kind, such that it is not conducive to fulfilling the needs of the present hour. It is a truth which can be made relevant and actual through the grace of God which is conferred upon us, and in this grace we patiently carry this truth with us into the future until it finds *that particular* moment of grace in which it becomes *our* salvation. When *this* moment comes then it provides a justification for that earlier moment in which the truth concerned was plucked – perhaps too early, perhaps too late, perhaps too hastily or too violently – from the tree of knowledge. This is not to assert, or even imply, that the ecclesiological subject-matter treated of in the Council is of this kind. How could anyone be in a position even today positively to assert such a thing? Nevertheless it is helpful to pose this question right at the outset and thereby to make it serve as an exhortation to prudence and discretion.

If we are to speak of the new image of the Church which has emerged since the Second Vatican Council, then we must regard all this not indeed as a necessary presupposition to our discussion, but as a proviso which it is prudent to bear in mind. Statements made about the Church at the Council have been so many and so varied, some old, some new, some important, some secondary, some belonging to the field of dogma, others merely at the level of canon law or pastoral theology, that it is *a priori* impossible to sum it all up in a single brief survey in which every statement is accorded its due value. In the light of this, as well as in the light of the somewhat startling question which we have just posed, it is therefore justified – indeed it is actually demanded of us – to search for certain *new* traits in the image of the Church which the Church herself holds up before her in order to become that which she is. 'New' here does not mean, in any primary sense, that which has not yet been said, for it is difficult to point to any element in the ecclesiology of the Council which could be called 'new' in precisely *this* sense. A very clear illustration of the point being made here is provided, for instance, by the theme of the synodal collegiality of the episcopate (the theme, therefore which, on a superficial view, was perhaps the most disputed in the whole Council). On close examination this theme turns out simply to have filled out with content a statement which was initially made at the First Vatican Council in the *relationes* of the defenders of the primacy of the pope, Bishop V. Gasser and Bishop F. M. Zinelli in particular. Not only was the statement in question not contested by these, it was actually formulated by them in so many words as a manifest truth.[2] In fact a further point is also quite clear. Where a Council gives up a doctrine previously upheld in the Church but not hitherto defined, rejecting it as false or inadequate, we can certainly not speak of a development from implicit to explicit truth. And of course instances of this are conceivable. But we hold fast to the principle that the Church does not attain any fresh revelations, but rather retains a vital hold on, and interprets the *one* Christian and apostolic revelation. And if we hold fast to this, then it follows that any new statement that is *positive* necessarily *must* – at least implicitly – have been present in the awareness of faith of earlier ages. It cannot therefore be the task of the theologians merely to praise the novelty of a truth that has come to be recognised in the Council or in theology, as though something *absolutely* new had been discovered. It follows that 'new' as used here is a single term covering two distinct factors, and the reality it signifies is just as important as a new discovery on some theoretical plane. The two factors are the new vitality which the truth in question has acquired in the *life* and activity of the Church, and the special effectiveness which the truth will presumably acquire for the Church in the *future*.

II

The first trait in the new image of the Church which must be brought out relates to the Church insofar as she is present in the concrete in the local communities and regional Churches. It is a strange text to which we have to refer at this point. It is to be found in No. 26 of the third chapter of the Constitution on the Church, and there gives the impression of being an interpolation in a context which is elsewhere concerned with the function of the bishop in conferring sacramental consecration. In this context the following statement is made without any convincing connection with the rest of the passage being apparent: 'The Church of Christ is truly

---

[2] For details of this cf. the author's commentary on the third chapter of the Constitution on the Church. *Das Zweite Vatikanische Konzil. Konstitutionen, Dekrete und Erklärungen* I (Freiburg, 1966), pp. 221–224.

present (*vere adest*) in all lawfully instituted local communities of the faithful who, united with their pastors, are actually called "Churches" in the New Testament itself. They are' (so the passage continues) 'a new people called by God each according to his own locality in the Holy Ghost and in the fulness of "utter conviction" (*plerophoria*, cf. I Thess 1:5); through the preaching of the gospel of Christ the faithful have been "gathered" into the local communities.' Brotherhood is instituted through the Eucharist. 'In these communities, however poor and small they may be, and even though they may live in the diaspora, Christ is present, Christ through whose power the one holy Catholic and apostolic Church is united.' Thus the text itself.

It is true. The Constitution on the Church viewed as a whole regards the Church primarily as the universal Church, the Church that is worldwide, as the union of all believers in the community governed by pope and bishops. Certainly this is not to deny the fact that the very nature of this universal Church is such that there is more to be said about it than merely the definition of its social and juridical composition (somewhat in the sense of Bellarmine's ecclesiology), and in fact something more actually is said about the Church from this aspect, above all in the first and second chapters of the Constitution. The universal Church is spoken of as a unity which is based upon the mystery of the triune God. Reference is made to the holy people of God, to the Body of Christ in which all share in the priesthood of Christ, in which each individual has his own charism and his own mission, and each one is called to bear witness to the grace of God. But even so, in explicitly defining the structures and composition of the Church, the Constitution precisely does *not* take the local and parish communities as its starting-point in formulating its conception of her. Of course it is no part of our task at this point to enter into the reasons which caused *this particular* basic conception to be adopted, whether these were conditioned by history, by the particular circumstances of the time, or by theological considerations. Doubtless there are reasons which make this basic conception both justified and necessary. But while recognising this, one point must be emphasised from the outset. When the Church gives expression to her teaching, even in the context of a Council, what is binding upon the faithful is initially and primarily *that which* is actually stated. The viewpoints and attitudes in the light of which the statements were made have a lesser binding force. The basic conception of the Church which is derived from the idea of the Church as a whole is, therefore, a legitimate one, and certainly not one to be discarded. But manifestly it does not represent the only possible view. For in this conciliar constitution the *alternative* viewpoint, in which the Church is regarded primarily as it exists in the *local* community and this is taken as the starting-point, is also present in the passage we have quoted above, even if it is only present there in the opening clause.[3]

Here too it cannot be our task to present the history of this insertion. It is noticeable, as we have said, that it has been interpolated at a relatively late stage into a passage the broad outlines of which had already been established. In other words it was inserted into an already ordered presentation in which the viewpoint spontaneously and unreflectingly adopted was characteristic of the whole trend of Catholic scholastic theology and canon law in the post-Tridentine age. This meant that it was, as it were, taken for granted that the authors of this passage should look initially to the Church in her universality, and even the New Testament passages relating to the Church were *a priori* interpreted in this sense. With regard to the genesis of this inserted passage we must confine ourselves to the following observation: the interpolation certainly has connections (though probably these are not the sole motives which prompted it) with certain desires which were put forward in the aula of the Council, for instance by Metropolitan E. Zoghby and the auxiliary bishop of Fulda, E. Schick. Probably it was not only considerations of the factors of dogmatic or biblical theology involved that prompted these desires or imparted to them their underlying tendency. Rather they correspond to the immediate and practical needs of the concrete situation. There was a desire to see the Church as she exists in the concrete in everyday life, as present where she actually celebrates the death of the Lord, breaks the bread of the word of God, prays, loves and bears the cross of human existence, where she acquires a reality that is truly palpable and unambiguous, and is something more than an abstract ideology or a dogmatic thesis or the overall pattern of organisation in a society. There was a fear that *this* Church would still not be represented clearly enough even though now reference was made no longer merely to the pope, but to the bishops as well. These interventions were, in principle, welcomed and favourably received. Moreover the interpolated passage never became the subject of any serious debate or opposition either in the theological commission or in the plenary session of the Council. But at the same time it was impossible, if only from the technical point of view and from the point of view of giving the decree as a whole the best possible chances of

---

[3] On this cf. the author's observations in *Handbuch der Pastoraltheologie* I (Freiburg 1964), pp. 179–189, II/1 (Freiburg 1966), pp. 166 ff.

success, to reconstruct the whole of it in the light of this different view-point. And it was precisely because of this that, as G. Philips (the secretary of the theological commission) subsequently confirmed to me once more, a place had to be found for this passage wherever the matter could best be accommodated. The question of whether the happiest place for the inser-tion was in fact devised can be set aside. The essential point is that the passage is there and that it says what had to to be said.

The highest truth which can, in the last analysis, be applied to the Church as a whole is in fact asserted of the local community itself, namely that in it Christ himself, his gospel, his love and the unity of believers are present. The Constitution recognises and explicitly states that the local and parish community, so far from being a mere minor administrative subdivision in a major religious organisation called the Church, is actually the concrete reality of the Church, the presence of Christ in which she achieves her highest fulness, and that too in the word, in the Eucharistic meal and (even in evangelical theology this point may perhaps not always be expressed with all the clarity that could be desired) in the love which unites the hearers and those who celebrate the Eucharist. Of course it could not be expected that in this passage something further should also have been said, namely how these three entities are united among themselves so as to form the concrete actuality of the Church as presence of Christ. But at all events what does clearly emerge in this passage is that the concept of the Church as the 'perfect society' is quite inadequate to provide a basic model for a theological understanding of the Church. The Church is more than a perfect society not merely because in and behind the social constitution of the Church as a whole the Spirit, divine truth and love are present and are constantly renewing their vital impact. Even if we confine ourselves to the actual nature of society in itself, even at this level the Church cannot be confined to the idea of the 'perfect society' inasmuch as it is precisely the Church (in contrast to every kind of secular society) that is truly present and achieves her fulness at the level of the word of preaching and of the sacrament, that is, still at the level of the social and sacramental life of the Church in itself. In other words the whole is truly present and achieves its fulness in the part. Now in view of the fact that in this connection the constitution goes back to the linguistic usage found in the Acts of the Apostles and Paul, namely when it states that the community, e.g. at Ephesus is '*the*' Church and not merely *a* Church (the plural 'Churches' carries no weight in view of the statement '*Haec Christi Ecclesia vere adest in omnibus . . . congregationibus localibus*') we are authorised, and indeed called upon to explore further this ecclesiology of the local Church, and to accord it a vital place in our lives.

Certainly the work that still needs to be done in this field is immeasurable. But we should consider the future that presses in upon the Church, a future in which the premium set upon the characteristics present in the local Church, her poverty, smallness and 'diaspora' mode of existence, will perhaps be higher even than it is in the present. And especially in view of this future we can freely and calmly develop the lines indicated here by saying that life in the Church in the new form which it will acquire in the future will first, and by anticipation, be experienced *here* in the local Church. For the Church will make its impact as a present reality there where the presence of Christ is made real and experienced in the authorised preaching of his gospel and in the commemoration of his death in the Eucharist. *Here* that religious and theological 'experience' of the Church which is the most basic and most direct of all will have its place. Here the Christian of tomorrow will come to realise the true nature of the Church. Of course such a community, which feels itself to be the concrete realisation of the Church as achieved through word and sacrament, will be conscious of being united to all other communities which likewise are this same Church, will according to the will of Christ give concrete expression to this union, this state of being united in the Spirit with these other communities, even at the level of communal and social life as such, and, moreover, will be conscious of having a duty to do this.[4] It will understand by its faith that it only preserves the truth of the word and its own reality, in which Christ is rendered present, in the hierarchically constituted union of the communities of Christ. It will therefore acknowledge and live by everything which is stated in this constitution on the Church with regard to the universal Church as such, though admittedly acknowledging and living by it according to its place in the hierarchy of those truths in which, as the Decree on Oecumenism lays down,[5] the individual doctrines of faith are connected with the true basis of faith in different ways. But the factor which will first and last be of decisive importance will precisely be the real fact that, and the experience of the real fact that, Christ the crucified and risen one becomes present together with his word, the word that deepens into the unfathomable mystery of God; and because he is made present in this sense the Church

---

[4] It is self-evident that in a new way the early Church's conception of *communio* can thereby be made a living force in the practice of the Church. For bibliography cf. the studies referred to on p. 8a n. 2.

[5] Cf. this important passage in no. 11.

constantly renews herself as a vital force in the midst of the lowliness, poverty and desolation of the community which believes in him in the vast wilderness of this human life. All further knowledge of the Church will draw its life, and will only be able to draw its life, from this basis and this centre. The Christian of the new age will experience what happens to him in his community no longer – as formerly – as something that takes place *in* the Church, but rather as the impact of the Church herself considered as a vital force.

III

If we regard this fresh trait in the image of the Church in its significance for the future historical situation, then we shall also suddenly find ourselves in a position to 'place', theologically and existentially speaking, a second 'new' statement in the ecclesiology of the Council. This statement, if taken in any other way, commonly threatens to degenerate somewhat into an ecclesiology which seems primarily to be concerned with the constitutional structure of the Church. The Church is called the *sacramentum* of salvation for the world, that which gives it its union with God and within itself (cf. Nos. 1, 9, 48). In order to see why the understanding of the Church expressed in this key word *sacramentum* is of immeasurable importance for today and tomorrow we must first consider a certain dialectical tension between two statements in this conciliar ecclesiology which seem to be irreconcilably opposed. On the one hand it is laid down that every man who acts in good faith according to his own conscience attains to the salvation of God in Christ whether he is a Catholic or not. He may belong to another Christian creed, live according to the tenets of a non-Christian religion, or even, through no fault of his own, not yet have arrived at any explicit acknowledgment of God (cf. No. 16). On the other hand it is also laid down that the Church of Christ which finds realisation (*subsistit*) in the Roman Catholic Church, is necessary for salvation (No. 14), is prescribed for all men and all men for her. In addition to the dialectical difficulties entailed in these two statements we have also to bear in mind a further point. In the Decree on the Missionary Activity of the Church, in the Pastoral Constitution on the Church in the Modern World, in the Decrees on Oecumenism and on the Eastern Churches, in the Explanations on Religious Freedom and on the Relationship of the Church to the non-Christian Religions the Council certainly does not expect that in some way and in some future age invisible to us the Church will effectively become *the* Church of *all* men in the sense of including them all in a visible society. She is conscious rather of continuing to be the Church in the *diaspora*, the Church that exists in a pluralistic society. Indeed, according to all estimates of what the future holds for her, she will become this to a still greater extent than in the present. Now it is precisely in the light of *this*, and by taking *this* as our starting-point in interpreting the two dialectically opposed statements referred to above that we can elucidate for ourselves, in terms both of theological theory and of actual living, the situation in which the contemporary and future Christian's awareness of the Church must remain a living force, and against the background of which it must be understood.

This Christian must know the Church as the sole source of blessedness. Within the world he knows he cannot discern any one Church which, as a visible society actually belonging to human history, either is now, or is destined to become in some future age still invisible to us, the Church of all men. Yet for all this he cannot, indeed he must not, entertain that half explicit half submerged idea of the Christians of earlier ages that at least broadly speaking those are members of the Church who have been summoned out of a *massa damnata* of the rest of the human race, and called to salvation. Similarly he must not adopt that position of ecclesiological relativism which is secretly upheld by so many Catholic Christians, and in which it is felt that in the last analysis the Church is not so very important. After all it is only *one* – even if one that is particularly strongly to be recommended – among many religious groupings, so that it is open to the individual freely, and according to his own taste, to choose *that particular* one which precisely best answers his needs.

In the situation we have been considering the Christian is not helped merely by considering baptism, soundness of faith and conformity to the Church's constitutional laws as the 'orthodox' way of salvation, while in contrast to this innumerable individuals outside the Church achieve salvation in an 'unorthodox' way and one that is 'against' the general rule. For such a Christian sees at the same time that simply *in terms of numbers* this 'exception' is in fact the *norm*. If Christianity is Christ, the absolute deed wrought by God upon humanity, in which God bestows himself, then Christianity, and therefore the Church, cannot renounce the claim to be of her nature absolute and to have a mission that is universal. However, neither the Church nor the individual Christian can regard this interpretation of the Church (considering it as something more than a mere ideological hypothesis) as something that will only achieve reality in a remote future which is invisible to us. They must be in a position to recognise that the Church, considered precisely *as* a real and effective bringer of salvation (and not merely as a well-meaning and experienced partner in a dialogue) has a relationship with the non-Christian world which is actual and positive.

It is at this point that the doctrine of the Church as the basic sacrament for the salvation of the world may be invoked, since it serves to reconcile the two dialectically opposed statements which we took as our starting-point and to provide a common ground between them. If we take in all due seriousness this statement that the Church is the basic sacrament of salvation for the world we shall realise that what it is intended to say is this: the Church is the concrete historical *manifestation*, in the dimension of a history that has acquired an eschatological significance, and in the social dimension, of precisely *that* salvation which is achieved through the grace of God throughout the entire length and breadth of humanity. The relationship between the Church and this salvation of the world is the same as the relationship between the sacramental word and grace in the process of salvation which takes place in the life of the individual. In this process of salvation in the life of the individual these two entities are intrinsically connected but not identical with one another. Inasmuch as this process is subject to the conditions of time either of the two entities involved can precede the other. Grace can already be present when the sacrament has not yet been conferred. A sacrament, even when validly conferred, can still have to wait for its fulfilment through the grace which is signified by it. In the same way the Church is the authentic manifestation of grace in history, a manifestation which offers itself as salvation *universally* and to *all*, a manifestation which is indeed intended to be presented and borne witness to as a visible historical entity with a sacramental significance, and as something that can be described and pointed to in the explicit preaching of the gospel. But at the same time the reality of the Church is not *only* present where it has already fully achieved this status of being explicitly and visibly a social entity, the nature of which can be reflected upon and described, in other words where it is fully ecclesiastical in character and so itself as a part of the Church achieving its own unique impact as a concrete historical phenomenon. But for this very reason the converse is also true. The manifestation of grace which achieves this objective reality in the Church is a *manifestation* and a *sign of* that grace wherever it may take effect. In other words the Church as manifestation of grace is a sacramental sign of the grace that is offered to the world and history as a whole. From the Christian point of view the world, mankind and human history can certainly not be understood merely as the sum total of of all those individuals who are each working out their own personal salvations, or of the private lives of such individuals in so far as salvation is being worked out in them. If this were the case then there would have been no need for the incarnation of the Logos in the unity of the human race. All that would have been necessary would have been a purely spiritual message of God directed to the depths of the individual's own private conscience, in other words the kind of salvation history that is susceptible of a purely existentialist interpretation. But against this the message of salvation addressed by God to mankind considered as a unity in this sense has the character of an *archsacrament* or basic sacrament. It embraces the individual and his personal history but is in itself Christ or the abiding continuity of his existence in history which is the Church. This message of grace to the world, which has this quality of being a 'basic sacrament' does indeed take effect in the lives of individuals. Indeed it is intended to be brought to reality at the individual and sacramental level in the explicit word of preaching and in the form of the concrete sacrament. In the same way, in fact, this message of grace to the world, with its fundamentally sacramental character, is constituted by the common life of those who have received baptism and celebrate the Christian Eucharist. But this message, does not achieve its effective force only in those contexts in which it is given concrete realisation in the explicit word of preaching and in the sacraments, in so far as these are addressed to or conferred upon the individual. Grace can always take effect in the world even apart from the individual instances of the preaching of the word and the conferring of the sacraments, but wherever it does take effect this grace is already visibly being signified as an element in saving history as realised in this world in virtue of the fact that the Church herself has this force of being a basic sacrament.

So far we have only been able to indicate our basic position. But taking this as our standpoint we can achieve an understanding of a new 'experience' of the Church, precisely the experience that the Church is still the basic sacrament of salvation for the world in just those contexts in which the world is not the Church. The Christian of today and tomorrow will experience his Christianity as *ecclesiastical* by thinking of it not primarily and essentially as one of many interpretations of the significance of the world which compete with one another in the world's marketplace, not as a sum total of theories which are put forward at the same level as statements about the realities of this present world, so that the attitude underlying the Christian theories appears to represent a negation of these other speculations about the meaning of human existence. The Catholic must think of and experience the Church as the 'vanguard', the sacramental sign, the manifestation in history of a grace of salvation which takes effect far beyond the confines of the 'visible' Church as sociologically definable. The sacramental sign of a Christianity that is anonymous, that is 'outside' the Church in the sense that it has not yet realised its true nature, but at the same time 'within' the Church even though it has not achieved its 'ultimate self-realisation'. This is not because otherwise there would simply be no Christianity at all outside the visible Church, but because the Christianity that does exist there has not come to its full maturity as an objective entity, and therefore has not yet realised its own nature in the explicit awareness and reflexive objectivity of the creed as actually formulated, of the sacraments as supplying objective reality, and of the visible Church herself as providing an organised structure definable in sociological terms, all of which is, in fact, achieved in the Church herself.

The Christian will regard the non-Christians (in order to simplify the problem we shall set aside the question of non-Catholic Christians) not as having no part in Christianity or as standing altogether outside salvation because they are not Christians, but rather as anonymous Christians who do not realise what they truly are in virtue of grace in the depths of their own consciences; what they are, namely, in virtue of something that they achieve at a level which is perhaps wholly unadduced, but is none the less real; something which the Christian too achieves in that *he* goes beyond this and recognises what he is doing as a matter of objective reality in the reflexive processes of his own conscious thought. All this must be so if it is not the case that God, with a view to bestowing eternal salvation on men, suddenly permits their good will to count in place of the reality itself. For basically speaking this view would render invalid the doctrine of the necessity of the Church and grace as mediating salvation and not merely as something which men are commanded by God to embrace. Here, there can be no doubt. The awareness of the *professed* Christian, his faith as able to be formulated in propositions, as 'in conformity with the creed', is something that empowers him and actually obliges him as a matter of duty, to incorporate himself as a member in the visible society of the Church. And this faith of his is a part of Christianity in its fulness, and is a grace which once more facilitates and renders more secure precisely that which is already present in the depths of human existence and human awareness, so that it is this that he is actually acknowledging by his faith. There can be no doubt that the Catholic rightly feels and values his explicit membership of the Church as an unmerited grace, as a blessing, as a promise of salvation. But it must be admitted that in doing this he is also aware of a fear that plumbs the very depths of his being. For the greater the grace the greater the danger, and more will be demanded of him who has received more. Again he never knows whether he is in fact measuring up to what is demanded of *him* in particular, as distinct from others. He knows – this too can be accorded its due importance – the words of Christ which tell us that many will come from the east and from the west, but the children of the kingdom shall be cast into the exterior darkness (Mt 8:11 ff.). Again the Constitution *Lumen gentium* invokes a saying of Augustine[6] (No. 14) to draw a distinction between 'heartfelt' (*corde*) and merely 'corporal' (*corpore*) membership of the Church. The Catholic Christian knows that he belongs to the Church *corpore*. But *what he does not know for certain* is that he is actually *living* in it by faith and love. This is something which he can only *hope* for and which he must hope for. But because the Christian hopes for salvation for others also, because he is sufficiently aware of modern theological developments to recognise that he can hope for this (even if he cannot know it for certain), because it is easier for him today than it was formerly to conceive in theological terms of how it is possible to be a 'Christian' (here this is intended to signify a man living in the grace of God and of his Christ even when he does not know the name of Christ or feels compelled to reject him) – because of all this, *therefore* he can only regard himself and the professed Christians, the Church, as the vanguard of those who are journeying towards the salvation of God and his eternity through the roads of history.[7] For him the Church is, in a certain sense, the uniformed section of the army of God. It represents that point at which the intrinsic nature of the life of God made Man as projected into the world is also made manifest at the historical and social level (or better, is made manifest most clearly, since to the eye enlightened by faith the grace of God is not totally devoid of all embodiment even outside the Church). The Christian knows that the light of morning on the mountains is the beginning of the day that lights up the valleys. It is not a day that is confined to the higher levels, and so condemns the darkness below.

We may recall the Christian teaching that there is no absolute principle

[6] For a detailed exegesis of this section of the Constitution on the Church cf. K. Rahner, 'The Sinful Church in the Decrees of Vatican II', *Theological Investigations* VI (London and Baltimore, 1969), pp. 270–294, especially pp. 282–283.

[7] For the purposes of this study the author has permitted himself in what follows to take over word for word certain observations which he has already published in an earlier volume: 'Dogmatic Notes on Ecclesiological Piety', *Theological Investigations* V (London and Baltimore 1966), pp. 336–365.

of evil, that evil is that which is not, that the one unique God is good, and that he wills what is good for the Church as well, that that which is real is also the good, so that it follows that a true realist must think well of reality. The Christian knows that it would be blasphemous to suppose that in the last analysis it is easier to do evil than good, or that on a 'sober' and realistic view of reality it is the evil that is in possession there and not the good, or that ultimately speaking evil will survive when good has disappeared. The Christian knows that it is not the humility of the creature but rather its pride that prompts such ideas, or that makes it suppose that it is able, at least by embracing the evil, to emancipate itself from God, for this is simply a stupid lie. The Christian knows that in fact it is precisely the achievement of his own existence that is demanded of him; to believe in the light when he is in the darkness, to believe in blessedness when he is in pain, to believe in God as the absolute in the midst of the relativity to which he is subject. He knows that revelation in its progressive unfolding lays bare our sins to us only in order that we may believe in the forgiveness of God. (Guilt *alone* and taken by itself is something that we could already have experienced in our pain, our death and our powerlessness to escape). When Paul regards the unbelief of the Jews as only temporary (Rom 9–11) we may ask how this is to be interpreted at least in a theology which, while it wants to do Paul full justice, can no longer think simply in 'collectivist' terms. This statement should not lead us to credit Paul with the opinion that it was only later generations of Jews who would be believers, while the earlier ones remained *totally without faith in any sense*. Only one who is 'collectivist' to the point of being unchristian can suggest this kind of uncompromising solution to the question. In Paul's own thought an idea which he held firm to, and which constituted the inner kernel of his own personal conviction, was that the grace of God would emerge victorious over 'unbelief'. He himself may or may not have regarded the process by which this was to be accomplished as already having explicitly and definitively attained its full development. But in any case it makes no difference to the point at issue how far he did actually hold this view. The faith of the people of Israel, which became manifest as a phenomenon only in their later history (admittedly even this is still not apprehensible to us in any assured sense as a predestination of the individual to salvation), must be a sign of the fact that in earlier ages too God had already had compassion on this people in a manner which we can neither discern nor comprehend (once more nothing definite is implied in this with regard to the salvation of the individual as such). For why otherwise should we take as the defining characteristic of Israel as a whole the faith of her later stages of development and not the unbelief of her earlier period? How otherwise could it be preferable to say: 'Israel as such will be overtaken by God's grace' rather than: 'This people has rejected God'?

In the light of this the Christian is fearless and untroubled in the view he takes of the world – that world which is filled with a thousand opinions and philosophies of life. He does not need anxiously to scrutinise the statistical data to see whether, not only in theory but in actual fact as well, the Church is the greatest organisation based on a philosophy of life, or whether her rate of growth is in proportion to that of the world population. Certainly he will regard the world with missionary zeal. And this is a point which is also included in the Constitution on the Church and the Decree on the Missions. These are especially concerned to ensure that the quite astonishingly optimistic note they strike with regard to the salvation of the world shall not obscure the need for the Church's missionary activities or weaken the missionary zeal of Christians. In this connection one question may be left open as not to be treated of here, that namely of whether we have already arrived at the clearest possible 'synthesis' between this optimism with regard to salvation and the inalienable duty of Christians to be missionaries of the gospel. In any case the Christian will bear witness to the name of Christ. He will be resolved to impart his grace to others, for he possesses a grace of which those others are deprived – are *still* deprived, precisely the grace namely of belonging to the Church *corpore* and not merely *corde*. Only when they have this grace will they actually be contributing to that basic sacramental sign that is the Church. Moreover it is this grace that summons the entire world to make space in human living in its dimensions of freedom and of physical concretion too for that divine life which has all along been at work at the very roots of human nature as the offering of God to communicate himself to man regardless of whether this offering is accepted or refused. It is this grace too which not only impels history forward to that blessedness in which its ultimate consummation is to consist, but is also intended to be incarnate in history itself in full measure and in manifest form. But the Christian is aware of a further point. His zeal has the greatest chance of success when his enthusiasm for his missionary vocation is tempered by calmness and patience. He knows that he must imitate the patience of God (which, according to Paul, is positively salvific rather than condemning in its meaning). He knows that God has willed this world to be as it is because otherwise it would not be at all, and that even that which is 'merely' *permitted* is simply permitted precisely as an element in something that is willed (and not merely permitted) by God. He knows further that this which is willed by God can and must be hoped for not merely as the revelation of God's justice but also as the revelation of his infinite kindness to man.

The Christian knows that God does not begin the work of his grace only at that stage at which man takes it up in the name of God. For this reason, when he is faced with one who, so far as his 'philosophy of life' is concerned, has no intention of being a brother, the Christian nevertheless goes to meet him boldly and hopefully as a brother. He sees in him one who does not know what he truly is, one to whom it has not yet been made plain what he nevertheless may be presumed already to be achieving in the depths of his own human living. (So true is this that we have an absolute duty to assume this in hope, and it would be a failure in charity to hold anything less about the non-Christian, for should I as a Christian simply and absolutely take it for granted that the non-Christian with whom I am in contact is devoid of God's grace?). In his fellow the Christian sees Christianity in its 'anonymous' or unacknowledged form at work in a thousand ways. He knows that man is always more and always achieves more in his human living than he himself can express. Ultimately speaking the reality of our existence as humans always goes beyond the interpretations we ourselves place upon it in theory. Now if the Christian recognises all this then he cannot consider it rash or out of place to assume that even though the non-Christian interprets himself quite *otherwise*, still by God's grace some kind of 'unacknowledged Christianity' is already present in him or even is actually, though all unconsciously, being put into practice. If the Christian interprets his own *self* (rightly understood) as *simul justus et peccator*[8] or as, arising from this, *simul fidelis et infidelis*,[9] even though he intends to be a *fidelis* and only this, then it is no impertinence either if he interprets the non-Christian as one who is perhaps *simul fidelis* even though he intends to be only an *infidelis*. If the Christian sees that the non-Christian is kind, charitable and true to his own conscience he will no longer be able to say nowadays 'All those are "natural" virtues,' for in fact, ultimately speaking, these only exist *in abstracto*. He will no longer say: This is certainly just the 'outward brilliance which the vices of the pagans display', as Augustine does. On the contrary he will think, 'There the grace of Christ is at work even

[8] On this cf. K. Rahner, 'Justified and Sinner at the Same Time', *Theological Investigations* VI (London and Baltimore 1969), pp. 218–230.

[9] On this cf. J. B. Metz, 'Unbelief as a Theological Problem', *Concilium* 6/1 (1965), pp. 32–42.

in one who has not yet explicitly called upon it but who, at the same time, has already hungered after it in the unexpressed and unacknowledged longings of his heart. There is one in whom the unspeakable groanings of the Spirit have already called in supplication upon the silent but all-pervasive mystery of existence which we Christians know as the Father of our Lord Jesus Christ!' Supposing that the Christian sees the 'heathen' dying willingly. Supposing that he notices how the other willingly submits, as though no other course were open to him (Oh yes, another course *is* open to him, for he can summon up the ultimate resources of his entire existence and use them to assume a last and absolute attitude of protest and absolute cynicism and doubt) to a death in which he falls into the bottomless abyss which has never been plumbed to the full (because in order to include God it must be infinite). Supposing that the Christian himself recognises in this basic willingness of the non-Christian, which is no longer an articulate attitude at all, that this abyss into which the non-Christian is falling is the abyss of a meaningful mystery and not of a despairing void. If the Christian sees all this then he sees also in one who is dying in this way him who is nailed to the saving cross of human existence *at the right hand* of Christ. And he sees that precisely *this* real situation in the concrete, in which this dying man finds himself, wordlessly utters the plea 'Lord remember me when you come into your kingdom'. Why should it not be so? The sheer transcendence of human nature need not always be used as a mere means with a view to asserting one's right to earthly existence. It can be accepted and endured, and then it can also be elevated by grace in such a way that, liberated from its downward tendency towards the finite, it becomes the dynamic impulse that urges us upwards towards the God of eternal life, inasmuch as he, in the ultimate reality of his own nature, considered as that which has been communicated and is to be communicated further, is the ultimate goal and destiny towards which man is supernaturally directed. This orientation towards God implanted in the spiritual transcendence of man by grace goes beyond his nature and liberates him from his earthly bent. Moreover it is sound Thomistic doctrine that it also alters the final goal, the 'formal object' of what the spirit can achieve. And because of this, even though it may not actually set any new object before man's vision it is *in actual reality* a 'revelation', and that too not a 'natural' revelation but one that is grace-given. Moreover in the sense that as revelation it is 'uttered' by God to man on the level of his freedom and personhood it can already be considered 'verbal' and, in so far as it is accepted at this level, as faith.

We are dealing, therefore, with the submission of a man in obedience and love to the infinitude of his own transcendence as to something which is beyond his control. Man submits himself to this transcendent dimension in his own being not in the measure that it can be grasped by us, but rather in the measure that we are grasped and contained by it as something beyond our control. Now if this is so, why should not this attitude of obedient and loving submission on the part of the individual be so transformed, even in the present by the ordinations of God's will to bestow supernatural salvation on men, as to become something more than merely the spiritual transcendence which is in this sense natural to man? Why should not God bring it about by his own act that this spiritual transcendence *de facto* becomes in us that interior tendency which draws us into the life of God? And supposing the individual accepts this tendency implanted in him in the sense that he willingly submits to the control of that which he cannot comprehend in its incomprehensibility, why should not this be enough? (Is it really necessary to insist that of course all the demands of natural and supernatural ethics are to be thought of as implicitly contained in this, though admittedly only in such a way that their authentic orientation to God can be achieved 'subjectively' speaking in the concrete life of the individual even in those cases in which the most far-reaching errors at the material level with regard to particular moral norms are to be found?[10] This is something which is shown in the experience of Christians as well as that of heathens).

Now on this showing, when the Christian preaches Christianity to the 'non-Christian' he will take as his starting-point not so much the basic attitude of wanting to make the other something which he simply has not been hitherto. Rather he will attempt to bring him to himself. Of course this cannot mean that Christianity is, as the modernists hold, simply the explicitation of the religious needs of man's nature. Rather it is because God in his grace, and because of his will to save all men universally, has already long before *offered* the reality of Christianity in its truest and deepest essence to the individual, and because it is perfectly possible, and even probable, that the individual has already freely accepted this reality without consciously adverting to it. These, then, are the factors which will influence the Christian of today and tomorrow in his view and experience of the Church. He will think of it not as making itself felt only infrequently and with difficulty, not as one of the numerous 'sects' into which mankind is divided, not as one of many elements in the pluralism

[10] On this cf. K. Rahner, *Handbuch der Pastoraltheologie* II/1 (Freiburg 1966), pp. 152 ff.

of society or the pluralism in the intellectual life of mankind. Instead of this the Christian will think of the Church rather as the visible and apprehensible form of that which already has a unifying force at the interior level, as the historical expression of that which is universal to all men and, in a true sense, evident to all (for all that it has been freely instituted by God, for it is precisely God and not any particular finite being which has instituted it!). The Church appears to the Christian as the sheer rendering present in visible form of the nature of man as subject to God's designs (that is, the nature of man as it exists in 'historical fact', and to which a supernatural calling has been vouchsafed). In short the Church appears to the Christian as the fundamental *sacrament* of a grace which, precisely because it is offered to all, presses forward to express its sacramental significance in history even where the individual sacrament (of baptism) has not yet been conferred. But precisely on this view of the Church this grace is never simply *identical* with that which constitutes its effective sign. Rather, in virtue of the particular concrete sign which it institutes in the present, and through which it is itself made present (both aspects must be expressed) it assures us that its power extends *everywhere*. We can say in all calmness: through the sign of the particular sacrament as it is conferred the grace of God assures us that its power extends everywhere, even to those areas where the specific sacramental sign has not yet been applied as such in the concrete to those specific individuals in whom we hope that the grace of God will powerfully take effect. For these individual sacramental signs taken together (and in unison with other factors contributing to the Church's make-up) precisely constitute the Church, since she is, in fact, the community of those who have been baptised and who celebrate the Eucharist. But in virtue of the fact that she is the *sacramentum* of salvation for the world, she is also the promise of grace to it. It must be remembered that the history of mankind is *one and single*, so that there is an intrinsic unity between everything that it contains from Abel to the last living human being, and each individual has a connection with all the rest, not merely those living at the same time or in the same place as himself, but with all human beings right through the ages. Now if this is accorded its due significance then the Church is to be thought of as the leaven working through the lump of dough that is the whole of humanity. And its influence is not confined to that particular part of the 'dough' where it can actually be seen taking effect and so which has itself been turned into an active element in the process of fermentation. On the contrary the leaven that is the Church is at work everywhere and for all. Its influence is extended to every age and is present precisely in those parts of the flour which, so far as we can see, have not yet been turned into leavened dough. To the kind of Christian whom we have in mind, therefore, and who belongs to the new image of the Church, the Church herself will appear as a promise extended to the world outside the Church. And this is true not only on the condition that, or to the extent that, this world has already itself come to belong to the Church. The promise is not only an assurance that this world will increasingly come to belong to the Church, but is the real hope that it will be possible for the world to be redeemed through the Church even in those areas of it where its inclusion in the Church has not acquired the status of a palpable fact of history.

IV

It is only in the light of this that we can clearly recognise the ultimate basis for that collegiate and synodal principle in the Church which figured so prominently in the discussions and teaching of the Council. This principle is the love of those who are united in Christ and so equal. And this is also the basis for all the hierarchical differences that exist in the Church. Of course that unity of love in the Spirit, that state of brotherhood which is a gift of God, was, in itself, always the centre and goal of the message of the gospel and the ministry of the Church. For she has always known and preached that the love of God and the love of neighbour fall under one and the same commandment, and constitute the one grace which justifies. And yet this truth, so obvious and yet so far beyond our comprehension, which constitutes the mystery of our existence, exercises in a manner that is quite new a determining influence upon the image of the Church and the Church's life of worship for the future.

We may regard the usual talk about the contemporary society of the masses as false, one-sided or premature. Nevertheless this term does point to a danger, the danger namely that precisely because of the ever-widening social interconnections in which the individual is inescapably involved, because of the constantly increasing influence of social forms and systems which arise, because of the increasing insignificance accorded to human life and because of the fact that in his function in society the individual is increasingly involved in specialisation, the individual himself no longer finds any concrete 'thou', any room for intimate relationships with his fellows. The only relations open to him are such as bring him a sense of abandonment and loneliness. He has a sense of being a tiny and anonymous cog with a function to perform in a huge social machine, a cog which can be replaced at any time. Of course independently of the Church and outside the Church's sphere of influence counter forces are already at work against this danger, and new kinds of informal groups are arising in society which make it possible for man to draw near to man and so protect himself agains this state of desolation. Certainly the family will only truly come into its own when it acquires that significance which is at once most ancient and most new, of being the sphere of a love that is personal and proper to the individuals within it. But precisely for this reason the Church too, as she exists at the local level, can acquire a quite new importance as the community of those who, gathered about the altar of Christ, are united by love among themselves. This will be achieved precisely in so far as the local Church of the future no longer appears primarily as the operator of administrative techniques on behalf of a vast institutional organisation designed to cater authoritatively for the spiritual wellbeing of the individual. The Church at the level of the local community will be the community of those who freely believe, of those who have taken their own personal decision. For these baptism is the expression and manifestation of the grace of a faith that is actually put into practice, or at least of acceptance into a family and community of believers in which the faith of the rising generation can really mature as something which they have committed themselves to of their own personal initiative. In such a community that brotherhood will be able to flourish which has its basis in Christ. This future community of the faithful must certainly not be sectarian in character, the sort of community, that is to say, which sullenly and fearfully takes shelter in the shadowy places of history and society like a little group of social inadequates. If such a community experiences its own significance as a sacrament of salvation for the world it can never fail to recognise its task of bearing witness, its function of being the salt of the earth and the leaven of the world, or its mission extending into all spheres of human life. But it can really experience itself as a community united by ties of brotherhood in Christ.

Measured by the physical, indeed the ideological strength of the future world powers or of *the* future world power in the singular, the universal Church will also find that it has less power than ever within its own sphere of human history, if we take power to signify the possibility of exercising a decisive influence over the individual in other areas of life apart from those of truth and love. While, therefore, we must obviously recognise the spiritual authority of the pastors and officials of the Church, these will be thought of in the future precisely not as vested with power in the social dimension, the sort of power, namely which would be really and effectively present independently of and prior to the faith, loyalty and trust of the members of the Church. The authority that goes with an official position in the Church stems from the mission of *Christ himself*. And this means that its real significance springs uniquely from that love that binds together those who are united among themselves as equal, as having been sanctified, and as sharing in community with one another the living experience of the love of Christ. Under these circumstances laity and pastors can become accustomed to meet and exchange ideas as members of a family, and it is this that is spoken of in the Constitution on the Church (No. 37). This is the love which unites the brethren who are one in their belief in the *one* Lord who sets them free for the incomprehensible and blessed infinitude of God. It is the deepest and most essential factor in their lives as Christians, and it will, much more clearly and much more directly than formerly, subsume, permeate and assimilate to itself all those institutional factors which necessarily must endure. In this community the unity between love of God and love of neighbour will be experienced in a quite new way. God will not be reduced to the level of the human by a process of demythologising. But because the fact of God becoming man is so central to Christianity, God will be found in man and man himself will be discovered anew as the mystery which projects out and beyond itself into the mystery of God. Thus man will find his true nature only in that which he himself is not, yet in such a way that when it is accepted in a spirit of love, it allows him to experience what is truly meant by God. Admittedly at first we have only weak and indistinct ideas of how such a community, formed by the new spirit of love of God and love of neighbour, will appear in the concrete; how a Church formed by love in this way will express her communal worship, seeing that she is neither a clan constituted by the local community with religious trimmings added to it, nor yet a cosy sectarian nest where the socially frustrated can take shelter, nor (and this is the mistake most often made today) an extremely select department-store of holiness in which the individual obtains moral strengthening for the wellbeing of his individual soul, and in doing this merely makes allowance for the fact that many are simultaneously claiming the services of this department-store, so that in fact, in this extremely individualistic interpretation of its purpose the Church's function as serving the community is made subordinate to its function as catering for the individual. The community of the new Church must be a community of love, and love is extremely practical. But it is better for us to admit to ourselves in all honesty that as yet we hardly know what outward shape a community living by practical love in this way can assume. We are only capable of obtaining something when we do not believe that we already possess it, and this applies here also.

v

What has been said so far is admittedly far from expressing everything that can be discovered, at least in principle, in the ecclesiology of the Second Vatican Council with regard to the new elements which will appear in the image of the Church. Indeed we have not yet said even half of what is to be said on this subject. This is particularly true because that which most of all pertains to the origins always remains the newest as well. This element in the Church, which is at once most ancient and most new, is that which she utters and imparts. But what she utters is, in the last analysis, not herself. She is the message that speaks of another and makes this other present and effective for us.

On this showing ecclesiology is related to the other departments of dogmatic theology as grammar, the techniques of poetry and semantics are related to poetry itself. The Church understands her own nature best when she is actually fulfilling her function, and this means when she is actually speaking of God and his grace, of Jesus Christ, his Cross and Resurrection and eternal life, and when, in the very act of uttering this message, she allows herself to be moved by the grace of God. We can also say that she realises her own nature as an 'institution' of salvation only when she understands herself as the *fruit* of salvation and acts as such. There is no doubt that in the Constitution on the Church this turning-point has been reached and passed. Certainly this document does speak explicitly – why indeed should it not? – of the Church as an institution, of its officials and its authority in various departments, of its hierarchical structure, of its teaching and pastoral offices, of the different degrees in which its members participate in its mission, of its authorities and their powers – in short of the Church as an institution of salvation and as a means of salvation. But all this is, nevertheless, subsumed and made subordinate to a more basic understanding of the Church, in which the Church is viewed as the people of God gathered together by God's grace, and the Church is interpreted as the outcome of God's grace, as the fruit of salvation. It is possible for the Church to be seen as the Body of Christ, as the people of God; for her to be understood as 'the people of God on their journey'. It is possible to recognise that she herself is still seeking to find her goal through history. It is possible for the Church to recognise her own nature as a reality which still bears in itself the form of this present aeon (No. 48), yet which is eager to raise herself above this level to the point at which the kingdom of God is 'all in all', and no longer merely a Church. It is possible for us to regard all those vested with hierarchical authority in her as being such only in virtue of the fact that the Church herself is *already in existence*, and to recognise that this view of them is at least as important as that in which they are regarded as those who form the Church. Now if we can view the Church in this light, then certainly we have achieved something more than a one-sided view of the Church as an authoritative institution of salvation. Then the Church appears not primarily as she who acts upon us, but rather as she whom we all *are* in virtue of the fact that the grace of God has moved and inspired us and bound us together into a unity.

Many further fresh traits in the image of the Church could be pointed to. Here however let us confine ourselves to mentioning a few of the minor ones. To a greater extent than in the ecclesiology of the official Church of earlier times the Church now appears as the sinful Church, the Church of sinners, so that she must constantly be turning back in repentance to her Lord. Even if it cannot be said that this presentation of the Church has been given all the importance due to it as a theme of ecclesiology, still it is a vital factor in the new image of the Church. The Church appears as a communion of faith, hope and love (Nos. 8, 64, 65), as a Church of the Trinity (No. 4). She is not merely the Church of hierarchical authorities and of the sacraments, but the Church of the free charismata as well (No. 12), the Church of martyrdom (No. 42). Moreover we are ready to recognise whole-heartedly that martyrdom is present in non-Catholic Christendom as well. The Church feels herself to be the Church of the poor and oppressed (Nos. 8, 41). Far more clearly than formerly, she has overcome the misconception which was tacitly present in the theology of the Fathers and the Middle Ages. This was the feeling that the difference between the clergy and the laity, or between the state of being ordained and that of not being ordained *ipso facto* and of itself implied a difference in the nearness to God which the individual could attain to, a difference, therefore, in the degree of his love of God and love of neighbour, and so of his holiness. The Church is conscious of being the Church in the eschatological phase of saving history, in which, to the eye of faith, the drama of the dialogue between God and man has already irrevocably been decided by God in favour of man's salvation (No. 48). But precisely by viewing herself in this light the Church is conscious of being one who bears in herself the form of the present age and of herself as still belonging to that order of creation which waits longingly for the revelation of the glory of the children of God. Thus she is not the permanent institution which mediates the future kingdom of God and the eternal life that goes with it to the individuals who receive salvation, in order that she may remain herself here below. Rather she is the pilgrim who is herself journeying through history to that eternity in which she will cease any longer to be an institution of salvation with an authoritative and sacramental system of this kind (No. 48).

We have only been able to bring out a few of the traits which are present in the new image of the Church. In this we do not mean to imply that other traits, familiar to us from earlier times, are no longer in force in this image, or that they no longer have any importance. It is also obvious that the application of these new traits in the image of the Church in the concrete realities of her actual existence still requires a long process of education until these traits can be made manifest in real and living form in the worship of the Church's individual members and in the practice of the Church herself. But the Church has already made a beginning in entering upon her new life of worship of this kind. Now the point of vital importance will be to ensure that the letter of this conciliar ecclesiology is really made spirit and life.

2

CHURCH, CHURCHES AND RELIGIONS

For modern Christians and for those of a religious bent the question of the relationship between the Church, the Churches and the various religions provides a thought-provoking subject for discussion. The society in which the Catholic Christian of today lives is a complex and heterogeneous one. He lives in the closest proximity to, and has the closest personal connections with, non-Catholic Christians. The sphere in which his life is passed is no longer a country which, in its social, cultural and even civic aspects, is homogeneously 'Catholic'. Indeed, where formerly the individual nations were independent of one another in their lines of historical development, nowadays these lines are tending to become fused into a single great world history. And the result of this is that the non-Christian religions and philosophies of life such as Islam, Hinduism and Buddhism, no longer constitute an area of foreign folklore which has no bearing upon the course of life modern man maps out for himself and raises no radical problems for him. Instead of this these non-Christian religions have come to be regarded as the philosophies of life of men who have become neighbours to modern man, men in whom he cannot fail to recognise just as high a degree of intelligence as that with which he credits himself. Moreover he is compelled to accept it as axiomatic, if he wants to be just and fair, that they in their turn have a certain knowledge of Christianity and an honourable resolve to strive for the truth. Now in this situation it is borne in upon him – and far more deeply borne in than in the case of a Catholic of earlier times – that these Christians who belong to other creeds, and these adherents of non-Christian religions, are, on the whole, quite undisturbed in their interior thoughts and dispositions by Catholic Christianity; that in spite of it they continue whole-heartedly to give their alliegiance to their own particular Christian confession or non-Christian religion.

Now we might conceive of a position in which the Catholic arrived at the judgment that all these creeds and religions are equally justified from the outset as expressions of a single basic attitude of 'faith'; that they all serve to bring men into a relationship with God that is salvific; that they differ from one another only in points that are more or less inessential; and that, just as in human society and culture in general the individual can choose to adopt any mode of life he likes, so too here it is open to him to select whichever one of these creeds or religions suits him best. *If* this were a possible position for a Catholic, then of course the fact that there is so much diversity in religion would not in itself cause him a moment's disquiet. But this is precisely a judgment which the Catholic Christian cannot make. An intrinsic element in his Christian and Catholic beliefs is the conviction of faith that now at any rate Christianity is the unique and absolute religion founded by God through Christ and prescribed by him for all men; that it is *the* way of salvation which God, of his salvific will, has created for all and made radically binding for all to follow. We cannot adopt that attitude of religious relativism which regards all religions as on the whole equally justifiable, and the confusion and disorder among them as relatively unimportant; or that attitude which considers that the variations and points of convergence between the different religions are, taken all in all, only concerned with inessentials. Such an attitude would, if pressed to its logical conclusions, represent the total overthrow of the Christian and Catholic faith. And this is no less true even though there may be no small number of Catholics who implicitly feel that they can combine a religious relativism of this kind in their concrete attitudes with an active practice of the 'Catholic' religion which may even, in some cases, be very enthusiastic. The really convinced Catholic, therefore, finds himself confronted with the question of how, without this religious relativism, he can reconcile his faith in the absolute nature of his Catholic Christianity and of his Church, and in the universally binding force which they have for all, with the fact that even after two thousand years of Christianity and the Church the greater part of mankind is neither Christian nor Catholic. For in facing up to this question he cannot deny that this greater part of mankind has both intelligence and sincerity of conscience. A further fact which he has to take into consideration is that he is bound by the terms of his own Catholic belief to hold fast to the fact that God truly and effectively wills all men to be saved. He cannot hold the opinion that God himself denies the possibility and the grace of salvation to a wide section of mankind. And yet it is only in Jesus Christ that this salvation is conferred, and through Christianity and the one Church that it must be mediated to all men.

To the extent that it is possible at all within the limits of this study, this question must be answered. The answer that is given must be based upon the orthodox teaching of the Catholic faith. What we are looking for, therefore, is an answer which we cannot, in any sense, attempt to find a basis for in the history or philosophy of religion, or from some position in which we remain uncommitted to the creed of a specific religion. On the contrary, we are seeking for an answer which the Catholic Christian must give on the basis of his own Christianity and according to the principles proper to this. Obviously in giving such an answer we cannot enter into any extensive development of the dogmatic principles on which it will be based. These can only be stated in bare outline. Obviously too a generalised answer of this kind, based as it is on a pre-existing system, must necessarily make use of ideas which cannot themselves claim to have dogmatic force but are only intended to be *reconcilable* with the dogmatic positions.

For the Catholic theologians of today, in contrast to those of former times, one not inconsiderable factor has made it easier to find an answer to this question. It is that the Second Vatican Council has had something quite fundamental to say upon this question. The relevant pronouncements are to be found in the Dogmatic Constitution on the Church, in the Decree on Oecumenism, in the Decree on the Missionary Activity of the Church, and in the Explanation Concerning Non-Christian Religions. The relevant pronouncements, even though there is a genuine continuity between them and the earlier traditions of Catholic teaching, are nevertheless both fresh and courageous. Moreover, while they are certainly brief, they are also fairly unambiguous.[1] The striking point in all this was above all the fact that although these pronouncements represented a very notable advance in the question with which we are concerned, this advance was achieved almost as though the necessity for it were self-evident, and the pronouncements were adopted without debate or opposition of any kind. It is neither necessary nor possible to expound the relevant passages at this point, or to provide a theological interpretation of them. Here we must confine ourselves to emphasising right at the outset that in the theological considerations which follow the author is conscious of finding support and justification in this explanation of the Council.

I

We must begin by stating the fundamental principle on the basis of which our question must be answered.

[1] For a more detailed investigation of this point cf. K. Rahner, 'Atheism and Implicit Christianity' in volume IX, (London & Baltimore, 1972), pp. 145–164.

1. With regard to this fundamental principle we must begin by refering to a conviction which is an intrinsic element in the content of the Catholic faith. It is the conviction that in spite of original sin and also the personal sinfulness of men God truly and sincerely wills *all* men to be saved, and that in virtue of willing the universal salvation of all in this sense he offers every man, whatever the circumstances of life in which he finds himself, a genuine possibility of attaining to his own salvation. This general offering of salvation attaches itself (at least if we set aside the question of the final destiny of children who die unbaptised) to salvation in the grace of Christ as its definitive mode, and it is this that Christian salvation properly means. It achieves its final consummation in a sharing through the life of God, and this in turn implies the enjoyment of the immediate vision of God and, as the concomitant of this, a love of God that is ultimate and eternal. It also implies that state which we refer to in the creed as the 'resurrection of the flesh'. Catholic theologians of earlier times often put forward the hypothesis that under certain circumstances men who had arrived at the use of their intelligence and free will could enjoy a merely 'natural' beatitude without sharing in the divine nature and the divine life in the beatific vision. They developed this hypothesis in order to find a way out of the difficulty of seeing how supernatural salvation could ever be attained by those individuals who, at least to all appearances, could not and did not attain to belief in the gospel as an act of supernatural grace. But today at least, in the light of the Second Vatican Council, it should be clear that this way out of the difficulty is no longer open to Catholic theologians. On this question we have to hold firm to the fact that the salvation which God offers to every man as genuinely possible for him is the Christian salvation that comes to him through supernatural grace and consists in a sharing in the life of God. The possibility of attaining to this salvation is such that it can only remain unrealised if it is frustrated by the real, grave and personal guilt of the subject to whom it is offered.

This will of God to save all men in Christ and through his grace can be characterised more precisely and more concisely as God's will to bestow himself on the creature who is endowed with spiritual faculties. What is intended to be conveyed by this may be stated as follows:

The salvation which God, of his will to save all men, offers and effectively bestows upon the individual is present now in its first principles and as a seed which is still undeveloped. (At this stage it is called 'justifying and sanctifying grace'). In the future this will be brought to its fulness in the form of eternal life (this is called the 'vision of God'). It can only fail to be brought to this fulness if man of his own free will sinfully rejects it. Now salvation in this sense is not a *created* gift of God, a mere creaturely state of sanctification and blessedness, but rather, in the deepest sense, God himself. For it is himself in his innermost and most mysterious life, and so in his divine glory that God gives man to have as his own. This self-bestowal of God in that form in which it is offered is both that which God offers and imparts to man as a gift of salvation for his own final perfection, and at the same time it is something more. It is the possibility which he imparts to the creature as endowed with spiritual faculties to receive what is offered with a freedom that is raised and intensified to a supernatural level; to receive it, therefore, in such a way that in the very act of accepting it man continues to recognise that which is actually offered him as salvation as divine. In other words he does not, in some sense, draw it down to the level or into the dimension of the purely finite and natural perfection of man and so deprive it of its true status. God himself *is* the salvation and at the same time the power to receive the salvation in such a way that this salvation really is God himself, and God remains not only the ultimate Cause but the real content as well of this salvation. This self-bestowal of God as the salvation of man and as the possibility of accepting this salvation in full freedom is something that, without derogating from the sharing in the divine life that it effects in the ultimate depths of man's nature, applies to the whole man in all the levels of his being, in that which unites all these levels and in the manner in which they mutually condition one another.

2. Thus the self-bestowal of God upon the creature as endowed with spiritual faculties implies two things:

(A) The divine self-bestowal (at least as offered and bestowed upon the free creature as that which makes it possible for it to act for its own salvation) penetrates to the ultimate roots of man's being, to the innermost depths of his spiritual nature, and takes effect upon him from there, radically re-orientating this nature of his towards the immediate presence of God. It imparts to this nature an inward dynamism and an ultimate tendency towards God himself that is a grace. It elevates the uncircumscribed transcendentality of the person as spiritual in such a way that this becomes something more than the condition proper to human nature as spiritual, personal and free. It becomes a transcendentality that reaches up to the immediacy of God himself. This divine finality and dynamic impulse present in the person as spiritual is indeed and in the most absolute sense a grace, because it owes nothing to the 'natural' nature of man. But this does not mean that it is to be conceived of as something which only exists here and there in some individuals but not in others. This 'supernatual existential' or mode of being (as we may call this finality and dynamic impulse which makes us tend towards the immediate presence of God) is indeed the outcome of grace. But it is inserted into man's nature through the salvific will of God to become an abiding element in his spiritual mode of being, and as something that is a living force in man always and everywhere, whether accepted or rejected by man's own free will. It radically influences the ultimate development of his existence as spiritual.[2] Admittedly this does not mean, and need not mean, that man must always have a conscious awareness of this 'supernatural existential' in his life, or that he must be able to create this awareness within him simply by a process of psychological introspection.

Just as in other contexts too man can never achieve, merely by reflecting upon himself, any adequate view of the full depths and heights of his own existence as a spiritual being endowed with transcendence and freedom, and can never objectify this to himself, so too it is with this supernatural existential of which he is aware, yet which he cannot on that account know in the sense of objectifying it to himself. It is a mode of being, or 'existential', which is constituted by the salvific will of God for all men, to become an abiding element in their spiritual existence and to belong inescapably to human nature as such. It is the ultimate, most vital and most interior reality and power of man's existence, even though in the average and everyday activities of his life he never consciously reflects upon the fact that he is living by it, and even though the way in which he experiences this grace is not one in which it becomes the object of his conscious awareness.[3] For he experiences it in virtue of the fact that constantly, and in all the exercise of his knowledge and freedom, he experiences himself as one who is orientated towards that which lies beyond all definable realities, namely towards the silent mystery of God. In order to have a single key phrase in which to sum all this up in brief we may call this self-bestowal of God, considered as the abiding existential of every human life, the transcendental self-bestowal of God.

(B) Now even at the natural level every spiritual mode of transcendentality that belongs to man is activated when man as a physical and social entity engages himself in the concrete realities of his life as

[2] On the concept of the 'supernatural existential' cf. F. K. Mayr and K. Rahner, 'Existential', *Sacramentum Mundi* 2 (Freiburg and London 1968), pp. 304–307.

[3] On this cf. K. Rahner, 'Reflections on the Experience of Grace', *Theological Investigations* III (London and Baltimore 1967), pp. 86–90; also the same author's *Alltägliche Dinge* (5th ed. Einsiedeln 1966).

conditioned by space and time, as belonging to history, and as involving communication with other beings on the same plane of existence. In other words this transcendentality of man as spiritual does not remain a separate department of human life *over and above* the historical context in which he is involved, and in which he brings his existence to its fulness. And this also applies to the process by which man develops to the full the supernaturally elevated transcendentality bestowed upon him, the 'supernatural existential'. This is not something that takes place apart from this historical mode of being, but rather something that is achieved in and through his existence as engaged in human living in the concrete.

The 'supernatural existential' in man has a history of its own which unfolds throughout the whole length and breadth of man's life as a historical being. It is in this life that it is imparted to man in his freedom, and it is in this life that it is made manifest. This manifestation does not necessarily or in all cases need to be explicitly and thematically religious. It is *ipso facto* present, albeit unconsciously and, in a certain sense, 'anonymously', everywhere where the transcendentality of the spirit and moral freedom are exercised, because the transcendental self-bestowal of God through the 'supernatural existential' is precisely one of the factors exercising a decisive influence upon this spiritual nature of man.

Thus the presence of the abiding 'supernatural existential' in man has the effect of making saving history coexistent with human history in general in its spiritual dimension, even though in many cases man himself does not consciously advert to this or formulate to himself what is taking place in this spiritual dimension.[4] To this extent we can and must say that either saving history or its opposite, the history of perdition, is taking place wherever man of his own free decision either voluntarily undertakes his own mode of existence or alternatively protests against it. And this is precisely because this 'supernatural existential', considered as God's act of self-bestowal which he offers to men, is in all cases grafted into the very roots of human existence.

Indeed we may go so far as to say that 'revelation history' is always and everywhere taking place because of God's act of supernatural self-bestowal considered as that which raises and re-orientates the transcendental dimension of the human spirit by the power of grace. The reason for this is that even though man himself may not have recognised this supernatural self-bestowal or reflected upon it in his conscious thought, nevertheless it still constitutes an element in his transcendental awareness.

[4] For a fuller exposition of this cf. K. Rahner, 'History of the World and Salvation History', *Theological Investigations* V (London and Baltimore 1966), pp. 97–114.

Certainly the reason that 'revelation history' is always and everywhere taking place is not simply that the spiritual level of man's being, with the still undeveloped resources and possibilities which it has of itself, *ipso facto* constitutes an authentic revelation in this sense. Rather it is that God himself, by the very fact of his own gracious act of self-bestowal, *constantly* communicates himself to man as the divine ultimate to which truth points, and as the very scope of love. And this transcendental self-bestowal of God is communicated (even if not as a definable idea) in and through the spiritual dimension of man's life.

What we have been speaking of is the progressive and purposive unfolding of salvation and revelation ('salvation' and 'revelation history') which derives from the presence in man of the 'supernatural existential'. Now it is possible for man himself to explicitate this in his conscious thought and to make it a religious theme for investigation. And this process of making the 'salvation' and 'revelation history' of the 'supernatural existential' an explicit object and theme for man's religious thought can be positively guided, or even demanded by God as part of his plan to save man. Over and above this it is possible for this process of explicitation to be of such a kind that man is supplied with relatively sure criteria enabling him to judge the rightness or otherwise of the development of his ideas in objectifying and interpreting this 'salvation history' and 'revelation history' taking place within his own nature. He can assure himself by these criteria that the gradual and progressive process of objectifying and reflexively interpreting this 'history' that takes place within him is correct, legitimate, and not a false interpretation or a distortion due to human error and human sinfulness. Now if, and to the extent that, we actually achieve all this we can move on to a further stage. Within the broader context of the 'salvation' and 'perdition' history which is universally present everywhere and all the time in mankind, and within the universal 'salvation' and 'revelation history' which is taking place throughout humanity, we attain to something more, something that we can call the *explicit* and *official* history of salvation and revelation, something which we are habitually accustomed to call simply 'salvation history' (*Heilsgeschichte*), something that is apprehensible to us as Christians in the salvation history and revelation history of the Old and New Testaments.

This explicit and official salvation history is still dependent upon the 'supernatural existential' present in all men and taking effect throughout humanity. It is dependent too upon the process of objectifying this which, unalloyed by human error, is attested by God himself. And this salvation history is brought to its climax and goal in Jesus Christ. In him, as the God-man in person, there takes place God's self-bestowal upon man and upon his history in its most sublime, most absolute and most irrevocable form. At the same time in this same Jesus Christ there takes place the most total and perfect acceptance of this self-bestowal of God, as well as the most sublime effects issuing from this acceptance. Thus in this God-man the self-bestowal of God upon the world, and the acceptance of this by the world (in other words the 'supernatural existential' and the reception of this into human nature) are present in history definitively, irrevocably and in a mode in which they can be apprehended in the concrete.

The 'supernatural existential', therefore, present in all humanity tends dynamically towards its irrevocable climax in Jesus Christ. It has this innate tendency of its very nature, but also in virtue of the fact that the dimension of transcendentality in man is realised in a progressive and purposive unfolding, a history. To the extent that this is true, and to the extent that every movement towards a goal derives its direction and force from the goal itself, it can be said that the whole of 'salvation' and 'revelation history' *both* as universally present in all men *and* in its explicit and official form is dependent upon Jesus Christ and derives its direction and its forward movement from him. To this extent and in this sense too the whole of this history is the history of the God-man. It follows that this latter is itself already present even in those men who have not attained to any explicit, conscious or objective knowledge of Jesus Christ.

Taking this as our first principle, therefore, we are now in a position to indicate, at least briefly, where the answer is to be found to the question which we have posed for ourselves.

II

First let us take that assertion of the Christian and Catholic faith which lays down that Christianity is *the* universal, absolute, and God-given religion, and that the one Catholic Church is, of her very nature, a sharer in this absolute quality of Christianity. Let us attempt to answer the question of what this means and how it is justified. When we attribute this absolute character to Christianity we do not intend to assert that the salvation history and revelation history of God is identical with that particular area in the religious history of mankind which is confined to the Old and the New Testaments or to those who have had an explicit faith in Jesus Christ. When we say that Christianity has this *absolute* character we are saying something quite different from this. First and foremost that the whole salvation history and revelation history of mankind is coexistent with the history of mankind as personal and spiritual and with all that is morally good in this. And inasmuch as it is coexistent in this sense with the history of the human spirit the whole of it is sustained in being by that transcendental self-bestowal of God which is grace-given and which finds its supreme and irreversible manifestation in history, and at the same time its free acceptance on the part of humanity, in the God-man Jesus Christ.

The God-man, then, is the supreme and climactic point in God's bestowing of himself upon mankind, such that he supplies meaning to the whole of this divine self-bestowal right from its inception. Right from its very inception God's plan and God's execution of this plan in the implementation of his will to save all men has proceeded from the God-man as its starting-point and to him as its goal. And because of this the whole of salvation and revelation history is Christian right from its inception even before there has been any conscious recognition of this in it, and even before that point in history is attained at which its Christian significance has been objectively formulated and made explicit, namely in the creed, in the Christian act of worship, and in the form of a visible Church.

Conversely, to postulate a salvation and revelation history of this kind is in no sense to deny the absolute character of Christ himself, of Christianity as an explicit faith, or of the Church as the visible expression of the abiding presence of Christ. For this history is in fact itself being impelled towards Christ, even though only in a hidden manner, by this forward movement, this historical unfolding of the grace that is offered to all and in all ages. That which is made effective (at least as something offered by God) always and everywhere throughout the history of mankind achieves its supreme expression as a comprehensible historical fact which can no longer be suppressed or denied in Jesus Christ and his Church. In Christ and in his Church man's transcendence is not merely present in the depths of his conscience in virtue of the 'supernatural existential'. Also, and more than this, this transcendence of his is actually opened up to the immediate presence and action of God in virtue of what has taken place in history and what has been explicitly uttered. Christianity and the Church can see their own significance as the effective presence of God's salvation in the absolute and of his grace, in history and as apprehensible to man. They can achieve this understanding of their own significance precisely because it does not entail any denial of the fact that salvation history both in the collective sense and as applied to the life of the individual, is present *everywhere*. On the contrary, Christianity and the Church understand this as the prior history that leads up to themselves and as the effect of that selfsame grace which has achieved its definitive and unsurpassable historical manifestation in themselves. Moreover the fact that it has arrived at this definitive mode does not mean that the grace referred to has been withdrawn from the universal history of mankind, or that it has ceased to be the inner dynamism latent in the very heart of this and making God present in it.

This divine dynamism, then, latent in the entire history of the human spirit, transforms it into saving history and revelation history. And in doing this it impels this whole spiritual and religious history towards that point at which it becomes explicitly apprehensible as the history and manifestation of Christ and of his Church. And even though this point may lie in a future that is remote and invisible, it is in fact ultimately identical with the end of history and the return of Christ in glory. This is the first point. The second point is that Christianity and the Church themselves have only arrived at their definitive fulness and historical maturity when the whole of salvation history and revelation history has visibly and explicitly been transformed into the history of Christianity and of the Church and has become a definable element in the Christianity that is explicitly embodied in the Church. So far we have been treating of two basic principles, and in the light of the synthesis which we have achieved between them it now becomes intelligible to us that even Christianity and the Church themselves are constantly in process of seeking the final perfection of their own nature. And because of this they are in a position to recognise in those tendencies within the spiritual and religious history of mankind which are religiously positive even though not yet explicitly Christian, that which Christianity and the Church must absorb and transform into themselves in order to become fully that which they already are: the manifestation in history of the grace of God now at its eschatological stage in history and in a state of purity which is divinely attested and assured.

III

In the light of the basic principle indicated above we can also acquire fresh insights in our deepening awareness of our Catholic faith with regard to the interpretation we should put upon non-Catholic Christians and Christian Churches outside our own. The Catholic Church cannot think of herself as one among many historical manifestations in which *one and the same* God-man Jesus Christ is made present, which are offered by God to man for him to choose whichever he likes. On the contrary she must necessarily think of herself as the one and total presence in history of the one God-man in his truth and grace, and as such as having a fundamental relationship to all men. She is conscious of herself as making abidingly present that which derives authoritatively and juridically, even from the aspect of historical succession, from *that* Church which Jesus Christ gathered about himself as the community of those who believe in him; conscious of herself as the Church which has remained faithful to her own origins in her sacramental system, in her moral principles and in the authority legitimately bequeathed to her by Christ himself. All this Christ has made an intrinsic element in his Church, although admittedly the manner in which she has preserved all this involves a process of historical unfolding and legitimate development. For this reason the Catholic Church cannot simply think of herself as one among many Christian Churches and communities on an equal footing with her. The unity which Christ indubitably willed his Church to exhibit is meant to be visibly and unambiguously present even in the dimension of history and social life. And the Church cannot accept that this unity is something which must be achieved only in the future and through a process of unification between the Christian Churches, so that until this point is reached it simply would not exist. But though he must hold this the Catholic Christian need not on that account regard the other Christian Churches and communities simply as entities which should not be there at all or as constituting a mere contradiction of the Church of Christ.

We must begin by stating a principle which should be fully and sincerely accepted as axiomatic, and which we have a duty in Christian love to accept in this sense. It is that absolutely speaking all Christians, together with the ecclesiastically organised communities to which they belong, have a will to be one and belong to the one true Church of Christ. Now to will this is a grace of God that is absolutely basic to salvation. As such it is undoubtedly more fundamental and more absolute than that will which causes non-Catholic Christians and their Churches to remain separated from the Catholic Church, from her teaching and from her authority, and to believe that they must maintain this separation in force. They believe this because in spite of that more basic will to unity which is present in their consciences, they still cannot see that the Catholic Church is the Church of Christ to which they too, absolutely speaking, owe their allegiance. It is not possible at this point to enter into the question of why, in spite of God's universal will to save all men, and in spite of this basic will on the part of all Christians to adhere to the true Church of Christ and maintain its unity, God himself in his saving providence tolerates this failure to recognise the one Church of Christ. Indeed, this saving providence of God recognises (though no doubt only indirectly and by implication) that this failure has a positive meaning for these Christians and for the Church herself in the sense that even though this state of disunity should not be, still a deeper significance can be drawn from it.

In any case, when we reflect upon this more basic underlying will to adhere to the true Church of Christ and its unity we can see that even when it has not yet found its proper object, which is precisely this Church as it exists as a fully concrete and visible entity, still it has already found something. For an ultimate unity, effective at the invisible and spiritual level, already exists between all Christians. And in fact this unity is already such that, precisely because it is sustained and brought about by the Spirit of God, it is greater than the unity of the Church considered merely as a society, such as, for instance exists or might exist between Catholics. It is perfectly possible for these to belong to one and the same Catholic Church so far as their external lives and social relationships are concerned, and still, through their own fault, not to possess the Holy Spirit of grace and justification, and so to be united to one another only by social and ecclesiastical ties of a purely external kind. Furthermore on the Catholic understanding of faith it is immediately apparent that all those Christians outside the Catholic Church who have not committed any serious fault against the claims of their own religious or moral consciences, do in fact possess the Holy Spirit of justification and grace. They have already arrived at a participation in the divine nature, the 'supernatural existential' which they have voluntarily accepted. In other words that interior dynamism which assimilates them to God, and is in this sense the seed of eternal life thrusting upwards towards the immediate presence of God, is already present at the innermost core of their being. All these, therefore, are in possession of precisely that to which everything in the Church is ordered; for her official life, her sacraments and the exercise of her authority are on the one hand simply the instrument and means for achieving this end and on the other that which enables her to manifest the reality concerned as a concrete phenomenon in history. All Christians both within and without the Catholic Church, therefore, simply in virtue of being faithful to their own consciences, are united among themselves in the Spirit of the Church, in the life of God that is extended to them. It is this life of God as extended to man, therefore, that everything in the Church is intended to point to as its appropriate manifestation. It is meant to be a sacramental sign in history of this life, without actually being identified with it.

The unity of men in the Spirit of God can, therefore, be present, and to a large extent actually is present, even where the manifestation in history and the imparting of this truly divine unity has not yet been achieved at least in its fulness, where this unity has not yet fully imposed itself in the dimension of the social life of Christians, their forms of worship and their adherence to one and the same explicit creed. An analogy may be invoked here from the sacramental teaching of the Catholic Church, according to which there are cases in which the reception of the sacrament as a formal act of worship is actually anticipated, and the *grace* of the sacrament concerned is already present before the sacrament is received. This grace does indeed demand its appropriate sacramental manifestation, but under certain circumstances no longer achieves such manifestation in the human and temporal life of the individuals concerned. In the case of Christians outside the Church the same relationship prevails. Let us consider this ultimate unity in the Spirit, to which, in the last analysis, all attain as the beginning of eternal life, as it exists among those Christians who are separated by their beliefs from the Church. Among them it does not exist as a mere unity, totally deprived of *any* kind of historical manifestation. It is only that the historical manifestation appropriate to it is rendered more remote. For everywhere where the word of God in scripture is acknowledged, where, in the deepest and truest sense (even though, it may be, with certain omissions or wrong interpretations) the living God, the grace of Christ the Lord and the Redeemer and the forgiveness of sins is preached, where this preaching is effective for salvation because it takes place in the name of Christ, where baptism in the Trinity is validly and effectively conferred and where, in some cases other sacraments too of Christ are likewise administered, there the Spirit of justification and unity among Christians *ipso facto* creates for itself a unity in the dimension of the social and ecclesiastical life of Christians, of their creed and of their formal worship, a unity which, even if it is not total, is still real. In all these areas of human life, therefore, this Spirit of unity is already beginning to clothe itself in visible 'Church' form, even when it has not yet achieved the full manifestation of its unity and the full unity which it is meant to have as a concrete historical phenomenon. Christians, even while they remain still separated from one another in terms of their express beliefs, are already in the here and now more united in the dimension of grace *and* in the dimension of the Church than they are divided according to outward appearances. That which already unites them in the here and now is more than that which still holds them apart.

A further point which the Catholic Christian must take into consideration is this. The non-Catholic Christian will, through grace, make experience of the Spirit which performs its atoning and sanctifying work in him through the imparting of those Christian elements which belong to the visible realities of human life as these are communicated to him in his own Church. Moreover these Christian realities which his own Church supplies also have in real fact as they apply to him the significance of true and positive media of salvation. According to the Catholic understanding of the Church the communication of salvation as found here consists formally not indeed in that which actually causes his Church to be separated from the Catholic Church but rather in those positive Christian elements which can exist even outside the Catholic Church and which are brought about by God's salvific will. On the basis of this experience of grace which is *de facto* communicated to him through his own Church the non-Catholic Christian arrives at the judgment (even though he may not formulate it precisely in *these* terms) that so long as he can, and indeed must hold firm to this Church in which grace and justification are communicated to him he cannot recognise in any clear, positive or unambiguous sense in his own conscience that this Christian communication of his justification and experience of grace is also to be found pure and unalloyed in the Catholic Church. Nor can he judge that over and above this *in* the Catholic Church they actually achieve their authentic fulness and are made fully apprehensible as elements in concrete human living in the way that Christ willed them to be, and that must be brought about by grace in order that they can be manifested with all the fulness appropriate to them. Even on Catholic principles the non-Catholic Christian who encounters the grace of God in, and indeed through his Church, must presume that until he encounters precisely this Christianity which he has experienced in the Catholic Church, and in a form that is equally pure and more fully and unambiguously apprehensible as a concrete historical phenomenon to the point where it genuinely convinces his own conscience – until he arrives at this position he has an absolute duty to hold fast to the Christianity which he has inherited. The Catholic Christian must, without prejudice to his belief in the necessity of his Church for salvation, recognise the position of the non-Catholic Christian who has arrived at this kind of decision as a result of the concrete circumstances of his life. For such a one, even without any fault on his part, the possibility of recognising the true significance of the Catholic Church to a point where it overcomes his earlier presumption is not necessarily given in all cases or inevitably, and may never be given throughout his entire life.

In the light of this it becomes apparent that non-Catholic Churches and religious confraternities too have a positive function to perform, not only for their own adherents but also in relation to the Catholic Church. For it is perfectly possible for the one Spirit of God to manifest its presence in objective historical occurrences in the other Christian confessions and communions, that same Spirit which works, sanctifies and creates unity in the Catholic Church *and* outside her as well. These objective manifestations do not have to be present in the Catholic Church with the same frequency, with an equal historical impact, or with the same clarity and power to convince the conscience. At the same time the Catholic Christian, on the basis of his own understanding of the Church, cannot concede that the Catholic Church has in principle set its face against, or still persistently sets its face against all cases of such genuine objective manifestations of the Spirit, which themselves serve in turn to impart the Spirit to others. To this extent the Catholic Church has something to learn from such genuine objective manifestations of the Holy Spirit in the non-Catholic Churches. They are, of their nature, a call and an incentive to watchfulness which the Spirit of God offers her because she herself, through the narrow-mindedness and sinfulness of her members, has not yet arrived at the full effectiveness of the part she has to play in human history or the full development of her own nature.

IV

Finally let us return to our basic principle in order to achieve from this standpoint a theological evaluation of the non-Christian religions. Since these, even when compared to one another, vary enormously in respect of the degree of religious feeling, purity etc. that they have achieved, what we have in principle to say at this point can obviously only validly be applied to the particular religions in this category in very different ways and with more or less strong reservations.[5]

Bearing this proviso in mind it can be said that if we begin by viewing

[5] On the considerations which follow cf. the more detailed arguments in K. Rahner, 'Christianity and the non-Christian Religions', *Theological Investigations* V (London and Baltimore 1966), pp. 115–134.

the non-Christian religions before the coming of Christ then certainly we can recognise the possibility that 'in themselves' and in principle they were positively willed by God as legitimate ways of salvation. For certainly the explicit and official salvation history of the Old Testament and the explicit and official means of salvation recorded there were not prescribed for all men. On the other hand, however, it follows from God's will to save all men that every individual must have had some positive means of salvation available to him, giving him at least the possibility of possessing true supernatural salvation. Yet the nature of man as a historical and social being was such that a way of salvation of this kind could not be followed in the concrete altogether in emancipation from the social and historical context of human life. Man will not work out his salvation simply by acts of religion which are purely interior. He can only do so through the sort of religion which must, of its very nature, find concrete expression in the social and institutional life of the community.

When we reflect upon what we have already said at an earlier stage with regard to the 'supernatural existential' present in every man in all ages, and with regard to the fact that the supernatural history of salvation and revelation are coexistent with the history of the human spirit, then it will become immediately comprehensible that the religions which *de facto* do exist outside Christianity and the Old Testament are not merely the outcome of human speculation, human wickedness or a self-willed decision on man's part to devise a religion for himself instead of accepting it from God. Instead of this the 'supernatural existential', the dynamic impulse present in man by the power of grace and impelling him towards the triune God, is at work in all these religions and plays a decisive part in determining the forms in which these religions are objectively expressed.

Of course this does not mean that these religions are thereby rendered 'pure' or unadulterated as objective expressions and manifestations of this transcendental self-bestowal of God. They continue to be through and through a mixture of disparate elements which defies all analysis: apart from the manifestation of grace there is the religious instinct naturally present in man, and also his sinfulness, corrupting and destroying the religious element in his make-up. But through them all the grace of God is nevertheless constantly at work, and even in the most primitive, corrupt or grotesque forms this grace still offers to man the ultimate possibility of activating in some way or other (however submerged or distorted it may be) that orientation towards the mystery of God which is implanted in him by grace. A factor which should not be overlooked in all this is that in one way or another, and however difficult it may be to perceive, the religions that man actually encounters in the concrete have a general upwards tendency from what is lower in human life to what is higher, and so certainly do set before man the possibility, and even the necessity, of freely deciding in his conscience to move towards what is higher. In a certain measure, therefore, this impulse in his life already by anticipation implicitly directs him towards the mystery of the inconceivable fulness of God.

V

It can and must be said that these non-Christian religions are in principle, and in themselves, overtaken and rendered obsolete by the coming of Christ and by his death and resurrection. This is because in fact all of them, even in those elements of truth and goodness which they possess, were only provisional manifestations, destined to be replaced, of that divine self-bestowal which is present in the innermost depths of the history of mankind and its religion, sustaining it, actively influencing the forms which it assumes, and finally coming to its full and definitive manifest-ation in Jesus Christ. But in saying that all these non-Christian religions have been radically abrogated we have still not made clear our position with regard to the actual point in concrete history at which these religions ceased to be a legitimate way of salvation for certain human groups.[6] If we regard the history of salvation and revelation in the first place as being in some sense a *collective* entity, then it can surely be said that this concrete 'moment' in time (naturally it may extend over a fairly long period) is arrived at at that point at which Christianity in its explicit and ecclesiastical form became an effective reality, making its impact and asserting its claims in history in the relevant cultural sphere to which the non-Christian religion concerned belonged. This means that the historical expansion of Christianity, which even today has not yet simply been concluded, coincides with a progressive abrogation of the legitimacy of these religions.[7]

[6] On these questions cf. also J. Heislbetz, *Theologische Gründe der nichtchristlichen Religionen* (Freiburg 1967), pp. 200–218. For a more detailed explanation reference may be made to other sections of this work (cf. also the bibliography supplied in it).

[7] For a correct concept of what 'mission' means cf. K. Rahner, 'Grundprinzipien zur heutigen Mission in der Kirche', *Handbuch der Pastoraltheologie* II/2 (Freiburg 1966), pp. 46–80, esp. pp. 52 ff., 56 ff., 69 ff., 71 ff., 76 ff.

But so long as these religions to a large extent determine the *particular* circumstances affecting the salvation of the individual, this reply concerning salvation history in its *collective* dimension is still not enough to answer all the questions that arise at the individual level. Let us therefore concentrate for a moment upon the individual. For him the non-Christian religion which he has inherited from past history, and which has been handed down to him in his own sphere of life, is only abrogated as the authentic way of salvation for him at that point at which the message of Christ so penetrates into his own conscience as an individual that it is only through a grave fault of his own that he can any longer reject it as the way of salvation offered by God and as the fulfilment that goes beyond anything that his former religion had to offer.

In no case can we define with absolute certainty the *precise point at which* such a moment effectively occurs in the concrete life of the individual. For if a given individual rejects the Christianity brought to him through the preaching of the Church, even then we are still never in any position to decide whether this rejection as it exists in the concrete signifies a grave fault or an act of faithfulness to his own conscience. If in such a case Christianity is accepted, then we can *hope* in all thankfulness that this acceptance was not merely the result of human influence, but rather due to the working of the grace of God and its effective manifestation, which really does unite this individual to God. But we have no absolute certainty whatever upon this point. Thus we can never say with ultimate certainty whether a non-Christian who has rejected Christianity, and who, in spite of a certain encounter with Christianity, does *not* become a Christian, is still following the provisional paths mapped out for his own salvation which are leading him to an encounter with God, or whether he has now entered upon the way of perdition. In any case even today, and *after* the coming of Christ, it is still perfectly conceivable that a non-Christian religion still exercises a positively saving function for the individual. Indeed the Second Vatican Council explicitly states that God does not refuse salvation to a man who, through no fault of his own, has still not attained to any explicit acknowledgment of God, who, in other words, so far as the level of his conscious awareness is concerned, must be called an 'atheist'.[8]

The paths by which mankind, and within mankind the individual, make pilgrimage towards God are long and devious. But only the gravest

---

[8] For an analysis of what this statement means and implies cf. a study of the author which has already been referred to, namely 'Atheism and Implicit Christianity', in volume IX, pp. 145–164.

sinfulness on the part of man himself – and about this we can make no final judgment – can turn them into ways that are really false, and which lead to perdition. And so long as this is not the case all these ways have a single secret orientation which is common to them all, however much they may seem to diverge from one another. Every way by which a man travels from genuine motives of conscience is a way leading to the infinitude of God. These ways are of various lengths, and not every one, not every age in history, and not every people either, progress at the same rate or arrive at the same point in their journey when these are compared one with another. But everyone who genuinely embarks upon such a way does arrive. But not only do all of these ways lead into the eternal life of God, all of them also lead first to a cross-roads and then to their finishing point, and at each of these points Christ and his presence in the Church are to be found. In union with the Church, his mystical body, he is the beginning and the end of all the ways of God. Whether a man reaches this final point in the way of God while still *within* history, or only attains to it when the way of his own history comes to its close – that is something which God himself arranges of his own free decision, and is a mystery hidden in him.

But whoever has already found Christ and his Church visibly present in the history of his own personal life cannot discover any reason for separating himself from Christ from the fact that so many men, through no fault of their own, have not yet found Christ and his Church. For Christ is the one source of salvation for all men. He is sought, all unknowingly, even by those men of good will who have not yet learned to call upon him by the name he bears on earth.

3

ON THE RELATIONSHIP BETWEEN THE POPE AND THE COLLEGE OF BISHOPS

THE Second Vatican Council has certainly made pronouncements of decisive importance in its teaching on the connection between the papacy and the episcopate, and its teaching on this point has now been ratified as the official teaching of the Church. But while recognising this, it must also be said that, for reasons which are very various, the actual pronouncements of the Council itself failed to supply solutions to many of the questions which were already being discussed among theologians even prior to the Council. Among these was the question of how we should define the *precise* relationship between the pope as the supreme pastor of the Church and the united episcopate who, as a college, are invested with the same supreme power in the Church as the pope himself possesses. Long before the Council I myself attempted to supply an answer to this question.[1] But as a result of the Council and the theological developments arising from it the problem with which we are here concerned has come to occupy a different place in our discussions, one in which it has a greater bearing on our concrete lives but which is, at the same time, more polemical. And in view of this it is necessary for us to undertake an expansion and development of the solution which we then put forward only provisionally.[2] As for the discussion which has emerged in the meanwhile, with regard to how far the thesis I proposed can be reconciled with the theology of the Council, I can for the most part only make any contribution to this to the extent that the further developments

[1] On this cf. K. Rahner (with J. Ratzinger), *The Episcopacy and the Primacy*, Quaestiones Disputatae 4 (Freiburg/Edinburgh/London 1962), pp. 11–36. cf. also *idem*, *Theological Investigations* VI (London and Baltimore 1969), pp. 317, 357 ff. 361.

[2] The following article was written with nothing further in view than the special occasion proper to itself, and before any positions hostile to it had yet been explicitly defined (cf. n. 3). For this reason I think it best at this initial stage to let this study, which is wholly confined to the actual subject-matter, and therefore non-polemical, to stand upon its own merits without further modification.

offered here prove fruitful for our understanding of the actual matter itself.[3]

I

In the Dogmatic Constitution *Lumen gentium* concerning the relationship between the papacy and the episcopacy the Council itself does not make any exhaustive pronouncement in the sense indicated because it leaves specific questions open to further discussion among theologians. It lays down that in accordance with the defined doctrine of the First Vatican Council the pope possesses *'plena et suprema potestas'* in the Church, and that he can exercise this plenary power even without any collegiate act in the true sense on the part of the united bishops. In this he is not bound by any juridical guidance which these bishops have to offer. It states further that the united episcopate as such, i.e. considered as a collegiate entity, is likewise the bearer of the same full and supreme power in the Church, though of course only to the extent that it is not simply the sum total of all the individual bishops, but a *corpus, ordo, collegium* that is constituted with and under the pope as its indispensable head and to the extent that it is only capable of a 'collegiate act' with the free agreement of the pope himself. This remains true even though in concrete fact and in the actual circumstances of history this may take place in very different ways.

In defining the relationship between the pope and the universal episcopate the Council does not go beyond this formulation. This means that the statement in question contains nothing else than what had all along been held clearly and explicitly as a matter of faith by the Church both before and after the First Vatican Council. For what is said here about the united episcopate and its relationship to the pope and the plenary power he enjoys as primate is precisely the same as what has all along been said about the relationship between an Oecumenical Council

[3] The opposition which my thesis has aroused is curious in one respect, namely that I myself am never cited as the defender of the thesis which is under attack. In so far, therefore, as I am being referred to at all, I must begin by defending myself against the interpretation that has been placed upon the thesis I have put forward. A full 'answer' in this sense would, however, assume such proportions that the apparatus of footnotes that it would entail would exceed the limits permissible in the present article. For this reason I must pass over the discussion which has arisen – chiefly with W. Bertrams and Kl. Mörsdorf. My assistant and student Karl Lehmann will take up the question in a special article (cf. *Philosophie und Theologie* 1968, the third number).

and the pope, vested as he is with this plenary power as primate. In this it is in fact obvious that it is not merely as a result of being summoned to assemble at a particular point that the Council acquires this *plena et suprema potestas* in the Church. Rather the united episcopate must already possess this power in order that they can hold a Council. If the bishops were in possession of such power neither as individuals nor as a body, then the mere act of coming together in a particular place could never bring it about that they suddenly acquired this power. This could never be the case even if we were willing to assume that they could only actually *exercise* this power (whatever their reasons for doing so) when they were actually assembled together in a particular place. If it were sought to suggest that the bishops as locally assembled only acquire this power belonging to an Oecumenical Council precisely as a result of being called together by the *pope*, then (and this is a point that we shall have to return to in greater detail at a later stage) we should have to say that the prior supposition on which this theory is based was false, because a power that is *transmitted* within the Church herself (as opposed to one that is imparted by Christ) cannot, by definition, be the *supreme* power, since the power of him who imparts it must in fact be higher than itself.

In the light of this it becomes self-evident that the teaching of the Second Vatican Council with regard to the united episcopate as the upholder of supreme and plenary power in the Church and with regard to the relationship between this united episcopate and the pope is simply a repetition of the classic doctrine concerning the power of a Council (and in fact with regard to that of the united episcopate) which has always been in force, and which was explicitly put forward at the First Vatican Council by Gasser, Zinelli etc. But precisely because of this it is also clear that those questions about the relationship between pope and Council (= united episcopate) which have been matters of theological controversy up to now were not touched upon, and therefore that they still remain matters of controversy today. The only increase in clarity that has been achieved is that the hitherto disputed question regarding the relationship between pope and Council is now presented in a better and more realistic form as the question of the precise relationship between the pope and the united episcopate.

Scholastic theology is accustomed to give precision to the form in which the question with which we are here concerned is presented by asking whether there are two 'incompletely distinct subjects' vested with full and supreme power in the Church or only one. Those who choose the *second* of these two alternatives as their answer to this question obviously presuppose that the *one* subject involved can only be the pope. Those who choose the *first* alternative as their answer equally obviously imply thereby that there cannot be two 'completely distinct subjects' vested with one and the same supreme power in the Church. For the purposes of the considerations offered here let it be explicitly acknowledged and taken as read that the two presuppositions here involved are valid, even though in themselves they are not sufficient to answer the question. For (and this is relevant to the first presupposition) let us suppose that the pope is not vested with this power in virtue of his own personal office, but instead of this that he derives this power of his (even though verbally acknowledged as supreme and plenary) from the united episcopate (= Council). For, in the scholastic controversy referred to, the power of the Council is commonly held to be derived from the pope in just this way. But on this hypothesis it is no longer possible to see in what sense this power could be the supreme power, and how it could ever be exercised by the pope even *seorsim*, apart from the Council and the united episcopate. There is something more to be said also which touches upon the second presupposition. If it were possible to conceive of two distinct subjects existing in the Church both vested with the supreme power, then it would cease to be comprehensible how the unity of the Church would not be, in essence, radically broken. Furthermore this would be tantamount to denying the truth that the united episcopate exists as a college only with and under the pope. In view of all this, therefore, let us take as read the validity of both the two presuppositions involved in the two answers given by the scholastics to the question which has been put. Even so, however, with regard to these presuppositions we still have a few further remarks to make, which are not unimportant for the further considerations which we have to offer.

With regard to that theory of the scholastics which maintains the absolute unity of the subject vested with supreme power in the Church the first presupposition is not so obvious as it appears. For in fact this position presupposes that there can be *one* subject such that it can be vested with supreme and plenary authority in the Church, although this power belonging to it is derived from another source (still *within* the Church), likewise vested with authority. For what is being asserted on this view is in fact that the Council is vested with such authority in virtue of being given a share of, or allowed to participate in the supreme plenary power of the pope. But if this does not involve any intrinsic contradiction then it would in fact be just as valid to hold the opinion that the pope was vested with plenary and supreme power in the Church even though he possessed this power as a result of having 'derived it' from the united episcopate or Council either by participation or by having it conferred upon him, or in some other way. Precisely according to the principles presupposed by this first scholastic opinion therefore the statement that the pope is the possessor of this supreme power in the Church could not, taken by itself, enable us to draw the conclusion with compelling force that he does not possess this power through having derived it from the united episcopate. This consideration is enough of itself to show what a dangerous presupposition precisely for the *papacy* itself underlies the opinion that the supreme power of the united episcopate or Council can be derived from the power of the pope.

With regard to the *second* principle mentioned above as presupposed in the doctrine of the two *incompletely* distinct subjects, this does, in fact, indisputably have some foundation in virtue of the incontestable truth that the pope himself is supreme and indispensable precisely as member and head of the college of bishops. But the other ground on which it is based, which is likewise not unimportant – is indeed in reality more fundamental – nevertheless does entail certain problems. The argument here is as follows:

The unity of a society is such as of its essence to exclude the possibility of two *completely distinct* bearers of supreme power over it. Purely from the juridical point of view this may in fact be wholly enlightening. But it is possible to hold the view that in the *Church* precisely as such this difficulty with regard to the unity of the society is removed through the power of the *Spirit* within her. In other words that the unity of the Church is sufficiently guaranteed by the Spirit in spite of power in her being vested in two completely distinct subjects. In support of this view it could be pointed out that precisely according to the Second Vatican Council it is the *Spirit* which preserves the 'organic structure' of the Church in spite of the heterogeneous character of this structure, and that this in turn is neither caused nor guaranteed by any formal juridical norm.

The least that can be concluded from this consideration is that when it is a question of how two different functions can exist side by side in the Church without mutually cancelling each other out or themselves in turn needing to be reconciled through the human application of some common juridical principle, caution is needed. We need not always, or from every aspect, demand a principle unequivocally applicable at the *juridical* level, in virtue of which we can test the Church's unity juridically. At the same time this is not intended to imply that the attempt we are about to make will lead to a 'spiritualisation' of relationships which necessarily are juridical, or that its primary aims lie in the sphere of Church politics. Against such objections we shall be *thinking out*, in what follows, the problem of juridical law involved in the relationship concerning which this question has to be raised. The only points which will concern us, therefore, in discussing opposed positions will be the actual arguments put forward and their power to throw light upon the problem.

II

With regard to this question an attempt will here be made to justify the following thesis:

The bearer of the highest and supreme power in the Church is the united episcopate with and under the pope as its head. This single bearer can exercise its plenary power either in a 'collegiate act' in the true sense, or through an act of its head, the pope, who even in this case acts precisely *as* head of the college, without having to be commissioned for this by the rest of the bishops (the mere fact that they are such does not in itself constitute them as a college) by means of a juridical act on the part of these other bishops. *Thus there is only one subject endowed with supreme power in the Church: the college of bishops assembled under the pope as its head. But there are two modes in which this supreme college may act: a 'collegiate act' properly so-called, and the act of the pope as head of the college.*

The first point to be made with regard to this thesis is that in no sense does it derogate from the significance and dignity of the primacy of the pope. In fact the Council explicitly declares that the pope is in possession of his plenary powers not as a private person but as head of the entire Church. In this statement, then, the position of the pope is not under-estimated by the fact that his office and the significance attached to this in general can be understood only in relation to the Church, though this certainly does not mean that it is given to him by the Church. Now if this is the case then we cannot in any way be derogating from the dignity and uniqueness of his office either by saying that he possesses this plenary power precisely *as* head of the college of bishops. In no sense is there any implication in this thesis of the idea that his office and the plenitude of power which goes with it is handed over to him by the college of bishops. It is given to him by Christ. But it is given to him together with all that is included in it inasmuch as he is the appointed head of this college, which apart from him would not exist at all. For this college is constituted as such in virtue of the unity it achieves through the presidency of the pope (Peter), and by being one with him. Without the pope it itself is nothing, and he is the pope in virtue of the fact that, and to the extent that he is its head together with all the rights which precisely belong to this headship. In virtue of these rights he can also act *seorsim*, i.e. by a separate act of his own as distinct from a collegiate one. But even so he is still acting precisely *as* head of the college. Of course the fulness of his power cannot be derived from any *abstract* concept of what 'head of a college' means. The pope is head of the college in precisely *that* manner which has been worked out in concrete fact as the faith of the Church through a progressive development of dogma, and which has been defined in the First Vatican Council. But the plenary power vested in him in this sense is precisely that of one who holds the prerogatives pertaining to the college of bishops as it actually exists in the concrete, so that however he acts he is still acting precisely *as* head of this college. This does not mean, however, that he has to be specially commissioned for the purpose by the rest of the bishops. When, therefore, we say that the pope holds his office as visible head of the Church, and only in union with her, this does not derogate from the importance and uniqueness of his primacy as bishop of Rome. Rather it is only in this way that we can arrive at an understanding of its true nature. And if this is the case, then we cannot be in any sense belittling the primacy either by saying that the pope holds his official position precisely *as* head of the college of bishops. A further point constantly to be borne in mind is that the Church of which he is head is a socially structured entity, and the papacy is not the sole factor in determining what this structure shall be. On the contrary the episcopate too is numbered among those elements in it which are *juris divini*. If, therefore, the pope is pope precisely because he is head of the Church and only in virtue of this, then it follows that he is head of a Church which is also episcopal in its constitution, and is this too *juris divini*, as a matter of divine right. It is, therefore, quite impossible for the pope to be head of the Church without at the same time and in virtue of this also being head of the united episcopate. If, therefore, the bishop of Rome enjoys his plenary powers precisely *as* head of the Church, then it necessarily follows that he also enjoys them in virtue of being head of the united episcopate. It is true of both these facts that the one implies the other in the *same* sense, and with *equal* validity: the fact that the office of the pope relates to the universal Church implies that it relates in the same sense to the united episcopate and vice versa.

That this interpretation cannot simply be false from the outset is also shown by the following fact: the pre-Conciliar version of the Constitution on the Church, even though it was composed primarily by Roman theologians, had stated unreservedly that the pope is endowed with infallibility precisely *as* head of the Church *and* of the college of bishops (No. 30 in this schema): '*Tamquam universalis ecclesiae pastor et doctor, et collegii episcoporum caput*'. It is true that in the final and definitive text of *Lumen gentium* (Nos. 22, 25) this passage was omitted, or rather the term '*collegii episcoporum caput*' was transferred to another place in such a way that the two phrases were no longer explicitly presented as interchangeable. But the reason for this alteration was not that the statement contained in the pre-conciliar text is false, but rather that it was felt that this question should be left open.

Even from what has been said up to this point it will be clear that the teaching of the First and Second Vatican Councils does not exclude the thesis we have put forward at least in any positive sense. This also applies to the term *seorsim* in the *Nota Praevia Explicativa*. Having regard to the total context in which it is used this term 'by himself' only serves to rule out any necessity for a 'collegiate act' on the part of the united episcopate. What is sought to be conveyed by it is that even when the pope makes use of the supreme power vested in him 'by himself', he is acting validly and in a manner which is binding upon the Church. He is not bound in this to seek any special agreement on the part of the rest of the bishops in such a way that this agreement would be prior to the act of the pope himself and its binding force, and that it would only have full validity in this sense in virtue of this prior agreement. A further and separate question is what the nature of such an act is considered *ontologically*. Is it *ipso facto* and of its very nature the act of the head of the united episcopate, or rather the act of an individual who is indeed also (*qui*) the head of the college, but precisely in this act is not acting *as* (*qua*) such a head? On this point the term *seorsim* as used in the Declaration remains indeterminate. The opinion that this question was not affected by the *Nota Praevia* is also shared by e.g. Y. Congar, O. Semmelroth, A. Grillmeier, who were members of the theological commission of the Council.

A further objection to our thesis which is raised is that the pope holds supreme power in the Church 'alone' and 'in person'. To this it must simply be said that this term 'alone' has exactly the same force as that of *seorsim*, so that this difficulty is to be met with the same answer as that given above. Even if it is true that 'the pope in person' possesses this plenary power, still we cannot see what consequences can be drawn from this which run counter to our thesis. In this context the phrase 'in person' can only mean 'as a concrete physical individual', since in fact 'in person' cannot mean 'as a private person'. When it is said that the pope 'alone' receives this supreme power from Christ, the word 'alone' here can only mean that he is given this power actually as a physical individual. But it cannot mean that the united episcopate does not have this power, since it does in fact undoubtedly possess it. 'Alone' and 'in person', therefore, mean simply that he possesses his power as a physical individual in the concrete, and that as such he is also the 'bearer' (certainly not merely the 'exerciser') of this power.

But in all this nothing whatever has been said in reply to a *further* question which might be asked: How can we find more precise terms in which to define what is distinctive in the position of the pope, if we are asked in what *official* (as opposed to private) capacity he 'alone' and 'in person' is the bearer of supreme power in the Church? If it is suggested that according to our version the pope exercises this power not 'in person' but 'in the name of the college of bishops', this latter being the unique bearer of this power, then we must reply that to formulate our position in these terms is most misleading. For this phrase 'in the name of the college' insinuates that in order to exercise his power the pope would need to be commissioned for the purpose by the rest of the bishops. But of course this is not the case, and is in no sense asserted by the terms of our thesis either. On the contrary what this states is: The act of the pope, which he exercises in virtue of the commission given to him directly by Christ, is *ipso facto and in itself* an act of the college (*not* a collegiate act), because this power conferred upon him 'in person' and on 'him alone' by Christ of itself makes him the 'mandatory' of the college. If it is stated that the pope possesses his primatial power not only independently of the individual bishops but also independently of 'all of them together' (DS 3060) this is, of course, correct. But it proves nothing against our thesis. The mere fact that this phrase *Simul omnes* of the First Vatican Council is, as applied to the united episcopate, precisely *not* equivalent to the term 'college' is in itself enough to establish this point. For the pope himself belongs to the college as such as a constitutive member of it and indeed the supreme member of the college itself. If, therefore, he were to hold this primatial power of his independently of the actual college as such, and not merely independently of the sum total of all the rest of the bishops, then he would hold it independently of himself also – a position which is meaningless. In the strictest and most precise sense the pope has a supreme power not as a figure over against the college or above it, for this college is in fact itself indisputably vested with this same supreme power. The position is, rather, that the pope exercises this same power as an individual also, and this is precisely why in his possession of this power he is set apart from every other individual bishop and also from the sum total of all the bishops (though these are not identical with the college of bishops as such).

III

The *positive* grounds for upholding this thesis will appear *per modum exclusionis* primarily as the outcome of a critical examination of the other and opposed theories with regard to the relationship between the united episcopate and the primate. Let us begin by stating the first of two complementary principles which apply here. Every attempt to derive the plenitude of power belonging to the united episcopate and therefore to the Council from a primatial power that is attributed to the pope will meet with difficulties, both on the theoretical plane and on that of historical fact, which are insurmountable. It should be noticed that on such a theory this primatial power of the pope would be as such a *different* entity from the plenary power transmitted by him to the united episcopate. A power which is derivable from another power, quite different from it but still within the framework of the Church, cannot, simply by definition and in the very nature of the concept, be the supreme power. In virtue of being derived it is necessarily subordinate to that power from which it originates. A power vested in the united episcopate which is conceived of as at the same time a permanent sharing in the primatial power cannot be supreme.

To this principle a second must now be added. The supreme and plenary power of the united episcopate belongs to it *juris divini*. Since the Second Vatican Council there can be no doubt upon this point, and in fact in the First Vatican Council no doubts were cast upon it. Now in the light of this we are justified in asking whether a power which is held *juris divini* can be a power in which the subject is merely allowed to participate. If this participation were based upon an act of will on the part of him who confers a share of his power and might equally well withdraw it, then the power which is participated in in this sense is certainly not *juris divini*. If, on the other hand, it is suggested that the pope must allow this power of his to be shared by the united episcopate *jure divino*, then such a statement can still only signify, in effect, that the will of God and of Christ, by which the Church is constituted, intends there to be a united episcopate which has the same power as the pope, and in his sight this united episcopate is such that it has this power only as united with and under the pope.

On any showing this is correct, but it says no more than what must be said and maintained in all theories that are advanced upon this question. But in that case participation in the power of the pope is nothing more, in effect, than having this power. It is no longer a question of 'participation', but instead, according to the will of God, two different subjects actually exist, both of them vested with the *same* power (in all logic therefore they must be as subjects 'incompletely distinct'), which they receive from God. But the first of these subjects is not one which itself concedes a share in its own power, since *ex hypothesi* it is quite incapable of with-holding this participation from the other. In any case we no longer see how it can be the case that according to this theory anything more could be involved than a strange play on words being used to express the fact that God imparts this effective plenitude of power to the united episcopate and in doing so always intends it to belong to the united episcopate only in so far as this constitutes a college, and as united with the pope.

A further point, and one which even J. Salaverri concedes, is that the view we are contesting here is, even from the *historical* standpoint, more than improbable. The idea that the Council (considered as the united episcopate) possesses supreme and infallible power in doctrinal matters in the Church was already held as an explicit doctrine in the Church when the doctrine of the infallibility of the pope in matters of faith was still far from having been recognised with the same clarity in the Church's conscious faith. Now if this doctrinal power vested in the Council was derived from that of the pope, the converse would have had to be true. In that case the papal authority, since it provided the basis for that of the Council, would actually have had to be recognised first. Certainly at the material and factual level that which is derived, that which is sustained in being by some factor beyond itself, can come to be recognised even before that which provides it with its basis and origin. But when we are discussing juridical powers the same cannot apply. In such cases the order in which the realities signified come to be, and the order in which they come to be recognised must be parallel to one another because the actual object of enquiry is itself a conceptual reality which cannot have any significant existence at all without being recognised. This also appears from the fact that the Second Vatican Council makes no attempt to derive the plenary power of the college of bishops from the plenary power of its head. It attributes this plenary power to the fact that the episcopate is descended from the apostolic college, and recognises that this same power was imparted to this apostolic college as such and in itself, and not to Peter as an individual. In the grounds it puts forward for its decision, therefore, it follows the same course as had been followed in the actual history of dogma itself.

Now let us consider the alternative point of view. One of the commoner interpretations is the doctrine that the full and supreme authority in the Church is vested in two incompletely distinct subjects. This thesis is justified in a certain sense to the extent that it makes no attempt to derive the authority of the united episcopate from that of the pope. It can be taken merely as a description of this state of affairs, saying namely that viewed simply from the point of view of the direct practical experience of the exercise of this authority the supreme power of decision in the Church is vested in two subjects which are incompletely distinct as physical entities. And if this is all that is being said, then there is nothing in this thesis to be objected to. But if what is being maintained in it – at least implicitly – is that this *description* of the difference between the two subjects in the actual exercise of their authority is also the *ultimate* that can be said at the juridical and theological level, such that there is no further and deeper truth to be attained to beyond this, then this thesis is false. In fact it expresses nothing more with regard to the more essential and more fundamental relationship of the two 'incompletely distinct subjects' of supreme power in the Church, and manifestly presupposes that nothing more can be said either, and that this actual concrete state of affairs must be accepted as a positive datum, and that we must remain at the merely positive level of juridical institution.

Against this, however, we must first put the following objection The concept of 'two incompletely distinct subjects' is, even from the purely formal point of view (and abstracting from the concrete case with which we are concerned), obscure and imprecise in the extreme. We might legitimately ask: 'What do the terms "distinct" or "incomplete" properly mean?' Are there really 'two' subjects, because this is, in fact, what is being maintained, or is it in the last analysis only a *single* subject, seeing that in fact we cannot regard them as distinct from one another in any 'complete' or effective sense at all? If it is true that ultimately speaking it is *quite impossible* for two subjects to be vested with supreme power in one and the same *single* society precisely considered as single, then what in that case can it mean still to assert that in this case there are 'two subjects'? Are we not being too hasty in concluding from the fact that the two parties actually endowed with this power are incompletely distinct as *physical* entities, that these same parties must equally be regarded as distinct precisely *inasmuch as* they are endowed with this power? But how can we conclude this, seeing that this power is one and single not merely in a specific but in a numerical sense, as pertaining to a society that is numerically one and the same? Of course the 'misfortune' of two such subjects being irreconcilably opposed to one another and so taking decisive action in completely opposite directions is prevented by the fact that they are, after all, only 'incompletely' distinct. But does not this precisely mean that *there are not really two subjects at all?* To the extent that (notwithstanding the assertion to the contrary) they are not really 'two', no problem exists. But to the extent that, in spite of whatever unity we may concede to exist between them' they must be 'two', we must at least still pose the question of what kind of relationship they can bear to one another, such that the unity between them (which must, in fact, be implicitly conceded after all) really and effectively exists and is also recognisable as such.

Surely the fact that the pope actually belongs to the college of bishops carries, in the main, only enough weight to supply an answer to this question with regard to the juridical machinery involved, and not sufficient to provide an answer with regard to the question of the true and precise '*essence*' of this unity belonging to 'both' subjects. We may invoke a dictum of St Thomas to the effect that unity does not, in the last analysis, follow from duality. On the contrary, the notion of 'two' only becomes comprehensible to us from the notion of 'one'. Now it must be recognised that the duality with which we are here concerned cannot be derived from the unity (as the exponents of the first view contend). Since the power that is in question is not regarded as belonging of its very nature and right from the outset to the head of the college, this could only mean that the pope allows his power to be 'participated in' by the college. And this is excluded. Again, the unity of power cannot be achieved by combining two originally separate powers (*non enim plura secundum se uniuntur*). In the light of this the real question we have to deal with here becomes evident. It is the question of a *more basic, more original* unity which must be *prior* to the 'duality' of the two subjects as they now exist. The saying about 'two incompletely distinct subjects' represents a practical rule of thumb and the initial description of a fact as it outwardly appears, namely that two different ways of acting are used in the exercise of the supreme power, even though in itself and considered formally this can only be *one* and single. This saying, therefore, is correct at its face value and considered purely as an empirical description or designation of the *phenomenon*. But if it is pressed any further than this it becomes not an answer but rather a question in itself, the question of what kind of unity belongs *in essence* to this subject which is vested with that power in the Church which is in itself necessarily *one*.

The *positive* answer to this question can only be given on the basis of the doctrine that there can of necessity only be *one* subject vested with the supreme power. Recognising this and taking it as our basis we can then go on to ask *how* we can arrive at a conception of this subject in which we accord it its due place as one of the facts *a posteriori* recognised as such in the teaching of the Second Vatican Council, and which we now have to deal with on the basis of this teaching. This *one* subject must be conceived of in such a way that it includes, from the outset and of its own nature, *both* the entities the unity between which we are discussing here. This means: Whether we say 'pope' or 'college of bishops' our conceptions of both these entities must be such that each implies the other. Whether therefore we say 'the united episcopate with the pope as the head of the college and also capable of acting alone and of his own initiative', or alternatively 'the pope who in his official acts acts in every case (even though he has two different ways of acting open to him) in such a way that through him the college is acting (though this does not necessarily mean in an act that is collegiate in the strict sense)' – whichever of these two statements we choose, the meaning remains the same. In such a statement we must always be referring to that *one* subject which as one is vested with, and exercises the one supreme power in the Church. The fact that in the thesis formulated above we have given preference to the first way of putting the matter does not imply any rejection of the second one. Our only reason for preferring the first formulation here is that it gives clearer and more direct expression to the subject considered in its concrete reality, and more clearly excludes the idea that in this thesis of ours we are treating of the pope as permitting the college to share in his power. This would mean that his power has priority over that of the united episcopate and has as its bearer the pope himself independently of his status as head of the college.

In order to understand this thesis a point that has constantly to be borne in mind is that in general and in principle it does not of itself imply any denial of the fact that the act of a 'moral' (collective) or 'collegiate' person is actually performed in the concrete by a single person in the physical sense. Nor does it imply that for this act to be validly performed the other 'persons in the physical sense' belonging to this collective body or 'moral person' must necessarily and in all cases actually themselves commission the first individual to perform it by a separate and distinct act of their own, physically prior to the official one of the whole body. We can think of an extremely wide variety of ways in which a person in the sense of a physical individual can be appointed to represent a collegiate body or 'person' in the juridical sense. In our case this is quite certainly made effective by God (Christ) and not by the sum total of the members of the college of bishops, at least inasmuch as the pope is the head of this college *jure divino*. The only question still remaining, therefore, can be at most that of whether this appointment by God himself also implies the capacity so to act in the name of the college that this act is in fact not a 'collegiate act' at all, but still an act of the college. In other words the pope acts *as* head of the college whenever he makes use of his primatial power. In any case a commissioning of precisely *this* kind (such that it includes this more precisely defined authority) to represent and act for a college, deriving as it does from a third party, namely God, cannot be rejected by this college. Now in this conception there is no intrinsic logical contradiction. Admittedly all this presupposes that he who confers an authority of precisely *this* kind can also ensure in the giving of it and for the exercising of it that the acts arising from it are *de facto* in conformity with the will of the entire college rightly understood. And this in turn does not exclude the principle that precisely this rightly understood will of the college is *recognised* from the decisions of him who is its head precisely in this sense.

The harmony we are presupposing here is present in the Church through the power of the Spirit within her. In fact *Lumen gentium* (No. 25) emphasises this connection between pope and Church when it says that in his decisions the pope is not bound by the (prior) agreement of the Church (for the juridical validity of his act), but still that he and his decisions cannot fail to have this agreement *'propter actionem ejusdem Spiritus Sancti'*. The same can also be said with regard to the relationship between the decision of the pope and the will of the college.

The *fact* that the appointment vested in the pope takes this form is of course to be deduced from the actual sources of revelation in the concrete. It is to be deduced from these first on the grounds that since the Church is *one*, only *one single* subject vested with supreme power can be conceived of within her, second because the primatial power of the pope and the supreme power in the college of bishops are established from these sources.

Additional support for the thesis is also to be drawn from the following consideration. The act of founding the Church is initially posited in the act of founding the college of the 'Twelve', and it is precisely *from* this college that a *member* of the college is appointed by Christ as its head. Now if we observe this order of events, which is also depicted by the Council (certainly we must bear in mind in this the indisputable fact that the college is in each case the bearer of supreme power in the Church), then it seems most consistent with the facts to say that Peter obtains his primatial authority precisely *as* head of this college. If we then go on to recognise that Peter can exercise his own personal power without any collegiate act on the part of the Twelve, still this further recognition does not invalidate the earlier realisation, namely that the authority belonging to him is that of the head of the apostolic college as such. On the contrary all that this adds is that this supreme power of his is now more precisely specified and concretised, so that it is seen to be one specific mode in which this head of the 'Twelve' can act. We can then go on to apply the same consideration to the relationship between pope and episcopate.

Of course what we primarily achieve by this is simply an understanding of our thesis at the formal level, a recognition of its formal meaning and of the fact that it involves no intrinsic contradiction.

IV

Perhaps a consideration of the content of this thesis that is *theological* in the true sense will enable us to advance a little further. The subject vested with supreme authority to lead and govern in the Church must reflect the distinctive quality of the Church herself. The first way in which this is made apparent is for visible expression to be given to the unity that exists in the multiplicity and to the multiplicity that exists in the unity. This is made especially effective if the Church considered as the 'sacrament' of love in the world, so penetrates into the world from the innermost resources of her own nature that she unifies that which is diverse in it, while at the same time according due recognition to this diversity. In order to point out a second way in which it is made apparent, attention must be drawn to a further constitutional factor: the unity and diversity involved in the very concept of 'Church'. This is constituted by the multiplicity of those who are using the freedom bestowed irrevocably upon each of them to work out their own salvation, and at the same time by the 'covenant unity' or comm-unity in which the individual, without any diminishment of his own uniqueness even in the actual achievement of his own personal salvation, finds salvation mediated to him.

Now if the supreme holder of the power to lead and govern in the Church is to reproduce and represent this quality of the Church in his own person, then as an individual his status must be both collegiate *and* personal at the same time. Naturally we cannot, by taking this as our starting-point, deduce the *de facto* constitution of the Church from it as a matter of logical argument. But confronted with it as an existing reality we can understand it. A point which we must always bear in mind here is that the pope, without prejudice to his unique position as visible 'representative' of Christ upon earth, is still a member of the Church, and precisely identified with the Church. In other words we should not expect him *merely* to reflect the relationship of Christ to his Church as distinct from himself. Thus it cannot be inconsistent with the nature of the primacy belonging to the pope if he is head of the Church precisely *inasmuch as* he is head of the college of bishops. In other words a specific element in the nature of the Church is constituted by the very fact that he has this function of being head of the college. Whereas in Christ himself the personal and the 'official' (functional) aspects completely coincide, in a member of the Church (as redeemed) this is not altogether the case. It is not, therefore, the case with the pope either. The personal factor is present and plays a part in his official function. For instance he acts of his own initiative in the sense that he does not need any special authorisation each time he decides to do so. But his personal action is still an act of the *bearer of the office as such*. (*'Non enim ut persona privata sententiam profert'*), and, by the very fact of being a person holding office in this sense, he is a member of the Church and head of the college of bishops as such. Now precisely because he has this position the pope represents in his own individual person both the unity of the Church *and* her diversity, a unity and diversity constituted by the fact that she is made up of a collection of many Churches.

If therefore we accept the position of 'head of the college of bishops' as belonging integrally to the primatial power of the pope as such, and as an intrinsic element in it, then it straightway becomes clear why this power is 'unrestricted' and in this sense 'full'. We can only designate a power as 'restricted' if it is limited by some other arbiter external to itself, and not in respect of that kind of 'limitation' which is inherent in the very nature of the power itself. Now in many respects the authority of the pope is certainly 'limited' even at the juridical level. For instance (setting aside its limitation with regard to the teaching authority which is bound by revelation etc.) it is 'limited' by the existence *juris divini* of the college of bishops, which the pope can neither abrogate nor, taking it in its entirety, inactivate. Now if this 'limitation' were not *a limitation arising from the nature of the papal primacy as such*, then we could not call his power 'full' in the true sense at all. But if this 'limitation' arises from the intrinsic nature of this authority in itself, inasmuch as the pope possesses this power proper to himself precisely as head of the college of bishops, then we can understand that it is not thereby 'restricted' in the true sense by any other juridical arbiter such as might restrict this power *ab externo*.

In terms of its content there is a further standpoint from which we can regard this thesis of ours. One of the special concerns of many of the theologians at the Council was to point out the unity which exists between all the official powers belonging to bishops, and also the fact that they all have their primary and basic roots in the sacrament of episcopal consecration. The Council then went on to ratify this point in an extremely significant manner. In the formulations of the mediaeval canonists the *'potestas ordinis'* and the *'potestas jurisdictionis'* have for the most part simply been juxtaposed without any connection between them being adverted to. Now, however, the real unity between these two powers has been made clear by the findings of the Council, and this raises many further questions for ecclesiology and canon law. Once the unity between these two powers is conceded and presupposed, the existence of the college of bishops as such, or membership of this college, cannot fail to have an important bearing on the further question of the manner in which the *'potestas ordinis'* is vested in the individual bishop. We must not be led astray on this point by the fact that in the validly consecrated bishop this *'potestas ordinis'* is present permanently and irrevocably. For in fact this irrevocability, to the extent that it really is present, means simply that in the individual bishop membership of the college too cannot be totally lost so as to leave no trace whatever (even if the *'communio hierarchiaca cum Collegii Capite et membris'* is removed, so that *full* unity with the college no longer exists). But it does not mean that the *'potestas ordinis'* has nothing to do with membership of the college of bishops, and therefore nothing to do with the college itself or with its head either. Even the *'potestas ordinis'* is an element in the one and full power which is originally present in the college of bishops as united with and under its head the pope, the power, therefore, in which the individual bishop obtains a share in virtue of his episcopal consecration. On the basis of this it may validly be concluded that the pope is the visible principle of the unity belonging to the college of bishops in relation to the *'potestas ordinis'* too, and not merely in relation to the *'potestas jurisdictionis'*. Furthermore it is precisely when our thesis is accepted as a principle that the pope stands revealed as the supreme and definitive bearer of the *'potestas ordinis'*. It is not the case, therefore, that he needs to be able to perform more individual sacramental acts than any other bishop, or to perform them with greater intensity. Rather he represents the unity of sacramental power in the Church. If we accept that the *'potestas ordinis'* is rooted in the united college of bishops in this way, we can then understand that even in the actual conferring of the sacraments too 'collegiate acts' are possible (if, indeed, not actually necessary). This is the case, for instance, in concelebration which must, in fact, be understood not as a synchronisation of many Masses, but as one *single* sacrifice even in the dimension of the sacramental sign. The reconciliation as practised in the early Church likewise had this force. In this the bishop, in union with the assembled priests or *presbyterium*, used the laying on of hands to confer the *pax* of reconciliation with the Church, and thereby the Spirit. Thereby forgiveness of sins in God's sight was likewise conferred by this rite. Now this can be understood as a 'collegiate act' in the full sense, even though, it is true, one that was performed not by the united episcopate but rather by the college that was accustomed to act in such a setting, and which was made up of the bishop and his presbyterium. The same is true of the anointing of the sick at Easter, in so far as this was conferred by several priests.

If, therfore, we unreservedly accept that a 'collegiate act' is in principle possible even in the conferring of a sacrament, then we can go on from this to say: the sacramental sign as established in the Church is constituted hierarchically, and it is in conformity with the nature of the Church herself that the act in which this sign is made effective (and which is always an act of the Church herself and of her college) can in every case be of two kinds: it can either be a 'collegiate' act in the true sense, or it can be the act of an individual. But in this latter case the individual performing the act is actually sharing in the sacramental power of the Church, and so performing this sacramental act in the name of the Church.

We can see, therefore, that the relationship between the pope and the college of bishops corresponds in certain respects to the position of one who has been vested with sacramental power, even though initially this relationship was considered only from the aspect of the *'potestas jurisdictionis'*.

V

We may now turn to the question of what differences the thesis we have expounded would make in practice. Certainly the importance of this question should not be exaggerated. The common ground between the different interpretations is too great for these differences to be very far-reaching. For in any case it is true that in the exercise of supreme power in the Church the pope can act *seorsim*, while it is equally true that a collegiate act on the part of the college of bishops is possible. But both of these constitute an exercise of one and the same supreme power in the Church. Nor is it legitimate to say that if we take a general view of the whole question, and accept the other interpretations as our starting-point, we shall come to the conclusion that something different takes place, or has taken place in the Church than if we accept the thesis presented here as our principle of interpretation.

But even with these reservations it does not seem that the thesis with which we are here concerned is totally without practical consequences of any kind. The concrete *way* in which various possible practical consequences which do follow from our thesis are to be drawn remains – from the juridical aspect – reserved to the *discretio* of the pope, and it must not be maintained even that a given way of applying the truth upheld here is possible only if our thesis is presupposed. To give a concrete example, it is to be enacted by positive law that the universal episcopate shall be given, even apart from its role in Councils, a share in the supreme government of the Church, as for instance in the convening of a Council, setting up the synod of bishops, arranging for the universal episcopate to be consulted by the pope, making it possible for the regional conferences of bishops to develop special ecclesiastical laws of their own, giving the universal episcopate a share in the work of the Roman Congregations by letting them have representatives on these, etc. But any such concrete way of exercising supreme power can be, both in its inception and in the practice of it (this may vary according to the particular circumstances prevailing at any given time), clearer to understand, less circumscribed and less strained if it it is regarded as an application of the theory we are upholding here. For on this theory we do not need constantly to be striking a precarious balance between two bearers of supreme power in the Church, both of whom, even if they are 'incompletely distinct', still have to be accorded their due effectiveness. Our theory envisages rather the exercise of power by the *one single* and supreme bearer of *all* power in the Church. And on this theory the only question remaining is how to establish more precisely the form this exercise of it should take in the concrete in order to be most effective.

That axiom is true which lays down that an authority which is never exercised is no authority at all. If there are *two* bearers of supreme power in the Church (even if these are 'incompletely distinct'), then the question constantly arises afresh of how, while maintaining both the two exercises of power as two quantitatively distinct activities, we can strike a balance between them in such a way that neither simply absorbs the other into itself and so, *in reality* (even if not 'in so many words') abolishes it. If there is only *one* supreme subject vested with supreme authority in the Church, (even though with two ways of exercising this authority which, though distinct, are interrelated in such a way that they can be interchanged or made to flow into one another), then two principles follow from this: first, the pope cannot feel that the active collaboration of the college of bishops (which may take the most diverse possible forms) is *ipso facto* a diminishment of his own authority. Second, the episcopate cannot feel that by recognising to the full the pope's authority in cases in which he acts *seorsim*, they are accepting a limitation imposed from outside their own body of the full scope of their own personal authority, for this activity of the pope is, of its very nature, an *act of the college* itself, even if it is not a 'collegiate act' in the strict sense. Of course it must be conceded as an ever present possibility that with regard to the 'independent' exercise of authority on the part of the pope in particular concrete instances individual bishops may still retain their own attitudes. They may wish that in such cases the episcopate might be allowed to share more manifestly, more actively and in a more directly practical way in the decision involved. Here, therefore, we have reached that point beyond which we cannot go in defining *juridically* the respect due to the episcopate in the taking of such decisions. This is likewise the point which may be taken as a starting-point in defining the scope of the para-canonical importance and effectiveness of the episcopate, which must not be undervalued. And we shall undervalue it if we blindly and rigidly confine ourselves to the question of whether the effective part to be played by the episcopate is sufficiently assured in juridical and legal terms. At this point too scope is opened up for the movement of the Spirit of God, which acts *fortiter, suaviterque* so as to ensure that in the exercise of this supreme power by the one supreme bearer vested with it harmony is preserved, at least in the long run, between the different ways in which it is employed.

4

THE PRESENCE OF THE LORD IN THE CHRISTIAN COMMUNITY AT WORSHIP

1. Presence' in General

IN this brief study[1] we shall be discussing the presence of the Lord in the Christian community at worship. The approach we shall be adopting is a systematic and synthetic one, and we shall take as our basis the work that has already been done on the theological sources. For this purpose due allowance must be made from the outset for the inevitable and insurmountable imperfections inherent in the concepts we need to use in such a study, as also for the fact that of their nature these concepts approximate only deficiently and analogously to the realities involved. Thus a point that strikes one immediately is that the idea of 'presence' admits of, and indeed demands an interpretation in terms of space and time. But this word 'presence' is capable of being extended further into all dimensions of human existence, and of being applied to man as a whole at his various levels as a being endowed with a body, with intellect, with free choice and decision, with a social life in common with his fellows, and with a place in history. Such a word, therefore, does not admit of any strict or precise definition, any more than does man himself. Every attempt at describing or defining what 'presence' means ends up by appealing to that basic and primary experience in which, the moment we make it, we recognise what 'presence' is, and yet which at the same time we are incapable of expressing. Such an experience, which is itself shifting and variable as it occurs in the unfolding of human history whether at the individual or the collective level, gives us an awareness of the way in

---

[1] For a bibliography on this question cf. the references in this volume, 'On the Presence of Christ in the Communities of the Diaspora', pp. 84–102. In addition to the documents of the Council mentioned there cf. especially the particularly important No. 9 (*Diversi modi praesentiae Christi*) in the '*Instructio de cultu mysterii Euchar-istici*' of the Congregation of Rites dated 25th May 1967 (the official Latin text is to be found in *Typis polyglottis Vaticanis* 1967, p. 13).

which 'presence' is achieved, and this in turn varies in intensity according to the particular level in human living which is involved. 'Presence' always implies a relationship between two entities or, more precisely, between three: the relationship namely between the two which are present to each other, and the relationship which both bear to the 'medium' or 'common ground' between them. It is this medium as such that provides the sphere in space and time which makes it possible for the two to be present to each other. This means that the very nature of what 'present' means is determined by these two (or three) entities, their distinctive qualities and the very different ways in which they may be related to one another. 'Presence', therefore, can assume very different forms and manifest very different properties. On this basis we can, perhaps, formulate here at the very outset the following propositions:

(a) 'Presence' cannot, in the first instance, be either regarded as, or deduced from the co-existence of two physical bodies which modify one another at the physical level. Presence, rather, is a concept that is originally and basically anthropological, one which belongs *a priori* – even though in different ways and different degrees – to those factors which determine the condition of man as a whole.

(b) In the context of human living, therefore, presence in its fullest and deepest sense is that which affects and causes that which we call 'presence' from all aspects and at all levels of man's being, and which removes that contrary state of 'absence' in which one entity exists and yet, so far as another is concerned, is as though it did not exist.

(c) The presence of two beings in space and time (that of men to one another or that of man to another being which is capable of being, in some sense, present to man and for him in space and time) certainly is significant and important for human life. But nevertheless, in the last analysis it can be accounted merely that which is presupposed, that which has the force of an 'ontological symbol' (is a *Realsymbol*) of the specifically human mode of presence, in which men are present to each other (and to others).

(d) Hence when we speak of a 'presence' through love, in the Spirit, in knowledge etc., what we are treating of is not some kind of metaphorical transference of the concept of presence, but rather the original and basic meaning of the word. For the initial datum of human experience is not the co-existence of two bodies in space and time but rather man himself as endowed with a consciousness of his own being, as set in charge of himself and made answerable for his own free decisions, as given responsibility for himself and at the same time achieving the fulness of his own existence in personal intercommunication with others. Now all original and basic concepts, which genuinely cannot be defined in other terms, have their origins in this experience.

(e) Nevertheless we must not regard the concept of 'presence' as one for which there is absolutely no substitute. This is true even at that level at which the concept of physical presence is involved. The term has hardly any part to play in modern physics because here, properly speaking, the investigator is concerned only with the existence, location, mutual interdependence in function, or ascertainability of physical particles. But it is true in a far deeper sense of that more basic concept of 'presence' which is anthropological, for this can be expressed in terms of that by which this presence is constituted (in terms of its actual content), and in relation to this the 'presence' itself is, as it were, only subsequent and secondary. Even in the case of the 'eucharistic presence' this still applies for the very reason that that by which it is constituted, namely 'transubstantiation', is not to be thought of as the introduction of the reality of Christ into a specific locality in the sense implied in the 'adductionist' theory.

After these preliminary remarks let us pass on immediately to a synthetic and systematic exposition of that kind of 'presence' in which the Lord is made present to us and we to him in the Christian cult.

2. On the Presence of Christ in the Cult

(a) What we are considering here is the presence to each other of Christ and the Church in her cultic activities. Now the 'medium' of this presence is the Holy Spirit of Christ. This statement must now be expounded in more precise detail.

(aa) It is necessary to have such a 'medium'. Usually we do not pay sufficient attention to this 'medium' and the necessity for it to obtain any clear idea of its significance. For we interpret every mode of 'presence' according to the conceptual model of a physical and local presence, a presence in space and time (the reason for this is that *conversio ad phantasma* which is indispensable in every act of intellectual cognition). Now certainly in this kind of presence the 'medium' is necessary too. But the very fact that it is always there (both objectively and subjectively) all along means that it is not adverted to. But let us suppose that something is present not as a constant and unvarying fact of existence but still in the realm of immediate possibility or, to put it another way, that there has to be a transition from a state of absence to one of presence or to a more intensive kind of presence. In such a case as this a medium of the kind we are speaking of is postulated as prior to the presence itself and as a necessary condition for it which is distinct from itself. This medium, then, is something that makes that which is to be 'rendered present' actually present, and that is, at the same time, different from it; something which, as one, makes two entities which are to be rendered present to one another actually present and at the same time maintains the distinction between them. It provides the unifying sphere or common ground for a mutual presence between them to be achieved. Now if it is pointed out that an entity which makes itself present to something else itself provides this medium or common ground necessary for mutual presence to be achieved, then in general and in principle we would have to concede the truth of this objection. But a point that should not be forgotten – especially in our present case – is that it is wholly conceivable that at least one of the two entities being made present to each other cannot, of its own resources, establish this access to the other, and the medium or common ground which makes this presence possible. Instead of this it has to be 'admitted' to this presence which is to be made actual. Now this means nothing else than the setting up of a medium of presence such as we have been speaking of, which is to be distinguished from the actual presence itself as the means and necessary condition for it to be achieved.

bb) In the particular case we are considering this medium (the dimension of the presence, its *ambience*) is the Spirit of Christ. It cannot be our task at this point to show how this statement is to be deduced from the positive sources of revelation. Here we shall be attempting to make comprehensible what this statement is intended to convey. Of course this previously existing medium of the presence of Christ in the cult can, already in itself, be thought of as a 'presence' of the Spirit of Christ which has been bestowed upon the Church, which 'indwells' her as a gift of God in the hearts of those who have been justified. From this point of view no distinction is to be drawn between the presence of Christ and that of his Spirit. Christ is present in the Church through his *pneuma*. *His* presence actually is *pneuma hagion*. But precisely as such this presence of the Spirit in the Church is the 'medium' which is the necessary prior condition for that further presence which is achieved precisely between Christ and the Church in the enactment of the *cult*. There are two reasons for this. First in the cult and through it there takes place a special presence of Christ over and above the 'habitual' presence of the Spirit and so of Christ in the Church. This special cultic presence of Christ is such that it does not exist with *this* degree of 'actuality' apart from the cult. The second reason is that the Spirit of Christ as 'habitually' present in the Church and her members can be, and in fact is, the onto-logical presupposition for the actual presence of Christ in the cult. For it is only in the *pneuma* of Christ that the Church can teach, pray, believe, hope, love and confer the sacraments. Now it is in these activities that the cult of the Church is achieved, and it is through this cult that Christ and the faithful are rendered mutually present to one another in the most actual and sublime form possible. But in what does this 'medium' consist, if we may so express it, in its ultimate essence? It is constituted by the fact that only the divine Spirit as 'uncreated grace' can cause a human act (and in the first instance the cult too belongs to this category) to become an act of such a kind that in it God is attained to in adoration and 'posses-sed' as he is 'in himself'. It becomes such an act through this grace working in it as an intrinsic principle. In other words the interior subject-ive principle of the cult must be the Holy Spirit of God himself in order that this cult really can enter into the holy of holies of the divine life itself, and in order that this cult may consist not merely in the adoration of a God who is infinitely remote and 'other' to ourselves, but may rather become that *commercium* which is, in a certain sense, interior to God himself, for it is through this that we share in the trinitarian life of God which goes back to the source without origin, the eternal Father.

(b) In this dimension of the Spirit a mutual presence of Christ and of the faithful to one another at the highest level of actuality is constituted through the cult of the local Church. The local Christian community which accomplishes the cult of God in Christ and through his Spirit is not merely one segment of the universal Church, analogous, for instance, to one particular political constituency in a state. Rather it is *the* Church as present at one specific place, so that through the local community in that place the Church realises to the utmost possible extent the perfection of her own nature, her 'actualisation', and experiences through the cult the presence of Christ in the Church in its most sublime form. Certainly we can speak of many ways in which Christ is 'present' in the Church. We can say that Christ is present in the Church through an exercise of the Church's teaching authority, e.g. in Councils. And he can be said to be present in all other acts which are acts of the one universal Church who extends her boundaries throughout the 'length and breadth of the earth'. But it should be noticed that when we are thinking of the cult of the Church considered as a whole we are thinking of it inasmuch as it includes the eucharistic sacrifice as the supreme mode in which the work of redemption is made present. And in virtue of this the cult is *capable* of being, in the subject taking part in it, the most sublime way of making real his faith, his hope and his love. And it is to this that the whole activity of the official Church is orientated as means to end. Now to the extent that all this is true we are justified in saying that there can be no act through which Christ is made more closely and forcefully present than the cult of the Church, and it is through this presence that the Church herself is constituted ('gathered together', as the Council puts it) as 'actualising' her own nature and bringing it to its fulness. This cult, in which the supreme 'actualisation' of the presence of Christ in the Church, and thereby the supreme 'actualisation' of the Church herself, is achieved, is different from the cult of the people of God in the Old Testament in that it takes place in every local community of worshippers. In this respect too an essential and formal difference appears between the Church and any other *societas perfecta*. From this in turn it follows that the concept of the 'perfect society' is totally inadequate as a characterisation of the Church even at the 'visible' and empirical level to which her cult too belongs. No secular society can achieve the supreme 'actualisation' of its nature in one individual segment or element in its total makeup. On the contrary this degree of 'actualisation' is only achieved through the cumulative process of all its elements and their activities being added together till, in a certain sense, the sum total of them all is finally arrived at. Yet in the light of the supreme 'actualisation' which is achieved with such intensity at the altar the whole Church is 'there' in the local community at worship, because in this local community which, according to all outward appearances and in the dimension of the merely juridical and 'social' is only a small segment of the Church, the most actual and the most intimate presence of Christ is achieved, that presence which actually constitutes the Church in his Spirit.

(c) The presence of Christ in the cult must be understood as *single* and *active*. No doubt this presence of Christ in the cult of the local community contains within itself very different elements. Yet it must be understood as prior to all these elements, and as unique. For Christ is also one in his relationship to men as sanctifying them, and man himself is also one in the midst of all the many dimensions in which he exists. The different elements in this single and unique presence must be comprehended as the intrinsic constitution of this presence precisely as *single*. They derive their meaning and their significance precisely *from* this one presence, and achieve it *in* this. Or (from many points of view this way of putting it is more exact) these elements must be understood as different degrees in the 'actualisation' and intensity of this one unique presence through which God and man become united for the glory of God and the salvation of man. This also applies to the presence of Christ in the Eucharist in which Christ is made substantially present under the forms of bread and wine through 'transubstantiation'. For it is not merely that this presence too, which is achieved in the dimension of the effective *sign*, is measured by the union which the faithful achieve with Christ in his *pneuma*. It is not only that this presence is always orientated to the actual consumption of the sacrament, so that Christ is adored precisely under the forms of bread and wine, these having the force of an *anamnesis* pointing back to his death and resurrection and making manifest the *meal* of eternal life. It is not only that this presence of Christ in the Eucharist is a real and bodily presence of a nature that is absolute and unique, and which cannot be understood on the analogy of a natural presence and co-existence of two bodies in the same sphere, to which both are related and by which they are limited. We must recognise, rather, that there is something beyond this and more important than this: the act by which this eucharistic presence of Christ is made effective in 'transubstantia-tion' is only rightly understood in the entire context to which it belongs, which is that of the cult taken as a whole. For the 'form' of this sacrament (which goes with the 'species' of bread and wine as an integral element in the sacramental sign of this presence) consists of the words of consecrat-ion which persist and endure (as valid) in the dimension of human living and human historicity (even when acoustically speaking they have ceased). Only as united with these words are the 'species' the sign of Christ's presence. Now these words of consecration can only exist, can only be uttered and understood (and without being understood they would not be human words at all) in the context of the Christian cult taken as a whole. Even the 'substantial' presence of Christ in the Eucharist belongs to the dimension of the 'sign' and so to the one cult taken in its entirety, even though it constitutes the supreme and ultimate reality which can be achieved in this cult.

This single presence of Christ in the cult must be understood as *actively taking effect*. What we mean by this is that right from the outset this presence of Christ in the cult must be understood not as the mere co-existence of two entities in the same place, something which is, in the last analysis, already achieved by the very fact of God's omnipresence taken by itself, and something which, taken by itself, has no significance for the glory of God and the salvation of man. This saving presence of Christ in the cult is constituted rather by the following factors:

1. The self-bestowal of God in his Spirit, through which God gives himself immediately as he is in and of himself as the 'subject' and

co-principle of that life in man which is a sharing in the life of God himself, and that too . . .

2. Through all the 'media' and mediating acts by which this divine self-bestowal is communicated, and which show forth this divine self-bestowal in sign and symbol at the historical and social, and therefore the cultic level. For it is through these signs that these media and acts of mediation take effect, and so make present this divine self-bestowal. We shall shortly be returning to these mediating acts to treat of them in rather more detail.

(d) This *single* presence of Christ in the cult considered as as an active sanctifying force is constituted by the following elements:

(aa) *By the word of the gospel*: a true presence of Christ is already *ipso facto* achieved wherever the word of the gospel is preached in power and heard in a spirit of faith. This is explicitly stated in *Lumen gentium* (No. 26). In fact the *kerygma* of the New Covenant is no mere handing on of a piece of human knowledge from one individual to another such that only the human concepts of the reality they stand for are present and not the reality itself. On the contrary the *kerygma* is the event in which the reality itself that is being proclaimed is imparted to him who hears of it in a spirit of faith through the words and concepts that are expressed. Christ (as he who was crucified and rose again on our behalf) imparts himself to us as the eschatological union between God and man as achieved in the Spirit and through faith, in an act of divine self-bestowal, and thereby makes himself present in preacher and hearer alike. All elements of human conceptuality in the preaching of the word of God are, so to say, only the 'flesh' through which the divine reality makes itself present by manifesting itself in effective signs, and so takes effect upon us in a (free and supernatural) act of self-bestowal. The word of preaching as delivered with authority and heard in faith and in the Spirit is a word that has an effective and exhibitive force, one which, through a process of *anamnesis*, renders saving history effectively present, and already in the here and now effectively promises to man a future of salvation that is absolute (*Verbum efficax rememorativum et prognosticum*). This effective and exhibitive force in the word that is preached (and the presence of Christ constituted by this) has, it is true, specifically different degrees of intensity. But this effective and exhibitive force in the word of preaching belongs to the very nature of that preaching which is the event of grace and so the presence of Christ. The supreme degree of this special kind of effective force is attained in that word which is the actual 'form' of the sacrament or the sacramental sign in itself.

(bb) *Through the sacrament*: Every sacrament can, and indeed must, be understood as that kind of exhibitive and effective word in which Christ, through the mouth of the Church, utters himself as the eschatological 'sacrament' of salvation to a specific man in a situation which is significant for his life as a whole and in a form in which it can be apprehended at the level of concrete human living. From this standpoint it is clear that every sacrament signifies and effects a presence of Christ. We can, if we like, call this presence 'dynamic' and 'non-substantial' (to distinguish it from the presence in the Eucharist). But this presence is not that of God alone as he exists in himself, but rather the presence of the incarnate *Word* as such. This is what is expressed in the doctrine of the 'instrumental efficacity' of the humanity of Christ in the sacraments and the imparting of grace, whatever further explanations we may choose to offer of this instrumentality. A further point for consideration is the following: the fact that an authorised human intermediary is involved in the dispensing of the sacraments is indeed an integral element in the constitution of the *sign* of the presence of Christ. Indeed the dispenser of the sacraments takes the place of Christ himself in the dimension of the sign that effects what it signifies. But since he does not himself, in any proper sense, bring about the sacramental grace, the actual *res sacramenti* as its effective source, he does not, in any sense take the place of the presence of Christ himself. In other words the human dispenser of the sacraments does not take the place of an absent Christ, but rather represents Christ as present in the dimension of the 'effective' sign, even though it is Christ himself who, of his own power, brings about the grace in his *pneuma*. Finally if we want to emphasise the 'substantial' presence of Christ in the Eucharist as distinct from a 'merely dynamic' presence in the other sacraments then, in doing this, we must not overlook the fact that this 'substantial presence' – accurately understood – belongs to the dimension of the sign, to the sacrament as such. It does not yet belong to the sacramental grace, to the the *res sacramenti* itself, and does not bring about salvation in man of itself (*edunt boni, edunt mali*) unless this 'substantial presence' is complemented by that effectiveness of the Spirit of Christ through which alone man is really united to God, and in which the presence of Christ attains its supreme point and its goal. This presence of Christ as achieved in the sacrament (in the dimension of the 'sign' and of the 'reality' signified) has not only the character of a gift of God to man, but also that of a cultic act to the extent that through the act of Christ the High Priest, which is in a certain sense 'made incarnate' in the action of the Church, man is consecrated more and more radically to the adoration of God through the cult, and to the extent that the reception of sacramental grace on the part of the recipient of the sacrament also and necessarily signifies the acceptance and exercising of this commission which man is given in the grace to take part in the cultic worship of God.

(cc) *Through the Eucharist*: We have already referred in brief to the connection which exists between the Eucharist and the proclamation of the effective word of God in preaching and in the sacraments. Taking this as our starting-point it already follows that the Eucharist constitutes the supreme event in which that presence of Christ in the midst of his people which is the Church is achieved. This supreme mode in which Christ is made present in the Church is not to be deduced solely or exclusively from the dogma of 'transubstantiation' as this dogma is understood by scholastic theologians. In the Eucharist the word of the gospel is present totally and in a supremely effective form. It is that word through which the proclamation 'showing forth' the death and resurrection of the Lord, the work of redemption which was achieved once and for all, is presented by the Church in visible cult and in the Holy Spirit (as a unity) to the Father, while at the same time the Body and Blood of Christ are brought to the believers. The special quality of this presence, which precisely belongs in a special and unique manner to the Eucharist, in many respects goes beyond those elements in the one presence of Christ which we have already mentioned, even though it is perfectly possible to understand it specifically as the supreme instance of the presence of Christ as we have considered it up to this point. In the Eucharist the presence of Christ achieves, through the sacramental word that 'shows it forth', the supreme and specifically distinct 'actualisation' of what it essentially is. In this two modes of presence are achieved: the death and resurrection of Christ are made present and actual sacramentally ('in the "mystery" ') and at the same time the Body and Blood of Christ are made present substantially. These two modes of a presence that is ultimately and most deeply one are achieved in such a way that this presence is related not only to the entry of Christ into the individual saving history of a particular person but also to the Church herself as such. This is made manifest in visible form in the community at worship, and in the celebration of the Eucharist it achieves its supreme fulness and 'actuality' both in the dimension of the 'sign' and at the same time in the dimension of the reality itself that is signified. This is because in the Eucharist the union of Christ the head with his body, the Church, is at its most intense, being in fact made visible in the sacrament and made effective in the grace that it conveys. Here then Christ is made present on the one hand in his relationship to the Father and the task he has received from him, and on the other in his relationship to the Church and the functions he performs for her.

(dd) *Through hope and love*: These are achieved through the grace of the Spirit and 'incarnated' in the cult. For the word of the gospel always has the character of an eschatological proclamation of the glory that is to come. Furthermore every sacrament is a 'prognostic' sign, and the Eucharist is the proclamation of the coming of the Lord in glory and an anticipation of the glory that is to come. And for these reasons every event in which the Lord is made present through the cult has the character of that sign and that actual event in which the Christian hopes of the people of God for a future that is absolute are born and made manifest in concrete form in the sacramental life of the Church. The same is to be said of the love of members of the Church for one another. For every word of God is the effective manifestation of the love of God as addressed to man, in which, by a true act of self-bestowal, he gives himself to man. *For this very reason* this effective manifestation of God's love brings about a genuine union between men. It follows that this applies above all to the sacramental word because every *opus operatum* unites man more interiorly and more deeply to the 'Mystical Body' of Christ. This is true in supreme measure of the Eucharist, which is the exhibitive 'symbol' of that Body, 'the head of which is Christ, and to which God has willed to unite us as the members of this Body by the closest ties of faith, hope and love' (N 875). Since the Eucharist is always to be interpreted in its 'context' (if we may so express it), in which its nature as effective sign is realised, it follows that as the sign of love it subsumes within itself everything which is necessarily included in the eucharistic cult, or is demanded as most properly due to it or as most needful for its proper celebration: the attendance of many at a specific place so as to form a local community of worshippers, the hearing of the word of God in common, praying in common, making profession in common, of faith and hope, caring in common for the needy and suffering members of the Church (through almsgiving, practical charity etc.). All this is the sign and the effect at the same time of the presence of Christ in the midst of his people, his effective presence in the hope and love of the believers.

After this fourth section we must reiterate once more what has already been said under (c). These diverse elements in the presence of Christ must not be regarded as so many different 'presences'. They constitute *one single* presence of Christ which, from the one deed of Christ performed upon the members united to him by faith, develops various modalities from within itself, yet all the same retains that original and basic unity which is prior to this process of development. This one presence of Christ is the 'actualisation' in both 'visible' and 'existential' form at the same time of that unity, and so that presence too, in which the faithful remain constantly united and so present to each other also, with Christ and among themselves. For this reason this presence, considered both as 'made visible' in the cult and in its 'existential' effects in grace, can assume increasingly *different* forms and degrees of actualisation and intensity. It can be present simply in the sermon and in the common prayer of the believers, in the conferring of the sacraments, in the celebration of the Eucharist. These *different* elements in the *one single* presence of Christ are interconnected among themselves, proceed from one another, and are mutually demanded by one another as the fulness of this unity. This is because it is a unity in which the *opus operatum* and the *opus operantis*, the deed wrought by God upon man, and the response of man in grace, the interior grace and its manifestation in all dimensions of human life both social and historical, are mutually interconnected and are given concrete effect by man in ever new forms. This one presence of Christ is, in a certain sense, both 'visible', i.e. precisely 'sacramental' as the historical and social level, *and* at the same time effective and exhibitive. It signifies the further projection and actualisation of a quite unique unity which is latent in saving history from the beginning of the world as presence and promise: God himself imparts himself to the world through his Spirit in that he 'descends' into the depths of the cosmos and of history and so, as it were, even upon Christ himself. But precisely through this invisible movement he not only remains the ultimate consummation of the whole of saving history, but brings this unity in Christ, the incarnate *Word* of God, to a unique and definitive climax, the climax of eschatological victory realised at a specific and concrete point in history, and so constituting an unsurpassable perfection. A presence of this kind is always constituted by two elements: by the sign as that which is objectively symbolic, and by the reality signified itself. The sign itself has certain variations of its own. It extends from the simple word of preaching to the Eucharist (considered as sign). The same applies to the reality signified to the extent that the inner unity with Christ in the Spirit is capable of unlimited intensification. And from these two aspects we can deduce and understand every variation in the one presence of Christ. But if, and to the extent that the sign, considered as an element in the presence of Christ, has a *cultic* quality, i.e. a communal and explicitly religious character, being *ex professo* orientated towards the worship of God (this is not, of course, always and necessarily the case), this presence of Christ can justifiably be called 'cultic'.

(f) In describing and laying special emphasis upon the cultic presence of Christ in this way we must not forget that this effective presence of Christ is not restricted to a cultic presence. For an individual may, in the 'medium' of the Holy Spirit, fulfil and make actual in the human activities of his life, the grace that has been imparted to him. He may, in a certain sense, give this grace a visible embodiment in history in his Christian activities, and whenever the individual does this there takes place a true, even though perhaps a so-to-say 'anonymous' presence of Christ in the world and its history even if this presence is then not cultic at all. For in that case this presence, even though it is in some sense represented by a 'sign', is, nevertheless, devoid of the specifically cultic qualities which would otherwise have belonged to it. From this it can be concluded that the Church is the abiding and ultimate sacrament of the world's salvation not only in virtue of the explicit preaching of the gospel, the conferring of the sacraments and the Eucharist, but also in virtue of every deed and suffering on the part of her members. For through these deeds and sufferings considered as a gift of grace this presence itself achieves a certain visible embodiment at the historical and social level. But wherever and however the Church is this ultimate sacrament of salvation for the world, there Christ is present in his Spirit, and there he makes this presence of his apprehensible also, even though, it may be, in a mode that is 'anonymous' or unacknowledged. It is because of this that the Lord himself says that he is present, though unrecognised, wherever one man shows compassion from his heart to another.

5

ON THE PRESENCE OF CHRIST IN THE DIASPORA COMMUNITY ACCORDING TO THE TEACHING OF THE SECOND VATICAN COUNCIL

THE subject which we have set ourselves to examine in this brief study[1] is apparent from the title itself. Moreover it is obvious from the outset that what has to be said about the presence of Christ precisely in a *diaspora* community applies either wholly or to a very large extent to every authentic Christian community which gathers about the altar of Christ and is the Church of Christ in its particular locality. At no stage, therefore, can there be any question here of attempting to find some reasons for attributing a special theological glory to the diaspora and the communities belonging to it, or of representing the diaspora as something that is altogether right and fitting. Under certain circumstances the diaspora can be frankly recognised and accepted by Christians as a 'necessity'[2] of saving history (and not merely as a sociological fact), but even

[1] Here the author is taking up afresh one of the topics which he has already treated of in an earlier article, 'Das neue Bild der Kirche', *Geist und Leben* 39 (1966), pp. 4–24, cf. in the present volume 'The New Image of the Church', pp. 3–43. At the same time reference must be made to a brief commentary of the author's, *Das II. Vatikanische Konzil. Konstitutionen, Dekrete und Erklärungen. Lateinisch und Deutsch. Kommentare, Teil I* (Freiburg 1966), pp. 242–244, where he attempts to interpret the text chiefly being considered here. In the study which follows the author cannot undertake to collect together all that the Council had to say about a 'diaspora' community. The presence of Christ in the community is the sole subject of the present considerations. Any comprehensive study would have to investigate other conciliar texts also: e.g. the Constitution on the Liturgy No. 42, the Decree on the Apostolate of the Laity, No. 17, the whole of the Decree on the Missions, which in fact describes the constitution which new Churches have initially to adopt, and how they are to be implanted in the midst of non-Christian peoples – in other words in a situation which is, for all material purposes, similar to that of the 'diaspora' communities. On this cf. also 'The Presence of the Lord in the Christian Community at Worship' in the present volume, pp. 71–83.

[2] On this concept cf. K. Rahner, *Sendung und Gnade* (Innsbruck, 4th ed. 1966), pp. 224 ff.

84

so it continues to represent a harsh fate for those who belong to it, and every local Church must, in order to fulfil its missionary vocation, have the will to grow and develop, and so to lessen the 'diaspora' conditions in which it finds itself.

I

After these preliminary remarks we must pass on immediately to the theme expressed in the title. But in doing so attention must be drawn to an unusual passage in the Constitution on the Church. We are referring to No. 26 in the third chapter of this dogmatic constitution of the Council.[3] The actual subject of this No. 26 is the function of the bishop as consecrating and sanctifying. But in this general context one passage has been included which refers to the individual community of worshippers in general, and not precisely to the local Church as subject to a bishop. However obvious this may appear to everyone who reads it attentively and with due attention to detail, it is a point that must still be explicitly emphasised here. For although the individual local community of worshippers is described in general terms, nevertheless certain specific characteristics of it are explicitly mentioned here which have a special relevance to our present theme. Thus it is said that communities of this kind are often small and poor, and not infrequently live in the diaspora. Certainly, therefore, we have here a passage which has a direct and explicit bearing on the subject we are treating of.

The passage we are treating of has been interpolated into the text at a relatively late stage. For in a passage concerned with the consecrating and sanctifying function of the bishop (and which falls between the description of his teaching function[4] on the one hand and his pastoral function[5] on the other) there is no compelling reason for including a description of the local community and its conditions. Even though this may not be the sole reason for including this passage, its insertion is certainly connected with certain wishes which were put forward in the aula of the Council, e.g. by Metropolitan E. Zoghby and E. Schick, the auxiliary bishop of Fulda. It was not only considerations of dogmatic and biblical theology that supplied the initial inspiration and the basic orientation of these wishes. Rather they were prompted by directly practical and pastoral considera-

---

[3] For an understanding of the observations which follow the reader should have directly before his eyes the conciliar texts which are referred to from time to time.

[4] cf. the Constitution on the Church No. 25.

[5] cf. ibid. No. 27.

tions deriving from the concrete situation. There was an impression that the theology of the Church as presented in the Constitution as a whole was too theoretical and so too far *removed* from the concrete realities of everyday life, and that this would be the case so long as it treated of the universal Church, the pope and the bishops without going on to treat of the individual Christian's concrete experience of the Church as affecting his own personal life from day to day. There was a desire that the Constitution should contain some message about the Church as she exists in the concrete circumstances of everyday life, in other words in the actual situation in which the death of the Lord is effectively celebrated, in which the bread of the word of God is broken, in which we pray, love, and bear the Cross of our everyday lives in the concrete, for it is in this situation that the Church as a reality really is unambiguously and palpably something more than an abstract ideology, a dogmatic thesis or a large-scale social organisation. Interventions of this kind and expressions of this kind of desire were in principle readily accepted and welcomed. Moreover the insertion of the passage we are treating of here provoked no serious dispute or opposition either in the Theological Commission or in the plenary sessions of the Council. It was felt that something should be said about the local community of worshippers in the concrete, and so the passage was inserted at that point at which the ideas which it was intended to express could most easily be fitted in. Admittedly whether this meant that the best place for these ideas was in fact found is another question.[6] But then this question is not so very important. The passage is there. That is the main point.

Even abstracting from its precise content and from its special application to the diaspora community, this passage is of the highest importance. When traditional scholastic theologians intend to speak of the 'Church' they always think immediately of the universal Church, of the unity, under the pope and bishops, of the Christian communities scattered throughout the entire world. And they never pause to reflect that 'Church'

[6] A further conclusion arising from the observations which follow is that it would in fact be perfectly possible to take as our starting-point the *individual* communities, regarding these as the Church of Christ. We could adopt this approach even if our intention was to present an ecclesiology in the true sense of the term. So too it would have been perfectly possible in the Constitution on the Church itself to speak – at least in the first and second chapters – of the individual communities, even if the Constitution as a whole was intended, in its basic structure, to have the universal Church in view. In fact, however, this approach has not been adopted. Even the 'Church' which is presided over by an individual bishop is always regarded as a 'subsection' of the Church (No. 23 ff.).

could have any other meaning than this. Admittedly it may be that the usual kind of scholastic theology does contain some brief mention, in a subsection on biblical theology, of the fact that in the New Testament the individual local communities too were called 'Church'. But in any ecclesiology of this type the local community as such is hardly treated of. In such ecclesiologies, and also in the average awareness of Catholics, it appears merely as a sort of administrative subsection of *the* Church, this being a social organisation on a cosmic scale. And even since the Church has come to be regarded (chiefly through the influence of Pius XII's encyclycal, *Mystici Corporis*) as the mystical body of Christ filled with the Spirit of Christ, something which is far more than merely a *societas perfecta*, still even as such, the Church has continued to be the universal Church which is world-wide, while the communities living in particular place and worshipping at a particular altar are precisely communities, parishes (and other '*segments*' of a similar kind within this one universal Church). The fact that the New Testament applies the designation used for the whole to these 'segments' in themselves is something that does not trouble or disturb these ideas very much. Scholastic ecclesiology has failed to draw any clear conclusions from this linguistic usage, even though for its particular theory it must appear strange, and even though, at least in the sphere of biblical theology, we can at least raise the *question* of which of the two usages is the more original in the New Testament, that which applies the term 'Church' to the local community in the concrete, or that which applies it to *the* Church as a whole. And even when the *Council itself* set out to expound its teaching on the Church it was unreflectingly taken for granted that the subject under discussion was precisely *the* Church (and only this), in other words the totality of those who believe in Christ throughout the entire world, as existing in that state of organised unity which Catholic believers hold to be indispensable for this totality according to the will of Christ. It was far from obvious at the outset that the Council would finally come to apply the term '*Church*' to the individual local communities of worshippers too. Nevertheless that is what has happened, and it is a fact of the highest importance. For in the case of a dogmatic statement the most important point is precisely *not* whether it takes a long or short time to arrive at it, or in what particular contexts or associations of ideas it (initially) makes its appearance. Nor can we pause here to explain a further point, namely what significance this recognition might have as providing a basis for working out an ecclesiology in oecumenical dialogue with Protestant theology (even though as it occurs in the Council document it is not presented precisely *as* a basic starting-point of this kind). Perhaps we are still far from being in a position to recognise this importance to the full.

In the passage we are considering one sentence in particular is crucial: '*Haec Christi ecclesia adest in omnibus . . . congregationibus localibus*'. The Church, the one Church of Christ, is present in its entirety in every local community.[7] In this local community *the* Church is made actually present in the particular place in question. Every local community is, each according to its particular locality, the new people called by God in the Holy Spirit, and in that *plerophoria*[8] of which Paul speaks in 1 Thess 1:5. What is asserted here is that *the* Church of Christ ('*Haec Christi ecclesia*') is present in the local community, so that the local community is not 'a' Church but 'the' Church. And this assertion is not weakened by the fact that the passage speaks of Church*es* in the plural, influenced in this by the linguistic usage of the bible as found in Paul. Certainly it should not be denied that this usage in which the plural 'Churches' is employed is also legitimate, and rightly serves to underline the fact that the local community constitutes *the* Church only in virtue of the fact that it is precisely

[7] The problem here is how, according to the New Testament, the universal Church and the local community are related to one another, seeing that the same word 'Church' can be used to designate both. There is no need to gloss over the fact that the words '*adest in*' (a more cautious phrase than a simple *est* would have been) represent an evasion of, rather than a solution to this problem. At the same time the Council could not reasonably have been expected to supply any ultimate or definitive solution to this problem, especially in the present context. In fact the New Testament itself does not offer us any further enlightenment on this point in so many words, when it produces such formulae as 'the Church of God in Corinth' etc. Presumably the question we are considering here represents a problem that is entailed by the innermost nature of the Church as a Mystery, and therefore one that ultimately is too great for any explanation purely in terms of human reason. In any case it certainly cannot be considered any part of our intention in the present modest study either, to supply any detailed or exhaustive answer to this question. A point which we return to again and again here is that the unity of the Church and of each individual community is constituted by the fact that Christ is one and his Spirit is one. And surely this is sufficient for our present purposes to indicate the general direction in which the answer to this question is to be found; the question, namely, of how and why one and the same Church is present in each local community, and that not merely in the sense that she causes the local community to represent or 'stand for' her, but in the sense that in each particular community she achieves the ultimate and supreme realisation of her own nature.

[8] Properly speaking the Latin word used in the conciliar document represents a reference to 1 Thess 1:5, and it is hardly possible to supply a really correct rendering of it because the Latin word itself in its turn renders the original Greek concept only very imperfectly. On the concept of *plerophoria* cf. especially G. Delling, *T.W.N.T.* VI (Stuttgart 1959), p. 309.

united by the common bond of faith, love and law with all the other communities of Christ. Nor should it be doubted that the Council too is justified in speaking of Churches in the plural. But conversely this must not be allowed to obscure the further truth, which is brought out no less forcefully in our passage (without any further attempt being made to produce a theological harmony between two statements which seem to be opposed), namely that the one Church is made present in the local community of worshippers. In other words what we have in this local community of worshippers is not merely one *section* of the Church, one of its juridical or cultic administrative subsections. For this is precisely the difference between the Church and any earthly society, namely that in the part the whole achieves the supreme fulness of *itself,* and at the same time its clearest manifestation. It is in this sense that *the* Church of Christ (to express the matter once again in the paradoxical terms employed by the Council) 'is there' in the local community.[9]

II

Now the passage we are considering goes on to say that in any such local community gathered about their altar in which the Church is 'there' 'Christ is present'. He is present through that which constitutes this community as such.

Two of the factors in this constitution of the local community are its union with its own bishop and pastor and its union with the universal Church. But when we look into our particular passage more closely we notice in addition to these three further factors[10] which are essential. The first is the preaching of the gospel of Christ (which takes place 'in assembly'. In other words the gospel is not merely preached in the community as gathered together but is itself the basis for this state of 'being gathered together'). The second is the mystery of the eucharistic meal, which is likewise designated explicitly as the basic cause for this brotherly unity

[9] When it is stated in the Constitution on the Church (No. 28) that the priests make 'the universal Church visible in their particular locality', this is probably a weaker version of the same basic thought.

[10] Having recognised as distinct these three elements in the constitution of the local community, we may justifiably set them apart from the other two elements in it: that it is, of its nature, subject to the authority of a bishop, and that it is in union (even in the juridical and sacral sphere) with the universal Church. The reason is that what is being treated of here is precisely that which constitutes the local Church *as such*, and as distinct from the universal Church.

and so as actually *constitutive* of the community. The third is the love[11] and the unity of the community which develops precisely from *this*. This love itself appears, once more, as constituting a sign ('symbol') of the one and universal church in which salvation is mediated as present in the local community. The further question of precisely *how* these three elements in the constitution of the local community of worshippers are united among themselves is one on which our passage has nothing more to tell us. At most we can find an indication of where the answer to this lies to the extent that it is said that this community is the new people called by God[12] in the *Holy Spirit*. For it is in fact, in a very real sense, quite evident that it is precisely the *pneuma Christi* which draws these three basic elements, which are constitutive of the community, into a unity. For all preaching of the word of God only becomes the word precisely of *God* (and not merely a word *about* God) when it is uttered and heard in the Spirit, when the Spirit of God itself in its own reality becomes the source of the utterance (with authority) and of the hearing (in faith). The fact that the celebration of the Eucharist must take place in the Spirit and that it communicates the Spirit to men is also evident in scripture (cf. Jn 6:63), and it is likewise evident that the Spirit is only there where love is, and love can only be achieved in the Spirit.[13]

From the whole tenour of the passage one point becomes clear. It may be stated as follows: Christ is present *through* this community as constituted precisely in *this* way. And this presence of his is the object for

[11] We may be permitted to point out that even in Protestant ecclesiology this aspect has probably not been worked out sufficiently clearly. For in this the Church is regarded as existing wherever the gospel is legitimately preached and the sacraments are rightly administered.

[12] Here too it is to be observed that the passage does not say (as a superficial interpretation of scholastic theology might lead one to expect) that the individual community is a part of the new people of God, but that every community *is* the new 'people of God, each in its own locality'. This is something which is quite different.

[13] Even in the 'Decree on the Ministry and Life of Priests' it is stated, in No. 4, that the people of God is assembled (and 'primarily' at that!) into a unity through the word of God. In No. 5 of the same decree it is explicitly stated that the Eucharist is the flesh of Christ as living and lifegiving 'in the Holy Spirit'. Here in No. 4 the unity of sacrament and word is also indicated inasmuch as it is stated that the sacraments are sacraments of *faith* which are born of the word and nourished by the word. There is nothing, therefore, to prevent us from regarding the sacraments themselves as the most radical instance of the exhibitive word of God effecting what it utters, a word, therefore, that does not merely speak of something which is simply independent of what is said, but rather causes the reality itself that is proclaimed in the *kerygma* to take place in the here and now. This makes plainer the unity that exists between the first two constitutive elements in the local community.

which the community exists. The passage is, in fact, developed in three stages.

1. It is stated that the local community is the presence of *the* Church as actual.

2. We are told why and how (precisely through the three constitutive elements already mentioned) the local community is the Church as present.

3. As a conclusion of the first two statements it is explained that Christ is present in these local communities.

The question of *why* the community as constituted in this way is the presence of Christ[14] is one that is not explicitly entered into or reflected upon. But even so we gather from what is said that since the Church (as a whole and as a local community) has Christ, she constitutes his presence. She does this in the two dimensions[15] which, according to the Constitution on the Church taken as a whole, belong to the Church and are essential for her existence: she is the hierarchically organised people of God, his Body, and she is this even in the dimension of history and society. *At the same time* she lives by his Spirit, which is given to her as the Church of eschatological salvation through the compassion of God which he will never withdraw from her, and it is given to her as a pledge of final and irrevocable victory. The Spirit is also conferred upon her as truth and love.[16] Of her very nature, therefore, the Church is the presence of Christ

[14] We have no intention here of discussing or disputing the question of whether it is better to say: 'the community *is* the presence of Christ' or 'Christ is present *in* the community' (as, on an accurate reading, our passage expresses it). Obviously the Church is not Christ. And in neither of the two possible formulations is this asserted. The simpler and less awkward formulation is certainly that of the Council itself. But on the other hand a further point must not be overlooked. The presence of Christ in the community takes place in the word that is heard and believed, in the effective reception of the Body of Christ, in the practical love of the members of the community for one another, in brief in the Spirit of Christ as really communicated and as received in faith and love. This Spirit not merely offers itself, but also brings about the acceptance of itself through its own power. Its presence, therefore, is itself in act *and* at the same time the sanctification wrought by the Spirit upon man as he brings to its fulness the freedom which has been bestowed upon him. On this basis we can also state freely that the community is the presence of Christ, provided only that we do not absolutely identify this presence (that through which Christ communicates himself to man as Saviour, and so becomes present 'for him') with Christ himself.

[15] On these two dimensions in the Church, which as distinct yet undivided are essential elements in her very nature, cf. e.g. the Constitution on the Church No. 8.

[16] cf. the Constitution on the Church No. 39, No. 48. cf. also K. Rahner, 'The Sinful Church in the Decrees of Vatican II'; 'The Church and the Parousia of Christ', *Theological Investigations* VI (London and Baltimore 1969), pp. 295–312.

in both dimensions (that of history and that of the Spirit which opens up to her, and assures her of, that dimension of transcendence in which she can attain to the immediate presence of God). She is the presence of Christ in each of these two dimensions, and in the modes appropriate to each respectively, so that both dimensions together constitute the single presence of Christ. In that in the word of Christ, his sacrament (including the 'real presence' under the sacramental forms of the Eucharist), visible love and unity are achieved, Christ is 'there' in the dimension of history. In that this presence is the historical communication of his Spirit, it is in virtue of this precisely that it achieves its goal, namely the immediate union of man with God in his justifying and forgiving grace, which, in the last analysis (as 'uncreated grace') is God himself in the immediacy of his act of self-bestowal. Both modes are one and at the same time distinct, just as the sacrament and that which is sacramentally signified (*sacramentum* and *res sacramenti*) are one and distinct. This unity between the sacrament and the reality it signifies is something that can no longer be destroyed in the Church as a whole (however much it may be lost in the case of the individual recipient of the sacraments: 'unfruitful sacrament'). This is because the Church is holy and endures through the grace of God as eschatologically victorious. And because this is so we can also make the following statement about the Church as a whole (and thereby, surely, about the individual communities as a whole too, at any rate in a presumptive sense[17]): it abidingly constitutes this unity of the presence of Christ in sign and in the Spirit. Because that which constitutes it also constitutes the presence of Christ we can say (and this is something that explicitly applies only here) not only 'in her Christ is present', but also 'she *is* the

---

[17] A question which will, in fact probably have to be left open is whether, in spite of being juridically authenticated, in spite of the true preaching of the gospel and the valid administration of the sacraments in it, an individual community can be as a whole sinful and unbelieving (and only this). The conciliar document takes as its starting-point the 'normal case' of a community in which the word of God really is heard in a spirit of faith and the sacraments are 'fruitfully' received. But since for the individual community as it exists in the concrete we can only 'presume' this to be the case (in exactly the same way as with the individual Christian as such) it also becomes clear that even on a Catholic understanding of the Church it includes an 'invisible' element, and that we must allow for this if we are not to understand the Church merely as a *societas perfecta* in a sense that is *false*. But it must be remembered that the Church as a whole is conceived of as *indefectibiliter sancta* (No. 39), and that as a whole she makes manifest to the faithful, even as a fact of history, the act of abiding in the truth and love of Christ (cf. D 1794). Because of this there are objective grounds for the presumption referred to above.

presence of Christ', even though perhaps it would be better to avoid speaking of the Church as 'Christ living on'.[18]

III

A further question has now to be asked: *for whom* is Christ present in this way? Obviously the presence we are speaking of here is not simply a local presence such as we might conceive of in terms of the conceptual model of two bodies placed close to one another in the same area. This presence, rather, is one that causes us to be saved, a presence 'for us'. In answering this question we must certainly begin by pointing out that Christ is present in the community for the community itself, and to bring salvation to its own members. The Church is, in fact, always the fruit of salvation and the mediatrix of salvation at the same time. The fact that as mediatrix of salvation she makes Christ present means that she herself receives Christ as her own salvation, and that at the same time she mediates him to others.[19] In fact the only way in which the word can be rightly preached is for the preacher himself to have heard it in a spirit of faith.[20] In the Eucharist the Church is always she who receives, as well as she who dispenses, the Body of the Lord. In the relationship of love unity is always maintained within her in such a way that love is both given

---

[18] On this mode of parlance cf. the commentary and bibliography provided by A. Grillmeier on pp. 168–174 of the volume of commentary on the Council referred to on p. 84 n. 1.

[19] We must achieve a clearer view than is obtained in the usual presentations of ecclesiology of the unity which exists between the imparting of salvation and its reception. The Church herself would cease to be the authoritative and indefectible mediatrix of truth and salvation if she ceased, or ever could cease, to be she who abides *through faith* in the truth, and she who is the holy one (in the love of her members for one another). She has authority and is indeed indefectible in mediating salvation precisely *because* she has herself already received salvation through God in an act which is eschatological and so irrevocable, and has thereby been constituted as the work of God's compassion in Christ.

[20] Obedience in faith is, of course, something that is legitimately demanded of each individual preacher in his preaching. But whether we apply what we are saying to a preacher of this kind, or whether even an unbelieving preacher can assert this word in the Church and for her, makes no difference to the point we are making. The statement is correct, at any rate as applied to preaching and the preacher in the Church as a whole, and it is true even of a preacher who in his own personal life is an unbeliever that he can only preach legitimately when he speaks in the name of the Church. And in the Church the word is not only preached but believed too. Preaching proceeds from faith as its basis.

and received at the same time, and that the one attitude cannot be present without the other.

But ultimately speaking it would run counter to the basic tenour of the constitution on the Church taken as a whole if we were to confine our answer to the mere statement that in the community which is the Church Christ is present for, and bringing salvation to, the Church herself and her members. For in fact the principle that the Church is the 'sacrament' of salvation for the *world*[21] is numbered among the basic tenets of conciliar ecclesiology. But this means nothing else than that in the last analysis instead of the Church making Christ present only to herself as *her* salvation, she makes him present to the world as the salvation of it. Now in order to understand this and appreciate it at its true worth we must advance beyond the stage of merely noticing in passing the explanation put forward relatively frequently and with numerous minor variations by the Council to the effect that the Church is the basic sacrament of salvation and, furthermore, of the salvation of the world. Over and above this we must realise a further conviction which is either expressed or implied[22] in the pronouncements of the Council, and that too in a manner which is notably clearer and more forceful than has been the case in tradition hitherto. This is the conviction that men can be and are justified without belonging fully to the 'visible body' of the Church (it should be noticed

[21] cf. the Constitution on the Church No. 1, No. 9, No. 48, No. 59; the Decree on the Missions No. 1, No. 5; the Constitution on the Liturgy, No. 5, No. 26; The Pastoral Constitution on the Church in the World of Today, No. 43. It is not possible here to enter into the precise nuances of this doctrine as presented in the various documents. On this doctrine of the Church as the 'basic sacrament' cf. the study of the author cited on p. 84 n. 1 of this article, on 'The New Image of the Church', now included in this volume, pp. 2–43. On the material and historical aspects of this subject cf. P. Smulders' important study, 'Die Kirche als Sacrament des Heils', *De Ecclesia. Beiträge zur Konstitution 'Über die Kirche' des Zweiten Vatikanischen Konzils*, G. Baraúna ed., German edition prepared by O. Semmelroth, J. G. Gerhartz, H. Vorgrimler, Vol. I (Freiburg/Frankfurt 1966), pp. 289–312 (with copious bibliography). cf. also *ibid.*, the studies of J. L. Witte and Abbot B. C. Butler. cf. the brief summary in the article 'Ursakrament' (O. Semmelroth), *L.T.K.* X (Freiburg, 2nd ed. 1965), pp. 568–569; the concept occurs in three distinct passages in the Constitution on the Church: No. 1, No. 9, No. 48. cf. in addition the comprehensive expositions of A. Grillmeier in the commentary referred to on p. 84 n. 1 of the present volume. cf. in the commentary pp. 156 ff., esp. 157 n. 4, 177 ff. also the remarks of O. Semmelroth, pp. 315–317. Also O. Semmelroth, *Die Kirche als Ursakrament* (Frankfurt, 3rd ed. 1963); K. Rahner, *Kirche und Sakramente* (Freiburg 1960). cf. also the bibliography below pp. 201/210.

[22] cf. e.g. The Constitution on the Church Nos. 15–16; the Decree on Oecumenism, No. 3; the Decree on the Missions, Nos. 1, 4, 7.

in parenthesis that in holding this the Council does not call in question the unique role of and necessity for the Church as mediating salvation on any true understanding of this role). Once we recognise this we can see that to call the Church the sacrament of salvation for the world means something far more than merely that she is the sign to all men of the grace of God as *offered* to them (as though this grace could become fruitful in salvation only when the individual concerned actually belonged to the visible body of the Church). Also, and more than this, she is the sign of the grace of God as actually having achieved its victory in the world, a grace, therefore, which can and does extend its justifying effects even to those areas in which the individual justified does *not* already fully belong to the Church in the visible dimension of history and society, thereby himself contributing to the constitution of the Church as the basic sacrament of salvation for the world. It remains true that grace can take effect in the sense indicated even though both inside and outside the Church we cannot arrive at any assured judgment as to whether a particular individual is justified or not. Thus we can say that the Church, and therefore the individual community that is the Church, makes Christ present to the *world* in that, through her whole existence as an historical entity (in preaching, sacraments and visibly active love) she constitutes a *reality* in human history that is *one and the same* for all, the unique sphere of existence in which the personal saving history of each individual is achieved. The Church also makes a further factor present in this way. It is through her that this same Christ, actually present in the world that is not the Church, has inserted himself into the innermost centre of the lives of men, to become, as justifying and sanctifying through his Spirit, the centre and source of their saving history. Even with regard to the presence of Christ through the Church for the world, therefore, we must pay due heed to the fact that the Church, and the presence of Christ as constituted by her, has a twofold dimension.

IV

Now evidently what we have already said so far with regard to the presence of Christ in the local community of worshippers which is the Church applies also to the 'diaspora' communities that are small. This point is explicitly emphasised in our passage. In fact it says '*even though* they are often poor and small and live in the diaspora'. Evidently the intention that lies behind this formula is to express sollicitude for such small and poor 'diaspora' communities. They *too* constitute the presence of Christ in the world even if, because of their smallness in terms of numbers, social prestige and power, they cannot impart that effulgence to the presence of Christ which is so often invoked by the practitioners of an unenlightened apologetics in order to prove the presence of Christ in the world and to make it appear splendid. But we can without embarrassment pass over the actual text of the conciliar document and sum it up by saying that such 'diaspora' communities, *precisely as such*, are a sign of the presence of Christ. We have only to read 1 Cor 1:26–31 to realise this. The insignificance of the community in terms of numbers and social standing is, in Paul's view, not merely something that 'regrettably' has to be put up with until the Church finally emerges in her full splendour and her victorious power. On the contrary it is something which God himself has 'chosen' in order that *he*, and not man, may be made manifest in his own autonomous power, and may bear witness to himself. God has precisely chosen circumstances of insignificance because he wants to attest the fact that his love has been rejected. The Christ who is to be present here is Christ crucified (cf. 1 Cor 1:22), who is a scandal to the Jews and folly to the Gentiles. In the Eucharist it is the death of the Lord that is to be proclaimed, for it is only through this that life is brought to the world. Of their very nature, therefore, truth love and light, to the extent that they really are of God and given by God as salvation, have a mysterious affinity with the mystery of the Cross and so too with the folly and scandal involved in it. Given that a community has the function of making Christ present through the word of preaching, through the sacraments and through love, how could it, in any true sense, fulfil this function by appearing in the world with power, with earthly wisdom or with social prestige? Is it not almost a necessity of the very nature of such a community to approximate to the form of the 'diaspora' community? To be 'small', 'poor' and few in numbers, and so to be living in the midst of those who have not already been touched by the grace of God at the actual level of the conscious awareness of truth and adherence to the Church as a society? Again the Council itself has repeatedly pointed to a connection between the Church and poverty (which, in the last analysis, can only be a real factor in a 'diaspora' community), even though it did not attribute to this connection the full scope and force which was desired, chiefly by the French and South American bishops.[23] We must avoid thinking of the presence of Christ through the Church in terms of an abstract ideology,

---

[23] cf. e.g. the Constitution on the Church, No. 8, No. 41 ff.; the Decree on the Ministry and Life of Priests, No. 17; the Pastoral Constitution on the Church in the World of Today, No. 42; the Decree on the Pastoral Office of Bishops, No. 13.

and think instead of the preaching of the gospel in the *concrete*, that gospel which will, as a necessity of saving history, meet with contradiction. Furthermore we must achieve a right understanding of the celebration of the Eucharist, seeing it not as a celebration of a sort of cosmic liturgy of the beauty and the unveiled *doxa* of God, but rather as an act in which the terrible death of the Lord in darkness and ruin is made present and takes possession of us. We must not misinterpret love as an idealistic philanthropy which is intended to conceal the brutality of human living from itself instead of helping to bear the pain of it. And if we do all this, *then and only then* (in spite of the reservations expressed at the beginning) we shall understand that the 'diaspora' community is capable of being, most clearly of all, the presence of Christ as the crucified one.

This will come as no surprise to anyone who reflects that in the last analysis the 'diaspora' situation is far from being extraordinary or exceptional for the Church as such from the point of view either of her own intrinsic nature or of the future which is destined to befall her. From the point of view of the Church's own nature it is not extraordinary, for in fact the Church is not the kingdom of God made manifest in glory, but rather the sign of this, the promise of this and the community which hopes against all hope as it waits for this kingdom to come. As a sign in this sense of a reality that is hoped for the Church can never for one moment expect that at some point in earthly time the world and the Church will simply become co-extensive so as to form a single homogeneous society which is both Christian and world-wide at the same time. But that contradiction to herself, her truth and her love which is an element intrinsic to her own life cannot be restricted in its manifestations to the interior and private dimension of the individual's own conscience, but must also, and of necessity, assume a social form. Today the Church is gradually entering upon a future in which she becomes a world Church in the true sense, and in which she is everywhere. This is because the individual histories of the many nations hitherto covering separate areas of human living have become united into a single overall world history. Nevertheless the Church must still remain the sign that will be contradicted because Christ, whom it is her role to make present, is himself destined to be contradicted. Now these two facts can only both be true simultaneously in that the Church as she exists everywhere is actually a 'diaspora' Church, however varied the 'diaspora' conditions may be and may continue to be, to which the Church is subject among particular peoples and in particular areas of human history.[24]

[24] On this cf. K. Rahner, *Sendung und Gnade*, pp. 24–47.

Certainly it is true that even in the future the Church must not become either sociologically or still less theologically a 'sect', or ever wish to become so in any sense. By 'sect' here we mean a group of individuals who are inadequate to meet the demands of life, and who do not have the courage to take an active part in shaping a developing world. Because of this they make a virtue of their necessity that is both false and cowardly. But while recognising the danger and temptation of misunderstanding the Church's true nature in this sense (by glorifying a ghetto-like way of life as lived in the nooks and crannies of history), still this does not prohibit the Church from recognising the fate which is in fact hers, that namely of living, whether exteriorly or interiorly in a 'diaspora' situation, as a disposition of God which, so far from running counter to her true nature, precisely causes it to be made manifest. If the Church understands her 'diaspora' situation as something proper to her own nature as being a sign of salvation to the world, then she can combine in the right sense the attitudes both of humility and pride: pride ('boasting') in her election to be a sign of the salvation of the world, and humility because she is chosen precisely and only as a *sign* of that salvation, which can also be attained to by those who do not (yet) belong to the Church in terms of visible membership of her as a social and historical entity. In other words what we are speaking of is the difference between the Church as sign of salvation to the world and the salvation which is present in the Church for herself and for the world. Now anyone who pays due heed to this difference and recognises it as essential and abiding has thereby understood also the *theological* nature of the 'diaspora' situation. He no longer needs merely to endure it as a sociological situation and a purely external fate to which the Church is subject.

V

The local community of worshippers is, in virtue of the word, the sacrament and the love that is manifested in her, the supreme 'actualisation' of the very meaning of 'Church' as such. It will still be a long time before the average Catholic Christian appreciates this, and before he understands that that which first and last provides the focal point and the initial impulse for his belief in the Church and his love for the Church is to be found not where the Church appears as a large-scale organisation endowed with great power, but where the centre of that worship is located which is constituted by the word, the sacrament and brotherly love. The amount that still remains to be done in order to arouse men to an awareness of this significance in the Church is immeasurable. Poverty, smallness and a 'diaspora' situation are singled out in the conciliar document as the characteristics of many local communities. But we ought to realise that these are destined to apply to the Church as a whole, especially in view of the future that is pressing in upon her, even more than we do at present. And realising this we should calmly and freely allow the full implications of the basic principle expressed in our passage to be unfolded. Thus we shall say that the new awareness of the Church which will come to prevail in the future is actually anticipated in this passage which we are considering.[25] The Christian of tomorrow will only encounter the Church as such, will only experience her as 'actual' and present where the presence of Christ is experienced and made real in the authorised preaching of his gospel, in the *anamnesis* of his death, and in that love which unites men in Christ.

It is *here* that the Christian of tomorrow will recognise what the Church is. He will understand the achievement of the Christian community in its fulness here not as something which takes place *in* the Church, but rather as the achievement of *the* Church herself. Of course he will be aware that this Church, in order to be able to achieve its own 'actualisation' in this sense, has a structure of its own prior to achieving the fulness of its own nature here. But at the same time he will, from the outset, regard this concrete reality and composition of the Church as a whole which is prior to the achievement of her own full 'actualisation', precisely as a condition which enables that to be enacted which comes to its fulness in the form of a community gathered about the altar. Of course a community of this kind, conscious as it is of itself as an event taking place in the Church through the word of preaching, the sacraments and the love of the brethren, will be conscious of being united with all other communities which likewise constitute this same single Church of Christ. The individual community will give expression to that unity with all other communities through the one Spirit which is according to Christ's will even at the level of concrete social living as such, and will also be conscious that it has a duty to do this. It will experience in faith that it only maintains the truth of the word which takes place in it, and its power to

---

[25] On this cf. K. Rahner, 'Konziliare Lehre der Kirche und künftige Wirklichkeit christlichen Lebens', *Schriften zur Theologie* VI, pp. 479–498; on the situation of the diaspora cf. K. Rahner, 'The Christian in his World', *Theological Investigations* VII (London and Baltimore, 1971, pp. 88 ff. For a comprehensive analysis of the situation of the Church in the present cf. now especially the author's *Handbuch der Pastoraltheologie* II/1–2 (Freiburg 1966).

make Christ present, in the unity of the communities of Christ as hierarchically organised. This of itself will ensure that it recognises and lives by everything which the Constitution on the Church has to say about the universal Church as such. It will think of the totality of the communities in turn as *the* Church, and precisely not as a secondary amalgam of communities originally existing in isolation from one another as though it was this combination alone that constituted the 'Church'. The community will recognise that even in the Church considered as the union of the individual communities truth and love must be achieved, and therefore too that for this purpose this 'universal' Church must have its organs at the level of social organisation and living, namely those appointed in her to exercise the teaching and pastoral office. For these do not only provide a final summing up of what is recognised and achieved in the faith and love of the individual communities as such. They are something more than the mere mouthpieces of these individual communities.

But a community of this kind will recognise all this as belonging to a Catholic understanding of the Church, and will be content to live by it, realising that though the truth of Christ is ultimately one, it is presented in the form of a structured hierarchy of truths. It will recognise and accept what is laid down in the Decree on Oecumenism,[26] namely that though this truth which is the authentic foundation and basis of faith is one, the individual doctrines of faith and their application to the concrete realities of human living are related in very different ways to this one true foundation, so that it is only from the basis of this that we can believe in these doctrines and live by these applications of them in the concrete. Now this basis (and this is something that concerns precisely the Christians living in the diaspora of today and tomorrow) is not the Church considered as a macrocosmic religious organisation with an extension that is world-wide (not even when we take due cognizance of its God-given authority and the fact that it orientates us towards the ultimate goal of our religion). Rather this authentic foundation of faith and love in relation to the Church will be the reality and the concrete experience that Christ the crucified and risen Lord is made present together with his word (including in this its sacramental and exhibitive force, its 'translation' into acts of love, and the witness it bears in this form), with its power to admit us into the unfathomable mystery of God. It is in the objective reality and the experience of this that the Church is made 'actual' ever anew in the midst of the insignificance, poverty and desolation of the community which believes in him in the vast wilderness of this human life. All other factors

[26] cf. the Decree on Oecumenism, No. 11.

in our awareness of the Church will draw their life from, and will only be able to live by this as their fundamental source and centre. The Christian of the future will experience that which befalls him in his community no longer – as formerly – as something that takes place *in* the Church, but rather as the 'actualisation' *of the* Church. Now this basic source and centre of the reality that is the Church and of faith in the Church can be, and actually will be experienced by non-Catholic Christians too (even though these may not give it its due by recognising it as a fully objective entity and as a social phenomenon expressible in 'this-worldly' categories). And because of this it becomes possible for the Catholic Church to enter into dialogue with the other Christian Churches and communities. There is a basis for this dialogue which God himself has provided in Christ, and which he brings to 'actualisation'. And only from this basis will such a dialogue hold out a real prospect of proving fruitful – fruitful in the efforts which are made on all sides to bear an authentic[27] witness to the presence of Christ in a Christian community. Even in the diaspora.

[27] In order to avoid a still greater increase in the footnotes to this article the author has decided not to repeat once again the relevant references to the findings of biblical theology and the witnesses of theological tradition. For these the reader may be referred to the wide-ranging and well-planned study of B. Neunheuser O.S.B., 'Gesamtkirche und Einzelkirche', *De Ecclesia* I (cf. above p. 138 a n. 21), pp. 547–573 (including a copious bibliography on the subject in all its aspects). Two approaches are possible, one in which the importance of the local community is stressed, the other in which we take as our starting-point a more universal conception of the Church. Now it is possible to regard these as two types of the 'theology of collegiality' as this has been developed e.g. by J. Ratzinger, cf. 'Die Bischöfliche Kollegialität' in *De Ecclesia II*, G. Baraúna ed., (Freiburg 1966), pp. 44–70, esp. pp. 56 ff. J. Ratzinger interprets my statement in *Theological Investigations* VI (London and Baltimore 1969), p. 335 as an extremely radical version of a theological conception that has only appeared in recent times. Moreover he finds that my own interpretation as set forth in 'The Episcopate and the Primacy', *Studies in Modern Theology* (Freiburg/London 1965), pp. 303–322, is in 'opposition' to his, and that even in developing the idea of collegiality it seeks to follow an exactly opposite path to that of the theology of the Fathers. But against this, my various statements on this subject (including those belonging to the present volume) show that I myself would prefer to regard these two types as 'conceptual models' which complement one another, although admittedly from many points of view, and precisely at the present time a certain priority may be attributed to the local Church. Admittedly too, difficulties do arise from the fact that for many reasons the structural forms assumed by the Church can no longer be based upon a territorial principle, while in view of the ever-increasing unification of the world an awareness of the Church as universal appears just as important. While the theological initiative of recent times may have led to an ecclesiology that is one-sided, and even produced certain effects in practice which are harmful, still there is *also* a necessary trait in this development which can be interpreted in a positive sense.

For example in the article referred to by Ratzinger I was concerned *amongst other things* with explaining in ecclesiological terms the significance of the *diocese*, and so here I took as my starting-point factors which I do not adduce in my other studies. In the light of what has just been said, namely the broader vision in which both elements have to be taken into account, I can whole-heartedly agree with the observations of J. Ratzinger with regard to the importance of the local Church. On the local Church cf. also H. Küng, *Die Kirche* (Freiburg 1967), pp. 105 f., 272 ff. etc.

6

DIALOGUE IN THE CHURCH

THE Second Vatican Council has had the effect of causing the question of dialogue between Christians to be raised as a subject for discussion and also actually put into practice. Everyone is speaking of dialogue, and of a dialogue between everyone and his neighbour. But in this there has already been a certain failure to arrive at any very clear idea of what the general term 'dialogue' really means, especially when it is intended to apply it to discussions which are properly speaking ideological and religious in character, and as these are conducted not merely between individuals but between social groups and institutions.

I

When the dialogue is to be conducted by that Church whose members are Catholics as well as Christians, and when it is concerned with the Christian faith and the principles deriving from this, then the basic difficulty consists in the fact that in this case it is not some favourite opinion that is being put forward. On the contrary, in such a case the subject of the dialogue is a teaching which is held with a total commitment of faith to have been revealed by God, and which is adhered to immutably by the Church and by the Christian believer. We can discuss among ourselves and exchange opinions and views. We can peaceably exchange ideas even when our minds are already made up concerning political, economic, cultural and artistic questions. And in all this we can, indeed we should, maintain an attitude of tolerance, recognising *a priori* that man in himself does not necessarily have to be right in all circumstances, that in the course of discussion he can alter his own personal opinion and allow himself to be taught a better one. In short in all these areas we can conduct an open dialogue. Nor does this need to turn into a mere disjointed discussion which is endlessly prolonged, and in which we never expect to arrive at any unity between us. Indeed an open dialogue of this kind is embarked upon with the aim of learning something and not merely teaching, with an attitude of being prepared, in certain circumstances, to revise our own opinions, to modify them in their details or even to alter them, to achieve new insights and to accord due value to factors which we have hitherto failed to perceive. The ultimate meaning of dialogue is such as to preclude treating of subjects of a purely factual nature. Rather it is a communication of ourselves which is aimed at mutual and loving acceptance. And to this extent an open dialogue still has a certain meaning even in those cases in which it does not imply that kind of unity which consists in mutually holding the same opinion, but rather in accepting the other person in his uniqueness and otherness, the difference of 'viewpoint' being only a very secondary expression of this.

But can an open dialogue of this kind also be conducted by Catholic Christians in matters belonging specifically to their faith, and with regard to a teaching that has been revealed by God, seeing that such a Christian holds firm with a total commitment of faith to this teaching in all that concerns the manner of its promulgation and its content as revelation? For in such a case is not the purpose of a discussion already decided from the outset: the victory of one's own personal convictions even over one's partner in the discussion, or else a breaking off of the discussion in which both parties go their separate ways 'unconverted' and with the convictions which they already held before the discussion took place? In questions of faith, then, is it impossible to have any open dialogue, and is a kind of 'missionary' controversy with the avowed intention of converting the other to one's point of view all that is possible – at least from the Catholic party's view of what discussion must mean? Is the only conceivable form of discussion which can exist, so far as we are concerned, one which is analogous to that which a Christian or a sincere humanist might hold with a Nazi who sought to defend the murder of the Jews, seeing that in this field a Christian cannot hold any open dialogue but is confined to avowing his faith and attacking or rejecting, however politely, contrary points of view, or else to sternly refusing to enter into any discussion at all?

The problem of why, and in what sense, the Church can, and indeed must conduct an open dialogue in such questions in spite of this cannot really be treated of *in extenso* here.[1] Yet we must draw attention to this question at this point because in the nature of the case it still recurs in the case of dialogue within the Church as we shall shortly be seeing. On the more general question we must confine ourselves here to saying this much: even in questions of faith, and in spite of the absolute character of divine

[1] On this cf. K. Rahner, 'Reflections on Dialogue Within a Pluralistic Society', *Theological Investigations* VI (London and Baltimore 1969), pp. 31–42.

revelation, the absolute nature of the Church's own assent of faith and her ultimately missionary purpose, the Church can conduct an open dialogue with all men and groups of men because in such a dialogue, without prejudice to the divine truth, the Church can and must be she who learns as well, she who is capable of being led into still deeper levels of her own truth and her understanding of that truth. In such a dialogue she can be purified from misunderstandings and distorted interpretations such as may have attached themselves to her understanding of her faith, and she can herself become more believing. It may be that it is only through such a dialogue that she can attain to that particular concrete historical form of the abiding truth which is to be the basis for her activity in hope and love, and which has to be worked out by herself in the particular circumstances of the present if she is to proclaim the gospel of God in Christ effectively to her own age.[2]

After these preliminary observations we must straightway raise the question of the necessity, the nature and the concrete form of this open dialogue which is to take place within the Church. When we speak of dialogue and the necessity for dialogue here we do not mean the sort of dialogue which is carried on everywhere and at all times, or which must be carried on (unless it is silenced by the atrophying of the human in man) because the very nature of man is such as to demand discussion and inter-communication with his fellows. When we speak of dialogue and the necessity for it here, then, we mean dialogue to the extent that it arises from a specific contemporary situation and is rendered necessary by this. From the very outset we are confining ourselves, therefore, to an aspect which, in itself, is wholly secondary. From this it is clear that even the dialogue within the Church can only be considered from this secondary viewpoint. The fundamental situation of dialogue between Christians as friends, as loving one another, as neighbours and members of the same community of worshippers – in other words the most important element in the dialogue between Christians – will be left out of consideration here. Here we shall primarily be concerned to discuss, on a broad basis, the question of an open theological dialogue within the Church, while the question of a dialogue within the Church in the spheres of pastoral

---

[2] For a fuller treatment of the subject of a right understanding of how insight into the faith can be developed even in the case of defined dogma cf. K. Rahner and K. Lehmann, *Mysterium Salutis* I, J. Feiner, M. Löhrer edd. (Einsiedeln 1965), pp. 693 ff., 698 ff., 731 ff., 756 ff., 780 ff.; K. Rahner, 'Zur Geschichtlichkeit der Theologie', *Integritas*, D. Stolte and R. Wisser edd., Festschrift für K. Holzamer (Tübingen 1966), pp. 75–95, now published in Vol. IX of this series, pp. 64-82.

theology and on social, educational and political matters must remain in the background.[3]

II

An open dialogue of the kind that can be conducted within the Church is possible and necessary. First: if the Church of today is to conduct a dialogue with the world, then it must not be overlooked that this 'world' is not simply 'outside', but is rather present in the Church herself. This means that the first, and perhaps the decisive dialogue with the world is that which takes place precisely within the Church.

In fact the 'world' which is to be the Church's partner in the dialogue that is necessary today is, in the first instance, not only present where non-Christian groups have already emerged as social organisations with a firm ideological basis of their own. No such social organisation needs to be achieved for the world to be constituted as a partner to a dialogue with the Church. Prior to the formation of any such ideological groups different from the Church herself, the necessity for a dialogue between the Church and the 'world'[4] arises from the almost incalculable pluralism of ideas which constitutes the situation in which modern man lives, and which on the one hand is prior to the formation of the ideologies and their upholders, and on the other cannot fail to have a bearing upon the faith of the Church. By the term 'intellectual pluralism'[5] as understood here we mean the sum total of the experiences, insights, impulses and human possibilities in all spheres of human living which are distinguished by the following characteristics:

1. As a sum total it is so immense and complex that it has reached a stage at which it is quite impossible for any one individual even to survey it all, let alone to organise it and reduce it to a single integrated system.[6]

2. It derives from the most diverse sources of knowledge and experience, for which no integrating factors can be found even if we go back

---

[3] In view of the fact that other works are available for consulation on these more concrete questions, the author has felt able to confine himself to the problems which are more basic.

[4] On the basic necessity for a dialogue between the Church and the world cf. *Handbuch der Pastoraltheologie* II/1–2 (Freiburg 1966), II/1: pp. 102 ff., 265 ff.; II/2: pp. 163 ff., 168 ff., 203–267.

[5] On the concept of 'Pluralism' cf. *ibid*. II/1: pp. 210 ff., 248 ff., 261 ff.

[6] For a fuller treatment with examples cf. the author's 'A Small Question Regarding the Contemporary Pluralism in the Intellectual Situation of Catholics and the Church', *Theological Investigations* VI (London and Baltimore 1969), pp. 21–30.

to their origins. Their complexity is such that no *a priori* theory of science can be found which is adequate to comprehend them, reduce them to a system or relate them one to another.

3. There is no one representative of this total complex such as might exercise authoritative control over all its elements (not even the Church).

4. All departments of this amorphous complex are – even though in various ways and different degrees – significant for the tenets of the Christian faith. All these elements are factors in modern man's picture of the world, and in his interpretation of himself, which in turn constitute the situation in which he lives out his Christian faith. They raise questions for this, and call it in question at the same time.

The world constituted by this intellectual pluralism also exists in the Church. For her members themselves live in the situation constituted by this intellectual pluralism, and for that very reason an interior dialogue is necessary in the Church. The situation of a world that is intellectually homogeneous and easy to comprehend is coming to an end within the Church as well. Since the French revolution and the restoration of the Church from the nineteenth century onwards a remarkable intellectual homogeneity (which has been still further strengthened by the definition of the First Vatican Council) has prevailed in the Catholic Church even though it has not been without certain ghetto-like traits. This has lasted for a whole century. It is the age of neo-scholasticism in theology and philosophy, the age of the theory of a natural law worked out in material detail, of a uniform and centralised form of ecclesiastical government in which the universal Church was ruled from Rome, the age of a Latin liturgy which was common to all, of a canon law which was common to all and by comparison with which all laws for particular Churches hardly entered into consideration, an age in which it was attempted to establish in the Church a way of life for Christians and Church members covering all areas and as far as possible self-sufficient, and to do this through social organisations in the Church, through schools, Christian literature etc. It was the age in which the Church was extremely consistent, relatively speaking, in preserving a negative attitude to much which modern man held dear, an age in which, relatively speaking, an attitude of mistrust was to a large extent general towards democracy, towards many social, political and economic tendencies of the future, towards the emancipation of women, woman's franchise, modern exegesis, the history of religions, the free and unrestricted study of the history of dogma and much else besides.

There was no need then for much dialogue to be carried on within the

Church, because all were already 'of one speech', and for this reason attention was directed outwards in an apologetic and defensive attitude. Of course even then the way was gradually being paved for change, above all after the pontificate of Pius X and the First World War under Benedict XV, when integralism as a force in ecclesiastical politics disappeared, the shock of the antimodernist controversy was overcome, and a return from this in some respects integralist attitude was demanded to a certain extent even by the pope himself (manifested in a more favourable attitude towards modern exegesis, in the demand for Catholic action, in the Lateran Treaties, in the fact that liturgical and oecumencial movements were first tolerated and then positively demanded etc.). But from the twenty years prior to the death of Pius XII this gradual process of change was, so far as the average awareness in the Church was concerned, still to a large extent concealed by something which might be called a certain 'Pianic monolithism'.[7]

Now since John XXIII and the Second Vatican Council it has become evident not merely to a few individual Catholics with deeper insight, but to the awareness of the average member of the Church and to the community in general that that intellectual pluralism which we have attempted to describe above has actually infiltrated into the Church herself and exists there.

It is plainly evident that in the Church's theology and philosophy questions are discussed no longer merely in neo-scholastic terms. Instead the problems and the terminology of modern philosophy have become a factor within the Church herself. It is evident too that Protestant theology is no longer merely the opponent against whom we have to struggle, but is the partner too with whom we share a common ground in face of the questions of the present-day intellectual situation, and from whom we can learn. We notice suddenly that Catholic exegesis too is readier to adopt the methods of rational and historical criticism in its approach to scripture, and thereby raises quite unaccustomed questions for dogmatic theology, so that theologians are far from being unanimous in the answers they give to these. We discover that there are innumerable questions of profound importance upon which we Catholics are far from being united among ourselves. These relate to our attitude in the fields of anthropology, culture, art, foreign and domestic politics and education. We are no longer pledged and committed to one and the same party. Churches are built and works of religious art produced which strike some as a religious revelation while others see them as an outrage. We are no longer united

---

[7] On this concept cf. the author's remarks in Vol. IX of this series, p. 86.

on the question of what properly constitutes, or should constitute 'Christian' literature and poetry today. What seems to one to be necessary and in keeping with the times as an interpretation of dogma seems to another to be bordering on heresy. What one considers to be the obvious way of life for a Christian of today appears to another as too cold or as a cowardly betrayal of every Christian ideal. All at once we discover that Christian principles, though everywhere assented to, are no longer so easy and unambiguous as was formerly believed to apply in the form of concrete imperatives which are likewise accepted by all. In short (we have mentioned only a few minor examples) the world of intellectual pluralism is present within the Church herself. And because of this a dialogue within the Church is inevitable and necessary even if it makes things far more difficult and toilsome for us than formerly, especially since this dialogue is in many respects more difficult than a dialogue with the world outside the Church. This is because however lovingly we may try to behave in a family dispute it still has a special sharpness and bitterness of its own. It is also because this dialogue within the Church is conducted among complex and heterogeneous schools of thought within a single body governed by the same Christian faith and by the one social organisation of the Church. Thus these 'limits' offer less possibility of avoiding the dispute than in the case of the dialogue carried on outside the Church.

In a Church which includes complex and heterogeneous schools of thought such a dialogue within its own ambience is necessary even when it is quite impossible to hope, and indeed not even a legitimate goal to strive for, that through this dialogue every kind of pluralism in the Church will be overcome and complete unity will once more be restored. For the Christians belonging to the Church must help one another to cope in a Christian way with the complexity of intellectual forces which today are present in an unintegrated manner in every individual. Christians must help one another to overcome the dangers for the purity and strength (both factors are involved here!) of their faith, which are entailed by this complexity and pluralism even though, or precisely because, their decision in terms of their own faith and Christian philosophy of life still has to be applied to it so that in a certain sense it is still 'neutral' ground. The Christians must have a common confession of faith. Even though this is not simply to be identified with the theology, the reflexive interpretation of their one faith and creed, because theology can certainly be extremely 'pluralistic' in character, still such close connections exist between faith and theology that these two entities can never be completely separated one from another. Theological reflection, therefore, has a real importance, representing either a help to or a danger for faith itself. For this reason, since Christians, in spite of their unity of faith, are pluralistic in theology, they must discuss their theologies at least in order to assure themselves sufficiently that in spite of the differences between their theologies the unity of their creed is maintained, a fact which today is far more difficult to establish than was formerly thought to be the case.

The Christians in the Church have connections with one another which are not merely theoretical. They must themselves act as Christians. They must take an active part in the single process by which the one Church achieves the fullness of her nature in the most varied dimensions and in the interior and exterior relationships in which the Church is involved. Now in view of the pluralism of ideas already present in the minds of the participators, a preliminary dialogue is required in order for there to be any action in common at all. In this dialogue we must do our utmost to unite ourselves for this common action. Dialogue is necessary in the Church because of the situation of a pluralism of ideas within the Church.

In order to achieve a still clearer view of this necessity it must be pointed out that neither the teaching authorities nor the pastoral authorities of the Church can, by their own act, supply any substitute for this dialogue.

In earlier times, which were more intellectually homogeneous, it might have appeared so. But in itself it was not so even then. For side by side with the authorities, their decisions as affecting doctrine and behaviour in the Church, there was always the inalienable initiative of the individuals, who are never merely carriers out of commands from above. There were always free charismata in the Church, which took effect, and necessarily had to take effect without any prior authorisation on the part of the authorities in the Church. And, though for different reasons, both factors are present and have to be present in increasing measure in the Church of today. But in those earlier times it could at least appear that in spite of the dialogue in council which of course always preceded official decisions in some form, the enactments of the teaching and pastoral authorities could be arrived at, and at least to a large extent actually were arrived at, without any preliminary dialogue. This is understandable. The situation in terms of ideas within which such decisions had to be arrived at was a relatively homogeneous one. Even such contradictions as there were were presented in a form that (at least to all appearances) was comprehensible as a clear 'yes' or 'no'. The actual content of the decision was presented in a form that was intelligible and easily applicable to the straightforward everyday experience of prudent mature men.

Today all that has changed. The subject on which the authorities have to take their decision no longer confronts them in the form of a simple 'yes' or 'no' so that one of the two is accepted as the authentic and authoritative teaching, and the other is anathematised. A whole range of possible prototypes on which to act presents itself, so that it is hardly possible any longer to gain a comprehensive view of them all or to relate them to one another in a comprehensible way. Neither that which constitutes a normal course of study in our formative years, nor our individual experience of life are any longer adequate to keep us sufficiently 'well informed'. Today in practice and in the concrete the authorities themselves presuppose a preliminary dialogue as necessary for their decisions, the sort of dialogue that informs them, gives them an initial understanding of the various systems of theology involved, systematically assembles and digests the relevant experiences and facts, and shows clearly for what they are in themselves those tendencies in the Church which are perfectly legitimate. All that which can be summed up under the term 'dialogue' is today included among those suitable human means[8] the application of which the Church has regarded as necessary for the decisions even of her teaching authority, in spite of the assistance she receives from the Holy Spirit. And these means are, of course, a fortiori indispensable for a realistic exercise of the pastoral authority of the Church.

Dialogue cannot be a substitute for the decisions of the teaching and pastoral authorities in the Church. The reason why it cannot be such a substitute is not merely that the officially constituted authority is necessary and still has a function of its own, but also that a dialogue in the strict sense, at the theoretical level, cannot of itself and in the last analysis overcome the cleavage that exists between the universal and the concrete, between ideas and existence, between possibility and actuality. But conversely, in the situation in which we stand today, whatever may formerly have been the case, the authorities themselves in their decisions presuppose that dialogue is a realistic means of arriving at a right decision in the sphere of their official authority. And the exercise of this authority by itself cannot be any substitute for the dialogue.

This is not to assert that the dialogue within the Church serves only as a preparation for the decisions of the authorities in the Church. There is no lack of topics which can be the subject of a dialogue within the Church, yet which are far from falling within the immediate competence of the

---

[8] cf. *Lumen gentium*, the Second Vatican Council's Constitution on the Church, No. 25.

teaching and pastoral authority.[9] What forms should Christian literature assume today? How should we judge the contemporary political parties in the concrete by Christian criteria? What type of school is to be preferred? Does the secondary school (*Gymnasium*) with a special emphasis on the humanities still have to be our ideal today? What should we think about the most recent tendencies in art? How should we judge of the Weimar Republic? etc. These and a thousand similar questions certainly do not fall directly within the competence of the official authorities of the Church, yet they are still most certainly not on this account questions which belong merely to the general sphere of cultural and intellectual life which Christians and non-Christians have in common. Rather they are questions which have to be thought out in a dialogue among Christians as such as well.

We must say this even if we hold the opinion that in such questions the Christian ought first and foremost freely to participate in the general secular dialogue in which all share. But the Christians should speak about such matters among themselves also, because they have to help one another to arrive at a better understanding of all these realities in the light of the criteria supplied by the gospel. Also because not infrequently through such a dialogue they can arrive at a common understanding and a common course of action, which can then also become the course of action of the Church considered as the people of God, even when it is not the act of the Church's official authorities. In such questions it will often turn out that we hold different opinions and that in spite of the dialogue we continue to hold them. The following pronouncement of the Council is relevant here:[10] 'Often enough the Christian view of things will itself suggest some specific solution in certain circumstances. Yet it happens rather frequently, and legitimately so, that with equal sincerity some of the faithful will disagree with others on a given matter. Even against the intentions of their proponents, however, solutions proposed on one side or another may easily be confused by many people with the gospel message. Hence it is necessary for people to remember that no one is allowed in the aforementioned situations to appropriate the Church's authority for his opinion. They should always try to enlighten one another through honest discussion, preserving mutual charity and caring above all for the common good.'

[9] For a fuller treatment of the problems involved here cf. K. Rahner, 'Grenzen der Amtskirche', *Schriften zur Theologie* VI, (Einsiedeln 1965) pp. 499–520.
[10] The Pastoral Constitution *Gaudium et spes* of the Second Vatican Council, No. 43.

Even this kind of dialogue in the Church, which seems to continue endlessly without result, has a fruitfulness of its own. Given good will on all sides, it educates us in intellectual modesty and prudence. It informs us, enriches our minds, and gives added precision to our ideas even though, for the most part, we continue to differ in our opinions and attitudes. Often it can be the case that a dialogue of this kind is the means by which we establish which group in the Church is to make its views and attitudes prevail in spite of opposition from others, and to cause the Church to conform her concrete decisions and actions to them, thereby rendering powerless and ineffective the contrary opinion. This too is now one of those factors in life which has to be accepted in patience.

When we come to the question of who is to carry on this dialogue within the Church we can think of the most varied groups or individuals, and in every conceivable kind of combination: individuals simply among themselves, formal and informal bodies within the Church, official functionaries, laymen, specialist theologians, the authorised spokesmen of organisations, those who come forward to speak of their own initiative and freely, but who may possibly have a 'charismatic' message to contribute, yes and even such non-Catholics or non-Christians as may be drawn into the dialogue within the Church because they have some 'specialist' contribution to make to this dialogue which is important, and indeed which may perhaps be indispensable as supplying information or something else that is necessary for the dialogue to take place.

III

Today a certain organisation of the dialogue has become inevitable. This does not mean that it has to be deprived of the elements of freedom, spontaneity and improvisation which are essential to it if it is not to degenerate into the sort of bureaucratic discussion and advice which takes place before official decisions are arrived at. On the contrary the institution itself is intended precisely to create the prior conditions in which the individual can freely come forward to make his contribution, in which the necessity for dialogue is neither overlooked nor forgotten in particular concrete cases, and in which the dialogue is never deliberately omitted on the grounds that it is uncomfortable.

Institutions of this kind, which make dialogue possible in the concrete, are already in existence to some extent. But they need to be tested for their effectiveness, and where necessary improved, in order that the dialogue really is made possible. The point of supreme importance for these institutions which are already in existence is that their leaders really shall open themselves to dialogue, neither stifling it nor manipulating it, that they shall respectfully and patiently allow other opinions to be expressed, that they shall themselves seek out partners to the dialogue who are genuine and bold and who have something to say, and that they shall not produce *pro forma* representatives' as a substitute for these. They must also bring into their deliberations laymen in the true sense, who have some special competence in professional matters, and encourage these to speak freely. They must choose these rather than those laymen who turn their status as laymen into an ecclesiastical hobbyhorse, or act as though they had official authority in the Church. In all these ways they must avoid any excess of ecclesiastical authoritarianism, and thereby create the outward conditions for a dialogue in which the participators really can speak openly.

All these institutions which are already in existence must be tested again and again to see whether they are effective in this sense in creating the conditions for dialogue, beginning from the conference of bishops and the diocesan synods, the diocesan officials and cathedral chapters, the boards of management, the social organisations, the Central Committee of German Catholics, and going on to the deanery conferences, councils of laymen, parish councils, advisory committees for radio, Catholic schools and so on. Institutions and the letter of the law can never be any substitute for the Spirit.[11] But if the Spirit is not to be dissipated, then it must be present in the institutions as well, and there must be a demand for it in these.[12] The Spirit, namely, of the love of God and Jesus Christ, the Spirit of fraternal charity, of mutual respect, of patience, of listening to one another, the Spirit which renounces all overbearingness, whether clerical or lay, the Spirit of self-criticism and modesty, the Spirit which makes us bold enough to preserve continuity with our historical heritage, and at the same time daring enough to make new experiments even when these have not yet proved themselves.[13]

---

[11] On this cf. K. Rahner, 'Do not Stifle the Spirit', *Theological Investigations* VII (London and Baltimore, 1971), pp. 72 ff.

[12] On the point that the Spirit of itself demands the institution cf. K. Rahner, *Theological Investigations* VI (London and Baltimore 1969), pp. 305 ff. Charismata can also be at work in the holders of office in the Church, cf. K. Rahner, 'Zur theologischen Problematik einer "Pastoralkonstitution"', *Volk Gottes. Festschrift für Josef Höfer*, R. Baumer and H. Dolch edd., (Freiburg 1967) pp. 683–703, now published in the present volume, pp. 293 ff. cf. also K. Rahner, *Vom Sinn des kirchlichen Amtes* (Freiburg 1966), pp. 33 ff.

[13] With regard to the attitude of boldness towards novelty cf. K. Rahner, *Hand-*

But in addition to those institutions which are already in existence it may be presumed that some others too will be needed in order that the dialogue within the Church may be made a concrete reality. Perhaps I may be permitted to focus the discussion on two in particular. Specialist theologians are, of course, constantly engaged in dialogue with one another, with varying degrees of enthusiasm and varying degrees of success through their books, articles, discussions at conferences and in private conversation. But I believe that what is missing and yet is urgently needed is a genuine panel of specialist theologians properly organised and appointed to supply information and theological advice to the German bishops so as to enable them to exercise their episcopal office of teaching in a way that is realistic and in keeping with the times. Something, therefore is urgently necessary. Today less than ever is the episcopate in any position to hand over its official responsibilities in matters of doctrine to Rome and its Congregations. The bishops must themselves fulfil these responsibilities, a fact which, indeed, becomes clear in the Letter of Cardinal Ottaviani to the World Episcopate.[14] This task of teaching which belongs to the bishops must today assume a form which is, in certain respects, quite new. It can no longer consist merely in the approving of catechisms, pastoral letters, measures of a political kind in the sphere of teaching, as for instance the approving or rejecting of those recommended for professorships and the censoring of books. At the same time, however, the bishops are no longer in a position today to rely for the maintenance of this teaching function of theirs merely upon a theological formation which individuals among them may have received in the past, on taking counsel among themselves or on a chance and subjective selection of theological advisers. The situation in theology is far too difficult, too complex and too obscure today to rely merely upon these aids.[15] For the official pronouncements and enactments which the bishops necessarily have to take – and they will inevitably be faced with the necessity for these – a more fundamental theological preparation is needed today. The very fact that they need to be informed about the

---

buch der Pastoraltheologie II/1, pp. 274–276, Im Heute glauben (Einsiedeln 3rd ed. 1965), pp. 24 ff., 32 ff., and also the study mentioned in n. 11 above.

[14] On this cf. K. Rahner, 'Kirchliches Lehramt und Theologie nach dem Konzil', Stimmen der Zeit 178 (1966), pp. 404–420, esp. 411 f., cf. Vol. IX of this series, pp. 83–100.

[15] On the theological situation immediately confronting us today cf. ibid.

various theological movements, schools of thought and different approaches to the problems involved etc. is in itself enough to make this necessary. Now for this a panel of specialist theologians is necessary which is assembled on an objective and representative basis, and is both able and willing to achieve a genuine and open dialogue. This is still necessary however true it may be that such a panel neither can nor should ever take the place of the bishops in the political decisions they have to take (if we may so express it) in the realm of doctrine as an exercise of their official function of teaching. Yet a panel of this sort, suitably composed to carry on a dialogue at the level of specialist theology, simply does not exist. Of course the bishops do seek information and advice, and even under certain circumstances and for specific questions convoke minor commissions of theologians. The Conference of German Bishops already includes an epsicopal commission for the teaching of the faith. But how far a sufficient number and the right choice of *periti* have already been incorporated into this to advise and assist in preparing its decisions is more than I can say. But even supposing some such body does already exist I may still be permitted to doubt whether this commission of theologians is already constituted in such a way in terms of numbers, a right representation of all relevant theological disciplines, learned authorities etc., that it can fully and effectively meet the demands which have to be made upon it. A further point is that such a panel should in no sense constitute a 'secret cabinet council'. On the contrary its composition must be known, and the names of the theologians included on it must be such as to ensure public confidence in its enactments, even though all that is envisaged here is an advisory body set up to undertake a 'study' of the questions concerned.

Certainly many panels and institutions do exist in Germany in which a dialogue about cultural and political questions is possible: the societies concerned with these questions, the Catholic schools, the central committee of German Catholics, the 'Catholic days', the relevant journals etc. Nevertheless I may be permitted to doubt whether these possibilities are sufficient for the preliminary theological work which is required for the support of the German bishops and for assisting them in their resolutions. On the one hand all these boards and panels have in fact no institutional connection with the commissions of the Conference of German Bishops for such questions, while on the other I doubt whether these episcopal commissions in themselves have available to them the group of specialists (i.e. in terms of number, competence, proportional representation etc.) working together in dialogue which they need. Perhaps I am merely ill-informed, but I ask myself whether, for instance, the problem of the

Church schools or the urgent question of the need for a change in the mixed marriage laws in Germany have been reviewed or debated in the work of any such board, which is equipped to do the preparatory work for the decisions to be taken in the Conference of Bishops, or whether even today the bishops are still paternalistic in their way of working, choosing their advisers in a rather chance and arbitrary manner. Today, in view of the difficulty and complexity of the questions and the necessity for upholding the rightness of the decisions taken in a manner that is convincing in public as well, this procedure is simply inadmissible. We must also bear in mind that the *de facto* existence of opinions on certain specific questions has an importance of its own, greater or less according to the weight carried by the upholders of such opinions and the degree of force with which they hold them. And these opinions themselves can, and perhaps should, represent a stage in the process by which the bishops form their opinions and arrive at their decisions, at least in those questions which cannot be decided upon unambiguously or exclusively in terms of dogma.

IV

We must now attempt to say something more upon the nature and the limits of the dialogue within the Church concerning theological questions in the stricter sense, that is to say problems of biblical, dogmatic and moral theology. This dialogue is necessary today. The reason for this necessity is to be found, as has been stated above, in the very nature of the case. Even in the sphere of theology in the true sense the situation of intellectual pluralism prevails. The multiplicity of the sources and methods of theology make it impossible any longer for any one individual to master them all. Theology must necessarily engage in a dialogue with the rest of the intellectual forces of the time. But these themselves are in turn so complex that the dialogue creates a difficult situation within the realm of theology. In practice there is no longer any uniform theological terminology, nor is it any longer so easy to devise any such if theology is to be placed at the service of preaching the one gospel to this world of today, so heterogeneous and pluralistic as it is in terms of ideas. There is no longer any one theologian who has a comprehensive mastery of the methodologies, sources, problems and conclusions of any single department of theology. On any given subject each one must constantly be increasing his knowledge, and this means that the 'subject' on which he should, as far as possible, know everything that there is to be known, becomes more and more circumscribed. Teamwork and dialogue are necessary in theology too.

Now theology does not exist as an end in itself, but is designed rather to serve the Church, her preaching and then her teaching office as well. Moreover theology derives its norms from this. It follows that the dialogue among theologians must be desired and demanded by the Church, and the theologians themselves must be constantly aware that their ultimate task is to serve the Church. This dialogue must not be regarded as a substitute for the task of the Church as the official teacher, and must not be intended to supplant the authority of the Church in her official function.[16] This dialogue must not transform the Church into a debating society. A theological dialogue within the Church achieves its true nature only if certain specific prior conditions are fulfilled: the participators must all submit themselves to the authority of holy scripture; they must really pay heed to its message even when they themselves are interpreting and translating this message. Officially defined doctrine must remain unambiguously the guiding principle and not be argued away as a mere 'interpretament' devoid of binding force. This remains true even in those cases in which the dogma (in a broader sense) needs to be explained and interpreted, where it is not simply too absolute to admit of revision, but still has to be sincerely accepted as an authentic pronouncement of the official teaching in accordance with the degree of binding force involved in each particular case, for there is a certain variation in this binding force. The personal and subjective work of theologians, which is necessary, inevitable and even justified in itself, must constantly proceed from the Church's teaching and be directed to this, and must constantly and sincerely be thought out afresh in the light of it even when this may be disturbing or painful. It must be contained within the greater awareness of faith of the Church herself as this exists in the present, and also as it finds authoritative expression and concrete force in the officially promulgated teaching of the Church. Everything else may be profound, stimulating and important for the history of human thought, but it would still have no place in a theological dialogue within the Church.

Since it cannot be considered as contrary to the nature of a dialogue within the Church if, on some particular question, it is not endlessly prolonged, but in a certain sense brought to an end by a pronouncement of the Church's teaching authority, this may open the way to, or even make necessary, a further dialogue. But the new dialogue is only a theological

---

[16] For an attempt at a thoroughgoing theological explanation in this connection cf. K. Rahner, *Vom Sinn des kirchlichen Amtes* (Freiburg 1966).

dialogue within the Church if it unequivocally and obediently takes as its starting-point and binding norm the new pronouncement of the teaching authority according to the degree of binding force intended by that teaching authority in each particular case.

It may be that bishops do not, from the point of view of specialist and scientific theologians, understand much of a theological question. It is right that in such a case they are morally bound to seek the information they need directly or indirectly from the scientific knowledge of the specialists when they wish to, or have to, arrive at a decision on the question concerned. But viewed from a strictly theological point of view this does not in the least alter the fact that as bishops they, and not the theologians, are the true 'judges' in questions of faith and morals when a pronouncement needs to be made for the sake of the unity of the creed in the Church and the purity of her faith. Even humanly speaking it is well that this is the case. Experts and specialists must give advice, but leave the decision to others who are in a position to achieve a comprehensive and unrestricted view of the realities involved as a whole.

In itself all this is a truism of Catholic faith and practice. But it seems that the time has come to emphasise that this truth which seems to be a truism is not, after all, so clearly self-evident. Even among us in Germany it is no longer sufficiently respected in oral and written dialogue, nor is the episcopal *imprimatur* any longer a sure guarantee today that this truism will really be observed.[17]

That is one side of the picture. But on the other side it has to be said that the authority of the official teachers cannot be any substitute for a theological dialogue. For today this is to be numbered among those means which are necessary, and, for the teaching authority of the Church, even morally prescribed, through which this teaching authority has to ensure that its own decisions are properly prepared and brought to maturity. This still does not imply in any sense a pre-judging of the precise question of what form this necessary theological dialogue is to take in the concrete, or how it may have to be consciously and deliberately organised or even institutionalised. To establish this in more precise terms is certainly in part a matter for the teaching authority itself. The task of establishing and judging how this duty which it has is to be fulfilled is, in the last analysis, still a matter for the teaching authority of the Church. This again does not prevent us from holding the opinion, which is based on historical fact, that right down to the most recent times the teaching authority of the Church has not always, or in all the ways

[17] On this cf. K. Rahner, *Stimmen der Zeit* 178 (1966), pp. 414 f., cf. here pp. 124 f.

that could be desired or that are necessary, created the conditions which make theological dialogue possible and meet the demand for it prior to the taking of official decisions.

In cases where it is ultimate decisions of faith which are in question and which have to be defined, even though in such a case the Spirit preserves the teaching authority from any actual error of faith, this still does not mean that any evasions of responsibility at the human level are made legitimate as such. But when such decisions on doctrine are taken, which, though authoritative are still capable of being revised, evasions of responsibility of this kind can have the effect of rendering the decision itself deficient, inadequate, or in need of reform. From this such evasions can lead further to difficult situations and to a state in which any genuine willingness to obey the authority of the Church in matters of doctrine *de facto* disappears.[18] I believe that many of Pius XII's doctrinal pronouncements would have turned out differently in form and even in content if they had been preceded by an adequate, open and free theological dialogue on the questions involved. Nor in fact can there be any doubt that Paul VI has recognised more fully the importance of promoting theological dialogue as a preparation for official decisions on doctrine (or else for the decision *not* to take any decision, which can also be an important act of the teaching authority of the Church) than was the case in the preceding decades, and this remains true even though, on a superficial view, he has made his own position more difficult by doing this.[19]

We can only hope that the bishops will follow his example in this precisely because they have authority to teach as well. They too have to recognise this, and it is less permissible today even than it was a few years ago, to abrogate their responsibilities in this in favour of the papal authority alone. But when such decisions on doctrine are taken, which though authoritative are still capable of being revised, there is a further question to be asked. How is unity to be established in the particular concrete instance between the two factors in the process by which truth is

[18] A theology of today that is credible and is conscious of its responsibilities will have to be increasingly aware of the fact that it is part of a developing history, though in this it will not lose its character as binding in any essential. On this cf. the bibliography on p. 105/n.2.

[19] The most important example is the commission for the study of the increase in population, the family and the regulation of births. It is also well-known that in deciding his general line of approach in other theological questions the pope avails himself of the advice of various consultative bodies (cf. the symposium (admittedly not of official status) working in an advisory capacity at Nemi near Rome in July 1966 on the subject of original sin and evolution).

arrived at or deepened? These factors are: the dialogue of the theologians on the one hand and the authority of the official teachers on the other. And again we may ask how long the debate should be prolonged and when and how it should be, in some sense, brought to a close by an official doctrinal pronouncement; when the doctrinal authorities should have the courage to keep silence and when they should be bold enough to come to a decision. All these are questions the concrete answers to which cannot be deduced from the general principles governing the relationship between the two entities involved. In these questions those concerned have constantly to return afresh for the taking of their decisions to the concrete instance. And the decision itself can never be arrived at at the theoretical level but only in practice. But from every side an attitude is demanded of courage, humility and the will to act in love according to the truth.

The dialogue or debate, therefore, when viewed in the context of the whole process by which the Church realises her faith to the full, has, of its nature, on the one hand an indispensable contribution of its own to make, but on the other its limits too. For it always remains subsumed under this more general process. And the knowledge of both these factors at once makes it a duty for the Church to engage in dialogue, and gives her the courage to do so with patience, attentiveness and a readiness to give a serious hearing to outside opinions. At the same time it serves to guard the dialogue from degenerating into mere empty talk in which only the opinionated who have no respect for the views of others receive a hearing. The dialogue must constantly be conducted in the awareness that it is taking place in the holy Church which is made up of sinners; that it is intended to conduce to salvation; that those participating in it will have to answer for the part they play in it before the judgment of God.[20] Once this is recognised it should be entered upon in the Church with all boldness. For it is much needed today.

[20] If a dialogue is to be really serious and sincere, then a vivid awareness has to be maintained throughout it of the constant danger of degenerating into ambiguity and mere talk. In a changed situation in the history of human thought the biblical exhortation once more becomes urgently relevant, that man will have to give a reckoning for every idle word.

PART TWO

Sacraments

7

PENANCE AS AN ADDITIONAL ACT OF RECONCILIATION WITH THE CHURCH

THE Second Vatican Council has laid down in two passages that in the sacrament of penance an additional reconciliation of the sinner takes place with the Church herself.[1] The Church, therefore, is not only the bearer of the effective word in which God pronounces his forgiveness and grace upon the repentant sinner. Also, and by the same act, she confers upon the individual that *pax* with her own self which was damaged or broken by his sins.

I

This declaration of the Council is an astonishing enactment. Almost fifty years ago the Spanish Carmelite B. F. Xiberta[2] initiated afresh the debate concerning the doctrine of the reconciliation of sinners with the Church[3] (and not only with God through the Church) in the sacrament of penance. Probably this was the first time the matter had been discussed since the Council of Trent. But when Xiberea sought to justify this doctrine he met only with rejection. J. Stufler,[4] the well-known expert on the history of the sacrament of penance, likewise rejected this theory after Xiberta's book had appeared. A. d'Alès[5] did the same. As late as 1957 it was summarily and unequivocally rejected by P. Galtier,[6] who certainly enjoys a great reputation as a historian and for his systematic expositions of the sacrament of penance. In E. Doronzo's[7] comprehensive theology of the sacrament

---

[1] cf. *Lumen gentium*, No. 11; *Presbyterorum ordinis*, No. 5.

[2] B. F. Xiberta, *Clavis Ecclesiae: De Ordine Absolutionis Sacramentalis ad Reconciliationem cum Ecclesia* (Rome 1922).

[3] Here the reconciliation of the sinner with the Church is taken to be the *res et sacramentum*, while the forgiveness of sins in the sight of God is the *res sacramenti* corresponding to this. [4] J. Stufler, *Z.K.T.* 47 (1923), pp. 453 ff.

[5] A. d'Alès, *R.S.R.* 12 (1922), pp. 372 f.

[6] P. Galtier, *De Paenitentia* (Rome, 3rd ed. 1957), p. 341.

[7] E. Doronzo, *De Paenitentia* II (Milwaukee 1951), pp. 131–153.

of penance, published in monograph form, Xiberta's theory is still accorded a relatively brief treatment (in comparison with the scope of the work as a whole), and . . . rejected. The great monograph on the history of the sacrament of penance by J. Grotz,[8] which has been published very recently, proceeds from the *a priori* view that originally reconciliation with the Church would not have constituted any essential element in the sacrament of penance itself, but would first have become established in the course of the second century, and then only in specific cases as something that was conferred *prior to* the sacramental act proper. He attempts to confirm this theory *a posteriori* by an immense display of historical learning. Even if we hold the opinion that in this large-scale and learned work the historical evidence adduced has failed to establish the author's thesis,[9] still the very existence of such a work from 1955 onwards shows precisely *how strongly* the idea of sacramental penance as a reconciliation with the Church had become foreign to the thought of theologians. The majority of treatises on this sacrament, extending right down to the most recent times, pass over this thesis of Xiberta's in silence, so that I myself was surely justified in speaking of a 'forgotten truth'.[10] In any case it has played no part in the average theology of the schools.[11] Even in the most

---

[8] J. Grotz, *Die Entwicklung des Bussstufenwesens in der vornicänischen Kirche* (Freiburg 1955).

[9] On this cf. K. Rahner, 'Die Busslehre im Hirten des Hermas', *Z.K.T.* 77 (1955), pp. 385–431; S. Hübner, 'Kirchenbusse und Exkommunikation bei Cyprian', *Z.K.T.* 84 (1962), 49–84; 171–215 (with bibliography).

[10] K. Rahner, 'Forgotten Truths Concerning the Sacrament of Penance' *Theological Investigations* II (London and Baltimore 1963), pp. 135–174; cf. also *idem*, *L.T.K.* II, 2nd ed., col. 836; *idem*, *Kirche und Sakramente* (Freiburg, 2nd ed. 1963), pp. 83 ff. The author may be permitted to refer to his earlier studies in the history of the sacrament of penance (cf. above, n. 9, pp. 138 f., 141). They have been collected in an Italian translation, *La penitenza della Chiesa* = Biblioteca di cultura religiosa, Seconda Serie no. 60 (Rome 1964, 2nd ed. 1968), 872 pp. A German edition of these historical researches is planned as *Schriften zur Theologie* IX. At the same time reference may be made to the author's comprehensive treatment of the subject *De paenitentia: Tractatus historico-dogmaticus* (Innsbruck, 4th ed. 1960, duplicated), XXIII–785 ff., which has still to be revised and published. For the evidence in concrete detail, therefore, the author must refer to his detailed investigations and the bibliography he draws upon there. On the matter itself cf. also the important investigations of G. d'Ercole, *Consortium Disciplinae. Le sanzioni nell' ordinamento canonico preconstantiano* I (Rome 1955); *idem*, *Penitenza canonico-sacramentale dalle orogini alla pace constantiniana* (Rome 1963).

[11] A typical example is to be found on p. 462 of S. Gonzalez's *Sacrae Theologiae Summa* IV (Madrid 3rd ed., 1956), no. 93, n. 4. Here Xiberta's thesis is rejected as 'contra communem theologorum sententiam'.

recent work on the question, that of McAuliffe,[12] while its author does not absolutely reject Xiberta's thesis, he still cannot bring himself to agree with it.

Thus it is, after all, an astonishing fact that the Council, with a marked lack of reserve, gives expression to this doctrine as a manifest truth. The fact that the Council felt no difficulty in doing this will appear in the course of this study, the purpose of which is to show that what the Council is asserting here belongs to the most ancient stock of tradition, in which evidence for the doctrine can be traced from scripture right through the theology of the Fathers and the Middle Ages as something essential and manifest.

Of course it is not the case that Xiberta met *only* with contradiction or an icy silence. We may take the case of B. Poschmann. While this author did not fully develop the thesis as a subject in its own right,[13] it still remains true that his historical studies on the history of penance in the early Church are influenced by the conviction that the practice of penance in the early Church and the institution of penance in patristic times are, in the last analysis, an insoluble mystery unless we constantly keep before our eyes a clear recognition of the fact that in the early Church the conferring of the *pax cum Ecclesia* was an essential element in the penitential practice of that Church considered precisely as a *sacrament*, and not merely as an associated practice prescribed by Church law. In addition to him individual theologians have claimed a hearing again and again who (either explicitly or implicitly) agree with Xiberta. Not only in the study mentioned above, but in my duplicated treatise (still unpublished) of almost 500 pages on the sacrament of penance I myself have already presented the doctrine of the additional reconciliation of the sinner with the Church as a key to the understanding of the entire history of penance in the early Church. Of the theologians who agreed with Xiberta prior to the Council

---

[12] C. McAuliffe, 'Penance and Reconciliation with the Church', *Theological Studies* 26 (1965), pp. 1–39. We are indebted to this painstaking study for references to the more recent writings on the question with which we are here concerned. But McAuliffe's study has not yet taken the pronouncements of Vatican II into account.

[13] cf. B. Poschmann, *Paenitentia Secunda* (Bonn, 1940), e.g. p. 11; 'Busse und Letzte Ölung' = *Handbuch der Dogmengeschichte* IV, 3 (Freiburg 1951); Apart from his other important and well-known works on the history of the sacrament of penance the following study by B. Poschmann is particularly important: 'Die innere Struktur des Bussakramentes', *M.T.Z.* 1 (1950), pp. 12–30. Poschmann shows a certain lack of terminological precision in his exposition of the teaching of the pre-Nicene Fathers. On this cf. K. Rahner, *Z.T.K.* 64 (1940), p. 162.

the following may be mentioned: de la Taille,[14] Cabrol,[15] de Lubac,[16] Mersch,[17] Schmaus,[18] Leeming,[19] Riga,[20] Dumont,[21] Schillebeeckx,[22] Courtney,[23] Palmer,[24] Anciaux,[25] Oggioni,[26] Marie-Benoit,[27] McAuley,[28] Cantwell,[29] Ratzinger,[30] Congar,[31] Vorgrimler,[32] Semmelroth,[33] Beumer,[34] Piolanti,[35] Alszeghy,[36] Leclercq,[37] Rondet.[37a]

[14] M. de la Taille, *Mysterium fidei* (3rd ed. Paris, 1931), p. 581; cf. *idem*, 'Conspectus bibliographicus', *Gregorianum* 4 (1923), pp. 591–599; further evidence in C. Dumont, *N.R.T.* 81 (1959), pp. 578–579.

[15] F. Cabrol, *Six Sacraments* (London 1930), p. 160.

[16] H. de Lubac, *Catholicisme* (4th ed., Paris 1947), pp. 61 f.

[17] E. Mersch, *La théologie du corps mystique* (2nd ed., Paris 1946), p. 304.

[18] M. Schmaus, *Katholische Dogmatik* IV/1 (Munich, 5th ed. 1957), pp. 591 f.; *idem*, 'Reich Gottes und Busssakrament', *Münchener Theol. Zeitschrift* 1 (1950), pp. 20–36.

[19] B. Leeming, *Principles of Sacramental Theology* (New York, 1956), pp. 361–366.

[20] P. Riga, *Sin and Penance* (Milwaukee 1962), pp. 111–113.

[21] C. Dumont, 'La réconciliation avec l'église et la nécessité de l'aveu sacramental', *N.R.T.* 81 (1959), pp. 577–597, esp. 578 ff., 583 ff.

[22] E. Schillebeeckx, *De Christusontmoeting als sacrament van de Godsontmoeting* (Anvers, Bilthoven 1957), p. 152; German ed., *Christus, Sakrament der Gottbegegnung* (Mainz 1960), p. 179.

[23] F. Courtney, 'The Sacrament of Penance', *Clergy Review* 40 (1955), p. 519.

[24] P. Palmer, 'The Theology of the *Res et Sacramentum* with Particular Emphasis on its Application to Penance', *Proceedings of the Fourteenth Annual Convention of the Catholic Theological Society of America* (Jonkers, N.Y. 1959), pp. 131–141; *idem*, *Sacraments of Healing and of Vocation* (Englewood Cliffs, N.Y., 1963), pp. 34–36.

[25] P. Anciaux, 'La dimension ecclésiale de la pénitence chrétienne', *Collectanea Mechliniensia* 46 (1961), p. 477; *idem*, *Le sacrament de la pénitence* (Louvain 1960), German edition, *Das Sakrament der Busse* (Mainz 1961), pp. 154–158, cf. also, pp. 44 f., 52 f., 72 f., 74, 76, 79, 111 f., 124, 136, 164 f., 168 f., 173 f., 179, 187 f.

[26] G. Oggioni, *Storia e teologia della penitenza: Problemi e orientamenti di teologia dommatica* II (Mailand 1957), p. 920.

[27] P. Marie-Benoit, 'Note sur le jugement exercé au sacrament de pénitence', *Études Franciscaines* 12 (1962), p. 145.

[28] G. McAuley, 'The Ecclesiastical Nature of the Sacrament of Penance', *Worship* 36 (1962), pp. 212–213.

[29] L. Cantwell, 'Pax Ecclesiae', *Clergy Review* 48 (1963), p. 617.

[30] J. Ratzinger, 'The Pastoral Implications of Episcopal Collegiality', *Concilium* I/1 (1965), pp. 20–34.

[31] Y. Congar, 'Über die Mutterschaft der Kirche', *T.Q.* 145 (1965), pp. 68–100, esp. 93–94.

[32] H. Vorgrimler, 'Der ekklesiastische (deprekative) Aspekt des Bussverfahrens', *Anima* 14 (1959), pp. 307–314. *idem*, 'Busssakrament', *Handbuch theologische Grundbegriffe* I (Munich 1962), pp. 204–217.

II

Now certainly it was natural for the Council to give expression to this truth, so ancient and yet so new, of the reconciliation of sinners to the Church in the sacrament of penance, because it was so extremely relevant in the actual *context* in which this was asserted. In chapter 2 of the Dogmatic Constitution *Lumen gentium* the intention was to speak of the 'priestly' functions of the people of God. These priestly functions are made actual in the sacraments and through the virtuous life which Christians lead. Whereas in earlier versions of the text not all the sacraments were treated of in this connection, the authors arrived, at a very early stage in their work of drawing up the text, at a decision to mention *all* the sacraments at this point.[38] In this connection,[39] therefore, not only the effect of all these sacraments as sanctifying man as an individual had to be brought out, but also the ecclesiastical aspect which they possess, the part they play in building the body of Christ. Now when it was sought to apply this to the sacrament of penance it was *quite impossible* to do this in any other way than that which was actually adopted, namely by saying: '*Reconcilientur cum Ecclesia quam peccando vulneraverant*'.[40]

At the same time it still remains astonishing that they were bold enough to express this doctrine so uncompromisingly, even though, to all appearances, they were unable to invoke any *consensus unanimis* in contemporary theology. It was even more astonishing that the statement was not the occasion of any debate in the aula of the Council, and that, as far as my own personal recollection goes, even in the theological commission it never became a point for discussion. Instead it was accepted even here without any opposition. Admittedly this fact, which is far from being

---

[33] O. Semmelroth, *Die Kirche als Ursakrament* (Frankfurt 1953), pp. 64 ff.

[34] J. Beumer, 'Die persönliche Sünde in sozialtheologischer Sicht', *Theologie und Glaube* 43 (1953), pp. 81–100.

[35] A. Piolanti, 'Socialità del sacramento della penitenza', *Studi Cattolici* 2 (1958), pp. 27–33.

[36] Z. Alszeghy, 'Carità ecclesiale nella penitenza christiana', *Gregorianum* 44 (1963), pp. 5–31.

[37] J. Leclercq, *La liturgie et les paradoxes chrétiens* (Paris 1963), pp. 87–104.

[37a] H. Rondet, 'Bemerkungen zu einer Theologie der Sünde', G.u.L. 28 (1955), 28–44; 106–116; 194–208.

[38] This decision was first adopted in the schema of 3.7.1964.

[39] cf. No. 11 of the Constitution *Lumen gentium*.

[40] The text in the Decree on the Ministry and Life of Priests (No. 5) is simply an echo of this passage in *Lumen gentium*.

simple or obvious, is in part to be explained once more by a special circumstance: the authors of the text deliberately avoided from the outset[41] any attempt at complicating this statement of reconciliation with the Church by the further question of the *precise relationship between* the '*venia offensionis Deo illatae*' on God's part, and the '*reconciliatio cum Ecclesia*'. The two effects are simply set side by side with the connecting word *simul*.

Thus the Council leaves open the questions of how the forgiveness of guilt in God's eyes (or, to express it more precisely, the forgiveness of guilt and the conferring of grace) on the one hand, and the additional reconciliation with the Church on the other are related one to another, whether these two factors are intrinsically connected by their very nature, which of the two effects (supposing this to be the case) can be thought of as the cause of the other (additional reconciliation with the Church *because* guilt has been forgiven, or conversely the forgiveness of guilt *because* reconciliation with the Church has been achieved), whether, therefore, reconciliation with the Church should be thought of as the *res et sacramentum* of the forgiveness of guilt (considered as the *res sacramenti*). This last-named theory is probably held by almost all modern theologians who explicitly teach that reconciliation with the Church is an effect of the sacrament of penance. Now while the Council does not enter into this theory, neither does it in any sense exclude it in enumerating these effects. Yet even allowing for its reserve on this point, the text of the Council is noteworthy in the highest degree: it teaches that *all* sins have an ecclesiological aspect, all 'wound' the Church. It teaches that in *every* exercise of the sacrament of penance a reconciliation with the Church takes place as well.[42] We may also be struck by the fact that in this statement no references are offered to any theological sources. In the passage it is left to the theologians themselves to think out precisely *what* distinctions are to be drawn in this ecclesiological aspect of sin according to whether it is grave or venial sin that is in question, how the damage done to the relationship between the sinner and the Church is to be defined in detail according to each particular case. They have also to think out, when it still remains an obvious fact that not every grave sin signifies a total cutting off of the sinner from the Church, how *this*

---

[41] cf. the *Relatio* to the Schema of 3.7.1964 (p. 45).

[42] The terms in which this is expressed are so general and so completely devoid of any restriction that it would simply be contradicting their objective meaning if we sought to interpret the text as applying, for instance, only to the (first) confession of grave sins.

precise reconciliation is to be distinguished from the removal of an excommunication (and the widely differing degrees of this) in the sense of contemporary canon law, and how the statement of the Council retains its truth even in the case of a mere 'repetitional confession'.

But all these further questions must not be answered by the theologians in such a way that their answer either contradicts or obscures the basic statement of the Council. The task of answering them is, incidentally, not so difficult as perhaps it might appear at first sight (and as, for instance, B. McAuliffe appears to imagine), for in such instances of the use of the sacrament we can meet with formally speaking the same difficulties as here, even when we confine our attention to the forgiveness of sins as such. Mortal and venial sins (the latter considered as *praeter legem*),[43] are, it is true, guilty in the sight of God. But even allowing for this the concept of 'sin' can only be applied analogously to the two types, and yet sacramental forgiveness is available for both. Why, therefore, should not venial sins too be a 'wounding' of the *holy* Church, seeing that she is holy not merely in an institutional, but in an 'existential' sense as well,[44] so that mortal *and* venial sins on the part of one of her members contradict her own nature and so 'wound' her, even though in ways which are essentially very different in the two cases? It is significant that the same guilt in God's sight can receive sacramental forgiveness several times over (in a repetitional confession). But if this is true, then it applies also to the guilt which consists in an offence against the Church. Finally – a point that must constantly and emphatically be borne in mind – if we can conceive of the Church not merely as an external juridical organisation but as a *holy* people of God, as a covenant of grace, as the Body of Christ vivified by the Spirit, then *every* sin on the part of a member of the Church contradicts the interior nature of the Church, and not merely those sins to which the Church attaches an excommunication properly so-called. This also finds expression in the fact that every mortal sin, taken in itself and before it is sacramentally cleansed, debars the sinner from the Eucharist, the central mystery of the Church, so that in every case it has an ecclesiological aspect (we do not propose here to go into the further problems connected with the question of whether this state of being debarred from the Eucharist prior to the *sacramental* cleansing of mortal sin is *juris divini* or *juris mere ecclesiastici*). Even taken by themselves these simple considerations are sufficient to

---

[43] We are presupposing that the reader is already familiar with the teaching of St Thomas on this point.

[44] cf. K. Rahner, 'The Church of Sinners', 'The Sinful Church in the Decrees of Vatican II', *Theological Investigations* VI (London and Baltimore 1969), pp. 270–294.

explain why the Council should have been able, without hesitation, to say what it has said.

The foregoing observations may suffice here so far as the immediate exegesis of the conciliar statements is concerned. Here we must refrain from entering into the second part of the statement with which we are concerned (*'quae [Ecclesia] eorum conversioni caritate, exemplo, precibus adlaborat'*), even though this second part of the statement too is quite unusually significant since it makes clear that in the concrete application of the sacrament of penance (which always includes the repentance, the *conversio* of the sinner as an essential element in it) the Church collaborates not merely through the priestly absolution but through much else in addition to this. In other words the *whole* Church (*exemplum, caritas, preces*) participates in this exercise.[45] One final point which still remains to be noticed is that the text (*'veniam offensionis Deo illatae ab Eius misericordia obtinent'*) formally and explicitly excludes that heretical misinterpretation which is pointed out by the Congregation for the Doctrine of the Faith in its Letter to the Bishops of the World, the heresy, namely, that in the sacrament of penance it is *only* reconciliation with the Church that is being treated of.[46]

III

There is something further which we would add to this statement of the Council and the brief exegesis of this provided in this article. This is something which, in a certain sense, could have been given a place in the conciliar document itself in the form of a 'note'. It consists of a few brief proofs from theological tradition supporting this statement to the extent that this is possible in a brief article. It may be asked, what is being treated of in these witnesses? Is it the simple fact that in the sacrament of penance a

[45] cf. K. Rahner, 'Forgotten Truths Concerning the Sacrament of Penance', *Theological Investigations* II (London and Baltimore 1963), pp. 135–174. This statement of the Council could be taken as a starting-point for achieving a new, positive and entirely orthodox understanding of that which is treated of in the History of Dogma under the headings of 'The Confession of Religious' and 'The Confession of Layfolk' (cf. *L.T.K.* VI, 2nd ed., cols. 741–742; VII, 538–539). An understanding of this kind would also be of great significance from the point of view of oecumenism. On this cf. W. Kaspar, 'Confession outside the Confessional?', *Concilium* 4/3 (1967), pp. 17–22.

[46] cf. *A.A.S.* 58 (1966), 659–661 (Letter of 24.7.1966). On this cf. K. Rahner, 'Kirchliches Lehramt und Theologie nach dem Konzil', *StdZ* 178 (1966), pp. 404–420, also Vol. IX of this series, pp. 83–100.

reconciliation with the Church is achieved as well, or do they go beyond this, thinking of this reconciliation with the Church as the *res et sacramentum* of the reconciliation with God (here it is the reality itself rather than the term *res et sacramentum* that is in question)? Though the question is legitimate, for the purposes of our present treatment we may be permitted to set on one side the distinction involved in this question. It is true that to some extent special emphasis will be laid explicitly on the second of the two theories summarised above, but this is justified on the grounds that this second theory necessarily includes the first. Here, it must be admitted, we have no intention of going into the more detailed arguments for holding that the *pax cum ecclesia* is to be thought of as the *res et sacramentum* of forgiveness in the eyes of God, this in turn being considered as *res sacramenti*. For such a line of argument would have first to show (and this is precisely what cannot be shown here) in *general* that in all the sacraments the *res et sacramentum* has an ecclesiological character, i.e. that it implies that the recipient of the sacraments has a specific relationship precisely with the Church. One further proviso may be mentioned. In what follows we shall often have occasion to speak of 'excommunication' (in quotation marks!) or release from 'excommunication' through penance. What we mean by this is not excommunication in the sense implied in contemporary canon law, but rather that state in which we no longer *fully* belong to the Church (or alternatively the conferring of a state of belonging to it which is in every respect full and complete) which is incurred by every mortal sin (and for which no other concise term exists). When *Lumen gentium* describes what *full* incorporation into the Church means, *one* of the elements in this apart from baptism, public confession of the faith and adherence to the laws of the community, is *also* the interior possession of grace (*Spiritum Christi habentes*[47]). Thus sinners remain in the bosom of the Church only *corpore* and not *corde*.[48] According to the teaching of the Council, therefore, there can be no doubt of the fact that even simple mortal sin, which allows the sinner to remain a member of the Church, as the Council of Constance defines, *alters* the relationship of the member involved to the Church.[49] This alteration[50] we

[47] cf. No. 14 of the Constitution *Lumen gentium*.

[48] *ibid.*

[49] On this text the conciliar commission has explicitly declared: '*peccatores Ecclesiae non plene incorporantur*'. cf. the studies mentioned on p. 131 n. 44, especially 'The Sinful Church . . .', pp. 291 f.

[50] Of course this 'alteration' in the relationship between the sinner and the Church has in turn two aspects or elements: the alteration which follows *ipso facto* from the nature of the sin as such, and the alteration in so far as this is constituted by the

shall here call (for want of a better word) 'excommunication' (in quotation marks!), and the sacramental removal of this 'excommunication' we shall call penance from 'excommunication'. Actually this is still conferred today in every sacramental absolution, because it is still true today that this also confers the right to receive the Eucharist, and even today to be excluded from this is the clearest expression of this state of 'excommunication'.

First we shall give a sort of *survey* of the 'history of dogma' of reconciliation with the Church, and then we shall go on to refer to a small selection of a few individual passages.

IV

This doctrine is already contained in scripture. We cannot embark upon a learned exegesis at this point. We must confine ourselves, rather, to this brief observation: if we were to undertake this our first task would be to

---

Church's reaction to this particular sin. For our present purposes it makes no difference whether this reaction on the part of the Church is necessary (*iure divino*, if we may so express it) or following from standards freely imposed by the Church herself, whether (to use a canonist's expression in a somewhat transferred sense) it takes place *lata sententia* or *ferenda sententia*. In any case the fact that by grave sin the sinner is debarred from the Eucharist and bound in duty to confess his sin shows that the Church always reacts in this way to grave sin. In every case of this kind the Church always exercises her 'binding' power even when she does not pronounce a sentence of excommunication in the sense meant in canon law. Of course a difficulty does arise here with regard to venial sins, which cannot be the subject of the Church's 'binding' power. But even with regard to these we can still say: venial sins as such (so long as we fail to rise above them), and in every instance of them, blur the relationship which man bears to the Church precisely as *holy*, a certain 'wounding' of the Church through man's own personal act (i.e. through the first element mentioned above). The fact that the Church cannot react to this as she does to a grave sin lies in the very nature of the case. If we find a difficulty in this, then it remains only because we are neglecting the ecclesiological side of venial sin. In order to make clear the character of absolution as a judicial act of the Church (cf. DS 1671, 1679) scholastic theology often emphasises that the reason why the plenary power of the Church in penance (which differs in this from baptism) is a judicial power, is that it consists in a power to decide in two opposite directions (*potestas bifaria*), a power of binding and loosing. However this argument can be applied without further qualification only to mortal sin, and has nothing to do with the question of an ecclesiological aspect of sin and absolution. Thus it appears that in any case the whole nature of the sacrament of penance is such that it is designed in the first instance for the forgiveness of grave sin and only secondarily for the forgiveness of venial sin. If we recognise this then the difficulty indicated above cannot be insuperable, and is to be solved in the same manner as with regard to the theological aspect of venial sin.

point out the 'ecclesial' aspect of sin which is clearly to be found in the Old and New Testaments.[51] The ethical system of the Old Testament is in fact explicitly a 'covenant ethic'. And this is equally true of the new 'people of God' in the New Testament. Nor can we here enter into any precise detail in the question of the relationship of dependence which exists between Mt 16:19 and 18:18 on the one hand and Jn 20:23 on the other. But in any case it is certain that the 'binding and loosing'[52] which is conferred as the authority of Jesus himself upon his community, and so upon the duly appointed functionaries of this, represents the counterpart in the synoptics to Jn 20. It is also certain that throughout the whole of tradition (also) it has been taken to refer to the same power to forgive sins[53] which, according to DS 1703, is expressed in Jn 20. This power of binding and loosing, which must not be thought of simply as an alternative way of expressing the power of the keys attributed to Peter, is to be interpreted against the background of Jewish theology at the time of Jesus. In the light of a more precise exegesis based on this it turns out that the state of being bound by sin signifies subjection to demonic powers.[54] Thus, applying this to the act of the Church, 'to bind' ('on earth') signifies 'consigning the individual concerned to the power of Satan' (1 Cor 5:5; 1 Tim 1:20), and so exclusion from the community of the saved, while 'to loose' ('on earth') signifies the dissolving of this state of demonic bondage and so being restored to the community of the saved, the covenant people with its power to ransom. The Church, therefore, has the power of the 'ban' and of the removal of this, and *precisely in this sense* has the power to forgive sins ('in heaven').

Without this idea of the ecclesiological aspect of the power of the Church in relation to the sinner, the penitential discipline and practice of the Christians of the early Church remain ultimately incomprehensible. Here we cannot fully develop the arguments justifying this point. But one

[51] cf. *L.T.K.* IX, 2nd ed., cols. 1170–1177 (with bibliography). In addition to the literature mentioned there cf. R. Knierim, *Die Hauptbegriffe für Sünde im Alten Testament* (Gütersloh, 1965) (with bibliography).

[52] It is impossible here to refer to all the literature in the field of biblical theology dealing with the question of what is properly meant by 'binding and loosing' in the bible. Here it must suffice to refer to H. Vorgrimler, 'Matthieu 16:18 s. et le sacrement de pénitence', *L'homme devant Dieu. Mélanges offerts au Père Henri de Lubac* I (Paris 1964), pp. 51–61. Here an accurate record is provided of the recent literature on the question in biblical theology, cf. also H. Vorgrimler, 'Das "Binden und Lösen" in der Exegese nach dem Tridentinum bis zu Beginn des 20. Jahrhunderts', *Z.K.T.* 85 (1963), pp. 460–477.

[53] cf. DS 1679.   [54] cf. DS 1520.

thing is certain. Sacramental penance as practised in the early Church was penance from excommunication. This was not the sort of excommunication that signifies a special punishment attached to a few particularly grave sins. This excommunication pointed rather to the fact that every grave sin (grave enough to remove the grace of baptism. This is the only kind of sin envisaged in the penitential practice of the early Church) also removes the *fulness* (something, therefore, that is concomitantly conditioned by *interior* grace) of the baptised individual's organic membership of the body of the Church through which the Spirit is conferred upon her members. This remains true even though he may still belong to the Church *corpore* as the present-day Constitution on the Church declares with Augustine. Such a state of 'being excommunicated' through sin itself was made visible at the level of social life by the 'ban' imposed by the Church, and the sinner was excluded from the celebration of the Eucharist. He was relegated (in normal cases) to a special class of penitents, and the performance of his penance was supervised by the Church. During the period of penance the penitent was supported by the prayer of the Church in the form of blessings, exorcisms, exhortations (a process which the Constitution on the Church regards as also continuing in the sacrament of penance as practised today when this is viewed precisely as a *whole*, for it states that the Church collaborates in working for the conversion of the sinner through love, example and prayer). After a specified period of belonging to the class of penitents, and when he had given proof of his repentance and conversion, he was once more reconciled *with* the Church, i.e. fully received back into her through the laying on of hands by the bishop, and *thereby* also once more obtained the Spirit which vivifies the *Church*, in other words grace and so the forgiveness of sins. The *pax* of the Church, the *reconciliatio* with her, was a sacramental sign of reconciliation with God.[55] This basic pattern of the penitential discipline of the early Christians clearly remained present in the mind of the Church down to the early Middle Ages. Throughout its troubled history the only question was whether this *pax* with the Church should be restored to every sinner, however grave his sin might be (the question of whether this was basically

---

[55] We can and must, of course, distinguish between two elements here: the sacramental conferring of the *pax* through the Church (in the person of the bishop together with the presbyterium) and the *pax* itself that was conferred. The former belongs to the sacramental sign (*sacramentum*), the latter is an effect of the sacramental sign (*res et sacramentum*). Thus in the case of baptism too we have in fact to distinguish between the rite by which the subject is received and the state of belonging to the Church achieved through this reception.

possible was, in general, no problem), how long the period of penance should last, whether in specific cases (e.g. in sickness) sacramental reconciliation with the Church and God should be conceded even before the time of penance had been fulfilled, and (towards the end of the patristic age) whether such a reconciliation with the Church should be granted *several times over* (after falling again into sin).

Then in the early Middle Ages the practice arose of *repeatedly* conferring reconciliation, and the external form of this was simplified (it was conferred by priests instead of the bishop, the reconciliation and the penance to be performed were given together at the outset of the period so that the performance of the penance followed *afterwards* etc.). As a result of this the ancient sacrament of penance assumed that liturgical and canonical form which is still familiar to us of today. But for all this the people of that time were still far from losing their awareness of the truth that the absolution in the sacrament of penance is also a reconciliation with the Church. It is true that in the main period of the Middle Ages the *precise connection* between the forgiveness of sins in God's sight and reconciliation with the Church was no longer so clearly recognised as in the early Church. But it was clear to all the great theologians of the Middle Ages, and was also explicitly asserted by them, that the absolution also constitutes a reconciliation with the Church. Even Luther[56] still recognised this. In the later Middle Ages this idea receded into the background. The teaching of the Council of Trent on the sacrament of penance was directed against the reformers, and here this ecclesiological aspect is not mentioned (though it is in the teaching on the Eucharist), but of course it is not denied either, and in recent times, with the religious individualism which characterises them, this aspect is to be numbered among the 'forgotten truths' concerning the sacrament of penance until, as has already been described, it once more appears and is given a place in the official teaching of the Church on this sacrament of hers in the Second Vatican Council.

v

A few individual references must now be added. For as early a writer as the *Pastor Hermae* penance, which permits the sinner to regain the seal of baptism which he has lost, constitutes his reincorporation into the 'tower'

---

[56] cf. E. Fischer, *Geschichte der evangelischen Beichte* I (Leipzig, 2nd ed. 1902), p. 132; further texts in L. Klein, *Evangelisch-lutherische Beichte. Lehre und Praxis* (Paderborn 1961), pp. 66 f. (Bibliography).

of the Church.[57] In *Tertullian* the two entities of reconciliation with the Church and forgiveness of sins in God's sight are set side by side more or less without connection, so that the exact way in which they belong to one another is not altogether clear. But in his theology of penance both aspects are plainly present. That the two are not simply identical is shown, for instance, from the fact that even though for Tertullian the Church has to refuse her *pax* to the sinner, he nevertheless finds it possible to hold out to him a prospect of eschatological forgiveness as the hands of God. On the other hand the judgment of the Church anticipates the judgment of God as a *praejudicium* (Apol. 29). There is a further point. In his polemic against the Catholics Tertullian, as a Montanist, does assert that it is possible (although it only *appears* that this is probable, or indeed has any prospect of success) for one who has committed mortal sin to be redeemed by God. At the same time he maintains that such a one forfeits any share in the *pax* of the Church. Now he can only hold both these positions simultaneously if both elements are not absolutely identical entities even for the Catholics. Nevertheless supposing that they do have some objective connection between them, then the only conceivable way in which this can be the case is that the peace of the Church is the cause of reconciliation with God. For only so are the two entities distinct from one another (as cause and effect). The peace of the Church must, in effect, be prior (as *prae-judicium*), and yet both entities are (for the Catholics) indissolubly connected. (Indeed they emphasise that penance would have no meaning if the peace of the Church were not imparted in it.[58])

The matter becomes clear in *Cyprian*.[59] Wholly in accordance with our exegesis of Mt 16:18, for him *ligare* signifies *ecclesiam cludere* while *solvere* means the imparting of the *pax et communicatio*.[60] But the connection between the *pax* of the Church and the effects of reconciliation in heaven is expressed with all the clarity that could be desired when he says: '*Pignus vitae in data pace percipiunt*'[61] or '*pace accepta accipere Spiritum Patris*'.[62] For Cyprian, therefore, we obtain the hope of salvation and the Holy Spirit *in virtue of the fact that* we obtain the peace of the Church. The second formulation, therefore, is particularly remarkable because it

---

[57] cf. The references on p. 126 n. 9, and n. 59 below to relevant works, esp. K. Rahner *op. cit.*, p. 410 ff.

[58] cf. K. Rahner, 'Zur Theologie der Busse bei Tertullian', *Abhandlungen über Theologie und Kirche (Festschrift für K. Adam)*, M. Reding ed. (Düsseldorf, 1952), pp. 139–167.

[59] cf. K. Rahner, 'Die Busslehre des hl. Cyprian', *Z.K.T.* 74 (1952), pp. 257–276; 381–438. cf. also p. 448, n. 9.

[60] cf. Cyprian, epist 57, 1.   [61] Epist 55, 13.   [62] Epist 57, 4.

is the only passage in Cyprian in which the imparting of the Spirit is explicitly connected with the usual reconciliation of the sinner. And precisely here the words are *'pace accepta'*.[63] We can go no further at this point in showing how closely this idea is connected with Cyprian's whole theology of the Church (exactly as with Tertullian). But in any case for Cyprian the peace of the Church is not a further effect of the forgiveness of sins and the imparting of the Spirit, but rather precedes this as their cause.

For *Origen* the relevant passages are so widely scattered and the theology of penance in Origen is so complex that reference must be made to special studies on the subject (especially those of Poschmann, Rahner and Teichtweier).[64] For Origen the essence of mortal sin, as distinct from other sins, consists precisely in the fact that man loses his place in the Church as the medium of salvation and so is excluded from the sphere in which a certain redemptive influence of creaturely powers can be brought to bear upon the sinner. For this reason he must be 'excommunicated' in order to make explicit the fact that the sinner is delivered over to the fire of God's judgment and the *interitus carnis* by the Satanic powers (though even this has a mysterious salvific meaning). Conversely, therefore, 'return to the Church' and 'redemption' are entities which are necessarily interconnected.[65] Again in Origen's view of ecclesiastical penance, even from the purely terminological point of view, 'return to the Church' occupies the foreground.[66]

'Loosing' signifies that the subject is once more acknowledged as fully a member of the Church. The sacramental quality in the removal of the 'excommunication' therefore, must be maintained precisely for him if we are to be in a position to maintain the sacramentality of ecclesiastical

[63] A survey of the relevant passages in Cyprian shows (against the view upheld by J. Grotz) that *pax* and *communio* as conceived of by Cyprian cannot be thought of as two separable entities in such a way that it would have been possible for a *communio* to take place (at the beginning of the carrying out of the penance) which nevertheless did not constitute a *pax* (this would of its nature be imparted by God through the Church at the end of the period of penance). The very fact that Cyprian speaks indiscriminately of *pax et communio* and *communio et pax* is of itself enough to rule this out, for it would be impossible to discover any objective reason inherent in the context for this interchange in the order in which the two terms are used.

[64] B. Poschmann, *Paenitentia Secunda* (Bonn 1940), pp. 425–480; K. Rahner, 'La doctrine d'Origène sur la Pénitence', *R.S.R.* 37 (1950), pp. 47–94; 252–286; 422–456. cf. also G. Teichtweier, *Die Sündenlehre des Origenes = Studien zur Geschichte der kath. Moraltheologie* VII (Regensburg, 1958) esp. pp. 294 f., 334 f., 336 f., 343 f.

[65] In Ps 36:2; *P.G.* 12, 1353.

[66] cf. K. Rahner, *R.S.R.* 37 (1950), pp. 255 ff., 422 ff., cf. also 436 ff.

penance in Origen at all. But we can only do this if we maintain (a point which is then very clear) that for Origen this reinstatement as a member of the Church is precisely the mode and the cause of reconciliation with God and the reattainment of the Spirit. This can and must be established as the theological and spiritual meaning of the reconciliation of the sinner with the Church. But this means that for Origen that effect in heaven follows from this that takes place on earth.[67]

Augustine's presentation of the matter is perfectly clear. '*Ecclesiae caritas quae per Spiritum Sanctum diffunditur in cordibus nostris, participem suorum peccata dimittit, eorum autem, qui non sunt eius participes tenet*'.[68] '*Sovitur qui cum columba* (the Church) *fecerit pacem, et ligatur qui cum columba non habet pacem sive aperte foris sit sive intus esse videatur*'.[69] '*Civitas Dei recipiendo efficit innocentes*'.[70] '*Pax Ecclesiae dimittit peccata et ab Ecclesiae pace alienatio tenet peccata*'.[71] These formulations are such as to give expression to the thesis we are upholding with unequivocal clarity, and all that they still need is to be translated into scholastic terminology. A further factor in Augustine's treatment makes this all the clearer. For him the reconciliation granted by the bishop only imparts the Spirit in virtue of the fact that by it the sinner is received into that Church of the saints which then (in a certain sense independently of the act of the official Church) acts of herself and precisely *as* this Church of the saints and as the possessor of the Holy Spirit in order to impart to the newly incorporated member a share in her own Spirit. Obviously this patristic conception is not contradicted by the fact that the connection between the forgiveness of sins and the act of the Church is asserted without the connecting factor of the *pax cum Ecclesia* being explicitly mentioned. The worthlessness of this as a counter-argument against our thesis appears when we compare it with the case of baptism and with the proposition that through baptism sins are washed away. In no sense can we deduce from this proposition any denial of the fact that the character in baptism is the *res et sacramentum*, and neither can we interpret the absence of any mention of the *pax cum ecclesia* as a counter argument to the patristic conception described above. Nor is there any need to deny the fact that here and there it may be that reconciliation with the Church is viewed rather as a consequence than as a cause of the imparting of the Spirit

[67] K. Rahner, *R.S.R.* 37 (1950), 436–452.
[68] In Joan. tract. 121, 4; *P.L.* 35, 1958.
[69] De bapt. contra Donatistas III, 18, 23; *P.L.* 43, 151.
[70] Contra Cresconium Donatistam II, 13, 16; *P.L.* 43, 476.
[71] De bapt. contra Donatistas III 18, 23; *P.L.* 43, 150.

through the forgiveness of sins. Precisely in terms of the ecclesiastical theology worked out by the early Church these two entities are so closely interconnected that it is not in the least surprising to find something of this kind.[72]

In spite of the changes in the exterior form of the sacrament of penance in the *early Middle Ages*, as a result of which the penance of 'excommunication' no longer found such clear expression, an awareness of penance as reconciliation with the Church remained alive right down to the high Middle Ages inclusive.

At this time a system of theology applicable to all the sacraments in general was being developed, which gave rise to such questions as those of matter and form and the interrelationship of *sacramentum, res et sacramentum*, and *res sacramenti*, and it is quite true that the explanation of this *pax cum ecclesia* as the *res et sacramentum* of penance did not emerge in the first moment that this systematic theology of the sacraments in general came to be applied to penance in particular. Since interest was primarily focussed upon the subjective aspect of penance, this (and not the act of the priest himself as representing the Church), was conceived of right down to the time of Thomas as the proper cause of the forgiveness. And so long as this was the case it was quite impossible to arrive at the formulation that the *pax cum ecclesia* was the *res et sacramentum* which still has to effect the *res sacramenti*. Given the general principles of the theology of the eleventh and twelfth centuries down to Thomas, it was quite impossible to arrive at any other conclusion with regard to the *res et sacramentum* of the sacrament of penance than that this *res et sacramentum* was the *penitentia interior*, and that it was through this that the *res sacramenti*, the forgiveness of sins was effected. For in fact, right down to the time of Thomas this *paenitentia interior* was, from the human side of penance, the sole effective cause of the forgiveness of sins as such. Then in the thirteenth century a turning point of decisive importance was reached, and it came to be acknowledged explicitly that in this sacrament taken as a whole the act of the Church played a decisive part as an effective cause of the actual forgiveness of sins. By this time, however, two distinct factors had come to have a radical bearing upon the state of the question. On the one hand the theological axiom with regard to the *paenitentia interior* as the *res et sacramentum* had become a formula deeply embedded in tradition, while on the other the idea of penance as reconciliation with the Church as well had been thrust into the background (even if it had not

---

[72] As an instance of such a case we may compare, e.g., the teaching of the *Didascalia Apostolorum*. cf. K. Rahner, *Z.K.T.* 72 (1950), pp. 272 f.

altogether disappeared). In the light of this we cannot be surprised that the traditional formulation was adhered to even though now (in contrast to the eleventh and twelfth centuries), in the light of the new theology and in fact only in the light of this, a different conception, namely the ancient one which had formerly been held, had once more become possible. To that extent, therefore, we cannot rely upon the whole of the teaching of the early scholastics, or the main stream of scholasticism down to the time of Thomas inclusive. Nevertheless we can invoke the teaching even of this period (down to Thomas inclusive) in support of our thesis at least to the extent that – in spite of a certain weakening which has already been explained – a living awareness did survive everywhere of the fact that in the sacrament of penance a reconciliation with the Church as well as with God takes place. It will be relevant to demonstrate this, therefore, with the help of at least a few examples and references.[73]

For our present purposes we must pass over the literature on penance of the Middle Ages prior to the Carolingian reform. But in saying this we must immediately point out that the doctrine of penance as a reconciliation with the Church is manifestly present in the *eleventh and twelfth centuries* as well. It is not possible here to give a comprehensive presentation of the theology of sin in respect of its effects upon the relationship between the individual and the Church. In many respects the quest for such a theology was still incomplete, and scholars were still striving for a balanced formulation in which to express it. Moreover we would have to enter into such further questions as the relationship between the Church and the Mystical Body of Christ and the distinction between belonging to the Church *merito* and belonging to it *numero*, as well as the question of whether the individual belongs to the Church through faith alone or only through faith and love combined. But in any case we can surely say without hesitation that in this period there is a general and manifest recognition of the fact that sin is an offence against the Church as well, an act of *Ecclesiam*

[73] Reference may be made to the following literature on the subject: A. Landgraf, 'Sünde und Trennung von der Kirche in der Frühscholastik', *Scholastik* 5 (1930), pp. 210–247; P. Anciaux, *La théologie du sacrement de pénitence au XIIe siècle* (Louvain 1949); also Z. Alszeghy, *Gregorianum* 31 (1950), pp. 275–283. A recent work which deserves quite special mention is also L. Hödl, *Die Geschichte der scholastischen Literatur und Theologie der Schlüsselgewalt*, Pt I (Munster 1960); cf. also von K. Fröhlich, *Formen der Auslegung von Mt 16:13–18 im lateinischen Mittelalter* (Diss. theol. Basel, 1960). Anciaux's work contains references to numerous sources, and these are briefly indicated in the following footnotes by giving simply the name Anciaux followed by the relevant page references; the numbers set above the rest of the type represent the footnotes in Anciaux.

offendere,[74] an *injuria Ecclesiae illata*,[75] and that in accordance with this it essentially alters the relationship of the sinner to the Church in such a way that he no longer belongs to it at any rate *merito*, no longer belongs as a member to the Body of Christ (or else only belongs to it as a dead member) etc. (Here a certain distinction is presupposed between the Church and the Body of Christ.) In accordance with this one of the reasons assigned (not the only one) for the necessity of the sacrament of penance is that the sinner must also make satisfaction to the Church, *ut satisfaciat Ecclesiae*, a favourite Augustinian formula in which to express this,[76] precisely because, in a certain sense he has separated himself from the church[77] and has departed from her,[78] becoming an *Ecclesiae debitor*.[79] In accordance with this view the power of 'binding' and 'loosing' which takes effect in the sacrament is also regarded not merely as the authority to impose penance or a censure (the power of excommunication in the juridical sense), but also as a power (which takes effect in the actual sacrament) of exclusion and readmission to the Church.[80] But this in itself is tantamount to declaring that the act defined as *sanum in Ecclesiam recipi*[81], *recipere in gremium Ecclesiae*,[82] *efficere membrum Christi*[83] is regarded as an essential effect of priestly absolution in the sacrament of penance and, moreover, precisely in virtue of the fact that *per sacerdotis absolutionem* there takes place an *Ecclesiae Christi consociari*,[84] a *per reconciliationem in Ecclesia inducere*.[85] This means, of course, that the function of admitting the sinner to the sacraments of the Church is also ascribed to this absolution,[86] as well as the function of admitting the sinner to the suffrages of the Church, by which his own personal penance is supplemented. (This is a factor which some authors actually declare to be absolutely necessary for the blotting out of sins.) It may be that the full significance of this *pax cum Ecclesia* in terms of grace was no longer clearly perceived by all; that the 'separation' from the Church gradually came to be regarded more as an effect of excommunication in the sense proper to canon law; that the statement that the *reconciliatio* with the Church is the *res et sacramentum* of reconciliation with God was impossible at this period for the very reason that it was absolutely denied that any act on the Church's part could have an effect on the actual forgiveness of guilt considered in itself

[74] cf. Anciaux, pp. 211; 214.   [75] *idem*, p. 506.

[76] *idem*, pp. 52[2]; 195[2]; 435; 445; 518, etc.   [77] *idem*, 52[2]; 53[1]; 174[3]; 245[1].

[78] *idem*, 211[3]; 214.   [79] *idem*, 218[4].

[80] *idem*, pp. 277[5]; 290[2]; 320[2]; 321[1, 2, 4]; 344[4]; 371[2]; 496; 499; 503; 504; 516.

[81] *idem*, p. 170[3].   [82] *idem*, 525; 537.

[83] *idem*, pp. 443[4]; 536.   [84] Richard of St Victor: *P.L.* 196, 1172.

[85] Anciaux, p. 453[1].   [86] *idem*, pp. 172[3]; 492; 499; 516; 443; 536.

(in other words for a reason which objectively speaking and from the point of view of dogmatic theology is certainly false). But while all this may be true, the one and decisive factor still remains in force for this period. It still explicitly recognised and asserted that in the sacrament of penance an additional reconciliation with the Church herself is achieved.

This truth was still not forgotten even at *the height of the scholastic movement*. Thus for instance we still find *Bonaventure* asserting[87]: '*Confessio ad hoc directo instituta est, ut homo reconciliatur Ecclesiae et ostendatur reconciliatus a Deo*'.[88] For Bonaventure this reconciliation with the Church is, together with the remission of temporal punishment for sin, the proper effect which the Church can bring about as an act of efficient causality by her power of the keys. By contrast it is not possible for her to effect the same remission in respect of the guilt incurred in God's sight. For in respect of this the keys can only exercise a dispositive causality. For Bonaventure too, therefore, this reconciliation with the Church is actually expressed in the indicative part of the form of absolution, while the part expressed in prayer form refers to the guilt incurred in the eyes of God himself (though even here there is a genuine sacramental causality).[89] Now on this basis, and since Bonaventure cannot ascribe any directly efficient causality to the absolution in effecting the blotting out of the actual guilt itself, it would have seemed natural to regard the reconciliation with the Church as that disposition for the forgiveness of guilt which he seeks. But for Bonaventure the various effects of the sacrament of penance are already interrelated in such a way that such an idea is foreign to him, the more so since he has to take into account the doctrine which (even though still relatively recent) is for him already in a certain measure traditional, the doctrine, namely that it is the *paenitentia interior* which is the object of the power of the keys (in its deprecatory form). For all this, however, due heed must still be paid to an observation of Heynck's to the effect that the *confessio reconciliativa* (for Bonaventure) is confession. And it is with this that the full effectiveness of the sacrament of penance is bound up, namely the lessening of the punishment due to sin and *reconciliation* with the *Church*. It is this that Bonaventure is usually thinking of when he speaks of *reconciliatio*.

[87] Studies which are of supreme importance for our understanding of Bonaventure (and which serve to correct B. Poschmann's interpretation of him) are: V. Heynck, 'Zur Busslehre des hl. Bonaventura', *Franziskanische Studien* 36 (1954), pp. 1–81; *idem*, 'Der richterliche Charakter des Busssakraments nach Johannes Duns Scotus', *Franziskanische Studien* 37 (1965), pp. 339–414, esp. 364 ff. cf. also below p. 170, n. 11.
[88] Bonaventure, IV Sent. dist. 17 q. 3, a.2 fundam. 2.
[89] Bonaventure, IV Sent. dist. 18 p. 1 a. 2 q. 1.

A work which was composed under the influence of Bonaventure, and which was widely diffused in the Middle Ages, is the '*Compendium theologicae veritatis*' of *Hugo Ripelin*, the Dominican of Strasbourg. This author, like Bonaventure, teaches that the deprecatory element in the form of absolution bears upon the actual guilt, while the indicative brings about the reconciliation of the sinner with the Church.[90]

The doctrine of reconciliation with the Church still retains its force for *Thomas*. Because he is lacking in charity, the sinner belongs to the Body of Christ as a member only *potentialiter* and *imperfecte*, not *actualiter*.[91] He is no longer in the Church in an absolute and unqualified sense, no longer in her *merito* but only *numero*.[92] It is true that Thomas differs from Augustine in that for him the 'Church's sanctification', which is applied to the sinner and so brings about his reconciliation with the Church,[93] consists not so much in the fulness of the Spirit possessed by the Church herself as in the sanctification which she actively imparts through her sacramental power. It is also true that Thomas' conception of the actual process by which this is brought about is one in which the grace that is mediated by sacramental power justifies the individual and *thereby* reconciles him with the Church. But while all this may be true, the point that is of such decisive importance for us still retains its force for Thomas too. He recognises a reconciliation with the Church as an effect of the sacrament of penance.[94] Now if one adds to this that, for instance, for Thomas it is the character in baptism which is the '*immediata causa disponens ad gratiam*,'[95] and if we maintain that the character has an essentially ecclesiological aspect, then it must, in effect, be consistent with the thought of Thomas too to hold that the *reconciliatio cum Ecclesia* is analogous to the character in baptism in that it too has the force of an *immediata causa disponens ad gratiam*, i.e. like the character in baptism is to be regarded as *res et sacramentum* for

[90] cf. L. Ott, 'Opusculum des hl. Thomas von Aquin de forma absolutionis in dogmengeschichtlicher Betrachtung', *Festschrift für Eduard Eichmann*, M. Grabmann, K. Hofmann edd. (Paderborn 1940), pp. 121 f.

[91] Thomas Aquinas, *Sum. Theol.* III q. 8 a. 3 ad 2, in which Thomas seems to identify 'Church' with 'Body of Christ' for this world and for the age after Christ. cf. also III q. 8 a. 4c.

[92] cf. Thomas Aquinas, IV Sent. dist. 16 q. 1 a. 2 q. 5 dubium. And corresponding to this, '*Per sacramentum homo non solum Deo sed etiam Ecclesiae oportet quod reconcilietur*', IV Sent. dist. 17 q. 3 a. 3 q. 2 ad 3.

[93] *ibid.*

[94] For an elucidation of the text cited cf. on the one hand A. M. Landgraf, *Z.K.T.* 51 (1927), 91 and on the other B. Poschmann, *Die Busse* = *Handbuch der Dogmengeschichte* IV/3 (Freiburg 1951), p. 93, n. 16.

[95] cf. Thomas Aquinas, IV Sent. dist. 4 q. 3 a. 2 sol. 3.

the reconciliation with God through grace. This is all the more true since in fact the material content of the Thomistic doctrine that the *paenitentia interior* is an effect of the sacrament must be regarded as unassailable. A further point is that in order rightly to interpret the doctrine of the *paenitentia interior* as the *res et sacramentum* of penance we must not forget that according to precisely this self-same doctrine the *votum sacramenti* is included in this interior penance. In other words it includes an orientation towards the Church and her power of the keys. Thus on any showing we can say that in any true penance the will to be reconciled with the Church is implicitly included. If, therefore, it is true that through the sacrament the *paenitentia interior* is intensified (or caused) then this also applies to the will to be reconciled with the Church (and this will is not in fact to be considered as a mere resolve to receive the sacrament as though it were involved in this *in indivisibili*, but is itself a grace-given act which can grow and pervade the depths of man's spirit and achieve supernatural power. Now if the *sacramentum* has (consistently with the ancient doctrine) this effect upon the will of causing it to seek reconciliation with the Church, then the sacrament must actually impart this reconciliation. But in any case on this showing the *paenitentia interior* has a twofold aspect. It relates to reconciliation with God and reconciliation with the Church. On the basis of these considerations too no grounds can be found for saying that our thesis is far removed from the mediaeval conception of the *res et sacramentum* of penance. We might say (departing in this from the actual words but not from the real meaning of Thomas) that the sacrament reconciles the sinner with the Church while he, with his disposition of *paenitentia interior* considered as a will to achieve reconciliation with the Church, precisely comes to meet this same Church. In virtue of this the sinner has the right to that *infusio gratiae* which makes it possible for him to achieve that *paenitentia interior* through which he is in a position so to appropriate the grace imparted to him in the actual conditions of his own personal life that it becomes his own in a manner that sanctifies and justifies him and that he is thereby liberated from his personal sins. Even abstracting from the earlier tradition, which explicitly demands this, it seems advisable to order the various elements logically precisely in this way because, of its very nature, this reconciliation with the Church must be still more immediate to the act of the Church in the sequence of effects than the *paenitentia interior* which, of itself, belongs rather to the sphere of the unique personal life of the individual than to the sacramental sphere in the narrower sense. *Res et sacramentum*, however, must have an immediate connection with the sacramental dimension, with the visibility of the

Church as such. Thus we should point to the *pax cum Ecclesia* rather than to the *paenitentia interior* as the *res et sacramentum* of penance.[96]

VI

From this point onwards the whole complex of ideas which we have followed through history seems gradually and slowly to become blurred and indistinct. It is not actually denied, but it is more or less forgotten. The 'private form' of penance cannot be the sole cause of this, though certainly it has been a contributing factor. But it cannot be solely held responsible for it. For absolutely speaking even in the present-day form of baptism the individual can still feel and experience very vividly that he is coming to the holy Church of Christ when he goes to the priest, that it is before *her* that he is accusing himself (however 'private' the accusation may be to all outward appearance), that the sin he is confessing is one through which, whether it be mortal or venial, he has sinned against the Body of Christ as well and has contributed his share in bringing it about that the Church is not fully that which she should be: the witness of God's sanctifying compassion in the darkness of the sinful world, the visible presence of the love of God in human history. The sinner can always experience even today that through his confession and the acceptance of this confession by the Church he now stands visibly[97] before the Church as he who he really is through his own fault: as a sinner who, in a certain sense, ceases to hide behind the sacred value attached to him as a member of this holy Church and so deceitfully to conceal his own sinfulness. Even today, therefore, the sinner can still experience the word of forgiveness in the sacrament precisely *as* the word of this Church, which forgives him his sin against the Church, which in that she forgives him helps to bear his guilt because in this forgiveness (as Origen taught) she truly takes upon herself the guilt of this her member and helps to bear it. She does this in the knowledge that Christ forgives *her* because he loves and sanctifies her even though in her children she shows herself again and again to be the Church of sinners. In making his confession, therefore,

---

[96] On the genesis and the theological significance of the concepts of *paenitentia interior* and *paenitentia externa* cf. esp. L. Hödl, *Die Geschichte der scholastischen Literatur und die Theologie der Schlüsselgewalt* I (Munster 1960). Summary with detailed references, pp. 376–391.

[97] We might almost say 'sacramental'. In the early Middle Ages the terms *sacramentum excommunicationis* and *sacramentum* of confession of sin were freely used: Anciaux, pp. 312; 146.

the sinner can experience even in the present-day form of the sacrament that he is freed from his sins in the eyes of God precisely in virtue of the fact that he finds the peace of the Church, enters once more (or enters more deeply) into the sole medium of grace and of the Spirit, the holy Church. He can experience that to be 'loosed' upon earth really is to be 'loosed' in heaven. The outer form of the sacrament (which had inevitably to become what it is in view of the size of the Church and her pastoral functions) cannot, therefore, be the sole cause of the ecclesiological aspect of confession having been thrust into the background. There must have been other causes apart from this, and it would be a valuable exercise to investigate the precise history of these. Yet surely they are not difficult to divine. The Church is seen more and more merely as the external juridical organization which is indeed endowed with divine right, and to belong to which is indeed the commandment of God. But she is no longer regarded as being in herself that sacrament filled with the Spirit which brings about salvation and grace provided only that we do not close ourselves against her Spirit through our own fault. The more, therefore, theology had to guard against the theories of Wycliffe, Hus and the Reformers, the more vitally necessary it became to emphasise that the juridical and visible constitution of the Church as well is of divine right. The more necessary it became to work out the precise nature of *that* membership of the Church which is still to be attributed even to the sinner, the more difficult it became to bring out the other side or to give it conscious expression. A further factor is the individualism of modern times, the origin of which can already be found in the late Middle Ages. Salvation and grace become more and more something which is worked out between God and the individual alone and taken in isolation. And in accordance with this view, when the Church does act as mediatrix in this, she acts at God's 'behest' in such a way that we no longer advert to the fact that the fulfilment of this behest also signifies her own authentic life and that it actually draws the individual more and more into this life of the Church herself.[98]

It cannot be said, therefore, that the fact that this doctrine was obscured constitutes an argument against its correctness. It was never properly speaking denied or replaced by any other doctrine which was better. Because the general conception of the Church as means of grace receded into the background of man's conscious thought the ecclesiological aspect of the sacrament of penance could no longer remain clear to him

[98] On this development we may compare e.g. the article by J. Ramsauer on the development of the concept of the Church in the post-Tridentine catechisms, 'Die Kirche in den Katechismen', *Z.K.T.* 73 (1951), pp. 129–169; 313–346.

either. Yet it belongs so essentially to the dogmatic tradition taken as a whole, and even to the teaching of scripture itself, that theology has the duty explicitly to advert to it once more.[99] In the Council this has been achieved.

[99] cf. also most recently L. Bertsch, *Busse und Beichte* (Frankfurt 1967) and in this the article by O. Semmelroth, 'Strukturen und Perspektiven im Busssakrament', pp. 68–88, esp. pp. 69 ff. on the ecclesiological character. On the theme of this article cf. pp. 76 f.

8

A BRIEF THEOLOGICAL STUDY ON
INDULGENCE

THE zeal to gain indulgences has certainly declined among Catholics. The non-Catholic regards anything like an 'indulgence' as quite alien to him. How could one express the matter in such a way that the other understood something about it? Admittedly it is only with great difficulty that something which springs from so complex a background of ideas can be explained to one who is unfamiliar even with those ideas which it presupposes. But at the same time, supposing that we did try to answer his question, and to answer it in such a way as not to presuppose too much in the way of specialist terminology and further theological knowledge – how, in that case would our answer sound? Tasks of this kind are difficult. It is a pity that they so rarely attempted. All of us, priests and laymen, should be better versed in such techniques. If we practised them we would come across many questions upon which we ourselves had never sufficiently reflected before in our precisely worked-out dogmatic theology, in which the difficulties are too often smoothed over by convention and familiarity. And here and there we would even find an answer which opened up to us ourselves the way to a deeper understanding of the very question which we had hitherto imagined we understood inside and out.

With this end in view, and taking these considerations as our starting-point, let us attempt to say something about indulgence, even though in doing so we incur the danger of merely exposing ourselves to all kinds of criticism, i.e. of failing to satisfy any of our hearers, whether it be those who understand nothing about indulgence (because even after reading about it they find it incomprehensible) or those who already have clear ideas about the subject (because these find that now the question has become more obscure instead of more intelligible). From time to time – this is something that every reader will notice – something will be said which is addressed not to those 'hearers' for whom this study is properly intended, but rather to the theologians who ask themselves whether what is said here agrees with the traditional doctrine on the question as this has been preserved. Such incidental remarks, therefore, should not be used as arguments purporting to show that the attempt we have undertaken is unsuccessful. Whether it really succeeds – that is a quite different question. Those who, having reached the end of this study, feel that it has failed, can always improve upon it by themselves making similar or different attempts, and can make them available in order that we can use them fruitfully to increase our knowledge. This is the sense in which we would wish this brief theological treatise on indulgence to be understood.[1]

I

Man is a complex being with many levels in his makeup. The decisions he takes and the acts he initiates from the source and centre of his personal freedom, from the innermost 'kernel' of his personhood, take shape in dimensions of his being which are not simply identical with the centre of personhood in his being considered as the source and origin of everything else in his makeup. He acquires attitudes and habits. He gives his character its distinctive mould and he 'objectifies' the acts in which he exercises his freedom, imposing them upon his 'environment'. The initial 'environment' which receives the impress of the act arising from his original decision, and in which it is objectified, consists of his own self in the external levels of his makeup. Here this objectified act is, so to say, frozen into permanent form and preserved. Hence when the innermost centre of the kernel of man's personhood is transformed by the grace of God – whereas previously, by a sinful decision, it was turned against God and his holy will – in other words when man 'converts' himself to God at the innermost and deepest level of his being, even then it does not always and *ipso facto* follow that all is once more well with him. It *can* be the case that all is immediately made well. It can be the case that this conversion is so powerful that it immediately transforms the whole man. *But it can also be the case* that this interior transformation of man is present in a certain sense like a glowing kernel at the centre of his personhood, yet that it does not simply and at one blow do away with all the ingrained attitudes,

<hr>

[1] The author has published several studies on the theology of indulgence. On the particular position he is adopting in this attempt, as compared with these other studies, cf., in particular, apart from the list of sources, the essay which immediately follows this one entitled 'On the Official Teaching of the Church Today on the Subject of Indulgence', pp. 166–198. Here an extensive bibliography will be found of works by the author himself as well as by others.

encrustations and after-effects of the earlier course of life led by the individual concerned. Even the history of salvation really is a history, i.e. a
process which requires time, and in which everything does not take place
all at once. Only one who thinks in purely abstract and formal categories,
one who imagines that time as a factor plays no part in conditioning our
personal history of salvation, as 'though God achieved his effects upon
us all at once in the sort of dimension beyond time which the Gnostics
imagined – only such a one can contest the truth of what we have said.
We must not therefore suppose that all that is needful has already been
achieved simply when we repent, whether within the sacrament of penance or apart from it, and in doing so genuinely do obtain the gift of
conversion (attained to by an act of unmerited grace coming from God
himself), and so are in the state of having once more found how to orientate ourselves to God in faith and love. This grace of conversion is, in fact,
intended to draw the whole nature of man into its sphere of influence,
extending this to the physical side of his nature, to the unconscious movements of his nervous system, to the submerged impulses in it, in order
that all may be healed and sanctified. Now this does not take place *ipso
facto* in every case of conversion, not even when this is genuine, and when
we can say: 'there is a man who has sincerely converted himself to God,
one who, in the midst of his freedom, yet liberated by the grace of God,
has 'radically changed the course of his life' and based his whole existence
upon the grace of God. Even in such a case the possibility always still
remains that 'I' am in many respects the old 'I', the one who is still unconverted or at any rate not wholly changed. In that state 'I' can still always
be myself with my own egoism, which I utterly fail to notice, and with
which, in many respects, I still continue to have an understanding; the 'I'
that retains the hardness of heart, pharisaism and cowardice of me, and all
the other attitudes and attributes which were made real in the sin of which
I was formerly guilty (and which I now repent). The result of this is that
I utterly fail to notice all this, or to achieve that state in which I really
separate myself from it all. Such a transformation of the whole man in all
his immeasurable complexity can, therefore, still mean that a long and
painful course lies before him. What anguish, what incalculable spiritual
developments, what deadly pains still remain to be endured in a process of
spiritual transformation, untill all is made different! Yet at the same time
how indispensable all this is! Without this how could one be 'made
perfect'?

These, then, are real factors arising from our sins, and they are present
in our personal human lives as these take shape in history. Springing as

they do from sin, they live on after it and constitute a just judgment upon it. We Christians call them 'the temporal punishments due to sin'. They are 'temporal' because they must be endured in a process of development over a period of time, and can only be overcome in this. They are punishments because they are the consequences of sin and a judgment upon it both at the same time. For when man, taking his own freedom as person as the centre and source of his action, misuses the (rest of) his personal makeup, violating and damaging it, then in this distortion of his own nature he experiences the contradiction and the opposition of this nature, its forms and its tendencies which were created by God and are therefore ineradicable, and which are prior to this decision which man takes of his freedom. There is contradiction between that in him which is free and that which, from the point of view of God, he is intended to be and which, moreover, he inalienably is; a contradiction which arises from the condition of man following upon his sinful act. Now this contradiction is necessarily productive of pain. It is the painful protest of the reality which God has fashioned against the false decision of man. Indeed it is quite impossible to define suffering in any other way. Thus in a certain sense sin gives birth to its own punishment. To the extent that this constitutes the refusal of creaturely reality to adapt itself to the way which we, as free beings, map out for ourselves, or to reproduce itself in the material constituted by our own human natures and the world in which we live (a refusal, therefore, which is precisely not that of God himself denying himself to the sinner) – to that extent we call this painful reaction against man's sins from the side of his own nature and of the other elements that go to make up his environment 'temporal punishments due to sin'. This is different from God's refusal of himself, which can likewise be either temporal or eternal according to whether man has finally turned away from God in an exercise of his freedom which has been rendered definitive and absolute *by death itself*, or whether it has not yet reached this stage.

Of course, even though such a punishment for sin is in itself 'temporal', we must consider how it is affected in cases where man's perversion has reached a fixed and final stage – in other words in which the original contradiction of the order of created reality within and without man has been renewed again and again, and even where it is immovably adhered to. In such a case this contradiction, which is itself temporary, i.e. able to be reversed, is transformed into an eternal punishment. It should not be thought that this implies any denial of the fact that these temporal punishments are decreed by God. The world (both within and without man)

with which man comes into contradiction through his own guilt as objectified in his own acts, is a concrete world which in its concretion was
created not by man and his freedom but by God. Who has not already
experienced the fact that a sin alters in its effects according to the particular
situation in which it is made actual? The sin as actually carried out always
consists of a synthesis which man himself cannot calculate beforehand of
two distinct elements: the original decision which he takes in his freedom,
and in which he freely exposes himself to this element of the incalculable
and the actual material in which the sinful act is made actual. It is only as
realised in this material that the sinful act is brought to the 'fulness' of its
nature. In the dimension of concrete reality this situation in which our sin
is committed is determined not by us but by God. And there can be no
mistaking the fact that in this concrete situation it is God's free disposition
that determines what kind of punishment this sin is to incur. This means
that this punishment for sin, considered as the reaction of 'extra-personal'
reality (both within and without man) to sin is also a punishment imposed 'from without', even though it was provoked precisely by the sin
of man himself. Once we have grasped this fact we can also understand
what is meant by the teaching of the Council of Trent (cf. DS 1543, 1689,
1712, 1715) to the effect that for the baptised Christian who has sinned
again after baptism the fact that his sin has been forgiven, whether within
the sacrament of penance or outside it, still does not mean *ipso facto* that
the temporal punishments due to sin are always and necessarily forgiven.
Relying upon the tradition of penance which has come down to her from
the time of the Fathers, the Church teaches that when one whose sins have
already been blotted out by baptism, and who has thereby become a
member of the holy Church, sins again, God is not prepared to bestow
upon him, or to offer him straightway, in the very act in which the sacrament takes effect, all those graces which he needs in the concrete in order
to accomplish the process of transformation and integration. Yet it is only
through this process that the debt of 'temporal punishments due to sin'
can be paid to the full and so wiped out. God, then, is not prepared simply
to bestow all the graces necessary for this in a single blessed moment in
which the whole human life of the sinner is transfigured, and in which the
process of transformation is a completely painless one. This is something
that we notice all too vividly in our own personal experience. Viewed from
this aspect it is much more difficult to explain how the baptism of an adult
can constitute a remission of this kind of all the temporal punishments due
to sin, as tradition teaches. This, however, is not the real question which
we have to investigate at this point, although we can say that this teaching

applies only to those cases in which all 'venial' (as well as mortal) sins really are repented of. And, as is shown by the findings of the individual's own concrete experience precisely of the after-effects of his former sins and because of these, this kind of repentance is not so easy. We should therefore reflect upon these truths, and recognise clearly the fact that probably all that is meant by the statement in question is that with regard to the grace of God in baptism all is indeed conferred all at once which is necessary for such a total overcoming of sin. Though probably the question remains open whether the individual really uses the opportunity offered to him in this. But in the sacrament of penance taken in isolation this opportunity is not offered to him in the same way at all. If, therefore, we recognise these facts, we shall not say that the statement in question would in any sense invalidate the explanations we have given so far.

The dissolving of the after-effects of former sin, with the sufferings they cause, the total integration of the whole person, including those extra-personal levels in his makeup, can take place in various ways in the 'fresh' radical decision on man's part to orientate himself towards God. It depends on other factors besides the 'good will' of man himself. His new act and the measure of its success are also conditioned by the situation, by the circumstances, the 'material' in which and upon which it has to be made actual. Now this situation and this 'material' are contingent factors. They are subject to change and can themselves become new and different. They depend, in the last analysis, on the dispositions of God, however we may think that these are applied in the individual case. Now according to the way in which, either through natural causes which are subject to his providence or through his own personal and gracious interventions, God forms this material which is in turn presupposed to the acts and decisions of man, and which influences these at the *interior* level, this process of dissolving and transforming the after-effects of sin becomes quicker or slower and takes place with more or less suffering and pain.

Certainly everyone has already experienced in the concrete what has here been stated in very abstract terms. Who, for instance, has not already noticed that the degree of his repentance in a given case, its power to remain constant, depends not only upon the 'good will' which 'commands' him to such repentance, but also upon the situation, upon the sudden light of knowledge which is not under man's own control, upon an inward disposition such as no 'despotic' control which man may exercise over himself by the use of his own intelligence and free will, is capable of giving. Every Christian knows that 'tears of repentance' are not simply something that man can count upon in the same way that he can take as his basis for the working out of his salvation the grace that is extended to him from above. Who has not already suffered from his own impotence really to turn himself into a different man? Who has not noticed after a 'good confession' that he has still, in many respects, remained the old man, that all the secret roots and impulses of his sin, the very sin that he has repented of and confessed, are still constantly present in him, and, moreover, not merely those which simply belong to man's lot, the circumstances in which he finds himself placed etc. from his birth onwards, but also those which effectively owe their existence to his own fault? God, therefore, can remit the 'temporal punishments due to sin' which we have incurred by giving us the best possible chance, the opportunity to rid ourselves as totally and swiftly as possible of the burden of our past which is at once the consequence of, and punishment for our sins. From this point of view we can, in many cases, interpret the disposition and course of a human life under God's hand as something that is almost visibly unfolding before our eyes. Throughout the life in question God is gradually breaking down false attitudes which we have sinfully built up within us. Those who were formerly overbearing, stupid and selfish through their sins he makes mild, wise and unassuming. It is true that under certain circumstances a supreme hour may arrive, such as that of martyrdom or some other ultimate decision, in which that which has still not been attained to after a long period of ascetical striving systematically practised can be brought to its full ripeness and purity in a man (of course in such a case it still remains true that perhaps the chance of such an hour of destiny may be missed if this ascetical striving, the faithfulness which is achieved in the pettiness and monotony of everyday life, has not gone before).

There too we are not masters of our own course. We cannot discover such paths of life or such hours of destiny simply by ourselves. They have to be bestowed upon us. We know that (since flesh and blood do not inherit the kingdom of God) in the case of every man whom God admits at all to a share in his eternal kingdom in the glory of his own holiness, he will so guide him either before or after his death that he arrives at the full ripening of his own nature precisely as that particular individual. But the actual process by which this is achieved can precisely be either swifter or slower, easier or more painful. How it takes place is under God's control. In effect, then, there is – as in the very nature of the case we are supposing there must be – a 'remission' by God, in the sense just indicated, of the temporal punishments due to sin. But we do not have to think of this as though some sentence of punishment had been imposed in a merely external and juridical sense, with no intrinsic connection (apart from the sin committed by the subject in the past) with his moral state. We do not have to think of the remission by God as granted simply in the way that a civic amnesty is granted (for this bestows 'grace and favour' upon the reformed and irreformable in equal measure). If this were the case then we would have to think of the temporal punishments due to sin as constituting a merely external and vindictive type of punishment such as leaves the individual who undergoes it wholly unchanged and the same man that he was before. Such a remission would only deprive the individual of the possibility of truly perfecting himself in suffering throughout all the dimensions of his being.

We have spoken above of a radical decision on man's part – we call it the love that is based on faith and hope – which has the power to justify. We have also spoken of a progressive process of integration. Now these two factors are mutually interrelated in such a way that each contributes to the other. The radical decision involves, of its very nature, the will to achieve this integration. The subject wills to achieve, in this radical decision of his, that love in which God and his neighbour are loved 'with his *whole* heart and with *all* his powers'. And conversely it is also true to say that this love is itself made perfect in virtue of the fact that it integrates within itself all the dimensions of man's being. The process of integration constitutes the mode in which this love grows and develops until it reaches the due fulness which is proper to it. In the light of this we can understand why the exponents of classic theology should regard it as immediately obvious that once it has reached this state of fulness the love of God and our neighbour also blots out all the 'temporal punishments due to sin'. This blotting out is not a 'reward' (which in the last analysis would be arbitrarily bestowed) for having achieved this fulness of love. On this interpretation how could even the theologians know that the attainment of such fulness in love had this effect? The blotting out of sin is rather the connatural consequence of this love, so that we might actually define it in the following terms: perfect love is that which has orientated 'all the powers', i.e. all the manifold levels of reality in the complexity of man's makeup purely to God, so that these, without themselves being suppressed or deprived of their true natures, become the 'material', the 'expression' and the 'manifestation' precisely of this love. If we have managed to understand what is meant, objectively speaking, by the term 'temporal punishments due to sin', then it is also clear that such perfect love blots out all these punishments, indeed that, ultimately speaking, this in the only way in which they can be blotted out. This in itself is enough to enable us to understand that an indulgence, whatever further precisions still remain to be added in defining its precise nature, must be an *aid towards* this perfect love which blots out all these punishments due to sin, and not a 'means' which excuses us from following this one essential way of compensating for our own past and the 'after-effects' (*reliquiae peccatorum*) which it has left behind.

It cannot be objected against this interpretation of the temporal punishments due to sin that it is inapplicable to the remission of them which we can obtain in the after-life. For this interpretation in no sense presupposes that after death man intensifies the depths of the radical decision which he took with the aid of supernatural grace in the concrete condition of his earthly life (in other words that he increases his 'degree of sanctifying grace'). Such a view would admittedly be irreconcilable with the doctrine that with regard to the possibility of an increase in supernatural grace and merit death constitutes the boundary beyond which we cannot go. All that this interpretation does presuppose is that this definitive decision for God, which remains unchanged in respect of its degree of intensity also, must (under certain circumstances) still continue to take effect even after death by permeating and shaping all those levels in the human person which are less immediate to his actual personhood. There is no doctrine of the Church which is controverted by this assumption. Even at the biological level growth and final maturity are not simply one and the same thing.

II

Now manifestly we can entreat God that he may, as far as possible, grant us favourable circumstances in his guidance of our lives, such as will as quickly and as beneficently as possible shape this process by which our whole sin-damaged being is transformed once the basic decision of conversion and repentance has been taken. Who has not actually uttered this prayer if he is a Christian (even if he has never hitherto regarded that which he prayed for from this point of view)? Who has not already entertained the idea: 'If I could only die one death, the "true death" in which my entire being with all that it has become throughout my entire life was made over to God in faith and love in an act of radical self-surrender down to the last fibre of my being, so that nothing was held back, nothing denied, but death was the total act of a totally committed faith!' No theologian will deny that through so intense a degree of love for God we would be liberated from all 'temporal punishments due to sin' as well if this grace was bestowed in its entirety upon the individual. Nor can anyone deny that one instance at least of a blotting out of the temporal punishments due to sin does exist, that namely which we regard not as *an* instance but as *the* definitive instance of this process.

We can, therefore, ask God to grant us the greatest and most favourable chance possible of achieving the maturity of the Christian man as a whole. Such a prayer need not for one moment spring from egoistical promptings or from the impulse to escape from these punishments as 'cheaply and painlessly' as possible. Nor need it involve any denial of the truth that for Christian living too there is a genuine attitude of 'standing by one's past' and 'bearing the consequences', so that to flee from this would be cowardly, unchristian and ultimately speaking futile. Time is, in fact, not only God's gift, through which the most important factor, namely salvation, must be achieved; it is also the restriction which ensures that that which must be achieved shall be achieved only gradually. Otherwise we could never in fact pray for the coming of the Lord by saying: 'Come soon.' The attainment of maturity can take place in various ways: in circumstances of anguish, toil and frustration or in the midst of a tempest which we nevertheless feel as blessed; in an attitude of freedom and enthusiasm in which we experience as the blessing bestowed by a powerful love that which seems to another the anguish of a weary process of 'dying'. Thus we can ask God that he may bestow upon us the possibility of a swift and happy maturing process.[2] But we cannot ask him to allow us to share in God's own holiness and beatitude when we are only half ready and immature. Surely we can in all reason ask God to work out the destiny of those who are to be made perfect by him soon and by the more joyful way. And what we can reasonably ask for ourselves that too we can ask – one might almost say still more readily and more selflessly – for others.[3]

This is a prayer to which the Church can lend her support. As a source of truth and a means of grace she has never merely been the external controlling organisation. She is the one Body of Christ in which all the members live for one another, suffer for one another and are brought to

[2] This point is in itself enough to show that a position adopted by the two doctors of the Church Bonaventure and Albert is incorrect. They supposed, namely, that the more perfect should not concern themselves with trying to obtain remissions of temporal punishments due to sin through indulgences, but that they should rather strive to wipe away these punishments by their own personal penitential practices.

[3] Hence it is that such highly esteemed theologians as Thomas Aquinas, Cajetan, Soto, Suarez etc. uphold the view that an individual can 'apply' the 'satisfactions' he has performed but which he does not need himself to another precisely as the Church does in the granting of indulgences; in other words he can, in a certain sense lend his own indulgences, as it were, to others.

perfection for one another. When God regards an individual he always sees him in his place in the whole, as one with Christ the head and as one with all the brethren of this one Christ. No-one lives to himself alone, no-one dies to himself alone. Each one is beloved by God by the very fact that God regards his Christ and his Cross – beloved as part of a single reality which God creates in the midst of mankind, destined as they are to be brought to perfection. Through her prayers, therefore, the Church can give her support to this entreaty for the 'remission of the temporal punishments due to sin'. And when she does this then she does it as that which she is, as the one great union of those who have been sanctified and redeemed, as the Bride of the Lamb, as Head and Body, the one Christ. When God hears her then he regards that which she is as she prays. She is the Church of the saints, the Church of the one Christ. He grants her a hearing for her prayer in virtue of that which he has bestowed upon her prior to any prayer, namely in virtue of the grace of Christ which has been made powerful and victorious in the Church. Indeed the Lord himself says with regard to the hearing of the prayers of the disciples: 'The Father loves you *because* you have loved me and have believed that I have come from the Father' (Jn 16:27). This is what is meant when we speak of an indulgence as coming from the 'treasury of the Church'.

The 'treasury of the Church' is God's own will to save – ultimately speaking, therefore, God himself – to the extent that this is present in the world with the force of an irrevocable victory in *that* Christ (as head) who has been decreed by God from all eternity, precisely *as* 'the firstborn among many brethren', in other words in union with his 'Body' which is the Church. Rightly conceived of, therefore, the significance of this idea of the 'treasury of the Church' is precisely not that some part of its contents is paid out as from some public fund which can be doled out in limited quantities and by instalments, something which otherwise the individual would have had to pay out of his own resources. And the fact that this is not the case means that the question of whether the treasury of the Church could ever be exhausted, seeing that so much is spent and paid out 'from' it, is utterly ruled out from the outset and therefore does not need to be solved by any subtle explanations. For the same reason it is also clear that God is not compelled to grant such a prayer for the remission of the temporal punishments due to sin *precisely on the grounds that* he can no longer demand that which he has already received (namely *out of* the treasury of the Church). He looks to the working of his own grace. This is the reason why he guides one to his perfection by this way and another by that. It is done according to his own free and incalculable measure, and in an order proper to him and decreed by him. But because in and through this sovereign power of divine grace there is a truly effective prayer – indeed, according to Christ's words an infallibly effective prayer – and because this prayer can be that of the entire Church, above all because it can and should be applied to the swift and happy attainment of the perfection of the whole man – for these reasons the Church can give her support as intercessor to the prayer of the individual for the remission of the 'temporal punishments due to his sins'. Where she does this in God's grace, where she does it well – for she must always perform such things through her members – where the individual is worthy of having his prayer heard through God's grace, there God hearkens too to the prayer of the Church of his own Son. It hardly needs to be specially emphasised once more that this takes place through the grace of God, who supplies the seed and the final flowering of this prayer and this worthiness according to the unfathomable decrees of his own good pleasure which is in no sense conditioned by any act on man's part.

With these provisos we can say that God gives the individual that which the Church implores on his behalf for his salvation. Thus the Church has always prayed for the sinner, who even as a penitent still bears the burden of his guilt. In the penitential practice of the early Church her intercession during and at the end of the period of penance belongs to the indispensable elements of ecclesiastical penance. She does not merely reconcile the sinner in that, by restoring him to harmony with herself, she imparts to him once more her own Holy Spirit which is the remission of sins; more than this, she actually prays with the repentant sinner for the forgiveness of the whole of his guilt with all its further effects. In view of the fact that it is, in fact, a *repentant* sinner that is being treated of, this applies in practice primarily (if we adopt the theological distinction and terminology current today) to the remission of the temporal punishments due to sin, to the total overcoming of the guilt. Even today this prayer is constantly being made. It is true that except for a small remnant it has vanished from the penitential liturgy used in the sacrament of penance itself because for practical reasons the accusation, considered as the initiating act of the penitential process, and sacramental forgiveness by the Church have been brought together in a single process, and the result of this is that the period of penance, the full overcoming of sin with all its consequences within man, is left almost exclusively to the Christian penitent who receives the sacrament. Yet for this reason the Church still continues constantly to be she who prays for the blotting out of the sins of her members and the punishment due to these sins, in the prayer of the

Our Father, in the sacrifice of Mass, in the penances performed by her saints and of all upon whom the guilt of the age weighs as the Cross of Christ and who bear this Cross in faith and love, in the explicit prayers of intercession which are constantly being made in the most varied forms on behalf of sinners. It is to be hoped that in the projected renewal of the liturgical forms of penance these aspects will be brought out still more clearly.

From such a prayer as this no-one can be excluded from the outset unless he has himself renounced his share in it by separating himself from the Church so that he can no longer be named in the liturgical intercessions in the manner in which the children of the Church have the privilege of being named (cf. 1 Jn 5:16). But in a special way we can include anyone in this prayer of the Church, and God's help can be extended to him in particular by means of an explicit and solemn intercession. Those who believe in the meaning of prayer, and who know what is meant by the Church, can be seized with awe at the following idea: the holy community of the redeemed, the Bride of Christ, stands at the throne of grace on my behalf! From her heart which is unceasingly and inalienably filled with the wordless sighings of the Spirit of God, prayer rises up on my behalf! It is *she* who says to me 'May Almighty God have mercy upon you, forgive you your sins . . .' It is *she* who promises this prayer to me, and she does this not merely in general terms or implicitly, but explicitly and as pledged by an act of her supreme authority to pray on my behalf.

III

Such prayer remits, 'bestows' not simply in an authoritative remission of the punishments due to sin as though it were a simple 'amnesty' of a punishment to be imposed in purely external terms that was in question, as though this punishment served *only* as a manifestation of the majesty of the law. In fact, as the Council of Trent explicitly declares, the Church does not ascribe to herself any power precisely of *this* kind, of granting an 'amnesty' from a punishment imposed in the sacrament of penance in a purely external ('vindictive') sense, even though precisely in this she is still exercising her power of binding and loosing as defined in Mt 16 and 18 (DS 1667 ff.). Even less, therefore, can she intend to use any such power outside the sacrament, especially since in fact the theologians commonly derive her power to grant indulgences from the same power of binding and loosing as spoken of in the gospels. But the holy Church which – as Tertullian has already said in a similar context – is always hearkened to, can assure the sinner in a special and explicit act, of a prayer of intercession such that it draws down a remission of the punishments due to sin. Now provided that we understand this *special* prayer in the right way and in the way in which we have attempted to interpret it, we can say: This is precisely what takes place in what we call an indulgence.

In earlier times the Church combined an assurance of prayer of this kind with the remission of a specific ecclesiastical penance which she had, of her own power, previously imposed upon the penitent in the sacrament of penance. But in a certain sense she replaced the effects of the performance of this penance by the penitent with her own intercession. And because of these facts she still gives expression, even today, to the intensity and urgency of this assurance of prayer in the form of sentences of the old canonical penances which in earlier times she remitted for the penitent in such a case. Because the Church prays, because she prays for salvation (and not for earthly things) – on these grounds she knows that she is 'always heard'. But because from the side of him for whom the prayer is offered the effectiveness of this prayer is always dependent upon his prior subjective dispositions (which themselves in turn fall under the powerful and also incalculable dispositions of the grace of God) – because of this we never know in the particular case when and how this prayer attains its goal. In the light of this we already see that the remission has not, and cannot have, the function of either diminishing or replacing the personal penance of the individual concerned. Of its nature the remission can only be aimed at securing that through the help of God that may really take place swiftly and easily which penance itself is also designed to achieve: the total cleansing and total maturing of the individual throughout his entire being, in which his initial endowment with grace is the heart and centre of the whole process. This remission, therefore, can only achieve its due effect where the individual genuinely has the dispositions necessary for penance. For without this there can be no question even of true repentance. Now if this is not the case even a forgiveness of the actual sins themselves is not possible, and therefore neither is it possible to obtain a pardon or remission of the temporal punishments due to sin.

We are presupposing that the process by which the individual is brought to full maturity, a process which is not merely psychological but in a true sense religious also, is not always and necessarily simply completed with death. This is not so even in the case of those individuals who, under the grace of God, have made their orientation towards God definitive and final in their lives and through their deaths. Even from the purely empirical point of view we cannot have the impression that a final and complete integration, in which the individual's basic decision pervades the whole of his being at all of its levels, coincides in every case with his death. Certainly according to Christian doctrine death is the end of that period in which an eternal destiny is worked out. What comes 'afterwards' is not a prolongation of the period or its continuation in an endless series of new ages, but rather the definitive fixing and the eternal validity of what has come to be in time. But unless we wish to regard man as simply 'coming to an end', so that we can then go on to say that he undergoes a 'resurrection' of the flesh, thereby becoming something absolutely new (which, however, would be tantamount to a radical denial of his continuing identity and of eternity as the fruit of time), then, precisely upon a Christian conception of the history man as an individual, we must recognise the existence of a further period of time between death and the final consummation of all things, during which the acts performed in freedom during man's time on earth are brought to their maturity. For this history of man precisely as human only attains its ultimate end and consummation in the resurrection of the flesh, in the transfiguration of all that is real in man taken as a whole, and not merely in a sort of Platonist history of the individual spirit. We cannot picture to ourselves what takes place in it, but this is no reason for denying such a possibility. Every attempt at describing this possibility serves in its result to show how impossible it is to deny that the possibility itself does exist. But even while renouncing any such attempt we can still say this much: supposing that the *history* of the individual as such is not simply terminated with death; supposing that with death considered as the outcome of a specific and determinate stage in this history belonging to the dimension of space and time man enters still more into an open relationship to the totality of the world (though he does not become 'liberated from the body' in the sense of a negative and empty separation from the cosmos); supposing all this is true, then he experiences the contradiction between the divinely ordained nature of his own being or that of the world on the one hand, and that which he still is through the still surviving effects of his own acts, in which his guilt has been objectified. He experiences these as the painful and punitive consequences of his sin. Now the painful process by which this contradiction is overcome is his purgatory. But just as in this life, so too even after death this process can be slower or quicker, more or less painful or happy, according to the particular circumstances and the prior conditions which determine this in each individual case. That the 'poor souls' may be granted a swifter and more happy maturing process – that is what we pray for when we pray for them, and that is the object of that intercessory prayer of the Church which is promised to us in an indulgence which we gain 'for the holy souls'.

An indulgence, then, implies that the Church agrees to offer her official intercession on behalf of the repentant sinner. And it is expressed in the form of a remission of some (hypothetically imposed) canonical penance (when it is a case of indulgences for the living). The necessary prior condition for this to be achieved is that the individual gaining the indulgence must perform some good work which is specifically prescribed. In earlier times, in which the indulgence properly so-called emerged, this good work constituted primarily some part of the canonical penance which had been imposed or else some other penance, generally easier, which had to be performed in place of the original one. Today the conditions laid down by the Church for gaining an indulgence consist only of some very small task, almost symbolical in its effect. This should not lead us to the point of no longer taking indulgences seriously, as though they were 'cheap' and to be had in great quantities. Many indulgences are offered. Whether many are also 'gained' in *reality* is another question. An indulgence is only gained in the definitive sense when the intercessory prayer of the Church achieves its goal. But in the last analysis this can only take place in a heart that is disposed to penance, in an individual who, working from a basis of faith and grace, strives through his actions and sufferings to ensure that he may become more and more a new creature fashioned after the image of Christ in all the dimensions of his being. It is in order that this may be achieved that the holy Church assures the Christian, by granting him an indulgence, of her help and intercession.

9

ON THE OFFICIAL TEACHING OF THE CHURCH
TODAY ON THE SUBJECT OF INDULGENCES

ALTHOUGH the theology and practice of indulgences was certainly most energetically discussed at the Second Vatican Council, no actual decision was arrived at. In the meantime a pronouncement has been issued by the pope, as a result of which a more practicable way has been devised of explaining the nature of indulgence, although admittedly certain basic theological problems still remain, which even this is incapable of overcoming. In connection with this new ordering of the question, we have set ourselves, in the investigation which follows, a relatively limited goal. The central and primary theme of these observations is the fact that the interpretation of the Church's teaching on indulgence as put forward by B. Poschmann[1] and the author[2] is perfectly

---

[1] Of B. Poschmann's works ;cf. especially: *Der Ablass im Lichte der Bussgeschichte* = *Theophaneia* 4 (Bonn 1948); also the reviews of this by H. Weisweiler, *Scholastik* 24 (1949), pp. 591–594, K. Adam, *T.Q.* 129 (1949), pp. 242–245, P. Galtier, *Gregorianum* 31 (1950), pp. 258–274, and K. Rahner (cf. n. 2); B. Poschmann, 'Busse und Letzte Ölung' – *H.D.G.* IV, 3 (Freiburg 1951), pp. 112–123; *idem*, 'Die innere Struktur des Busssakraments', *M.T.Z.* 1 (1950), pp. 12–30.

[2] cf. K. Rahner's review of B. Poschmann's *Der Ablass im Lichte der Bussgeschichte* in *Z.K.T.* 71 (1949), pp. 481–490; *idem*, 'Remarks on the Theology of Indulgences', *Theological Investigations* II (London and Baltimore 1963), pp. 175–201 (= a slightly revised version of the review of Poschmann's work); *idem*, 'Über den Ablass' *St.D.Z.* 156 (1955), pp. 343–355, also in this volume, pp. 150–165; *idem*, 'Ablass', *L.T.K.* I (Freiburg ,2nd ed. 1957), 46–53; *idem*, 'Sündenstrafen', *L.T.K.* IX (Freiburg, 2nd ed. 1964), 1185–1187; K. Rahner, H. Vorgrimler edd. 'Indulgence', *Concise Theological Dictionary* (Freiburg/London 1965), p. 277; K. Rahner, 'Indulgences', *Sacramentum Mundi*, III (Freiburg/London 1969), pp. 123–129. In the meantime other theologians have probably become adherents of the interpretation put forward by Poschmann and myself, cf. M. Schmaus, *Katholische Dogmatik* IV/1 (Munich, 5th ed., 1957), para. 272, esp. 609; G. Muschalek, 'Der Ablass in der heutigen Praxis und Lehre der katholischen Kirche', *Gespräch über den Ablass = Arbeiten zur kirchlichen Wiedervereinigung, Kirchengeschichtliche Reihe* 2 (Graz 1965), pp. 13–37; B. Häring, *Das Gesetz Christi* I (Freiburg, 7th ed. 1963), p. 518; L. Ott, *Grundriss der katholischen Dogmatik* (Freiburg, 7th ed., 1963), p. 525 ff.; P. Anciaux, *Das Sakra-*

reconcilable with the Apostolic Constitution *Indulgentiarum Doctrina*[3] of 1 January 1967. The task of demonstrating this fact, however, will probably bring to light certain further problems in the Church's current teaching on indulgence and its theological interpretation, and these too are of central importance. Because of this broader horizons will spontaneously open up, and our investigations will carry us far beyond this particular theme. It hardly needs to be said that in the 450th anniversary, the jubilee year of the Reformation, we shall also implicitly be bearing in mind the views of other Churches on the subject of indulgence, even though the more directly controversial problems entailed in this theology will not explicitly be presented.

I

1. We are presupposing that the reader is already familiar with the interpretation of the Church's teaching on indulgence up to the present as presented by us in connection with B. Poschmann's view. Here we shall not be repeating this. The reader will only be able to understand what we have to say here, therefore, if what has already been said about this theory of indulgence is familiar to, and still fresh in his mind. For our present

---

ment der Busse (Mainz 1961), pp. 175 to 192; E. Schillebeeckx, 'Der Sinn der katholischen Ablasspraxis', *Lutherische Rundschau* 17 (1967), pp. 328–355; probably O. Semmelroth too is taking a similar approach in his commentary on the Constitution on Indulgence (see below p. 170, n. 11). In all the material statements he has made on the subject of indulgence in his own published works during the course of the last twenty years or so the author has at no time adopted any approaches which are basically different from the present one. At the same time, however, notable variations can be perceived between the individual works in his conception of the temporal punishments due to sin, his interpretation in the concrete of the special intercession of the Church and the part played by love as the basic unifying force in his understanding (which is at basis both anthropological and theological) of the process by which the whole man is matured. It is in the context of these basic factors that the true theological nature of indulgence is to be sought. For this reason the author may also be permitted to adduce numerous references in this study in order to bring out in precise and concrete terms the fact that his theory of indulgence is in harmony with the current official teaching of the Church on the subject.

[3] cf. *A.A.S.* 59 (1967), pp. 5–24; in addition a separate edition of the Constitution has also appeared: *Constitutionis Apostolicae Indulgentiarum Doctrina. Breve Commentarium*, auctore E. Mura, R.S.V. (Vatican City 1967). This edition, published in both Latin and Italian with a commentary, was not available to me at the time this article was written.

purposes we shall call this theory the 'new theory' because it has already been called so by others.[4] But we do not intend by this to assert that it is new in its material content. On the contrary, as B. Poschmann has shown from the aspect of the history of dogma, it is a revival of a teaching which, historically speaking, belongs to the origins of the theory and practice of indulgence viewed as a whole. The revival of this ancient teaching has been made possible only by purging the teaching on indulgence which has been usual since the Middle Ages of an exaggeratedly legalistic element which has been found repellant. The only reason we ourselves have for calling this teaching 'new' is so that we may have a brief formula for it ready to hand. Nor are we concerned in the study which follows to take up any particular position with regard to the judgments passed upon this interpretation by other theologians. This would lead us too far afield. The question which concerns us, therefore, is not how, for instance, R. Masi's[5] judgment on the 'new theory of indulgences' is itself in turn to be judged.[6] Here let us merely notice in passing that even Masi concedes that the 'new theory' does not contradict any of the defined doctrines of the Church, and does not even, in any obvious sense (*nettamente*), run counter to the teaching of the *ordinary magisterium*. One further point may be noticed, namely that (from the opposite point of view) certain

[4] Thus cf. R. Masi, 'La dottrina tradizionale delle indulgenze', *Osservatore Romano*, 19 February 1966; *idem*, 'Nuove idee sulla dottrina delle indulgenze', *Osservatore Romano*, 26 February 1966. cf. also C. Journet, *Teologia della indulgenze* (Ancora, Rome 1966). These studies had, of course already been published *prior* to the promulgation of the Apostolic Constitution, and accordingly efforts were not spared in them to bring their influence to bear upon the new official pronouncement. In the investigation which follows we shall be concerning ourselves only indirectly to show that these efforts to present the theory of indulgence put forward by Poschmann and myself as irreconcilable with the official teaching of the Church did not in fact have any real influence upon the official pronouncement.

[5] cf. Especially the last article by R. Masi, 'Nuove idee sulla dottrina delle indulgenze', *Osservatore Romano*, 26 February 1966, p. 6.

[6] We are also compelled to refrain from entering into the discussion on the differences in the presentation of the nature of indulgence put forward at the Second Vatican Council. If we were entering into this question we would have to point particularly to the interventions of the Cardinal Patriarch Maximos IV Saigh and of Cardinals Alfrink, König and Döpfner. On this cf. L. A. Dorn, W. Seibel, *Tagebuch des Konzils. Die Arbeit der vierten Session* (Nurenberg 1966), pp. 233 f., 237 f., 248 ff., 260, 264 etc. The most important passages are now to be found in the work edited by J. Ch. Hampe, *Autorität und Freiheit. Gegenwart des Konzils und Zukunft der Kirche im ökumenischen Disput* Vol I (Munich 1967), pp. 436–449, 440–442 (Intervention by Cardinal-Patriarch Maximos), 442–449 (Vota of Cardinals Döpfner and König).

circles among Protestant theologians[7] have found it possible to regard our interpretation as a preliminary foothold for a more positive understanding of the Catholic doctrine of indulgence.[8]

2. This study is not presented as a commentary on the Apostolic Constitution viewed as a *whole*. The question under consideration here, rather, is simply whether the teaching of this Constitution[9] on indulgence amounts to a rejection, whether expressed or implied, of the teaching on indulgence put forward by B. Poschmann and myself, or alternatively whether, having regard to the actual text of it (for this alone is what

[7] cf. K. G. Steck, 'Ablass', *R.G.G.* I (Tübingen, 3rd ed. 1957), pp. 64–67 (cf. the conclusion: 'How they (Poschmann and K. Rahner) will succeed in getting their views accepted remains to be seen'). The present investigation seeks to show that the earlier efforts were not altogether useless, and also that even apart from our direct contribution they have left at least some traces in the official documents.

[8] cf. especially H. Bornkamm, 'Thesen und Thesenanschlag Luthers', *Geschehen und Bedeutung* (Berlin 1967), pp. 60–63. This article includes, on pp. 65–70 certain observations on the Constitution on Indulgence of Pope Paul VI of 1 January 1967.

[9] Of course the question of the theological standing of the Constitution would have to be discussed in general and in specific detail. Here, however, we shall not be treating of this in any explicit sense. The Constitution certainly contains no infallible doctrinal decision but is, nevertheless, an authentic presentation of the official teaching of the *ordinary magisterium*, so that its particular pronouncements still carry a certain degree of binding force. In estimating the standing of these pronouncements the stated purpose of the Constitution should not be overlooked. In it the *Sacrarum Indulgentiarum recognitio promulgatur* – the title of the Constitution – in other words it constitutes the new prescription for *practical* purposes for defining the nature of indulgence in the concrete. For this purpose, therefore, the preliminary doctrinal part serves merely as an extended introduction. But however this may be, we are taking the teaching of the Constitution as established and (though we do not intend to determine its precise theological standing any more closely here) as 'binding'. Admittedly we do hold the opinion that even a 'binding' doctrinal pronouncement on the part of the Church's teaching authority can and must have its meaning illumined and have its full implications brought out. What is binding in our understanding of the Constitution is the actual text of the *A.A.S.* We shall not, therefore, be taking into account the brief anonymous commentary which was appended to the text of the Constitution in No. 7 of the *Osservatore Romano* of the 9th and 10th of January 1967. We do not regard this commentary as having much authority, and feel that it has little to do with the real intentions underlying the Constitution. Why, for instance, is Mt 16:18 f. quoted once more as a proof of indulgence, when it is manifest that the Constitution itself deliberately avoids this? Why does the commentary speak of a '*potere di giurisdizione*' when the Constitution says nothing of this? Why does it speak of a '*porzione del tesoro*', when this is not really in conformity with the approach of the Constitution itself? Why is the commentary silent on the subject of the *sancta et justa libertas* when the Constitution makes full allowance for this in the use of indulgences by Christians? cf. also H. Bornkamm, *Thesen und Thesenanschlag Luthers* (Berlin 1967), p. 65, n. 220.

concerns us) this is not in fact the case. If we had to try to give a commentary on, and evaluation of this Apostolic Constitution taken as a whole, very many points would have to be discussed which cannot be treated of here, or which can only be touched upon very briefly, even though they may deserve the greatest attention from theologians: the question of the nature of the development of dogma in general, for certain noteworthy observations on this question do occur, such as are hardly to be found in any official documents of the Church prior to this one; points concerning the nature of indulgence, the necessity of adapting it or subordinating it to or under the Christian's task of working out his salvation viewed as a whole, in which love is first and last the determining factor; concerning the more ultimate 'roots of revelation' from which first the practice of indulgence[10] and then the theory of it gradually (*paulatim decursu saeculorum*) developed; concerning the concept of the *thesaurus Ecclesiae*, any quantitative interpretation of which is explicitly rejected; concerning the division (so strongly adhered to) of indulgences into plenary or perfect and partial (not imperfect!) ones; concerning the 'holy and justified freedom of the children of God', in virtue of which Christians can themselves decide whether they wish to avail themselves of the indulgences that are offered or to follow the Church's recommendation to gain them, etc. All this cannot be treated of here, even though in itself and viewed objectively it could, perhaps, be more important as a subject for investigation.[11]

[10] A further point that is discussed more freely than hitherto in this official document of the Church is the historical abuses in the practice of indulgence. At the same time, however, it must be recognised that at least from the pre-Nominalist period onwards a critical attitude had all along been adopted in the theory of indulgence. (See below p. 198, n. 58.) Moreover the Fourth Lateran Council (cf. D.S. 819) and the Council of Trent (cf. D.S. 1835) had already adopted a clearly critical attitude towards abuses (cf. the further inclusion of these quotations in No 8 with notes 41–42). It is explicitly conceded that there have been indulgences which were 'indiscreet and unnecessary', through which the attitude and the practice of repentance were deprived of their pristine force ('enervated'). Besides this it is also explained that because of the 'perverse quest for gain' the word 'indulgence' has been rendered obnoxious (we may contrast this with the formulation of the Tridentine text of D.S. 1835 adduced as a basis for the statement: *ab haereticis blasphematur*!). In considering these concessions it must be born in mind that such indulgences were still granted precisely by the Church (by whom else?). On the concrete practice of indulgence in the period immediately preceding the Reformation cf. E. Iserloh, *Luther zwischen Reform und Reformation. Der Thesenanschlag fand nicht statt = Katholisches Leben und Kämpfen im Zeitalter der Glaubensspaltung* 23/4 (Munster, 2nd ed. 1967),2 pp. 16 ff., 22 ff., 30 ff. (with bibliography).

[11] We may draw attention to one further point here, namely that it is also important from the point of view of theology to notice what the Constitution does *not* say,

3. While, therefore, in the following considerations we shall be arguing that our own theory of indulgence is reconcilable with the teaching the Papal Constitution, this in no sense implies that this theory is actually put forward in the Constitution itself. It is not the purpose of these considerations to assert, far less to prove, any such thing. The reconcilability of which we are speaking here is not based upon the fact that both interpretations coincide with one another on all material points. On the contrary it is based upon the facts on the one hand that no position whatever is taken up in the papal teaching on the question of the 'new' theory of indulgence, and on the other that this 'new' theory does not come into conflict at any point with what the pope has to say about indulgence. Its teaching is the same, even though, it may be, in one point of detail or another it may be presented under different aspects or with different formulations. Moreover in the position we are adopting here that the 'new' theory is reconcilable with the papal doctrine, we are not asserting even implicitly that the papal doctrine is irreconcilable with the traditional scholastic theology of indulgence. The case here is the same as with many other theological questions. What is formulated in the official teaching of the Church is that

---

contrasting in this with the ideas of scholastic theology. Thus for instance nothing is said about the idea that there is such a thing as a penance which can be performed by the Christian even though there is no question of applying its value in terms of 'satisfaction' as a blotting out of the temporal punishments due to sin since the individual himself has no need of it, so that so far as he is concerned it is 'extra', and *precisely for this reason* can be applied to others. The use at one point (cf. Norm 3) of the expression '*in modum suffragii*' (in the case of the indulgences applied to the dead) without any further explanation is certainly striking. The expression *per modum absolutionis* or *per modum solutionis*, however, are not used. Whereas in scholastic theology it is customary to invoke the support of Mt 16 and 18, this is avoided here, even though the expression '*claves Ecclesiae*' at one point (cf. No 8) does occur. This, however, cannot *ipso facto* be identified with a *potestas jurisdictionis*. On the development of the theology of the power of the keys cf. L. Hödl, *Die Geschichte der scholastischen Literatur und der Theologie der Schlüsselgewalt* I (Munster 1960); V. Heynck, 'Der richterliche Charakter des Busssakramentes nach Johannes Duns Scotus', *Franziskan. Studien* 47 (1965), pp. 339–414; *idem*, 'Die Diskussion über die Notwendigkeit und Begründung der Beichtjurisdiktion bei dem Anonymus O.P. des Cod. Vat. lat. 985', *Wahrheit und Verkündigung. Michael Schmaus zum 70. Geburtstag*, L. Scheffczyk, W. Dettloff, R. Heinzmann edd. (Paderborn 1967), Vol I, pp. 1049–1071. Up to the present I have not yet heard of any extensive commentaries on the Apostolic Constitution. I should, however, draw attention to the commentary of O. Semmelroth which has appeared in the meantime under the title 'Apostolische Busskonstitution. Bussordnung der deutschen Bischöfe. Apostolische Konstitution über die Neuordnung des Ablasswesens' as number 2 in the series *Nachkonziliare Dokumentation* published by the Paulinus-Verlag (Treves 1967), cf. esp. pp. 51–71.

common ground which either precedes or else arises from the teaching of the various schools, and which can be reconciled with several of the interpretations of these. The official teaching of the Church may be presented from a different perspective and formulated in different terms than those which we ourselves would uphold, and which we consider to be the more accurate. It may even be (and this is particularly noteworthy) that the terms in which it is formulated belong to a more traditional theory than our own. But as every theologian knows from numerous examples drawn from the history of dogma and theology, this in itself is very far from being a condemnation of the particular theological opinion we are upholding. Let it be willingly and explicitly conceded that something of this sort may be the case here, for instance in expressions such as *dispensare*, *clavis Ecclesiae*, in the rules for distinguishing between plenary and partial indulgences etc. But no theological argument can be drawn from any such differences to prevent us from placing a different theological interpretation upon a doctrine of the Church which we all hold in common.[12]

II

Critics of the 'new' theory of indulgence have oversimplified and distorted it, regarding the pith and essence of it as consisting in the fact that according to this theory the remission of the temporal punishments due to sin – as distinct from penances imposed by the Church – is achieved not by an official exercise of the Church's (and especially the pope's) jurisdiction but (in so far as it takes place at all) through the 'prayer' of the Church. The traditional doctrine on indulgence, on the other hand, so these critics maintain, upholds this act of the Church's jurisdiction and regards this precisely as constituting the decisive difference between indulgences and other ways of wiping out the temporal punishments due to sin. It is just this difference between the conceptions that the Constitution seems to take cognizance of in No. 8. On this point it seems to decide in favour of the traditional doctrine, and so too to adopt that definition of indulgence which is set forth in No. 8 and in No. 1 of the norms: An indulgence is an *auctoritativa applicatio et dispensatio 'thesauri Ecclesiae'* for the remission of the temporal punishments due to sins in God's sight, and this authoritative application and act of dispensing (*dispensare*) is something different from a mere prayer of the Church (*non tantum orat*). Now the question is

[12] The phrase *'resistere potest'* of D.S. 3010, for instance, cannot be adduced either against a Thomist conception of efficacious grace, even though the formulation of it was originally 'Molinist'.

whether this explanation involves any *real* contradiction between the teaching of the Constitution and the 'new' teaching on indulgence. The points which we shall need to take into consideration in order to arrive at an answer to this question fall under several distinct heads.

III

What strikes one first on a careful reading of the Constitution is that in it the granting of indulgences on the part of the Church is not characterised as an act precisely of her *jurisdiction*. The Church's power of granting indulgences is designated as '*potestas ministrae redemptionis Christi*' (No. 8), and as a power '*auctoritative dispensare et applicare*' in relation to the treasury of the Church (No. 8 norm 1). Now this is all the more striking in view of the fact that no support is claimed from Mt 16, the classic text for the Church's power of jurisdiction.[13] Certainly it might be said that a *potestas* which is exercised with 'authority' is, of its very nature, a jurisdictional power. It might be explained that the authors have deliberately avoided qualifying the authority to grant indulgences any more precisely than this because it is necessary to conceive of this power in such a way that we realise that indulgences are possible for the dead also, even though these are no longer subject to the jurisdiction of the Church. But against this we must first reiterate once more that not every *potestas auctoritativa* is a *potestas jurisdictionis* (we may recall the *potestas ordinis* as exercised, for instance, in the power of consecrating and dispensing the Eucharist). Those, therefore, who wish to identify the '*potestas auctoritativa*' of the Church referred to here with a specifically juridical authority have first to prove their case. For this identification is not expressed in the actual text of the Constitution itself, at any rate explicitly. A further point is that the whole presentation of the nature of indulgence from No. 8 to norm 1 is manifestly intended to describe indulgence as capable of being 'applied' to the dead as well (cf. norm 3). But in such a context how can it be supposed that it is an act of 'jurisdiction' that is intended, especially in those cases in which the indulgence can be gained *only* for the dead (cp. norm 15)? It cannot refer to the dead person himself (cf. norm 3: '*in modum suffragii*'). But in such a case *how* precisely can it refer to the living who gain the indulgence? If, therefore, this question is to be answered in the affirmative

---

[13] On the interpretation of this text cf. the works of L. Hödl (cf. above n. 11), P. Anciaux, *La théologie du sacrement de pénitence au XIIe siècle* (Louvain 1949), K. Fröhlich, *Formen der Auslegung von Mt 16:13–18 im lateinischen Mittelalter* (Dissertation, Basle, 1960).

at all, does this not imply that in order to support such an answer constructions have to be placed on the text of the Constitution which are no longer credible. In the case supposed is it the Church herself who performs the *suffragium*? If so then in this case also the general definition of indulgence must still apply. In other words *suffragium* must be able to be combined with the exercise of the Church's *auctoritativa potestas*. If, on the other hand, a negative answer is given to this question, in other words if the living person who gains the indulgence is the one responsible for the *suffragium*,[14] still, even then, we can say that it is the dead person himself who gains the indulgence *precisely as such*, and in that case what does the *potestas auctoritativa* of the Church bring about in this living individual? Is that which, *ex hypothesi*, is brought about in this individual while still living itself an indulgence?

Thus if we accept the idea of the *applicatio et dispensatio* of what is contained in the 'treasury of the Church' merely at its face value and merely as an exercise of some *potestas autoritativa*, and then seek to interpret this primarily as an act of *jurisdiction*, we shall lose ourselves in a whole thicket of thorny questions. A further and final point is that the concept of a jurisdictional power in this sense and with so wide a range of possible applications is somewhat obscure when its application is extended beyond the 'visible' society of the Church and used to relate the members of the Church to one another as subordinates or superiors in respect of *all* the activities of the Church considered precisely as a *society*. This becomes clear, for instance, in the controversial question of what is implied by saying that the absolution given in the sacrament of penance has a 'judicial' character.[15] If we do think of the authority of the Church

---

[14] In No 8 mention is made of the fact that the *believers* undertake a '*transferre indulgentias in suffragium defunctorum*'. In norm 3 it is not so clear who precisely is the subject who 'applies' the indulgence to the dead (cf. also norm 15).

[15] cf. also K. Mörsdorf, 'Der hoheitliche Charakter der sakramentalen Lossprechung', *T.T.Z.* 57 (1948), pp. 335–348; *idem*, 'Der Rechtscharakter der iurisdictio fori interni', *M.T.Z.* 8 (1967), pp. 161–173; on the problem cf. also E. López-Doriga, 'Die Natur der Jurisdiktion im Busssakrament', *Z.K.T.* 82 (1960), pp. 385–427. cf. the bilibiography already given on p. 170, n. 11. When, for instance, Mörsdorf sees the power of jurisdiction (*L.T.K.* V, 2nd ed., 1220) as consisting in the enacting of laws, pronouncing of judgment and government (this is his account of the Church's supreme authority), how is it then possible to apply any such concept so as to throw light upon the *potestas auctoritativa* with regard to the remission of the temporal punishments due to sin in God's sight – especially as, for one thing, the effect of a jurisdictional act in the true sense, as directed towards a subordinate, is independent of his assent, whereas the blotting out of a punishment due to sin in God's sight is possible only with the voluntary collaboration of the recipient of the

in this way we are in constant danger of reducing the terms we use to the level of clichés, the precise meaning of which as we apply them in general and in particular can no longer be verified. Our course should be, rather, to leave open the question of whether the *potestas auctoritativa* spoken of in the Constitution is to be identified with the jurisdictional authority, and to avoid losing ourselves in a process of conceptual acrobatics which is rich in verbiage but ultimately devoid of content. And if we take this course with regard to the meaning of the term *potestas auctoritativa* we shall straightway be in a position to deduce from the text of the Constitution simply the following two facts:

1. What the Constitution emphasises again and again is the 'dispositions' of the recipient of the indulgence. But once we have accepted the importance of these we come to what is proper to the Church herself, and to the part she has to play in the granting of indulgences. She has an 'ability' (*potestas* from *posse*!) which is real, valid and effective in God's sight with regard to the blotting out of the temporal punishments due to sins, and the Church achieves this by having recourse to the 'treasury of the Church'.

2. This 'ability' and this recourse consist not merely in 'prayer':[16] '*Non tantum orat sed . . . auctoritative dispensat*'.

So far as the first definition of this *potestas* is concerned the 'new' theory of indulgence certainly does not come into conflict with this in any respect. For the exponents of this theory have expressly emphasised that the Church's act is not confined merely to the remission of the canonical penances which have been imposed, but relates to the temporal punishments due to sins in God's sight. They have further emphasised that this activity is infallibly effective[17] – that is so far as the Church's part is concerned and leaving aside the 'dispositions' of the recipient of the indulgence – and indeed that in reality even according to the 'new' theory of indulgence this activity can be brought under the general concept of the *opus operatum*, provided this is rightly understood. In other words it certainly is

---

indulgence? To the extent that a *potestas jurisdictionis* is made effective in the sacraments, its effects bear upon the communal life of the Church, not upon the relationship of the individual to God. The concept of the *potestas auctoritativa* as applied to indulgence must therefore be developed independently of any speculations about the Church's power of jurisdiction. On this problem cf. the observations of E. Schillebeeckx, *op. cit.*, pp. 336 f., 342 f., 345 f., etc.

[16] The anonymous commentator speaks of a '*semplice preghiera deprecativa*'.

[17] cf. K. Rahner, *Theological Investigations* II (London and Baltimore 1963), pp. 185 f., 199 f.; *idem*, 'Ablass', *L.T.K.* I, 51–52; *idem*, 'Über den Ablass', *St.D.Z.* 156 (1955), pp. 351–353 etc., in this volume, pp. 150 f.

a *potestas auctoritativa*.[18] Thus we see that the only question at issue can be whether the 'new' theory of indulgence does come into conflict really (and not merely in the sense that it seems merely from the form of words to contradict the Constitution) with the second determination of what is meant by the *potestas auctoritativa*, in which it is said not to consist merely in 'prayer alone'. This is a point on which we must now speak further.

IV

This brings us to an initial point of very real importance, even if it is not the ultimate and decisive one with which this entire investigation is concerned. The exponents of the 'new' theory of indulgence will certainly be of opinion that when the Constitution rejects the idea that the essence of indulgence consists merely in 'prayer alone' on the Church's part this does not imply a rejection of the 'new' teaching on indulgence in itself. Is this in fact correct? The answer to this question needs to be worked out very carefully.

1. First we may permit ourselves a few preliminary remarks with regard to method and approach. In theological controversies there is always a strong possibility that any conflicts that may arise are merely apparent, merely verbal ones. At first two statements are set against one another as affirmation and denial because they use the selfsame words to

[18] For a more precise interpretation of such an act of subsuming cf. K. Rahner, *Theological Investigations* II (London and Baltimore 1963), pp. 192 f., 200 f. with n. 2; also 'A Brief Theological Study on Indulgence' in this volume pp. 150 f., 163. The actual *concept* of *opus operatum* was used less or not at all in the earlier studies. The primary reason for this was that we were making every effort to exclude the misunderstandings which could so easily arise, and which would give the impression that indulgence took effect in an automatic and magical way (see *L.T.K.* I, 51; *Theological Investigations* II, pp. 175 ff., etc.). What is at issue here was expressed perfectly adequately *from the very nature of the case*: 'Always sure of being heard', 'an infallibly effective prayer' etc. cf., for instance, *Theological Investigations* II, p. 178: '... And a "prayer" of an authoritative kind need not necessarily lack the efficacy of an *opus operatum*' (thus already in the article as originally published in *Z.K.T.* 71 (1949), p. 485). For the rest I have already drawn attention, in my review of B. Poschmann's book in 1949 (*Theological Investigations* II, p. 199), to the fact that Poschmann's theory of indulgence needs to be developed and set on a broader basis precisely with regard to the 'precise nature of an '*authoritative* prayer of the *Church* as distinct from a private intercession'. For a fuller treatment of this cf. the later study of K. Rahner, 'Some Theses on "Prayer in the Name of the Church" ', *Theological Investigations* V (London and Baltimore 1966), pp. 419–438; and particularly *ad rem*, pp. 428 ff., *idem*, *Kirche und Sakramente* (Freiburg, 2nd ed. 1963), pp. 22–30; *idem*, *Theological Investigations* II (London and Baltimore 1963), pp. 109–133; cf. also p. 179, n. 26.

assent to, or alternatively to reject, the proposition involved. Both parties (or at least one of them) presuppose that the meaning of these words is self-evident. They have this in mind when they use them and so do not pause to enter any more closely into, or to analyse their meaning. Each of the two parties, therefore, regards his own unreflecting understanding of the terms involved as 'obvious', and in doing so perhaps invokes the support of an alleged 'common parlance'. He regards this particular interpretation of the term, therefore, as already granted by the other party. In spite of this, however, the actual situation is that both parties are understanding the term in two different senses, and the contradiction is only apparent, or at any rate not established beyond doubt to be real.[19] The present-day situation in theology is in fact such that the differences between the different departments of it, the problems they raise and the aspects from which the objective theological factors involved can be viewed, are immense. As a result a situation has arisen almost perforce in which one can find little common ground between theologians with regard to the objective meaning of the terminology they use. So that even when they use the same words we can never be too hasty in assuming that they are using them in the same sense, nor yet shall we find it easy to establish whether this is in fact the case or not. The reason is that every explanation of what particular sense is intended is itself in turned expressed in words which, once more, remain undefined and perhaps are still not in all cases 'clear'.[20]

[19] The present-day controversy with regard to the concept of 'transsubstantiation' and 'transsignification', their significance and the extent to which they are or are not identical with one another is probably a good example of the methodological difficulties which arise in contemporary theology and which we have in mind here. On this cf. O. Semmelroth, 'Eucharistische Wandlung' *G.u.L.* 40 (1967), pp. 93–106; E. Schillebeeckx, *Die eucharistische Gegenwart* (Düsseldorf 1967); J. Ratzinger, 'Das Problem der Transsubstantiation und die Frage nach dem Sinn der Eucharistie', *T.Q.* 147 (1967), pp. 129–158; W. Beinert, 'Die Enzyklika "Mysterium fidei" und neuere Auffassungen über die Eucharistie', *T.Q.* 147 (1967), pp. 159–176; I. van Hout, 'Fragen zur Eucharistielehre in den Niederlanden', *Catholica* 20 (1966), pp. 179–199; P. Schoonberg, 'Transsubstantiation : How Far is this Doctrine Historically Determined?', *Concilium* 4/3 (1967), pp. 41–47.

[20] cf. for instance the problems entailed in the use of the concept of 'person'. On this K. Rahner, *Mysterium salutis* II (Einsiedeln 1967), pp. 342 ff., 349 ff., 353 ff., 364 ff., 385 ff. I have attempted to point out that this situation has the most radical implications for contemporary theology and for the Church's official teachers. I have done this in a major study which appeared in 1968 (*'Häresien in der Kirche heute?'*, Quaestiones Disputatae, Herder, Freiburg 1968). cf. also K. Rahner. 'Philosophy and Philosophising in Theology', *Theological Investigations* IX (London and Baltimore, 1972), pp. 46–63.

2. The Constitution speaks of an activity defined as '*tantum orare*', and sets this idea in opposition to that of a *potestas auctoritativa*. But it is not very easy to establish from this opposition exactly what is meant by the idea of 'prayer alone'. For it has already been shown that *potestas auctoritativa* is itself an idea that includes several different dimensions. Now it is not less true that 'prayer' alone taken in itself is a concept with several different levels of meaning, so that it is not straightway or *ipso facto* clear from the use of it in the Constitution that every conceivable level of meaning is intended to be excluded in defining the nature of indulgence. Even if we do not think of the private prayer of the individual Christian, since in fact in this context it is the prayer of the *Church* that is being referred to, still even this concept of the prayer of the Church contains many different levels of meaning.[21] It can be the prayer of a monk reciting the prayers of the office and praying in choir 'in the name of the Church'.[22] It can be an official prayer or collect, for instance for fine weather, recited by a priest. It can be the sort of prayer through which a blessing or some other sacramental benefit is conferred. It can be the form of prayer which as such constitutes the ritual of the anointing of the sick as *opus operatum*, and precisely as such it is an act of the supreme, that is of the actual sacramental 'power' of the Church acting from her 'authority'[23] (*potestas ordinis*). In any case the 'prayer of the Church' is an extraordinarily variable entity. It varies in respect of those in the concrete whom it is intended to support, in the way in which particular members of the Church are commissioned to perform it in the name of the Church and as the prayer of the Church, in the 'object' prayed for,[24] in the way in

[21] cf. K. Rahner, 'Some Theses on "Prayer in the Name of the Church"', *Theological Investigations* V (London and Baltimore, 1966) pp. 419–438.

[22] On this cf. the Constitution on the Liturgy of the Second Vatican Council, Nos. 84, 85, 90, 98, 99.

[23] On this cf. D.S. 1695 and the well-known theological considerations on the anointing of the sick.

[24] This aspect too is of great importance. Where the object of the prayer is *certainly* salvific (this is generally not the case, but remains in doubt) it is far easier to conceive that the 'prayer' (as, for instance in the anointing of the sick) is identical with an act of the Church's *potestas auctoritativa*, as for instance in the case of a prayer (even of the Church) for fine weather physical health etc. In the light of this alone it becomes clear that we must distinguish between the 'prayer' of the Church in indulgence and the prayer of the Church in the sacramentals. The commentator on the Constitution totally fails to perceive the real problem, therefore, when he suggests that the 'new' theory of indulgence is affected by the fact that a '*semplice preghiera deprecativa*' is ruled out in it. On this cf. p. 175-176, n. 17 and above all 18, p. 179, n. 25, and n. 26, where attention is drawn to earlier arguments put forward by the author.

which it takes effect and in the degree to which its effect can be said to be 'assured'. So variable is it, indeed, that one particular 'species' of this prayer can be conceived of – indeed actually exists – which (so far as the part played by the Church is concerned) is perfectly reconcilable with the element of infallible effectiveness and even with the concept of the *opus operatum*.[25]

Is it then the case that the terms of the Constitution are such as to assert that of all the conceivable 'varieties' of the Church's prayer not a single one enters in any sense whatever into the nature of indulgence, or are only some varieties excluded in this sense? To this question the Constitution itself supplies no answer. Yet it is legitimate to raise this question because there is a prayer which involves no real opposition to a *potestas auctoritativa*, but actually itself *constitutes* such a potestas and in a *particular* case can actually make the nature of this in the *concrete* more comprehensible than when the concept of *potestas auctoritativa* is used merely by itself. For if we take this latter course the idea which seems to be implied by it is legalistic in a sense which in reality is not intended for one moment, or at any rate is not positively inculcated as part of the Church's official teaching. To this legitimate question, therefore, to which no explicit answer can be found in the Constitution, we can, without strain, supply the following answer: the *only* kind of 'prayer of the Church' which is excluded as inadequate to define the nature of indulgence is that which is not conceived of as an act of her authoritative power.

3. Now the 'new' theory of indulgence has all along had this particular 'species' of the 'prayer of the Church' in mind when it has sought to define the nature of indulgence as a prayer of the Church for the remission of the temporal punishments due to sin in God's sight. Materially speaking, therefore, it does not run counter to the teaching of the Constitution. The exponents of this theory have never had in mind 'just any kind of' prayer of the Church.[26] They intended to refer to a prayer in which the

---

cf. also K. Rahner, 'Ablass', *L.T.K.* I, 51, 'A Brief Theological Study on Indulgence', in this volume, pp. 150–165.

[25] Apart from the evidence adduced in n. 18 cf. also *Theological Investigations* II (London and Baltimore 1963), pp. 185, 199; *Theological Investigations* V (London and Baltimore 1966), pp. 433–435.

[26] In view of the evidence already cited or referred to this is indisputable. cf. also *L.T.K.* I, 51: 'The essence of indulgence, therefore, consists in the *special* prayer of the Church . . .' (italics by the author). Furthermore everything depends upon the actual manner *in the concrete* in which such a 'prayer' is understood and proves to be effective in the case of indulgence also. For a more precise statement of the theological nature

Church, exploiting her nature to the full as *Ministra Redemptionis* (cf. the Constitution on Indulgence No. 8 norm 1) and as *Ecclesia ut unum Corpus Christo Capiti iuncta* (cf. No. 6) stands as intercessor on behalf of her member. They intended to refer to a prayer of a quite specific kind, one which of its very nature can be infallibly sure of being heard. It is this for four reasons: because of the indefectible and assured holiness of the praying Church[27] (though these attributes are certainly not present in the individual man), because of the task entailed by this very nature which she has to act as intercessor on behalf of her members,[28] because of the gift for which she is praying, which is certainly salvific in a positive sense[29] (this is something which we cannot know in the case of many other gifts which are prayed for), and because the pope, so far as his contribution is concerned, has given his authorisation to this prayer in the highest possible sense. It was emphasised by the exponents of this new theory – albeit in a different context – that such a prayer can actually be identical with the exercise of a supreme authoritative and sacramental power and also that in the case of indulgence it is capable of having the force of an *opus operatum*.[30]

A prayer precisely of *this* kind transcends the situation in which we have to opt between two alternatives, 'mere prayer' on the one hand and the act of a *potestas auctoritativa* on the other. And for this reason it is not excluded by the teaching of the Constitution. At most, therefore, it could be said that the Constitution rejects a particular interpretation of the 'new' theory which, however, even apart from its being rejected here, oversimplifies and falsifies the theory itself, and goes against its true meaning to an intolerable extent (indulgence = *any* kind of prayer of the Church). Already at this stage in our considerations, therefore, we can boldly put

---

of this prayer cf. especially apart from the references already adduced, K. Rahner, 'A Brief Theological Study on Indulgence', this volume, pp. 150–165.

[27] On this cf. the proof passages adduced on pp. 175–176, 178–179 and in nn. 17, 18 and 24–26. For further illumination on the theology of the subject cf. above all K. Rahner, 'The Church of the Saints', *Theological Investigations* III (London and Baltimore 1967), pp. 91–104; 'Church of Sinners', 'The Sinful Church in the Decrees of Vatican II', *Theological Investigations* VI, pp. 270–294.

[28] cf. K. Rahner, 'A Brief Theological Study on Indulgence' in this volume, pp. 150–165; *idem, Theological Investigations* V (London and Baltimore 1966), pp. 419 ff., *idem,* 'Why and how Can We Venerate the Saints?', *Theological Investigations* VIII (London and Baltimore, 1972), pp. 3–23 *idem,* 'One Mediator and Many Mediations', *Theological Investigations* IX, pp. 169–184.

[29] cf. above p. 178, n. 24 with references.

[30] E. Schillebeeckx regards the essence of indulgence as consisting also in an 'assurance of the intercession of the whole Church given by the authorities of the Church' (p. 352), though admittedly he does not explain any further the specific character of this prayer.

forward the proposition that the Constitution and the 'new' theory cannot be proved to be irreconcilable.

4. This becomes still clearer when we explicitly remind ourselves of precisely *why* the 'new' theory seeks to interpret indulgence as a prayer of the Church (made with authoritative power and 'in itself' infallibly effective). Two principle reasons are assigned for this.

(a) If the indulgence *precisely as such* is conceived of as a prayer of the Church, but precisely as *prayer*, then the danger of misinterpreting the nature of indulgence is essentially diminished. It is all too easy to represent the effectiveness of indulgence in terms which are extremely mechanical and automatic. Often the role of the personal penance of the recipient of indulgence is reduced to a minimum and regarded merely as an *external* prior condition for its reception rather than as an *intrinsic* element and as a *concrete* measure of the objective way in which the gaining of the indulgence takes effect in its recipient. It cannot be contested that there have been, and that there still are, theologians who conceive of indulgence in these terms. It has still to be shown that their theories, so far from being demanded by the Constitution, are actually ruled out by it, if we understand it rightly and work out all its implications to the full. The misinterpretation in question is excluded right from the outset, however, if indulgence is understood as a prayer of the Church (of a quite specific kind), because however infallible a prayer made on behalf of another may be in itself, in its objective effectiveness *in the concrete instance* it depends upon the dispositions of that other. Furthermore these dispositions must also correspond to what the 'object' of the prayer is which the petitioner seeks to attain to in the specific case. There is a possibility here, therefore, of misunderstanding the act of the 'authoritative power' of the Church in a sense which is extremely dangerous for the practice of indulgence, the possibility, namely, of holding that this authoritative act is absolutely incapable of failing to achieve the ultimate effect which it is intended to achieve, provided only that on the part of him for whom it is intended a few conditions are fulfilled which are easy to fulfil and also easy to ascertain. Now in terms of our objective statement of the case and of our religious teaching, this danger is not sufficiently guarded against when we speak *only* of the *potestas auctoritativa* of the Church. Once this is realised we can speak easily and in terms which can be understood of the immediate, and not merely of the ultimate object of this prayer: of the grace which the Christian receives to perform his penance in a spirit of love[31] in order

[31] This exercise of penance under the power of grace is the immediate 'object', analogous in a certain sense to the *poenitentia interior* which constituted the *res et*

thereby to attain to the blotting out of the temporal punishments due to sins.

(b) Once we have recognised that the 'prayer of the Church', understood in the right sense, enters into the very nature of indulgence, this should have the effect of unequivocally ruling out one quite specific conception of what a 'jurisdictional act' means as applied to indulgence, a conception which, if it is not actually directly and explicitly ruled out by the Constitution, certainly forms no part of its teaching. The conception we have in mind is this:[32] that the indulgence takes effect simply and *only* in virtue of the fact that a specific part of the 'treasury of the Church' is assigned to an individual (*per modum solutionis*: the Church 'pays' what the sinner would have to pay), and this acts as a substitute for the *reatus poenae temporalis* which has been imposed by the justice of God in its purely vindictive aspect. This part of the treasury of the Church is simply bestowed upon the sinful individual provided only that he has no actual attachment to sin as *reatus culpae*, without him himself having to change anything else. Now precisely *this* conception of indulgence as being essentially jurisdictional is excluded from the outset once we admit the element of 'prayer'. For this prayer – authoritative, uttered in 'power' and in itself infallibly effective – is a petition on behalf of the repentant sinner for that grace which is necessary in order that he may more swiftly, more 'surely' and more happily overcome the 'reliquiae peccatorum' which are something more than a *mere* external debt of punishment conceived of in purely legalistic terms.[33]

At this point we arrive at questions which carry us beyond the problem of a 'terminological' discrepancy between the Constitution and the 'new' theory of indulgence and of how this apparent contradiction is to be overcome, and which bring us directly to a question which is central to the matter itself. Just as the purpose of interpreting indulgence as prayer of the Church is, properly speaking, twofold, so too here we are concerned with the problem of how precisely we should interpret the dispositions necessary for the effective reception of indulgence, and also with the question of how the blotting out of the 'temporal punishments due to sins' is more

---

sacramentum for Thomas, and brought about by the *potestas ordinis* of this sacrament. The blotting out of the temporal punishments due to sins, therefore, is the ultimate 'object', analogous to the *res sacramenti* in the sacrament of penance.

[32] It is found, for instance in L. Billot, cf. K. Rahner, *Theological Investigations* II (London and Baltimore 1963), pp. 185, 191 ff., 199–200 with n. 14.

[33] On this cf. K. Rahner, 'A Brief Theological Study on Indulgence', in this volume, pp. 150–165.

precisely to be conceived of. This latter question in turn entails a consideration of what precisely these temporal punishments themselves consist in. Naturally these two questions are closely interconnected. But they must be treated of one after the other even though this procedure must inevitably be a laborious one.

V

1. The Constitution lays special emphasis upon the fact that in order for the indulgence to become objectively effective the recipient of it must have the right dispositions. And it treats of these dispositions in an extremely penetrating way, and far more fully than in previous official pronouncements of the Church on the subject of indulgence. In order to gain the indulgence the believer must be 'apte dispositus' and (cf. No. 8, norm 1) '*debitis dispositionibus praeditus*'[34] (cf. No. 10). A '*sincera metanoia et coniunctio cum Deo*' is demanded as a necessary prior condition (cf. No. 11). It is stated that for the most part the dispositions for a plenary indulgence can only be attained in a '*congruum temporis spatium*' (cf. No. 12) – certainly an insight which has hardly been given any emphasis in earlier teaching on indulgence. In norm 5 it is demanded as a condition for gaining a particular indulgence that the believer shall be '*corde saltem contritus*', though here it still surely remains an open question whether this is intended to refer merely to a necessary disposition or to an attitude which is already adequate from all points of view.[35] In norm 7 it is required that '*omnis affectus erga quodcumque peccatum etiam veniale*' shall be

[34] The explanation of these dispositions put forward here in No. 10, namely love for God, abhorrence of sin, veneration for the communion of saints, is certainly of basic importance both in itself and as a prior condition for the gaining of indulgence. But it still leaves the question open of whether the conditions mentioned here are enough. We shall be able to answer this question in the negative, for in norm 7, to which we are just coming, it is made clear that more is demanded for a '*plena dispositio*' of this kind. On the whole question cf. K. Rahner, 'Disposition', *Sacramentum Mundi* II (Freiburg/London 1968), pp. 92–94.

[35] Ultimately we can answer this question in the negative. Even the justified who, as such, is *corde contritus* can undoubtedly entertain such an 'inclination' ('*affectus erga peccatum*' norm 7), so that as a result the possibility is excluded, so far as he is concerned, of any blotting out precisely of the *reatus poenae temporalis* with which he is still burdened in the concrete. On this cf. K. Rahner, 'A Brief Theological Study on Indulgence', p. 158 f. of this volume; *idem*, 'Sündenstrafen', *L.T.K.* IX (Freiburg, 2nd ed. 1964), 1185–1187; *idem*, 'Ablass', *L.T.K.* I, 52 f. On the historical background cf. now E. Schillebeeckx, *op. cit.*, esp. pp. 333–349 (Bibliography).

excluded in order to gain a plenary indulgence. Certainly this is understood as a demand arising *ex natura rei*. Nevertheless one question still remains obscure, namely how – at any rate with the majority of Christians, for after all these are regarded as capable of gaining a plenary indulgence, this condition can be fulfilled in practical terms, even though it is stated in No. 3 that *all* men engaged in their earthly pilgrimage commit at any rate minor sins, and commit them every day.[36]

We must avoid adopting a line of thought which is impossible the psychological point of view, and have due regard to man's real existential situation as it exists in ontological fact.[37] This means that we must recognise that man cannot suddenly, swiftly and at will change his attitude (this is something which, once more, would run counter to the ideas of the Constitution itself) from a sinful inclination on the one hand, or a total conversion on the other to the opposite attitude, from any *affectus erga quodcumque peccatum etiam veniale* to a total conversion or vice versa. We must recognise that the achievement of any such radical conversion cannot be conceived of otherwise than as a gradually maturing process (this is also important for any genuine understanding of what is meant by the blotting out of the temporal punishments due to sin). And if we do recognise this then we shall recognise also that, to say the least, such arduous and elevated dispositions are required in order to gain a plenary indulgence that they can surely be fulfilled only in a very few cases by the individual who is, and who continues to be, a sinner.[38]

[36] In this we rely primarily upon D.S. 228 and *Lumen gentium* No. 40, where the most important passages for a Catholic understanding of the doctrine of *Simul justus et peccator* are to be found. On this cf. K. Rahner, 'Justified and Sinner at the Same Time', *Theological Investigations* VI (London and Baltimore 1969), pp. 218–230; *ibid.*, p. 279 (with bibliography).

[37] On this cf. K. Rahner, *art, cit.*, pp. 225 f. etc. The whole range of problems involved is discussed in H. Reiners, *Grundintention und sittliches Tun* (Freiburg 1966) (with extensive bibliography, pp. 204–212 of the same work).

[38] In passing it may be noticed that norm 7 presupposes that if a plenary indulgence is not obtained by reason of some deficiency in the totality of the dispositions required, a *partialis indulgentia* will be gained. But in that case, according to norm 5 and No. 12 the extent of this would have to be conceived of in such a way that through the intercession of the Church as taking effect in the indulgence 'as much' of the temporal punishments due to sin would be blotted away 'as' the actual *work* of gaining the indulgence itself was capable of wiping away. But surely this must imply some limitation of the effectiveness of such a 'plenary' indulgence which has failed to attain its goal, which presumably represents a departure, to some extent, from the usual idea of this effectiveness as previously taught. Hitherto it was probably assumed that such an indulgence blotted out at least all the temporal punishments due to those sins which really were repented of. Did the theologians responsible for this Constitu-

Now when we consider these statements in the Constitution with regard to the necessary dispositions for an indulgence to become effective, surely we can lay down the following conclusions:

(a) The necessity for such dispositions is emphatically insisted upon.

(b) It becomes clear, at least from norm 7, that a temporal punishment due to any given sin cannot be blotted out so long as any kind of *affectus* towards it still survives. Finally we shall have to conclude from No. 3 that in actual fact this is generally the case in the life of the individual Christian.

(c) In the Constitution the question of how the relationship between these necessary dispositions and the blotting out of the temporal punishments due to sin is to be conceived of in more precise terms is left completely open. As we shall have to show at a later stage, very different ideas can be arrived at as to what the precise nature of this relationship is. No particular position is adopted upon this question in the Constitution itself. And this means that it cannot be invoked *against* any particular interpretation of what this relationship consists of such as, for example, is assumed in the 'new' theory of indulgence. What is really meant by this in concrete detail can only be made completely clear in the sixth section of these considerations.

2. The questions of how we are to think of the 'dispositions' in the 'new' theory of indulgence, and how, on the basis of this, we are to conceive in more concrete terms of the relationship which they bear to the effectiveness of indulgence have still to be answered. But we shall be in a better position to develop these questions and to make them comprehensible in connection with the next topic which is to be treated of in the following section. For this question of the dispositions, and of the precise relationship they bear to the manner in which the indulgence is made effective, is most closely connected with the question of the actual temporal punishments due to sins, and how we are to conceive of these in more precise terms. But for this latter question (and the different opinions which theologians hold upon it) we shall have to refer to earlier presentations and to go into these fairly thoroughly. At the same time it is equally essential and unavoidable to repeat certain points here too, and to compare them with the teaching of the Constitution. This in itself is enough to serve as some indication of the subject which we have to treat of in the section which follows.

---

tion really think out this question? In any case we see here also how arduous the dispositions are which are demanded as appropriate for the indulgence to become effective.

VI

1. How does the Constitution conceive of the 'temporal punishments due to sins' and, *arising from this* – a point which is obvious – of the manner in which they are blotted out? The first point that strikes us as manifest is that in the Constitution there is no question of distinguishing precisely between the different terms which occur in this context. The term which is, of course, used most often is *poena temporalis pro peccatis* (cf. norm 1 and frequently), but side by side with this other terms too are used such as *poena*, this term being employed in a more basic sense than the German *Strafe* (punishment),[39] and implying everything that is hard to bear in the way of toil, pain, death etc. (cf. No. 2, No. 11); 'reliquiae peccatorum' (No. 3[40]; 7; 8); 'peccatorum sequelae poenales' (No. 3).

In our present context this variation in the use of terms is not unimportant. It is in itself sufficient to show that the Constitution appears to regard the 'painful' (*poena*) consequences of sin ('reliquiae peccatorum') as something that is *interior*, connatural and arising from the very nature of sin itself rather than as a punishment which has come to be attached to sin merely *ab externo* and *merely* imposed by the 'vindictive justice' of God, which would mean that it was also capable of being remitted by a mere external act on God's part. This point will become still clearer when we consider the arguments adduced by the Constitution for the existence of such *poenae temporales pro peccatis debitae*. They are presented not merely as imposed by the vindictive justice of God (this being conceived of according to the image of a judge imposing penalties in the context of social and civic life) as something that is supplementary, external to the sin itself and independent of those consequences which flow from the very nature of its guilt. Instead in the Constitution these *poenae temporales* are considered as the consequences of the sin itself, though naturally they also serve to manifest the holiness and sublimity of God, and in that sense also

---

[39] We would have to consider in greater detail the fact that the German term *Strafe* (punishment) and the Latin term *poena* are very far from being completely equivalent concepts, and from this point of view alone difficulties arise from the aspects of psychology and religious pedagogy. 'Painful consequences of sin' would be a more accurate translation of *poena temporalis pro peccatis*. In this we would need never for one moment to overlook the fact that these 'painful consequences of sin' are an expression and an effect of the justice and holiness of God, and that they can and must be experienced and interpreted precisely in *this* sense in faith. cf. also p. 183, n. 35.

[40] In this passage it is not made clear whether the '*vel*' between '*poenae*' and '*reliquiae*' is to be taken in an explicative or a disjunctive sense.

have, or are capable of having, a vindictive character.[41] Even when a radical conversion has taken place in the sinner the temporal punishment due to sins can, and for the most part actually does, remain at first as a connatural consequence which, considered as the residue of the actual sins themselves (*reliquiae peccatorum*), is still not *ipso facto* removed even by the sinner's conversion. It is laid down (cf. No. 2; No. 3) that every sin causes a disturbance of the *ordo universalis* and constitutes an injury to the immeasurable benefits received by the individual and by the human community as a whole.[42] These consequences of sin which achieve objective reality in the 'world', and which are painful to the sinner, are the concrete manifestations of the '*poenae temporales pro peccatis debitae*', and they are not *ipso facto*, necessarily or in all cases removed by the conversion of the sinner however radical this may be. For this reason these *poenae temporales* can also survive even after this radical conversion on the part of the individual, a point which the Constitution emphasises as a dogma of the Church, agreeing in this above all with the Council of Trent.

Now if we think out the full implications of these indications in the Constitution, if we realise that the *poenae temporales* are realised in the

[41] Because these consequences of sin arise from the painful experience of running counter to the abiding nature of man and of the world in the concrete, these being created by God and being maintained by him in their nature as hostile to the decision of the sinner, it can and must also be said that according to this conception the *poenae* are '*a divina sanctitate et justitia inflictae*' (No. 2). It is easy to recognise that these two aspects and statements are not mutually contradictory from the fact that in the same context these *poenae* are given concrete expression as *dolores, miseriae, aerumnae hujus vitae, mors*, factors which are undoubtedly themselves connatural consequences of our own or another's guilt. One further point may be noticed here, namely that the concept of punishment as a connatural consequence of sin does not exclude the concept of an 'external' punishment, but rather includes it: human acts (even the most 'interior') are always brought to their fulness by being objectified in the 'world' (to which the physical side of the nature of the spiritual person also belongs). For this reason too all human activity necessarily experiences the 'repercussion' of this world with its concrete structures so that of its very nature such activity is always constituted as an indissoluble unity of action 'from within' (expression) and *at the same time* passion 'from without' (impression), *actio* and *passio*.

[42] Once we recognise that the gracious self-bestowing of God upon the world and its history, and at the same time the personal and physical nature of man are also to be reckoned as part of the *ordo universalis*, we can say in all freedom (even though the Constitution itself does not take this into account) that any violation of God's law and any personal offence offered to God, who wills to bestow himself in Christ through grace (these are aspects of sin which are emphasised in the Constitution), are, in a true sense, identical with, and *ipso facto* involved in this damage and distortion done to the *ordo universalis*.

concrete first and foremost in the *dolores, miseriae, aerumnae hujus vitae* and in death (cf. No. 2), then the conclusion which follows logically and inescapably from this is that the blotting out of these temporal punishments due to sins cannot be conceived of according to the conceptual model of an amnesty from a merely externally imposed punishment, a sentence which has so far not been carried out, and imposed by a justice which is, in its turn, external, vindictive and coercive. These injuries and distortions of the *ordo universalis* cannot be removed by a mere 'amnesty'. They must themselves be removed, though this can take place either more slowly and with greater difficulty or more swiftly and easily (cf. the '*citius*' of No. 5 and No. 10, the '*facilius*' of No. 9) according to the possibilities that are offered and the efforts made by the individual. This is the basis from which we must, in all logic, form our concept of how indulgences are made effective, and which still remains to be explored in its own right.

The idea of the blotting out of the temporal punishments due to sins (whether with or without indulgences) sketched out above is based on what the Constitution itself has to tell us about the nature of these temporal punishments. It can now be seen to be wholly in line with the indications supplied by the Constitution. Certainly one point must be conceded with regard to the presentation in the Constitution itself. After a long theological development in No. 8 it arrives at the formal concept of indulgence as an '*auctoritativa dispensatio*' of the '*thesaurus Ecclesiae*' '*ad poenae temporales remissionem*'. It then proceeds to use this formal concept in its further developments without reflecting any further upon its own previous indications with regard to the nature of the punishments due to sins and how these punishments are blotted out. In other words it is not explicitly brought out what precisely are the *middle terms*, demanded by the very nature of these indications themselves, which link the authoritative interposition of the treasury of the Church by the Church herself (cf. norm 1, '*Ope Ecclesiae . . . quae . . . thesaurum . . . dispensat et applicat*') on the one hand with the actual blotting out of the temporal punishments due to sin on the other, seeing that these latter must bring about a positive restoration of the *ordo universalis* in its full integrity. But the fact that this is not explicitly brought out does not prevent us from paying due heed to the indications supplied by the Constitution *prior* to the theological development in No. 8 with regard to the blotting out of the temporal punishments due to sin. We must not forget that these also have an application when it comes to the blotting out of such punitive consequences of sin precisely through indulgences. The purpose of these temporal punishments is defined as '*ad purificandas animas*' (No. 2), so that it still has to be concluded that the soul would remain 'unpurified' if these punishments were simply remitted by nothing more than the 'granting' of an amnesty in the purely legalistic sense. It is laid down that according to the witness of the Fathers the aim of the prayer of the Church is that the penitent shall be 'washed and purified' (cf. No. 6). Even the faithful in purgatory are described as members of the '*Ecclesia* (*se ?*) *purgans*';[43] in other words a punishment in the purely vindictive sense is not conceived of even in the case of purgatory. For such a punishment would simply have to be endured without having any saving or enriching effect upon the soul itself. It is laid down that the souls in purgatory '*purificantur*' (No. 3). In accordance with this in No. 11 *every* kind of blotting out of the temporal punishments due to sins (in other words through indulgences also) is qualified as '*sanctificatio et purificatio*'. A further point of importance is that the other 'means' of blotting out the temporal punishments due to sins mentioned in the Constitution cannot be reconciled, without the help of arbitrary and artificial devices, with any idea that this blotting out is a purely legalistic amnesty for a mere vindictive punishment imposed *ab externo* but still not carried out. These 'means' consist in an ever closer union with God and Christ (as head and body) in the unity of love,[44] though admittedly this can be achieved in the most divers ways (the celebration of the Eucharist, the sacrament of penance, the scaramentals, works of devotion, penance and charity: No. 11). Even the temporal

[43] cf. No. 10. The expression is somewhat strange, unusual and lacking in clarity, but this is inevitable in view of the reality with which we are here concerned. It would be better if we could speak of the *Ecclesia purganda* or the *Ecclesia se purgans*.

[44] cf. No. 11. In this connection it must, of course, be realised (even though in the treatment of indulgence in the actual Constitution itself there is no clear consideration of this point) that this love consists not merely in that initial and basic orientation to God which must necessarily be present in every true repentance (*corde contritus* Norm 5), and which removes the *reatus culpae* as such. More than this, this love must be understood as a love which in increasing measure subsumes the individual, with all the complex realities of his makeup, within itself and in *this* way blots out the *reliquiae peccatorum*. This precise point is plainly stated when it is explained in No. 11 that all the means of blotting out the punishments due to sins have this in common ('*hoc unum commune*'), '*quod sanctificationem et purificationem eo validius operantur quanto aliquis arctius Christo capiti et Ecclesiae corpori per caritatem conjungitur*'. This is also the basic pattern of the blotting out of the punishments due to sin through indulgence, and this not merely because what is being spoken of here is all the *subsidia* of the blotting out of the temporal punishments due to sin, but also because it is explicitly stated that the blotting out which takes place though *indulgence* too is subsumed under (*inseritur*) the *ordo caritatis* (No. 11). On this cf. K. Rahner, 'A Brief Theological Study on Indulgence', pp. 158 ff.; *idem*, 'Indulgences', *Sacramentum Mundi* III (Freiburg/London, 1969), pp. 123–129.

punishments due to sins, therefore, are blotted out – whether through indulgence or without it – through that 'purification and sanctification' which takes place through the increase of that love which unites us with God in Christ and the Church. This is to be understood not as a mere 'sentiment' or attitude of mind, but as a power which gradually permeates the whole reality of man in his concupiscent and hitherto sinful nature, and orientates him to God.[45]

In the light of this conception of how the punishments due to sin are blotted out we can look *backwards*, as it were, and obtain a clearer view of the real nature of these punishments due to sin. This is a point which by this time has already repeatedly been made in contexts in which we reject a purely legalistic conception. On the other hand when we direct our gaze forwards it becomes clear precisely *how* we are to think of the blotting out of the punishments due to sin, including that which is achieved through indulgences. Indulgence too must be one of the ways in which the Church can contribute to bringing it about that an ever deepening love, and one which more and more integrates all within itself, is increased in the individual. It is a love which 'sanctifies and purifies', and *in this way* overcomes the 'temporal punishments due to sins' considered as the con-natural consequences of the sins themselves. When, therefore, we think out the full implications of the indications supplied by the Constitution with regard to the punishments due to sin and the various ways in which these are blotted out, it becomes clear that in fact there is both a distinction (analogous to the distinction between *sacramentum validum* and *sacramentum fructuosum* or that between *sacramentum* and *res sacramenti*) *and at the same time* a middle term between the action of the Church in granting the indulgence and the effective blotting out of the temporal punishments due to sin in the recipient of the indulgence. This middle term is the increasing of love.[46] The act of the *potestas auctoritativa* of the Church in the indul-

---

[45] For further investigation into this cf. especially K. Rahner, 'The Commandment of Love in Relation to the Other Commandments', *Theological Investigations* V (London and Baltimore 1966), pp. 439–459.

[46] It is also clear that what is formally the same effect cannot have several formally distinct causes. But if (a point which no-one will contest) the increase in love is *one* way of removing the '*peccatorum sequelae poenales*' (No. 3), then it necessarily follows that according to a right understanding of the nature of love on the one hand and the basic and self-evident metaphysical axiom mentioned above on the other, that this way must be *the* way of diminishing the temporal punishments due to sin. All other '*rationes seu viae*' (No. 8), all '*subsidia*' (No. 11) of this process of blotting out, can be, understood merely as forms and expressions, or as various means by which this growth in love is achieved or made manifest. This applies to indulgence also. But the

gence, therefore, is to be defined in such a way that it can contribute to this increase in love, and in such a way that it becomes comprehensible why and how it can do this. It is true that in its definition of indulgence (cf. No. 8, norm 1, norm 2, norm 5) the Constitution passes over this 'middle term'. But this is not surprising, and certainly cannot be adduced as a counter-argument against the existence and necessity of this middle term. The fact of the omission may perhaps be attributed to the further fact that it was never sought in the Constitution to take up any explicit position on a controversial question of theology. Alternatively it may have been the intention of the Constitution to formulate the meaning of indulgence precisely in the terms which have up to the present been traditional of a theology which fails to perceive, or even which denies, this middle term. But this does not mean that the Constitution itself identifies itself with any such denial. The omission of this is just as unremarkable as, for instance, in the case of a definition of a sacrament which passes over the significance of its character as *sacramentum et res*, and regards the sacramental sign and the ultimate sacramental effect as connected directly with one another without any middle term.

2. From this we can now see that the agreement, or at least the lack of contradiction between the Constitution and the 'new' theory of indulgence clearly goes far beyond what we have already established at an earlier stage, chiefly in section IV. The true pith and essence, the really central significance of the 'new' theory does not come to light so long as we reflect merely upon the key term 'prayer'. We shall only come to understand what is the really central point in the whole theory if we take as our starting-point not a juridical concept of the temporal punishments due to sins (after the model of the vindictive punishments imposed by the civil powers *ab externo*) but a genuinely theological, and so too a genuinely anthropological concept of what these punishments consist in. This also makes it clear how every blotting out of these punishments, and so too that achieved in indulgences considered as a means, really is subsumed (*inseritur* No. 11) under the *ordo caritatis*. We have already said enough on this point here and elsewhere, so that what has just been said does not need any further development or justification.

Once we have realised that indulgence has its due place in this sense in the *ordo* and the increase of that love which blots out sins and also the punishments due to sins, an apparent contradiction in the Constitution

---

theologian must not confine himself merely to describing the material differences between these *subsidia*. He must also work out the formal identity of their cause.

itself is also removed. At one point (cf. No. 9) the Constitution states that through indulgence a closer union with God is attained to *'facilius'*, in other words that the blotting out of the temporal punishments due to sins takes place more easily through indulgence than apart from it. This is reminiscent of an idea which often occurs with wide variations in the common conception of indulgence, and which has undoubtedly played a major role in the practice of indulgence hitherto. In earlier conceptions of what indulgence means this 'easier' (and 'cheaper') way of being freed from the punishments due to sin is presented plainly and without any further preamble: the debt of punishment is conceived of as a reality which can exist side by side with *any and every* interior attitude or condition on the part of the individual who is in a state of grace ('dispositions'), including that particular disposition which is demanded as an external prior condition for the effective gaining of the indulgence. The indulgence itself is conceived to remove this debt of punishment (through something else being substituted for it from the treasury of the Church *per modum solutionis* without anything further being demanded beyond the 'dispositions' (the conditions for gaining the indulgence taken as a whole) already mentioned, even though these of themselves do nothing to remove the debt of punishment. In all this the individual concerned does not have to grow and mature in love amid the pains involved in this process of maturing. All this is implied in the common theory of indulgence. But if it is really the case, then admittedly the blotting out of the temporal punishments due to sin is indeed 'easier'. In fact it is even 'cheaper' than when it takes place in conditions of pain through the individual's own penance, in which love matures until it gradually subsumes the whole sinful and concupiscent being of the individual within itself and so 'purifies' him from the punishments due to sin.

Now against this Paul IV lays down in his Letter, *Sacrosancta portiunculae*:[47] *'Non est igitur indulgentia facilior via . . .'*, but at basis the assistance offered by the mystical Body of Christ to the sinner in his weakness in order that he may really achieve that radical metanoia which still

---

[47] cf. *A.A.S.* 58 (1966), p. 632. In note 39 the Apostolic Constitution actually quotes this text: *'Iis vero christifidelibus, qui paenitentia ducti hanc "metanoian" adipisci nituntur, eo quod post peccatum eam sanctitatem affectant, qua primum baptismate inducti sunt in Christo, obviam it Ecclesia, quae etiam largiendo indulgentias, materno quasi complexu et adiumento debiles infirmosque sustinet filios. Non est igitur indulgentia facilior via, qua necessariam peccatorum paenitentiam devitare possumus, sed est potius fulcimen, quod singuli fideles, infirmitatis suae cum humilitate nequaquam inscii, inveniunt in mystico Christi corpore, quod totum "eorum conversioni caritate, exemplo, precibus adlaborat"* (Const. dogm. de Ecclesia *Lumen gentium* c. 2 n. 11)'.

always remains difficult. Indulgence, therefore, is not a *substitute* for the difficulties involved in the exercise of love, and it is not in *this* sense that it is the 'easier' way of blotting out the temporal punishments due to sin. Rather the indulgence is the assistance of the Church which supports the works of love, always difficult as these are, and precisely in *this* sense renders them 'easier'. The indulgence does not make it easier for the individual in the sense that it is a substitute for *that metanoia* which can actually in itself constitute a blotting out of the punishments due to sin, or in the sense that it takes the place of this *metanoia*. On the contrary it makes it easier for the individual precisely by demanding this same *metanoia* of him. The indulgence is not a substitute for the acts of love and penance in the concrete circumstances of the individual's life, but rather the assistance which he needs in order to perform these, and therefore it achieves its true purpose to the extent that these concrete exercises are brought to their fulfilment by the power of grace and through the free will of the individual concerned. If, therefore, on the basis of certain pronouncements of Paul VI, we have rightly interpreted the term *facilius* as used in the Constitution, then the apparent contradiction in it is resolved. But it does become apparent that even this explanation of Paul VI's only achieves its full force when it is taken in full earnest and accorded its due value on the basis of the 'new' theory of indulgence. According to the common theory of indulgence it can be said that through indulgence we can *devitare* the *necessaria peccatorum paenitentia*, at least in part, those penances, namely, which, were it not for the indulgence, we would have to perform in order to blot out the punishments due to sin. But even this point is contested by Paul VI. The 'new' theory states that indulgence is the assistance offered by the Church in order that the sinner may perform, and may fulfil more resolutely and more radically those necessary penances without which there can *never* be any blotting out of the temporal punishments due to sins. According to the common theory of indulgence indulgences and penance are – at least in part – two alternative means of blotting out the punishments due to sin set side by side for the individual to choose whichever he likes. So that the believer acts prudently when he avails himself of the first means, namely indulgence, because this way is simpler and 'easier'. According to the 'new' theory of indulgence indulgence is one 'means', namely the assistance of the Church, by which we can achieve the other 'means' (namely penance), this second being always, everywhere and without exception indispensable.

In the light of this a further difficulty can now be resolved which seems to tell against the 'new' theory (and also against the pronouncements of the Pope quoted above). This is one and the same problem as that which is also to be met with again and again in the theology of the sacraments when we seek to bring 'sacramental' devotion and the 'existential' devotion which we achieve in the concrete individual circumstances of our lives into a genuine relationship one with the other – in other words when we reject the false conception of the *opus operatum* as a more comfortable *substitute* for the *opus operantis* and instead conceive of the *opus operatum* as the sacramentally effective sign of the grace of God precisely *in order that* the *opus operantis* may effectively be fulfilled in the concrete circumstances of the individual's life.[48] Certainly, on any true understanding of the 'new' theory we can make the following assertion: That state of soul in which, as the ultimate *effect* of indulgence, a specific 'measure' of the temporal punishments due to sin are blotted out (for the sake of clarity this 'material' or 'quantitative' way of speaking of indulgence cannot be avoided), has this same effect of blotting out even when no indulgence is gained, provided only that it is really present or is really achieved.[49] If we did not have to say this, then indulgence and sacrament would precisely be a substitute for the exercise of the free will in faith and love, and at basis we would be putting forward an impersonal, in fact a magical conception of sacrament and indulgence. We would no longer be in a position to say with Paul VI: '*Non est igitur indulgentia facilior via qua necessariam peccatorum paenitentiam devitare possumus*'. But this does not mean that indulgence and sacrament are rendered superfluous. They are, in a special way of their own, God's offering of grace ('a grace which is offered') made manifest in the act of the Church to make the act of belief more possible and to intensify it in the concrete circumstances of the individual's life, that act of belief in which man responds to, and so achieves, salvation (as 'a grace that has been accepted').

VII

This harmony or (at least) this lack of contradiction between the two conceptions of indulgence must be still further illumined by another point in the teaching of the Constitution, its teaching namely concerning the 'treasury of the Church'. In No. 5 the Constitution reacts sharply

[48] cf. the references to more details expositions cited above, p 176, n. 18 and p. 179, no. 25.

[49] It is also important to recognise this in order to arrive at a right theological interpretation of what is meant by the new definition of a partial indulgence in No. 12 and in norm 5. However we cannot enter any further into this point here.

against a material or unquantitative idea of the treasury of the Church: *'Non est quasi summa bonorum ad instar materialium divitiarum quae per saecula cumulantur'.*

To say this is neither so obvious or so superfluous as it might appear to a man of our own times. In the earlier theology of indulgence the question was explicitly raised – and solved again and again – of why this 'treasury of the Church' was not exhausted, especially as it was thought to be made up of the 'superfluous' penitential practices of holy Christians who did not need the benefit of these exercises for themselves, so that they were applied as indulgences on behalf of others in the manner of an individual payment made from a large general fund.[50]

The treasury of the Church is the one total Christ (*'est ipse Christus Redemptor'*, No. 5) as head and members, upon whom, from whom and in whom God is gracious to the individual sinner. The doctrine of the treasury of the Church is, as is clear from the Constitution (No. 5), materially speaking identical with the *'perantiquum dogma'* of the *'communio sanctorum'*.[51] Now this interpretation of the 'treasury of the Church', if its

[50] On the treasury of the Church cf. K. Rahner, 'Kirchenschatz', *L.T.K.* VI (Freiburg, 2nd ed. 1961), p. 257 (with bibliography); *idem, Theological Investigations* II (London and Baltimore 1963), pp. 182, 184 f., 193, 199 f.; *Theological Investigations* V, p. 428 f.; *L.T.K.* I, 52; *Sacramentum Mundi* III, pp. 123–129; *'A Brief Theological Study on Indulgence'*, pp. 223–229; cf. the study by O. Semmelroth mentioned on p. 170, n. 11, 'Theologie des Ablasses', II. 'Der Kirchenschatz.' On the historical background cf. E. Schillebeeckx, *'Der Sinn der katholischen Ablasspraxis'*, especially p. 343 with n. 58, 349. On the interventions at the Council on the subject of the concept of the treasury of the Church cf. the documents already cited above p. 168, n. 6. In this certain considerations put forward by Protestant theologians on the concept of the treasury of the Church are also particularly valuable, e.g. B. M. Lackmann, 'Überlegungen zur Lehre vom "Schatz der Kirche" ', *Arbeiten zur kirchlichen Wiedervereinigung* (Graz 1965), pp. 75–157; P. E. Persson, 'Der wahre Schatz der Kirche', *Lutherische Rundschau* 17 (1967), pp. 315–327.

[51] It is striking that in the description of the 'treasury of the Church' the Constitution does not particularly draw upon or emphasise the value of the salvific deed of this Christ (made up of head and members) in terms of 'satisfaction' and precisely for the blotting out of the *punishments due to sin* as such. The treasury of the Church is simply Christ's deed of salvation (including the salvific works of all the justified to the extent that this has a salvific significance for all others). On this view of the treasury of the Church it would perhaps have been better to avoid the word *'dispensare'* (No. 8, norm 1) and perhaps to use the term *'applicare'* (norm 1) alone. 'Dispensare' does have too strong a connotation of a sharing out of this 'treasury' portion by portion. And this is precisely not intended. But can one *dispensare* that which is *'Christus ipse'*? At this point the problem of the theological terminology in the doctrine of indulgence becomes extremely acute. The Constitution passes over (and in the context with which it is concerned justifiably so) that question which is of such urgent importance

implications are freely thought out to the full, is very far from that interpretation of the meaning of indulgence which strives to overthrow the
'new' theory of indulgence. The 'treasury of the Church' is, in fact, not
divided into small 'portions' (as the anonymous commentator in the
Osservatore Romano still formulates it) in indulgences, and so distributed
to the recipients of these. This point has already been emphasised, for
instance, by P. Galtier, who certainly cannot be suspected of being a seeker
out of novel movements in theology.[52] And in fact no-one can conceive of
the matter in these terms either, who is really prepared to accept the full
implications of the description of the 'treasury of the Church' in the
Constitution. For this treasury is not anything which is susceptible of
being divided into 'portions' and so distributed. It is applied to each in its
entirety, for it is *ipse Christus*. This application, therefore, in which Christ
applies himself through the medium of the *potestas* of the Church to the
sinner, can only be subject to a finite limitation in the achieving of its
ultimate effect because of the finite limitations of the recipient himself,
because of his 'dispositions' with which he responds to this application and
voluntarily attains to what is intended precisely under its *influence*.[53]

---

for theologians and historians of dogma and theology, namely of why and how the
concept of the 'treasury of the Church' has been arrived at and formulated, seeing
that in the last analysis the reasons for it in the history of the theology of indulgence
are quite secondary ones. Moreover at basis this term is very far from being necessary
in order to express the reality it is used to signify, and constantly incurs the danger of
those very misinterpretations which the Constitution guards against and actually has
to guard against. cf. also p. 195, n. 50.

[52] cf. P. Galtier, *De paenitentia* (Rome, 2nd ed. 1950), pp. 517–546.

[53] This statement does not exclude the fact that – on the *analogy* of intercessory
prayer made by an individual, which appeals to the *infinite* kindness and compassion
of God – the intercession of the Church too also has, of its very nature, different
degrees. In other words even prior to the question of whether the finite dispositions
of the recipient are sufficient for the application of Christ to take effect the prayer of
the Church itself is also finite and has different degrees. In the light of this, and taking
a basic view of the matter, the distinction between plenary and partial indulgences
(which is in itself possible) should not be rejected out of hand. The question must
remain open here of whether this distinction is as important in terms of the concrete
reality of Christian living as the conceptual difference seems at first sight to be. It has
already been pointed out above that according to the Constitution itself it will not be
easy really to gain a 'plenary' indulgence. The majority of 'plenary indulgences' are in
fact probably only gained as 'partial' ones (cf. norm 7, second paragraph). In the case
of the partial indulgence, if the conditions necessary for gaining it really exclude
'*omnis effectus erga quodcumque peccatum etiam veniale*' (norm 7, first paragraph), and
accord this withdrawal its real and radical force, then in practice this indulgence is
really 'more perfect' because then that love is made real in it which in any case blots

In No. 11 the Constitution emphasises that Christians have a *'sancta et iusta libertas filiorum Dei'* either to gain indulgences or not to appropriate them for themselves. It emphasises that there is much else in the life of Christians considered as the working out of salvation which, by comparison with indulgences, is 'better' and 'more effective' because it is necessary. But, saving the teaching of the Church, this is not to make the actual objective existence of indulgences in the Church simply dependent upon the freedom of the children of God. Thus the all important point is rightly to explain the nature of indulgence, to assign it its proper place in Christian living as a whole, and to incorporate it into the *ordo caritatis*. Only in this way do the possibility and the hope remain that the Christians of today and tomorrow will maintain a living and personal attitude towards indulgence, or will acquire this anew, an attitude which can also be translated into practical works. We may properly doubt whether the usual scholastic theology of indulgence is suitable to achieve this.

The Apostolic Constitution makes us free to enter upon ways of achieving a better understanding of indulgence. Indeed it itself opens up such ways. Thus indirectly it supplies a fresh stimulus to oecumenical dialogue, and this too – in spite of all the obstacles that remain – should not be too lightly esteemed. When, for instance, the Constitution explains that Christ the Redeemer *is* the *'thesaurus Ecclesiae'*, then it is taking over almost word for word elements in the early Lutheran theology of indulgence,[54] even though, when we come to interpret this definition more closely, we have to recognise once more that more profound differences make their appearance. On the basis of an *approfondissement* of the Catholic theology of indulgence it is possible to achieve a more balanced understanding of the theological position at least of the younger Luther.[55]

---

out all the punishments due to sin. A similar problem also arises in the case of the offering of Mass with regard to a limitation of the effectiveness of the Church's act. On this cf. K. Rahner, *Theological Investigations* V (London and Baltimore 1966), pp. 436–438; but especially K. Rahner and A. Häusling, *Die vielen Messen und das eine Opfer* (Freiburg, 2nd ed. 1966), pp. 51 ff., 56 ff., 75 ff., 80 ff. (Opus operatum and Disposition), 91 ff.

[54] In this context it is altogether noteworthy that Martin Luter, in his theses on indulgence (58th Thesis, 72nd Thesis with explanation) can repeatedly explain that 'Christ' himself is 'the sole treasury of the Church', 'that he himself is the true treasure'. For references and further details cf. P. E. Persson, *'Der wahre Schatz der Kirche'* (cf. n. 50), pp. 318 f.

[55] cf. also E. Iserloh, *Luther zwischen Reform und Reformation* (Munster, 2nd ed. 1967), pp. 30 ff., 41 ff., 56 ff. cf. also the judgment of Iserloh's (*Luther zwischen Reform und Reformation*, p. 40) on the theory of indulgence maintained by the

But more than this, this *approfondissement* will have the effect of causing a discernible change in the situation as a whole, from one of endemic controversy to one of genuine dialogue.[56] In spite of numerous incontestable reservations[57] and points of detail in the papal Constitution which may seem inadmissible, it should not be forgotten that certain genuine and original principles of the Reformation have found official acceptance in a formal document of the Church.[58] Not the least of the points with regard to this document which will be of concern to the theologians of the different Churches is that they must not let the good will for a critical reappraisal shown here fail, or the considerable potential of this beginning, modest certainly, yet encouraging too as it is, to be wasted.

---

younger Luther; H. Bornkamm, *Thesen und Thesenanschlag Luthers* (Berlin, 1967) pp. 48–60.

[56] cf. the words of H. Bornkamm on the contemporary situation in theology: 'They are still always the same questions to which Luther had already pointed. And it is most impressive to listen today to his objections against the doctrine of indulgence of that time coming from the mouths of Catholic cardinals and theologians. In a whole series of key points a clear agreement has been manifested with Luther's criticism in the ninety-five theses' (*op. cit.*, p. 61).

[57] Thus for instance we would still have to enter particularly into the problems of how indulgence is to be measured. On this cf. the position adopted by U. Semmelroth, *Zur Theologie des Ablasses*, section V (cf. p. 170, n. 11), pp. 69 ff.

[58] It should not be forgotten that, especially in the early and the main periods of the Middle Ages the differences in the practice and the teaching of indulgence were often startling in the extreme. On this cf. L. Hödl, *Die Geschichte der scholastischen Literatur und der Theologie der Schlüsselgewalt* I (Munster 1960). The same findings appear in E. Schillebeeckx's article, '*Der Sinn der katholischen Ablasspraxis*', especially pp. 336 ff., 339, 346, 348 f.

IO

MARRIAGE AS A SACRAMENT

In the current scene both within and without the Catholic Church marriage constitutes one of the most popular topics of discussion. Admittedly in this, even in the case of discussions within the Catholic Church, it is only rarely that the discussion centres upon marriage as a sacrament. Here, however, it is precisely this question of dogmatic theology, however 'theoretical' and out of touch with current thought it may seem to be, that is to be treated of. This question and no other besides. For in fact that which has been forgotten, neglected and thrust into the background is still very far indeed from being less important than that which fills the columns of the newspapers and the Church's periodical literature, or even which has been made the subject of a papal commission. Perhaps it is not altogether useless from the 'practical' point of view too to enquire into what is, *precisely on a Christian understanding,* the heart and centre of marriage. What does it mean to say that married love is sanctified by God's grace? How does that which every marriage is in any case and of its very nature acquire new and deeper roots in virtue precisely of what takes place at the *sacramental* level? What part does marriage as understood in this sense play in the life of the Church at the level of theology and faith? Is it not necessary to view the institution of marriage once more in its theological and spiritual origins, seeing that at the deepest level it is on this basis alone that the concrete problems of life can be endured and solved? In the article which follows an attempt will be made to take a first step in this direction.

A valid marriage between two baptized Christians is a sacrament, one of the seven sacraments of the Church of Christ. In what follows we shall be exploring, to some extent, this straightforward statement which has been defined as part of the faith of the Catholic Church.[1] For in fact it

---

[1] cf. D.S. 1001, 1801. For a more detailed treatment on this (with bibliography) P. Adnès, *Le Mariage = Le Mystère chrétien. Théologie sacramentaire* (Tournai 1963), pp. 100–104; H. Rondet, 'Introduction à l'Étude de la théologie du mariage' = *Théologie, Pastorale et Spiritualité. Recherches et Synthèses* 6 (Paris 1960), pp. 97 ff.,

cannot be said that we have really understood this statement merely on the grounds that we 'know' about it in the sense that it strikes us as well-known and familiar, and to this extent is firmly rooted in the contents of our catechism, whether in its printed or unprinted form. The aim we have set ourselves is not directly or properly speaking to establish that this statement is contained in the 'sources' of revelation.[2] Nor shall we be defending it as a matter of theological controversy against the theology of the Reformation.[3] Here we shall only be attempting simply and straightforwardly to understand precisely *what* this statement really means and says. It is inevitable in the very nature of the case that in this we will have to concern ourselves with questions which are both extremely difficult and extremely obscure.

I

We must begin by enquiring briefly into the nature of the *sacrament in general.* In doing so we are conscious of the fact that we are embarking upon a way which is, from the aspect of the history of dogma, as also from that of the methodology employed in this field, a dangerous one. For the general concept of 'sacrament' is – historically speaking and from the point of view of the subject matter itself – a subsequent abstraction which has emerged at a relatively late stage from those seven sacred realities which take place in the life of the Church, but which, when we compare them with one another, turn out to be of very different kinds. An ill-thought out application of this concept which has subsequently been abstracted from them, therefore, in which it is taken as an overall model which is capable only of secondary variations, can make it extremely difficult for us to perceive the real nature of the individual sacrament. However our only purpose in beginning with a consideration of sacrament in general is thereby to acquire an initial orientation. The significance

---

175 ff.; H. Volk, *Das Sakrament der Ehe* (Munster 1952); M. Schmaus, *Katholische Dogmatik* IV/1 (Munich, 6th ed., 1964), pp. 767–828; E. Schillebeeckx, *Le Mariage* I (Paris 1967).

[2] cf. also the manuals of dogmatic theology, e.g. in P. Adnès, *Le Mariage, op. cit.,* pp. 135 ff.; M. Schmaus, *op. cit.,* pp. 781 ff.; cf. also J. Michl and H. Volk, 'Ehe', *L.T.K.* III (Freiburg, 2nd ed., 1959), 677–684; W. Molinski, 'Marriage', *Sacramentum Mundi.*

[3] This is set forth in P. Adnès, *op. cit.,* pp. 95 ff. (with bibliography); cf. also P. Althaus, *Die Ethik Martin Luthers* (Gütersloh 1965), pp. 88 ff.; O. Lähteenmäki, *Sexus und Ehe bei Luther = Schriften der Luther–Agricola–Gesellschaft* (Turku, 1955).

of it is that in a certain sense it makes sure that in our treatment of marriage as such certain definite aspects of it will not be able to escape our notice from the outset.[4]

The first point to be recognised about a sacrament is that it is essentially something that takes place in the *Church*, i.e. not merely something which the Church brings about, as it were, externally in the life of specific individuals, but an event in which the Church realizes her own nature and thereby 'actualizes' herself. A sacrament is something that takes place at that manifest level which belongs to the nature of the Church, not a 'private treatment' in which the Church merely collaborates in some way. This event has the force of a cultic manifestation, an objective symbol, a physical embodiment. It belongs palpably to the historical dimension of space and time, as well as to that of God's self-bestowal in grace upon man.[5] At the same time it also belongs to the nature of the Church which in Christ is the arch-sacrament, eschatologically victorious and indefectible, of precisely this same self-bestowal of God.[6] And finally it is also the free act by which this gracious self-bestowal of God is accepted by him who allows the sacrament to take effect in him, and by his act plays his own part in constituting it as such. In accordance with this we have to distinguish in the sacrament between the sign and that which is signified, between the manifestation and that which is manifested and which has a message to proclaim in hidden form in the manifestation. In the order of the physical person endowed with freedom as he exists in space and time, and in the order of the incarnation, both elements have a connatural relationship to one another, yet are not identical with one

---

[4] For more precise details on the emergence of the general concept of 'sacrament' see G. van Roo, *De Sacramentis in Genere* (Rome 1957), pp. 1–61; J. Finkenzeller, 'Sakrament' III, *L.T.K.* IX (Freiburg, 2nd ed., 1964), 220–225 (with bibliography). On the problem of the sacramentality of marriage in particular cf. P. Adnès, *op. cit.*, pp. 43 ff., 71 ff. (the Fathers), 89 ff. (the Middle Ages), 104 ff. (Post-Tridentine), 132 ff., 134 ff. (Systematic theology); H. Rondet, *op. cit.*, pp. 79 ff. (Middle Ages), 97 ff. (Trent), 145 ff., 153 ff. (Systematic theology); H. Volk, *op. cit.*, pp. 7–18; M. Schmaus, *op. cit.*, pp. 787 ff.

[5] On this cf. K. Rahner, 'The Word and the Eucharist', *Theological Investigations* IV (London and Baltimore 1966), pp. 253–286. My reason for referring to my own works in the course of this article is to give the reader the opportunity to achieve a better understanding of unusual and difficult lines of thought in the context of the general theological system which I have worked out.

[6] On this K. Rahner, *Handbuch der Pastoraltheologie* I (Freiburg 1964), pp. 118 f., 121 ff., 132 ff. See also below, p. 202, n. 7, 210, n. 20, p. 211, n. 21, n. 22 cf. in addition E. Schillebeeckx, *Christus Sakrament der Gottbegegnung* (Mainz 1960), pp. 17–95.

another.[7] The sacramental sign proceeds from the will of God truly to save men, and from the nature of the Church as the arch-sacrament of the grace of God, eschatologically victorious and indefectible. And as rooted in these this sign always has an 'exhibitive' force as the effective and unconditional offering of salvation by Christ and the Church. In this sense, then, the sacramental sign is *opus operatum*.[8] But since grace is only the event of salvation as brought about when it is accepted in freedom, and since this free acceptance can precisely be withheld by man, the sacramental manifestation of grace remains radically indeterminate *precisely from the human aspect*. It can remain an 'empty' manifestation. It can be an invalid or ineffective sacrament, or alternatively it can have the force of really being that 'exhibitive' word which carries what it expresses within itself, the word in which and through which that which it signifies takes place in very truth. Certainly this is far from being an exhaustive description of the nature of the sacrament in general.[9] But nevertheless certain aspects of it have been indicated to which we have to pay due heed in any consideration of marriage as a sacrament.

Marriage is a *sign*. It possesses this character prior to any theological consideration and prior to its bearing upon the relationship between Christ and the Church, because in itself it has a physical and social dimension of reality. Here we have the incarnation, as it were, the real symbol, the manifestation, the 'space-time' dimension, the expression of the most interior and most personal union in love of two individuals at the very roots of their being as orientated in freedom to God. Already here, then, we can perceive that difference and that unity in the elements which go to make up this sacrament inasmuch as this too is the sign at the physical and social level of a personal faith and love manifested in the appropriation of the grace of God as addressed to the individual in the sacrament. Considered purely in itself marriage already constitutes such a unity, in which the two elements remain distinct, of personal love, on the one hand, and its sign at the physical and social level on the other.[10]

---

[7] Apart from the treatments mentioned in nn. 5, 6 with references, cf. on this also K. Rahner, 'The Church and the Sacraments', *Studies in Modern Theology* (Freiburg/London 1965), pp. 206–215; *idem*, *Handbuch der Pastoraltheologie* I, pp. 323 ff.

[8] cf. K. Rahner, 'Personal and Sacramental Piety', *Theological Investigations* II (London and Baltimore 1963), pp. 109–133; *idem*, *Kirche und Sakramente*, pp. 22 ff.

[9] cf. G. van Roo, *op. cit.*, pp. 62 ff., 82 ff., K. Rahner, 'Sakrament' IV, *L.T.K.* IX (Freiburg, 2nd ed., 1964), 225–230.

[10] This is precisely what we mean when we use the term 'real symbol', cf. K. Rahner, 'The Theology of the Symbol', *Theological Investigations* IV (London and Baltimore 1966), pp. 221–252.

This sign, therefore, is both the 'other factor' in which and through which the personal love expresses itself, declares itself and makes itself manifest, and also, under certain circumstances, the *mere* sign which remains 'empty', deprived of its true basis, in which case it precisely does *not* carry with it what it signifies. Obviously this applies to marriage considered both as the sealing of a covenant and as the 'concluding of a contract' (as the canonists put it), and it also applies to married life as such. In both respects we can speak of the unity and the difference which exist between the sign and the reality signified.

II

For the present we shall still be remaining in this dimension of marriage in itself, without explicitly adverting to the precise *sacramental* significance of this sign. The question for us is, therefore, in view of what has been said, precisely *what* is made manifest in marriage in the dimension of the physical, of space and time, and of social living? Up to this point we have concluded that it is the most intimate and personal unity in love between two individuals (of different sexes). We must now see a little more deeply into what this statement signifies. Admittedly this could be achieved in various ways and at various levels. For instance that personal love which forges the most intimate possible unity between two human individuals would have to be considered in its own distinctive nature. Every word of this definition is capable of yielding the deepest insight into the meaning of marriage. Here three further specific aspects are particularly to be brought out: how this love relates to God, the process by which this personal love acquires fresh roots through that which we call grace, personal love as uniting us with the whole community of men.

    1. We would have to begin by saying something about how this personal and unifying love relates to God. To do this we would have to give an account of the entire theological problem of the unity which exists between love of God and love of neighbour, of the relationship which we bear to God, and of our intercommunication among ourselves. And of course this is not possible here.[11] Love of God and love of

---

[11] cf. K. Rahner, 'Reflections on the Unity of the Love of Neighbour and the Love of God', *Theological Investigations* VI (London and Baltimore 1969), pp. 231–249; *idem, Der eine Mittler und die Vielfalt der Vermittlungen = Institut für Europäische Geschichte, Mainz. Vorträge Nr. 47* (Wiesbaden 1967), also Vol. IX of this series, pp. 169–184.

neighbour *mutually* condition one another, even if at first we do not explicitly reflect upon the fresh roots which both acquire through grace. Love of neighbour is not merely a moral task and a duty which is demanded by love of God. More than this, it is the means without which love of God, a right knowledge of God and of our true and total commitment to him, is quite impossible. The transcendental reference which man bears to God can only be realised to the full, can only be experienced for what it truly is and as such freely entered into, in the experience which we have through love of our neighbour. For the 'world' in and through which, according to Christian philosophy and theology, God can be 'recognized' is precisely in its ultimate depths, not merely our material environment, but first and last the world of personal interrelationships. Only one who has encountered this world as a matter of concrete experience, has accepted it in love and freely committed himself to it, can make real to himself and freely accept that transcendental orientation of the spirit in terms of knowledge and freedom, the ultimate basis and absolute goal of which is that Mystery upholding all and upheld by none which we call 'God'. It is this that makes it possible to realise what it is to be so orientated. In this context it is a question of secondary importance (in the light of what is ultimate) how far we succeed in arriving at a free and loving commitment to the world of personal interrelationships such that this involves, at least as something included in it, an experience of our own transcendence, and in this of God also. The question, in other words, of how we succeed in objectifying in conceptual and thematic terms, and setting out in propositional form, that orientation to God which we realise and accept as something that is included in our personal relationships. Even the atheist who truly loves makes experience in his love (provided only that it is what it must be) of God, whether or not he can express this to himself in his conscious thoughts or words.[12] Even in his case the absolute quality of personal love for the 'thou' of his fellow man utters a silent 'yes' to God. It has that quality of self-surrender which is achieved, and necessarily must be achieved, in love, and which can only take place provided that its basic origin and its ultimate goal consist in that which we call God. Or, to put the matter in another way, a love of this kind between human beings is based in its ultimate and connatural depths precisely upon this orientation to God. These ultimate and connatural depths of love consist in its power to attain to the other at the very deep-

[12] For more exact details on this cf. the author's recent work, 'Atheismus und implizites Christentum', *Handbuch des Atheismus*, J. Girardi ed. (Munich 1967), also Vol. IX of this series, pp. 145–164.

est and most ultimate levels of his personhood and his uniqueness. Thus there is a hope of the two beings as they actually exist arriving at what is ultimate and definitive in the existence of them both, and in a love of this kind this hope is positively affirmed. This too has its basis in the ultimate orientation to God as also has the basic faithfulness which such love involves.

2. Now this personal love, which creates the state of marriage as the mode in which to manifest itself, is in fact[13] in the present order of salvation sustained by the grace of God which *always* imbues this love with its salvific power, exalts it and opens it to the immediacy of God himself. Now this can take place even before this love encounters the message of the gospel proclaimed and made known as such in explicit words.

We cannot here set out the special reasons for holding this. Instead we shall assume it as an application of a more general theological principle.[14] This can be formulated in the following terms: *in the present order of salvation a moral act that is truly positive ('actus honestus') is in fact also a salvific act ('actus salutaris') in the proper sense in virtue of the grace which always exalts it and which is offered always to every man by the universal salvific will of God.* This more general principle is, it is true, not universally accepted in Catholic theology. Nevertheless in different forms it has already been maintained in it for a long time, for instance by Vasquez and Ripalda,[15] and materially speaking should certainly be accorded recognition as a prolongation of what the Second Vatican Council teaches with regard to the possibility of salvation for the non-Christian and the inculpable atheist.[16] Doubts have been cast upon, or opposition offered to this principle hitherto by theologians only because they were incapable of rightly appreciating how it is possible, outside the sphere of the *explicit* preaching of the gospel, for that true faith to exist which is necessary for salvation, and also for a salvific act in the true

---

[13] The character of this grace as unmerited is not destroyed by the fact that this *de facto* situation is inescapable. Nor can this be presented as a 'demand' arising from human nature as such at the purely natural level. On this cf. the author's article, 'Concerning the Relationship between Nature and Grace', *Theological Investigations* I (London and Baltimore 2nd ed. 1965), pp. 297–317; 'Nature and Grace', *Theological Investigations* IV (London and Baltimore 1966), pp. 165–188, cf. also p. 219 n. 37.

[14] On this cf. K. Rahner, *Zur Theologie des Todes* = *Quaestiones Disputatae* 2 (Freiburg[5] 1965), pp. 79 ff., 85 ff.

[15] On this cf. Patres Societatis Jesu in Hispania professores, *Sacrae Theologiae Summa* III (Matriti, 3rd ed., 1956), pp. 516–512 (bibliography).

[16] More precise details are provided in the study referred to on p. 204, n. 12.

sense to be posited. But if, for reasons which cannot be treated of here and now,[17] we accept the fact that revelation, and therefore faith too, can also be granted to him who has not been touched in any direct sense by the historical message of the Old or New Testaments, then neither the general principle already mentioned nor its particular application to the special question we are considering here continue to constitute any insuperable difficulty. In other words we can say: in the order of salvation as it *de facto* exists there are no merely 'natural' moral acts on man's part. These acts are *de facto*, when they are posited at all, also upheld by grace and supernaturally orientated to God in his direct act of self-bestowal, and indeed are already in themselves acts which have been made possible by this self-bestowal even though this has not become objectified or explicitated in terms of man's own conscious awareness.

The situation as set forth above applies primarily to the love between human beings where this is made real in the form of a personal and selfless union between two individuals. But this means: *genuine love is* de facto *always that theological virtue of* caritas *which is sustained by God himself through his grace.* In this virtue love is extended to both God and man both in a mutual interrelationship and according to their respective conditions *in such a way that in this relationship the lover achieves his salvation in the event of justification. In this salvation of his he wills salvation for the other also, and in both God is attained to immediately as this salvation in person.* The human love of which we are speaking here, therefore, 'intends' God not merely as a transcendental (not explicitly objectified) origin and goal in his infinite remoteness, but rather attains to God in that absolute proximity in which he imparts his own self – and not in the form of any merely creaturely gift – as the innermost mystery and life of man. In virtue of the fact that it is *caritas*, therefore, this love is also the event of the loving self-bestowal of God upon us which alone empowers us to love God and man. *Caritas*, therefore, is the event of the love of God for us and of our love for God taken as a unity. Unfortunately here we must forego the attempt to translate this statement, which has been made in very abstract terms and on the basis of theological data, as it were into phenomenological terms and to express it as an existential and ontological fact. In this way, and on the basis of the experience of this radical love in itself, we could show that these theological implications of the nature of

---

[17] Apart from the article referred to on p. 204, n. 12 cf. K. Rahner (with J. Ratzinger), *Revelation and Tradition* = *Quaestiones Disputatae* (London 1965), pp. 9–25; idem, *Zur Theologie des Todes*, pp. 80 ff.

love are actually present in it, or at least we could demonstrate the possibility of this.

3. But this love signifies at the same time a unity with mankind as a whole also. This needs to be shown from various aspects. We are accustomed to attribute to married love the character of a special intimacy and exclusiveness in relation to others outside the married partnership itself. We actually go so far as to regard these qualities as constituting what is special in married love as opposed to other forms of love such as love of neighbour in general, comradeship, friendship etc.

Now we do not for a moment intend to deny that married love has this character. Certainly it is consonant with the nature of married love. Nevertheless we ought to ask ourselves precisely *whence* the character of this somewhat startling exclusiveness derives. Is it based upon the ultimate nature of this personal love or are there *also* less basic reasons for it which have to do, rather, with the concrete physical forms and manifestations of this love as these are limited by space and time? Or can it even be that still further determining factors in this exclusiveness are the cultural, social and sociological factors of human living? In other words are some of the factors which go to determine this exclusiveness susceptible of alteration?[18]

But in any case it must be of service to point this out, if only because of the fact that it would be false if we sought to understand married love from the outset as an act of withdrawing behind closed doors where the two partners are isolated from the rest, for this would be, at basis, an egoistical state. Marriage is not the act in which two individuals come together to form a 'we', a relationship in which they set themselves apart from the 'all' and close themselves against this. Rather it is the act in which a 'we' is constituted which opens itself lovingly precisely to *all*. This aspect of the basic essence of such love 'appears' already in the very fact that those united by married love themselves already come from a community. In their love they do not abandon this – indeed they must not abandon it. And their love becomes fruitful in the child that they produce, which for its part in turn must not become enclosed within the 'we' relationship, but must be set free to enter into the wider community of the

---

[18] From this point of view we would have to concern ourselves with certain aspects of the 'crisis' in marriage as this is defined principally by sociologists. It is only by ridding our minds of certain specific patterns of marriage which have arisen in the course of social history that the true essence of Christian marriage can be established in its pristine force.

'all'. Married love, therefore, is, even in respect of its concrete physical forms, a source of, and an initiation into a wider community, and must therefore itself also intend this right from the outset.

This idea needs to be still further deepened. Married love cannot be so intimate and exclusive that it ceases to be love at all. Now of its very nature it is love only when it does not exclude, but rather opens itself to and includes, when it really commits itself ever anew to that which is strange in the other even before it has explored and seen into it; when it trusts itself without condition to accept that which is really 'other' in the beloved as its own (which, in fact, must also constantly be taking place in the intimate partnership of the marriage itself). In the *specific* love for the *concrete* individual man must precisely *experience* what 'love' is in general. He must experience that this is possible really as love and not as flattery, behind which, contrary to all appearances, only egoism and self-assertion lie concealed, in order that he may be able to trust himself in his relationship with the other. But then when he has achieved this his love must not be smothered by both the married partners becoming egoistical to all others. They must not seek to use their mutual love so as to justify a position in which they precisely do *not* love others. They must maintain an openness to all, however much their finite powers and possibilities may in fact impose limitations upon them in this.

Married love too is a readiness, an exercise, a promise and a task, to *love* man *in himself* – something which is more than merely 'respecting' him, merely giving him 'his due' instead of being ready again and again to trust him with one's *self*, to commit one's self to him 'with one's whole heart and with all one's resources'. We are always in debt to all, often, perhaps to those most remote from us even more than to those who are closest. Marriage is the concrete state in which we begin to pay this endless debt, not a dispensation from this endless task which can only be fulfilled by God's help.

A further aspect must now be added to what has just been said. That grace which, as we have seen, sustains married love and renders it open to God in his radical immediacy is the grace of a covenant, which constitutes the innermost dynamism of the world and of the history of mankind in its unity. It is a grace which establishes the one dominion of God over all. So individual a grace, which, in its ultimate depths, is God himself, is directed to the individual in his uniqueness, and this is true however much it may also be the case that, while never ceasing to be this, it is at the same time an 'universal concrete', a unifying grace through which the individual is intended precisely as *belonging to* the *unity* of mankind, as having a place in the people of God.[19] This is not surprising. For the true uniqueness of the existence of each particular individual consists, if it is genuinely to be brought to its fulness and not to lead to an egoistical self-gratification of one's own 'personality', in the unique singleness with which one actually *loves* all. If grace is in this sense the event in which God becomes, for the particular individual, *his* God, it is also, and precisely in virtue of this, the event in which grace not only breaks out of the bonds of egoism in a 'moral' sense and, so to say, at the external level of man's life, but does so in such a way that thereby man is *set free* to transcend the possibilities of his own nature and to attain to *that* infinitude of the freedom of God in which *all* are comprehended in love from the very roots of their existence, and in God can actually be loved in this way even by the creature.

Married love, therefore, is – in spite of, and in its intimacy or exclusiveness – of its very nature and on the basis of the grace of God which sustains it, a state in which we achieve union with mankind, impelled as it is by the selfsame grace. It follows, then, that right from its very origins married love, if its true nature is really attained to, also constitutes a relationship with God, an event of grace, a loving concord with that basic movement in which, through grace, mankind considered as the people of God arrives at the unity of the kingdom of God.

Marriage, as we have said at the outset (1), is the physical manifestation, the sign, the real symbol and the embodiment of this married love, which achieves reality through this manifestation of itself. Marriage – this is what we now have to conclude – is the sign of *that* love which is designed in God's sight to be the event of grace and a love that is open to all. Yet even this insight is still only at the provisional stage in its development. The actual structure of 'sign' in itself has now to be examined more precisely, and that in its *sacramental* character. To accomplish this we shall first compare the sacramental structure of the Church and of marriage in general.

<h2 style="text-align:center">III</h2>

What has just been said about marriage considered as a 'real symbol' of the love which has thus been specified can now also be asserted of the *Church*. Of course in drawing this parallel we have to maintain the force of the distinction which exists between the individual (or a few individuals)

---

[19] Attention has once more plainly been drawn to this aspect in the Constitution on the Church, *Lumen gentium* (Chap. I–II).

and the community made up of all. But this distinction as applied to mankind is not *ipso facto* the same as that between a unity merely in the numerical sense and a numerical multitude. The mutual relationship which exists between the individual and mankind as a whole is different from this. In every individual man everything is present (*homo quodammodo omnia*), and the whole achieves a unique manifestation of itself in each particular individual. The community of mankind for its part is not the agglomeration of the many – all too many, but the unity in love of those, each of whom is unique in his own right, a love which sets each free for his own, which assembles all this and so once more unifies it. In the light of this it is not surprising that we can make the same assertion about the Church *and* about the individual, the more so seeing that even from the point of view of the individual it is a genuine community that is in question.

Allowing, therefore, for the general differences in the relationship which the individual bears to the community and that which the community of all taken together bears to the individual, we shall put forward the following proposition: the same 'sign' function which is found in marriage is also present in the Church. For the Church is, in Christ, the archsacrament, the basic sacrament: in him the love of God for mankind in his act of self-bestowal achieves its historical manifestation through grace in the loving unity of mankind.[20] In this parallelism which exists between the 'sign' function in marriage and in the Church respectively, one further particularly noteworthy element, as well as a difference which will be of importance in our later considerations, must be brought out. The special aspect in this parallelism is the following one. We have said that in marriage a difference exists between the sign and that which is signified, between the marriage as it exists at the physical and social level and married love. This difference can be so far-reaching that in the individual case the two entities – even though this is against the mutual relationship which is connatural to them – can actually be torn apart. The same is also true of the Church. Here too the sign ('Church as basic sacrament') and the reality signified are not simply identical. For what the Church points to is not herself. Rather as sign, i.e. as a socially organised community constituted by a common creed, a common cult and common works of charity, she is precisely the sign of that humanity, consecrated and united by grace (in interior faith and justification), the grace-given unity of which

[20] On this cf. J. Alfaro, 'Cristo, Sacramento de Dios Padre. La Iglesia, Sacramento de Christo Glorificado', *Gregorianum* 48 (1967), pp. 5–27; P. Smulders, 'Die Kirche als Sakrament des Heils', *De Ecclesia* I, G. Baraúna ed. (Freiburg 1966), pp. 289–312; *idem*, 'Sacramenten en Kerk', *Bijdragen* 17 (1956), pp. 391–418.

extends far beyond the social organism of the Church.[21] On the other hand a further and more essential distinction is to be found within this common difference: the 'sign' function in the case of a particular marriage can sinfully be degraded into a lie when that which it is intended to manifest and to render present is not present in itself, namely the love that is grace-given and unifying. In the Church as a whole the intrinsic connection between sign and reality signified can no longer radically be destroyed in virtue of the eschatological victory of grace in Christ. Nevertheless the basic parallelism between marriage and the Church continues to exist. The following proposition applies just as much to the Church as it does to marriage: she is the sign, at the palpable level of historical and social human life, of the fact that *that* love is being made effective and victorious throughout the whole of humanity which is the love of God for us and of us for God, the love which comprehends and unifies all so long as no-one sinfully denies it.

We cannot develop any further the doctrine of the Church as the basic sacrament of salvation (and therefore of that love which is salvation) at this point.[22] Here we must be satisfied with what has already been said, since what we are concerned with is the parallelism between marriage and the Church. When we compare the Church with marriage we are thinking of the Church simply as she is, the Church who is what she is simply in virtue of the mutual love between her and Christ. But while Christ is in this sense included, at the same time it is not *merely* a summary description when we say simply 'Church'. For she is also the basic sacrament of grace and of the love which unites us all precisely in virtue of the fact that in her a *social* unity of truth, hope and love is brought about among men in themselves. This aspect belongs just as much to her character as basic sacrament as her unity with Christ which she expresses in creed and cult, and which thereby constitutes the manifestation of her unity with Christ in the *pneuma*.

Indeed we can actually make bold to proceed a stage further: the unity of the Church which she presents as the model and basis for the unity of marriage – in the dimensions of the sign and of the reality signified alike – is, nevertheless, so far as that precise aspect is concerned which we are considering here, *de facto* constituted through the love of men in the Church and the manifestation of this at the level of social and communal

[21] On this cf. K. Rahner, *Handbuch der Pastoral Theologie* I, pp. 121 ff., 132 ff.; *idem*, 'The New Image of the Church', pp. 3–43, esp. pp. 12–25 in this volume.

[22] On this cf. the studies quoted on pp., n.6, 201 and 7 and p. 210, nn. 20, 21 In addition, K. Rahner, *The Church and the Sacraments*, pp. 193–201.

life. But this love is not something that belongs to another dimension altogether, but rather precisely that same love which unites married spouses – including all that deeper theological dimension which belongs to it. But in that case we can also say: *the love that unites married spouses contributes to the unity of the Church herself because it is one of the ways in which the unifying love of the Church is made actual. It is just as much formative of the Church as sustained by the Church.* The term 'Church-house', signifying the sort of local Church which is constituted by a family unit, is more than a mere pious image.[23]

This correspondence and parallelism between Church and marriage, therefore, is not merely an external similarity between two entities each of which exists on its own and independently of the other. On the contrary the conformity between the two is due to the fact that both have a common root. For marriage as such is, taken as a whole, the manifestation which is creative of *that precise* love which, as the love of God and for God in the divine act of self-bestowal, is constitutive of the union of mankind with one another and with God, and constitutive too of the basic sacrament of this which is the Church. In this we must not overlook the fact that the Church and humanity as made manifest, sanctified and unified in her are in no sense mythical entities but precisely those concrete individuals in themselves who love God and love in God, and give their intrinsic unity a manifest expression in the dimension of history in the unifying society that is the Church.[24]

Now let us see what happens when, on the basis of this fundamental conformity marriage takes place precisely in the sphere of the Church. It becomes precisely that which we are seeking to express when we explain that it is a 'sacrament'. In the light of the principle we have laid down this statement acquires the force not merely of a principle which we already know and understand. Rather this principle only truly becomes intelligible to us in the truths which it itself is intended to express, so that it is no mere abstract concept of sacrament which is applied to the institution of marriage *ab externo*. We must now attempt to clarify this point.

[23] On this cf. the Constitution on the Church, *Lumen gentium*, No. 11. This passage deserves greater attention, and not merely in the context with which we are here concerned.

[24] On the concrete problem thereby entailed cf. K. Rahner, *Theological Investigations* VI (London and Baltimore 1969), pp. 289 ff.

IV

Two baptised individuals voluntarily bind themselves in marriage. In this something takes place in the Church too. Here we do not need to adopt the approach of canon law, or to ask what precise conditions are required by the divine or human law upheld by the Church and from the nature of the case in order that such a bond of marriage (let us not call it a 'contract'!) may take place precisely *in* the Church and in the context of her life as a 'visible society'. But at basis all this is already given in virtue of the fact that it is two baptised individuals that are involved, and a marriage between them, something which always has a social relevance. Because married love has the character of a pointer and a sign, marriage itself is never a mere 'worldly affair'. For this love itself is no worldly affair, but rather the event of grace and love which unites God and men. When a marriage of *this* kind, therefore, takes place in the Church, it is an element in the process by which the Church fulfils her own nature as such, one which is brought into being by two baptised Christians who, through their baptism, have been empowered to play an active part in this self-realisation.[25] As baptised, therefore, they act in a manner which is precisely proper to the Church herself. They make manifest the sign of love in which *that* love is visibly expressed which unites God and men.

Now when the Church achieves the fulness of her own nature in this way precisely at this *essential* level, making it effective in the concrete and decisive living situation of a human individual, there we have a sacrament.[26] In that case there is no need for this purpose of any *explicit* words of institution uttered by Jesus (we could never establish as a matter of historical fact that he ever uttered such words, nor is it even probable that he did so), such as for instance are to be found in the case of the Eucharist.[27] The 'word of institution' in this case consists in two factors: on the one hand in the fact that the religious relevance of marriage is acknowledged and that it is recognised that this too is something that is achieved through the word and the deed of Jesus himself.[28] It also consists

[25] On this cf. K. Rahner, *Handbuch der Pastoraltheologie* I, pp. 146 ff., 151 ff.; *idem, The Church and the Sacraments*, pp. 269–272, 289–294.

[26] cf. K. Rahner, *Handbuch der Pastoraltheologie* I, pp. 323–332; *idem*, The Church and the Sacraments, pp. 202 ff.

[27] On these problems cf. K. Rahner, *The Church and the Sacraments*, pp. 258–264, and M. Schmaus, *Katholische Dogmatik* IV/1, pp. 75 ff.; E. Schillebeeckx, *op. cit.*, pp. 117 ff.

[28] On this cf. the brief survey by J. Michl, 'Ehe', *L.T.K.* III (Freiburg, 2nd ed., 1959), 677–680 (bibliography); P. Adnès, *op. cit.*, pp. 7–42; M. Schmaus, *op. cit.*

in the fact that marriage has been instituted by the Church as an eschatological sign of salvation for the kingdom of God (considered as the absolute proximity of God to man) until the end of time.[29] On the other hand
marriage itself and of itself carries with it its own profoundly significant
theological dimension.

Those theologians who invoked the support of Eph 5 for the sacramental nature of marriage were unable to perceive this point clearly. And
because of this there has always been a certain embarrassment about this
theology which, ultimately speaking, proves to be utterly unnecessary. For
the saying from Gen 2 : 24 which is quoted in Eph 5 appeared to raise marriage *in general* – not merely that between Christians – to a sign of the unity
between Christ and the Church, and it was believed that this could not be
conceded without difficulty. In reality this is perfectly possible if we think
out exactly the full implications of what we have said with regard to the
character of marriage as a sign referring to married love and the special
theological dimensions belonging to this. In Christian theology, in fact,
we certainly do not have to maintain that a sacramental marriage is related to a non-sacramental marriage as a sacrament to a purely secular
human activity. On the contrary both are related to one another as the
opus operatum to an *opus operantis*, and this latter too is wholly an event of
grace.[30] The order in which the one stands to the other here is similar, for
instance, to that relationship which a sacramental forgiveness of sins bears
to a non-sacramental one achieved merely through repentance. For this
too takes place as the outcome of grace and in grace.[31] Marriage does not
become an *event of grace* only at that stage at which it acquires the status of
a 'sacrament'. On the contrary the event of grace in marriage becomes a
sacramental event of grace as *opus operatum* in those cases in which it takes

---

pp. 781 ff.; J. Dupont, *Mariage et divorce* (Bruges 1959); P. Grelot, *Le couple humain
dans l'Ecriture* (Paris, 2nd ed., 1964); cf. also pp. 210, nn. 34 and 35.

[29] On this cf. K. Rahner, 'The Church and the Parousia of Christ', *Theological
Investigations* VI (London and Baltimore, 1969), pp. 295–312.

[30] On this cf. K. Rahner, *Theological Investigations* II (London and Baltimore
1963), pp. 114–133; *idem, Handbuch der Pastoraltheologie* I, pp. 330 ff.; *idem, The
Church and the Sacraments*, pp. 206–215 (supplement with A. Häussling); *Die vielen
Messen und das eine Opfer* = *Quaestiones Disputatae* 31 (Freiburg² 1960), pp. 208–
253.

[31] On this cf. K. Rahner, 'The Meaning of Frequent Confession of Devotion',
Theological Investigations III (London and Baltimore 1967), pp. 177–189; *idem,*
'Die Priesterbeichte', *Knechte Christi. Meditationen zum Priestertum* (Freiburg 1967),
pp. 208–253.

place between two baptised individuals in the Church. The case here is exactly as with the faith which justifies of itself even *prior to* baptism, and which then becomes *opus operatum* in baptism.[32] Up to the present, if I am not mistaken, there has been a strange naiveté among theologians in their approach to marriage in that that distinction and that unity which is familiar to every theologian in the case of faith – baptism, penance – sacrament of penance has not consciously been worked out and applied here. In the two former cases the grace-given event of justification is initiated not merely at the moment when the sacrament as such is conferred, but already prior to this at the stage of faith and repentance. *On the other hand* in the dimension of historical manifestation as such this sign only acquires the character of an *unconditional* pledge of grace from God, in other words that of an *opus operatum* and so of a 'sacrament', when it takes place in the Church and takes its place in the concrete in the context in which such a pledge acquires its historical manifestation. This is the Church herself considered as basic sacrament. When a marriage takes place between baptised people in the Church it constitutes an element in the Church's role as basic sacrament, so that the parties actively share in and contribute to the Church's role as basic sacrament, for both give manifest expression to the unifying love of the grace of God, and a marriage of this kind between them achieves this precisely *as* an element in the social unity of the Church herself. Now because of this the marriage as an event of grace gives rise to a 'sacramental' event of grace in which this sign actively contributes to the irrevocable manifestation of God's pledge of grace to mankind, that pledge which is constantly in force and of which God himself never repents. And this manifestation is nothing else than the Church herself.

On the basis of this conception of the 'institution' of this sacrament we can now proceed more freely to evaluate the findings of dogmatic tradition with regard to the doctrine of marriage as a sacrament. We do not need to force the evidence here so as either to postulate or to construct for ourselves any explicit doctrine hypothetically supposed to have existed right from the outset, in which marriage would always have been considered as a 'sacrament' and as such subsumed under a general concept of sacrament. The less we make use of any such idea – so long as we still understand and experience the 'sacramental' nature of a sign of salvation in the Church – the better it will be. When, therefore, we find this also confirmed by the

---

[32] Apart from the studies already mentioned in n. 30 cf. K. Rahner, 'The Word and the Eucharist', *Theological Investigations* IV (London and Baltimore 1966), pp. 253–286; *idem, The Church and the Sacraments*, pp. 269–272.

dogmatic tradition we should regard this as neither surprising nor shocking.[33]

[33] On the dogmatic tradition of the sacramentality of marriage cf. especially P. Adnès, *Le Mariage*, pp. 43 ff., 71 ff., 76–110; H. Rondet, 'Introduction à l'étude de la théologie du mariage', *op. cit.*, pp. 11–135; E. Schillebeeckx, *Le Mariage* I (Paris 1967). The principle we are stating here could also be taken as the starting-point for a new oecumenical approach. Many Protestant theologians maintain that marriage is not indeed a 'sacrament' but is, nevertheless, a *sanctum*. (Thus, for instance E. Brunner.) In view of this, and setting aside all polemical attacks against an alleged Romish 'sacramentalism' – which, however is based upon a wrong interpretation – the question has still to be raised whether a serious discussion, or even a mutual enlightenment is not possible on this point, to the extent that from the Catholic side we understand how rightly to interpret the sacramentality of marriage. In any case we should not simply apply to it a general and abstract concept of 'sacrament'. This procedure is adopted, for instance, by M. Schmaus, *Katholische Dogmatik* IV/1, pp. 803 f., 806 f., and probably also by K. Mörsdorf, *Lehrbuch des Kirchenrechts* II (Paderborn, 10th ed., 1960), pp. 238–249; cf. also *Münchener Theologische Zeitschrift* 9 (1958), pp. 241–256, esp. 248 f. These authors believe that they have to evaluate the function of the presiding priest in dogmatic terms, and so to treat of marriage in a way which is exactly parallel to the treatment appropriate to the other sacraments. K. Mörsdorf enters quite explicitly into the question with which we are concerned in his article 'Der ritus sacer in der ordentlichen Rechtsform der Eheschliessung', *Liturgie. Gestalt und Folgzug. Festschrift für J. Pascher*, W. Dürig ed. (Munich 1963), pp. 252–266, esp. 265 f. Mörsdorf sees an intrinsic connection between the marriage liturgy and the juridical form of marriage, with the result that he posits the closest possible relationship between the solicitude to ensure the juridical validity of marriage, and the activity of the Church in her function as mediator of salvation. Mörsdorf regards the more recent history of the Church's practice in the case of mixed marriages (especially as a result of the decree *Ne temere* of 1907) as the expression of the Church more and more realising her own power with regard to the forms by which marriage is validly celebrated. In this, according to Mörsdorf's own interpretation, the fathers of the Tridentine Council were not yet able to attain to this realisation. The active assistance of the priest in the liturgical sense is raised to the function of the priest as an active contributor (*persona agens*), so that the 'collaboration of the priest presiding over the marriage is an essential element in the performance of the sacramental sign' (*op. cit.*, p. 266). Mörsdorf is followed in his views by his pupil, G. May, *Die kanonische Formpflicht beim Anschluss von Mischehen* (Paderborn 1963), p. 42. At this point we shall not undertake any investigation of the historical aspects of this problem, even though these continue to be of decisive importance (the function of the marriage customs and rituals in the early and main periods of the Middle Ages, the interpretation of the decree *Tametsi* etc.). Nor can we examine the ways in which Mörsdorf and May use the concepts of 'passive' and 'active' 'assistance'. Nor do we propose to challenge these authors on the question of whether, and to what extent, the Church has the right to decide (in part) the external signs or form of the sacraments. A more important point is the fact that there are phenomena or factors in the Church's theology and practice of marriage which it is hard to reconcile with this thesis: marriages of baptised non-Catholics are

MARRIAGE AS A SACRAMENT

indeed not bound by the canonical form, but are rather valid and sacramental as *matrimonia rata* even without the priest playing any part in them. The marriages between persons of different confessions prior to 1918 in Germany were valid and sacramental even without any Catholic ceremony taking place. Finally reference may be made to canon 1098 (the possibility of concluding a marriage without any collaboration by the priest). When, therefore, Mörsdorf seeks to regard the active intervention of the priest as an '*essential* element' in the sacramental act, then this term 'essential' cannot be taken in a strict sense. For with regard to a requirement that is essential in the *true* sense in the context of the sacraments, the Church has *no* power of dispensation. But if the priest has no constitutive function in the concluding of a sacramental marriage in the strict sense, then it is not immediately clear what is meant here by 'essential element', '*persona agens*', 'active contributor' etc., or whether this in fact demands any theological interpretation. In any case from the standpoint of a sacramental theology such an interpretation is quite unnecessary. With regard to those cases in which the priest plays no active part, or at any rate not an 'essential' one, it is not asserted that the Church has no mediating function at all, as is proved from the example of valid baptism by laymen. Even in historical terms it must be maintained that the introduction of the form made obligatory by the Council of Trent derives primarily from the Church's anxiety for the welfare of the Christian community (clandestine marriages), but in no sense has this anything directly to do with the progressive development of the Church's authority. On this cf. *C.T.* IX, 639 f., 682–685, 761–764, 668f. Precisely with regard to the problems which are raised today on the subject of mixed marriages, the acceptance of this theological interpretation of the essence of marriage would in practice raise a fresh difficulty which, from the point of view of dogmatics, is quite unnecessary. On this problem cf. also L. Hofmann, 'Formpflicht oder Formfreiheit der Mischehenschliessung', *Catholica* 18 (1964), pp. 241–257, esp. 245 f.; F. Böckle, 'Das Problem der Mischehe', *Lutherische Monatshefte* 5 (1966), p. 342 with n. 6; P. J. Kessler, *Die Entwicklung der Formvorschriften für die kanonische Eheschliessung* (Diss. iur. Bonn, 1934, Borna-Leipzig 1934); H. Portmann, *Wesen und Unauflösigkeit der Ehe in der kirchlichen Wissenschaft und Gesetzgebung des 11. und 12. Jahrhunderts* (Emsdetten/Westfalen 1938); R. Lettmann, *Die Diskussion über die klandestinen Ehen und die Einführung einer zur Gültigkeit verpflichtenden Eheschliessungsform auf dem Konzil von Trient =* *Münsterische Beiträge zur Theologie* 31 (Munster 1967), pp. 166 ff. (Conclusion). Unfortunately even with regard to the historical aspects Lettmann does not adopt any position with regard to Mörsdorf's works (for his only remarks on this cf. p. 19, n. 21), and attaches himself without any discussion of other attempts at a theological interpretation to the theses of Wilhelm Bertram, which are primarily influenced by factors of social philosophy. In reply to the more recent hypothesis of K. Mörsdorf I can only offer the present outline of a theology of marriage in general and in numerous points of detail as an alternative suggestion. This could then constitute a starting-point for a further attempt to solve the dogmatic problems entailed in the question of mixed marriages. Even on the interpretation of the form made obligatory by the Council of Trent the last word has not yet been said from the point of view of the history of canon law, a fact which is brought out strikingly in the inaugural address of P. J. M. Huizing, the official canonist for the diocese of Nijmegen, *De Trentse Huwelijksvorm* (Hilversum/Antwerp 1966).

V

What has been said, however, still needs clarification to some extent in terms of what is familiar to us from the catechism as a formal statement of what constitutes marriage as a sacrament. It is customarily said that marriage is an image of the unity of Christ and the Church, and that it is a sacrament in virtue of this. On an initial reading of Eph 5:22–33[34] we may, perhaps, receive the impression that the vital common basis for the similarity between the relationship which Christ bears to the Church on the one hand and that involved in marriage on the other consists in the fact that the husband represents Christ while the wife represents the Church. In that case the unity of marriage as such would itself be a relatively secondary reflection of the unity between Christ and the Church, which in turn would be based on a reflection in which the married partners were regarded as separate from one another precisely in respect of the different roles they play. But surely we would still have to say that even for Paul himself this way of viewing the matter is secondary, conditioned perhaps by the parenetic context and more or less conditioned too by the sociological factors prevailing at the time. On this showing, then, it would not simply be the text quoted as a whole which would constitute a statement of central theological importance, but rather the particular passage of 5:29–33 that would have primary importance in it, for these particular verses bear upon the unity of love as such, as constituted in *one* flesh and body. The relationship of leadership and subordination as expressed in the love of solicitude and help on the one hand, and in obedience, submissiveness and 'fear' on the other, is not the objective factor that is decisive in this parallel.[35] If for our present purposes we can take this as

[34] For the exegesis of this cf. especially H. Schlier, *Der Brief an die Epheser* (Düsseldorf, 2nd ed. 1958), pp. 252–280.

[35] In view of the number of studies a detailed exegetical cannot be undertaken here. On this cf. N. A. Dahl et al., *Kurze Auslegung des Epheserbriefes* (Göttingen 1965), pp. 68–72; F. Foulkes, *The Epistle of Paul to the Ephesians* (Michigan 1963), pp. 154–163; H. C. G. Moule, *Ephesian Studies* (Michigan, 2nd ed., 1955), pp. 281–296; F. F. Bruce, *The Epistle to the Ephesians* (London 1961), pp. 114–120; J. N. Sanders, 'The Theology of the Church', *Studies in Ephesians*, F. L. Cross ed. (London 1956), pp. 64–75, esp. pp. 71 ff.; H. Schlier and V. Warnach, *Die Kirche im Epheserbrief* (Munster 1949), pp. 25 ff.; H. Conzelmann, *Die kleineren Briefe des Apostels Paulus = N.T.D.* 8 (Göttingen, 9th ed., 1962), pp. 86–88; F. Mussner, *Christus, das All und die Kirche. Studien zur Theologie des Epheserbriefes = Trierer theolog. Studien* 5 (Trier 1955), pp. 147–153; E. Kähler, *Die Frau in den paulinischen Briefen* (Zürich 1960), pp. 88 ff.; J. J. von Allmen, *Maris et femmes d'après Saint Paul = Cahiers théologiques* (Nauchâtel/Paris 1951), pp. 28 ff.; P. Grelot, *Le couple humain dans l'Écriture* (Paris,

established, then all that needs to be clarified here is where, in more precise terms, Christ is to be fitted in in the basic conception put forward in this study. First in the case of Paul it is clear that he regards the order of creation depicted in Gen 2 as belonging to the order of grace and redemption,[36] so that right from the outset that order of creation, and so too of the marriage of Adam, had the significance of pointing forwards to this order of grace. In our terms this is implicitly asserted – albeit on quite different theological principles – when we emphasise that every moral attitude on man's part (and this includes also what is presupposed to such an attitude) is everywhere and in all cases sustained and subsumed by the bestowal of grace by God upon the creature. 'Covenant' is the more sublime and more ultimate factor which, by comparison with the creation considered as the positing of a creature still not determined in a specific direction, has in turn the character of unmerited grace.[37] But precisely because of this 'covenant' is the goal and the all-embracing factor which sustains and subsumes creation as the positing of the condition which makes covenant possible, since it provides the potential covenant partner. This means that objectively speaking everything that takes place in terms of human morality has a hidden relationship to Christ, in whose being and work precisely this imparting of grace finds its eschatological culmination and manifestation. Because he is the goal of it all he provides the basis for the whole dynamism of human history as imparted to it through grace, impelling it towards the immediacy of God.

We are speaking, then, of a unity in love between two human individuals. They are united in a love which consists not merely in the fact that both are aiming at a single common goal in this earthly dimension. This unity, rather, refers to the persons themselves in so far as their orientation to the last end has an eternal validity. And where the unity of love in this

---

2nd ed., 1964); P. Adnès, *Le Mariage*, pp. 39 ff.; H. Greeven, 'Zu den Aussagen des N.T. über die Ehe', *Zeitschrift für evangelische Ethik* 1 (1957), pp. 109–125, esp. 121 ff.; P. Colli, *La pericopa paolina ad Eph. V 32 nella interpretazione dei SS Padri e del Concilio di Trento* (Parma 1951). cf. also n. 36.

[36] On this cf. H. Schlier, *Der Brief an die Epheser*, pp. 262 f., 276 ff. Most recently, especially R. Batey, 'The μία σάρξ Union of Christ and the Church', *N.T.S.* 13 (1967), pp. 270–281; N. A. Dahl, 'Christ, Creation and the Church', *The Background of the New Testament and its Eschatology* (Festschrift for C. H. Dodd), W. D. Davies and D. Daube edd. (Cambridge 1965), pp. 422–443, esp. 437.

[37] On this, in addition to the articles mentioned on p. 524, n. 13, cf. esp. K. Rahner, 'Erlösungswirklichkeit in der Schöpfungswirklichkeit', *Sendung und Gnade* (Innsbruck, 4th ed., 1966), pp. 51–87, esp. 52–75 = *Handbuch der Pastoraltheologie* II/2 (Freiburg 1966), pp. 203–228.

sense is achieved, there we have the operation and manifestation of that grace which constitutes the unity of men in the truest and most proper sense. But the converse is also true. Precisely this same grace, considered as establishing a unity between God and man, is manifested in the unity between Christ and the Church, and that too in a manifestation which has an absolute and eschatological force, and which as goal provides the basis for all other graces and their function as establishing unity in the world. For this reason there exists not merely an external similarity between the unity in love of two human individuals on the one hand and the unity between Christ and the Church on the other, but also a relationship between the two unities such that they condition one another: the former exists *precisely because* the latter exists. Their mutual relationship of similarity is not subsequent to the two but is a genuine relationship of participation due to the fact that the unity between Christ and the Church is the ultimate cause and origin of the unity of marriage.

In the light of this we can also understand that the more precise quality of the relationship between Christ as the *directing and controlling head* on the one hand, and the Church as the *obedient* and submissive *bride* on the other is not simply projected in precisely the selfsame sense into the unity of those united in love through marriage. The unity between Christ and the Church is the basis for the unity between husband and wife prior to the question of whether, and to what extent this unity which is brought about also carries with it all the special attributes of the unity which brings it about. To the extent that the unity of Christ and the Church itself has its source in God's gracious will to bestow himself, both *this* unity *and* the unity of marriage have their basis in the selfsame grace of God, which unites mankind to God and men among themselves. To the extent that the goals of this *one single* will to bestow grace are related to one another as 'cause' and 'effect', since precisely *in* the will by which God intended Christ and the Church everything else is willed, this one particular effect of this grace-giving will (namely married unity) is also brought about by the other effect (the unity of Christ and the Church).

By reason of this mutual interrelationship of the two unities, the unity of marriage achieves its *full* manifestation precisely in the unity of Christ and the Church. And because of this much that would otherwise perhaps have remained obscure and unrecognised in the unity of married love can be deduced from the unity of Christ and the Church. And this remains true in spite of the caution which is necessary in adopting this approach. Thus with regard to the relationship of leadership and subordination between husband and wife in marriage Paul had already, and rightly, perceived that the basis of this was the unity of Christ with the Church, even though it may be true that the relationship which he was seeking to justify in part belonged to *that period alone*, and to that extent cannot have been a *moral demand* in the same sense at all periods. But if we were to take the same principle as our starting-point we could recognise other and similar parallels too: the character of the Cross with which both are imprinted; the irrevocability of the covenant; the provisional nature of both measured by the final and eternal consummation for which the Church[38] and marriage[39] are still waiting. However we cannot delay any longer in this article in explaining and rounding off this point.

Marriage, therefore, reaches upwards into the mystery of God in a sense which is far more radical even than we could have guessed merely from the nature of human love as unconditioned. Certainly all still remains hidden under the veil of faith and hope, and all this may still not be lifted from the lowly circumstances of our everyday lives. There is no question that such a truth does not take place either at a level which is utterly beyond man, his freedom, and his interior assent. There is no doubt, therefore, that those united in married love experience this reality in the same measure as they open their hearts to it in faith and love. Surely it has become clear that such a theology of marriage cannot be understood in that sense in which we introvertedly make it our own 'private affair'. On the contrary genuine Christian marriage has at all times the force of a real representation of the unifying love of God in Christ for mankind. In marriage the Church is made present. It is really the smallest community, the smallest, but at the same time the true community of the redeemed and the sanctified, the unity among whom can still be built up on the same basis on which the unity of the Church is founded, in other words the smallest, but at the same time the genuine individual Church. If we were able to recognise[40] and to live out such a truth in its full significance then we could return somewhat more consoled and more bravely, in a spirit of truly Christian freedom, to our 'married problems', so urgent as they are, yet almost talked to death.

[38] cf. the Constitution on the Church *Lumen gentium*, No. 48.
[39] cf. *ibid.*, No. 35.
[40] On this cf. K. Rahner, *Glaubend und liebend* (Munich 1957); *idem*, 'Vom Gottgeheimnis der Ehe', *Geist und Leben* 31 (1958), pp. 107–109 = K. Rahner, *Glaube der die Erde liebt* (Freiburg, 2nd ed., 1967), pp. 125–128.

I I

THE TEACHING OF THE SECOND VATICAN COUNCIL ON THE DIACONATE

T HE subject which I have been asked to examine here is concerned with the teaching of the Second Vatican Council on the diaconate and the restoration of this.[1] So far as I know, in the various documents of this Council three texts in particular treat of this subject. The most important of these is, of course, article 29 of the 3rd chapter of the Constitution *Lumen gentium*. In addition to this two further texts have to be taken into consideration, namely a passage which falls under No 16 of the Scheme on the Missionary Activity of the Church, a Scheme on which there is still some little work to be done. Here the restoration of the diaconate is treated of from the point of view of the necessity of such a restoration in the missions. A further brief reference to this restoration is to be found in Article 17 of the Decree on the Oriental Catholic Churches, which has already been promulgated. Here it is stated that where the institution of the diaconate as a permanent state has ceased to be the practice it should be introduced once more.

First let us concentrate upon the principal of these passages, that which occurs in *Lumen gentium*. It is not possible for me here to set forth the history leading up to this passage. Here I would only recall the fact that this question is numbered among the five so-called 'test questions' which were laid before the Council on the 3 October 1963. The fifth question asked whether the fathers were agreed on the point that mention should be made in the Constitution on the Church of the diaconate and the necessity for its restoration. To this general question, which was intended merely to provide a general direction for a further working out of this decree, an affirmative answer was given, 1,588 of the fathers voting in favour of it with 525 against. It was, therefore, a notable majority. The work of the theological commission went forward along the lines indicated by this

---

[1] For the concrete occasion in view of which this lecture was composed cf. the list of sources attached to the end of this volume.

vote, with the result that that text was produced which – apart from a few small alterations – we now read in the Constitution.

In a vote taken on the 28th September 1964 the radical necessity for, and possibility of a restoration of the diaconate as a permanent state in the Church was accepted by an overwhelming majority. On the 29th September following the precise points of detail involved were laid before the fathers of the Council. These agreed by a comfortable two-thirds majority that even married men of mature age could be admitted to the order of deacon. On the same day, in the aula of the Council, the fathers rejected, by a majority the extent of which is not known, but which was substantial, the idea that younger men too could be admitted to the diaconate without any obligation to remain celibate. This must be sufficient here with regard to the history of the text. For the time appropriate to a brief lecture does not admit of entering any further into the manner in which these documents emerged and acquired their existing form.

Let us turn our attention to the actual *texts* themselves. In this we shall, normally speaking, be referring to the Constitution *Lumen gentium*. But where it is a question of entering into the reasons which the Second Vatican Council had for believing that the diaconate should be restored we must also refer to the Scheme on the Church's Activity in the Missions which was prepared, because in my opinion the reasons are set forth more clearly and more profoundly there than in the Constitution on the Church itself. I shall be saying a few words more on this point at a later stage.

I

The first point to be made with regard to the teaching of the Second Vatican Council on the diaconate is concerned with the question of the essence of this as a permanent official state and as a sacrament in the Church. In this teaching it is laid down first that the hierarchy of orders in the Church does in fact include, or at least could include, a state which, though subordinate, does constitute a genuine and permanent degree of the sacrament of order. In spite of this, according to the teaching and practice of the Western, as opposed to the Eastern Church, the diaconate has come to be regarded ever since the Middle Ages (apart from a few isolated cases which we cannot enter into here) merely as a necessary stage in the process of being raised to the priesthood. Now in the teaching of the Council, which is in conformity with the earliest and most universal teaching, it is expressly laid down that there is, or at least there could be, a degree in the hierarchy of orders, genuine, permanent and sacramental, which is something more than a mere stage on the way to priestly ordination. It is one which could be, and, under certain circumstances actually ought to be, recognised as a state and a degree in the hierarchy of orders, albeit a lower one, which has a genuine and essential function of its own distinct from that of the order of priest. From this point of view, therefore, the nature of the diaconate is such that it belongs in very truth to the hierarchy of order in the Church herself. It is not a lay state, but belongs to the three official states or degrees in the hierarchy of order itself, so that in all truth and reality deacons belong to the officially instituted and sacred orders which Christ founded in his Church. When, therefore, we distinguish between laymen on the one hand and the hierarchy of the Church on the other, we should certainly not assign the deacons to the lay state, nor should the diaconate itself be understood as in some sense designating the status of outstanding lay functionaries in the Church. On the contrary, the diaconate is, in very truth, a degree, albeit a subordinate one, in the hierarchy of order itself. Now with regard to the tasks which are, in practice, attached to this order of deacon, the passage with which we are concerned distinguishes between these various tasks of the diaconate in almost the same way as in its presentation of the official functions of bishops and priests. A new division has been introduced here according to which three general official functions are envisaged: the function of teaching, the function of sanctifying and the function of leading. It is true that with regard to the third function certain more precise distinctions and provisos have been introduced. But it is still quite evident that in the Constitution on the Church these three general official functions which apply to every official state in the hierarchy of the Church are attributed to the office of deacon also.

This appears from what is said here about the function of preaching the word. It is stated that the deacon's part in this is to read the sacred scriptures to the faithful and to instruct and exhort the people. In other words the function of preaching the gospel is attributed to the deacon too, though of course in union and cooperation with the Church under the direction of the bishop and, in some respects, of the priest too. Thus with regard to the first function, which is attributed to all those who have been officially ordained in the Church, this applies to the deacon too. In the passage under consideration here the function of sanctifying is likewise attributed to the deacon clearly enough. In fact it is stated that it is his task solemnly to confer baptism, to have custody of and to distribute the Eucharist, to assist at and to bless marriages in the Church's name, to carry the Viaticum to the dying, to preside in the liturgy and prayers of the faithful, to dispense the sacraments and to conduct the rites of burial. Again with regard to the function of guiding and leading, we can find something in our text which has reference to the deacon. For in it the task of directing and administering is explicitly adduced. Now it is true that this task of the deacon belongs to the service of the Church and not, strictly speaking, to the guiding of her, this being, in a certain sense, confined to the bishops alone. Nevertheless the deacon does, in a certain sense, share in this task, and it actually belongs to the very nature of the diaconate itself to the extent that explicit mention is made of the task of administration. Of course this is expressed only very briefly and in a few words. On the other hand the task of charitable activity receives just as brief a mention even though this does undoubtedly belong, according to the very earliest traditions of the Church and with a firm basis in holy scripture, to the office of deacon.

Nevertheless we are compelled to say in all honesty that the text itself does not supply much information on this question. Perhaps, on the other hand, the Scheme on the Missions, *Ad Gentes Divinitus Missa* can help us, for these official functions of the deacon are likewise mentioned here. The function of preaching the word is expressly mentioned. It is said that in the missions deacons have the duty of preaching the word of God as cathechists. The function of sanctifying receives slighter mention in that particular Scheme. But to compensate for this it is expressed all the more clearly that the activity of deacons can, in a certain respect, be understood as a function of providing official guidance and leadership, or at least a sharing in this. This is what is meant when it is said that it is the task of the deacons in the missions to act in the name of the parish priest or the bishop in giving guidance to the widespread communities. Again the official function of performing works of charity is expressly mentioned here. It is said that it is the deacon's responsibility actively to engage himself in works expressive of love in the form of social and charitable activities. In this Scheme, therefore, this aspect is developed on a broader basis than in *De Ecclesia* itself.

Now with regard to the essence of this order of deacon, the essential point, and one which finds expression in all the texts we have mentioned, is the sacramentality of the diaconate. On this point the documents leave no room for doubt. What is in question here is a sacrament, a genuinely sacramental consecration, a sacramental grace which is imparted through the laying on of hands.

II

The topic which is being treated of in the main text, and also in the texts on the Eastern Churches and on the missions, is the restoration of the diaconate. In article 29 of the Constitution *Lumen gentium* two sections are devoted to this. The first concerns the theology of the diaconate, the second speaks explicitly of the restoration of the diaconate on which we shall now have something more to say.

This restoration is characterised in the Scheme on the Missions as useful and to be recommended, and in the Decree on the Catholic Eastern Churches it is urgently advocated. The reasons which the texts adduce for this deserve to be considered first. The presentation of these reasons appear, as I have already indicated at the beginning of this article, to have brought about a salutary development between the Constitution *Lumen gentium* and the Scheme *Ad Gentes Divinitus Missa*. In the Constitution on the Church it is stated that the tasks of the deacon as enumerated here are certainly supremely necessary for the life of the Church, and that even though, in the current administration of the Latin Church, there are many areas in which these tasks can only be performed with difficulty, still in the future the diaconate can be restored as a special order in the Church's hierarchy existing as such in its own right. The reason adduced in the Constitution, therefore, is to be sought primarily in the difficulties of the concrete situation. It is said that there can be no question that these tasks are necessary: baptising, preaching, the works of charity etc. And it is further stated that the restoration of the deacon is necessary because, owing to the lack of priests today, it has become extremely difficult to fulfil these tasks. The Scheme on the Missions has not yet achieved final completion. But the reasons put forward here, while they do not run counter to this text in the Constitution on the Church, still differ from it nevertheless in certain notable respects. For this Scheme treats of those individuals who already, in effect, are actually performing the official functions of the deacon by acting as catechists and so preaching the word of God, by acting in the name of the parish priest or the bishop to guide and administer the scattered Christian communities, or by performing the works of charity in social or philanthropic activities. Such individuals, the Scheme states, should be fortified by the laying on of hands as handed down from the apostles so that they may be able more effectively to perform their diaconal functions through the grace of the sacrament. Here, therefore, it is not any actual difficulty, for instance the lack of priests etc. which is adduced, rather it is asserted that the official functions appropriate to deacons already in practice exist in the Church. Now it is assumed as self-evident and actually asserted that since these individuals are actually performing these official functions which already in practice exist in the Church they should, as a matter of necessity or at least of suitability, be further fortified with that sacramental grace which, according to the doctrine of the Church, is truly designed precisely for these official functions. In other words it is simply stated: 'The official functions already exist. We know from revelation that the diaconate also has a sacramental status. Why, therefore, should those individuals who already exercise these official functions of the deacon be deprived of that grace which does *de facto* exist in the Church as a sacramental grace?' The Scheme on the work of the missions, therefore, abstracts from the question of whether or not the external circumstances and difficulties, the lack of priests etc., are so great that fresh resources are necessary to come to the help of the Church's priests and hierarchically ordained ministers in their work. It is simply stated that these official functions are actually in existence in practice and in effect, and that those who perform them should do so in that specifically sacramental power with which Christ has *de facto* endowed his Church.

Now with regard to the restoration of the diaconate itself, the authority appropriate to this is mentioned in both texts. It is said that the conferences of bishops instituted in various forms and over different areas can undertake this restoration. Similarly in the Scheme on the Missions it is said that the appropriate conferences of bishops who have regarded the restoration of the diaconate as beneficial must be the ones to put it into practice. We must, therefore, lay down clearly and unequivocally that according to both texts the proper authority to act in this matter is not the pope but the conferences of bishops. It is to these conferences in themselves, here taken as the bodies from which such action must appropriately proceed, that power is ascribed to decide in this question as to whether it is opportune to bring about such a restoration in the different areas. Of course this must take place, as is also explicitly laid down, in full agreement with the pope or with his assent. Nevertheless it is the bishops who have to take the initiative in this matter, and who therefore have the responsibility of examining and judging as to whether it is opportune to bring about such a restoration in the different territories. It would be mistaken, therefore, for the bishops to suppose that the initiative has to come from the Holy See. On the contrary, the task with which we are here concerned is not directly that of the actual restoration itself, but rather of investigating and judging whether restoration is opportune. And this task is assigned, by the passages from *Lumen gentium* dealing with the missions, to the bishops. Now once such an authorisation has been given there can be no doubt that, for all the difficulties, a manifest duty exists to act upon it also. I do not say that there is a duty to bring about a renewal of the diaconate, but rather a duty to take all possible pains to examine and to judge whether or not this is opportune in a given area.

In the light of this it also becomes clear what is being laid down in these passages with regard to the manner in which the restoration should take place. With regard to the territorial spheres it is immediately evident that these passages do not presuppose that the restoration must necessarily take place everywhere in the world at the same time. There can be no doubt that a given conference of bishops can arrive at the judgment that in their particular area such a restoration of the diaconate is necessary and would be extremely beneficial, whereas another conference of bishops may arrive at the opposite judgment so far as its area is concerned. We have seen that the authorised bodies who have the power to bring about this restoration are the various conferences of bishops. And to this extent it is obvious that it need not necessarily be expedient for a uniform restoration to take place simultaneously throughout the entire Catholic Church. But no conference of bishops can say, 'Since our colleagues in another country are not restoring the diaconate we too can peaceably abide by the practice which has been customary up to the present.' Right from the outset and of set purpose, the text itself provides for the possibility of the restoration of the diaconate being confined to a particular region. But since this is within the power not of the individual bishops but of the bishops' conferences and territorial assemblies of bishops, there is no doubt that in a given country or in a greater area a certain uniformity is necessarily required. I do not believe that an individual bishop can set himself up in opposition to such a restoration against the majority decision of his colleagues who belong to the same conference of bishops. Otherwise it would not in fact have been stated that it is for the conference of bishops to judge of the expediency of this restoration. The idea that this question is within the competence of an individual bishop to decide is certainly contrary to the spirit and the letter of the passages concerned.

After prolonged discussions the decree decides that in any such restoration the diaconate can be conferred upon more mature men as well, and even when they are married. On the other hand it is explicitly laid down that younger men too, when they are suitable, can be raised to the order of deacon, though in this case they are bound to celibacy. In view of this it is evident that the text with which we are concerned itself envisages various classes of deacons. Naturally this now opens the way to further and more far-reaching discussions, the subject-matter of which no doubt presents difficulties of its own. Nevertheless we must accept the text as it stands, and recognise that in any such restoration at least two classes are envisaged: younger deacons who are bound to celibacy, and others who are of more mature age and married, upon whom this sacramental ordination can likewise be conferred. Surely no-one will deny that the diaconate as conferred upon these more mature men will, in practice and in the concrete, have a greater significance and more influence from the pastoral point of view in the life of the Church than the other case which is likewise envisaged in the text concerned.

III

We must now briefly enter into certain further questions which are still left open by the texts themselves. First, the question surely arises of who these men of more mature age are. What actual *age* is envisaged here? The actual terms of the text are extremely general and somewhat vague, and probably this is deliberate, because in this field, after all, there is need for a little further experience in deciding how old married men should be in order to be ordained deacons. Next a further question arises as to what conferences of bishops or regional assemblies of bishops of various kinds the texts intend to refer to. Here too the answer is not easy. The conferences of bishops are so different from one another in respect of the number of their members, their status, the extent of the regions they represent, that in this respect many questions can suggest themselves. On the other hand even this difficulty could, without great effort, be removed because even after they have come to their judgment as to whether a restoration of the diaconate is opportune, it is only with the agreement and assent of the pope himself that this restoration actually takes place.

The text says nothing about the kind of *formation* which the future deacons should undergo. Here too there is much that still needs to be considered and examined in greater detail. Nevertheless I believe that in view of the fact that the Scheme on the Missions envisages men who are already performing the tasks appropriate to deacons, we should regard this in itself as an indication of what kind of formation is required. Those individuals ought to be put forward for ordination who have already *de facto* acquired sufficient formation and experience in the Church's work, and who are already performing the official functions of deacons. On this view not so very many difficulties will arise in our considerations of what sort of formation deacons should undergo as might otherwise be expected. *De facto* such individuals already exist. *De facto*, therefore, they are already, to a large extent, formed and prepared for their diaconal functions and experienced in them. The form and manner of formation, therefore, which has hitherto been considered sufficient for the formation of such individuals will also to a large extent be no less adequate for the formation of the future deacons. Otherwise those who already perform the official functions of deacons would, in fact, have been unable to perform them at all.

A further question which has been left open in the texts with which we are concerned is that of the diaconate as a 'lower' *degree* of order. One statement which has a certain relevance here is that passage in the Constitution on the Church which states that deacons would be ordained not as a preliminary to the priesthood but for a ministry of their own. Nevertheless, with regard to this 'lower degree' several theological questions still remain unanswered. It is stated that the deacon exercises his ministry in union with the bishop and his priests. But what, in more precise terms is the relationship which the deacon bears to the bishop or to the priest or to both together? How can we define more precisely the reasons for representing the order of deacon as a 'lower' degree of order? Much in the way of theological exploration and examination is still needed in order to establish this. Of course it is true that the deacon does not have those functions which, according to the official teaching of the Church, and especially that of the Council of Trent, belong only to the priest, as for instance the administration of the sacrament of penance and the consecration at the Eucharistic Mystery. And to this extent there is a palpable and easily comprehensible difference between the diaconate and the priesthood. From this basis, therefore, we can easily go on to say that the status of the deacon is lower as compared with that of the priest. Nevertheless this does not necessarily or *ipso facto* imply that the diaconate is simply a 'lower' degree from every point of view. When we think of the ministry on behalf of the poor, and of many other tasks which belong primarily to the deacon, it is no longer easy to perceive how the diaconate could be designated in this connection as a lower degree. Moreover, a point which we should particularly notice is that the Constitution *Lumen gentium* carefully avoids saying that the episcopate (*munus episcopali*) is a 'higher' degree, above that of the priesthood. On the contrary, it regards the episcopate as constituting, of its essence, the plenitude of an order that is, though hierarchically structured, integrally one, and that exists in the Church in virtue of a divine institution. Now if we make this way of regarding the matter our own, then we can consider the diaconate too as constituting in its own right an authentic and special mode of participation in this one integral order in the Church. From this it follows that on the one hand we both can and must say that the diaconate is a lower or more restricted mode of participation in this order than the priesthood. But at the same time we do not necessarily have to say that this is the case in every respect. My belief is that the bishop has the most solemn duty of making the love of Christ present in the world in relation to all who toil and suffer, who are poor and weak, who have to bear persecution etc. Now if this task belongs, in a quite primary sense, to the bishop himself, the deacon has no less vital a share in it than any priest. I have decided to mention this one point alone in order to show that the text with which we are concerned still leaves many questions open, both for further theological investigation and also so far as the Church's practice is concerned.

In conclusion perhaps it will be appropriate to return once more to something which has already been said in order to enlarge upon it a little further. When we look more closely into the texts relating to deacons in the Constitution on the Church and the Decree on the Missions, we find that it is not permissible, theologically speaking, to say that the tasks there ascribed to the future deacons can also be performed by laymen, or perhaps by those who, at some point in the future are to be equipped with the lower orders. In my opinion any such conception would be, from all points of view, quite untheological. In the sacrament of order a threefold division exists both in the sacrament itself and in the official functions that go with it, and no-one can deny that from apostolic times onwards the Church has been aware of, has recognised, and has actually exercised her God-given right to impose this division. Now if, and to the extent that, this is true – and it cannot be denied by anyone without danger of heresy – then in my opinion a further point manifestly follows, and one that is clearly stated in the Decree on the Missions. It is that when certain individuals in the Church are in fact fulfilling certain specific functions, then the Church herself must supplement this by conferring on them that grace which our Lord specially instituted precisely for these functions, and which he gave his Church authority to confer in sacramental form. This is the fundamental point for consideration in this whole question of the restoration of the diaconate. It is not some arbitrary question of what functions can or cannot be exercised by whom. It is not some kind of romantic revival which is in question here, of a reality which did in fact exist in the early Church. Rather what we are asking here is whether in our Church of the present day the office of deacon is *de facto* being performed. If, and to the extent that we have to answer this question in the affirmative, or if and to the extent that we have to say that it is absolutely necessary for there to be such an office, given the circumstances of the present day, then this office is to be set up. And if an individual is already suitable for this office, then it seems to me to be necessary on theological grounds that that grace should be conferred upon him which does exist in the Church precisely for the official functions which he is *de facto* performing. Moreover it appears that all other considerations are, from the outset, excluded from this genuinely theological one. We are not in the least concerned with the question of whether absolutely speaking it is possible for laymen too to give Holy Communion to others. No-one will deny that this is possible. But the question that is being asked here is whether the Church really needs individuals who will have the duty of doing this and much else besides as part of their official and permanent functions, and as part of the normal life of the Church. If such individuals are needed, if such a permanent office, together with its functions, can be provided for in the Church, or if, indeed, it actually already exists, then the matter is already decided. The Church already has, in her possession, that sacramental grace which is designed for this office, which is already present and being exercised in her. And this sacramental grace must be conferred on those individuals. Theologically speaking, no other factors enter into the question. This may suffice by way of introduction. Since other theologians will be exploring the nature of the case from the theological point of view, I have been able to confine myself to certain aspects which have, of their very nature, been raised by the relevant conciliar documents.[2]

[2] For a fuller treatment of this cf. the conference report entitled 'Le diacre dans l'église et le monde d'aujourd'hui', P. Winninger and Y. Congar edd. = *Unam Sanctam* 59 (Paris 1966). The concrete occasion for which this lecture was composed was such that it was not possible to enter into the new prescriptions for the diaconate set forth in the *Motu Proprio 'Sacrorum Diaconatus Ordinem'* (cf. the *Osservatore Romano* of 28 June 1967, p. 1). For a more detailed interpretation of this document I may draw attention to the edition with commentary which is to be brought out by Herbert Vorgrimler and published by the Paulinus-Verlag, Trier (= *Nachkonziliare Dokumentation* No. 9). On the situation in Germany cf. K. Rahner, H. Vorgrimler, J. Kramer, 'Zur Erneuerung des Diakonats in Deutschland', *Stimmen der Zeit* 180, (1967), pp. 145–153. For further information on the current movements attention may be drawn to a series of documents entitled *Diakonia*, and produced by the *Internationale Diakonatskreis* at Freiburg im Breisgau (Directors: Mgr. Georg Hüssler and Hannes Kramer).

PART THREE

Eschatology

12

A FRAGMENTARY ASPECT OF A THEOLOGICAL
EVALUATION OF THE CONCEPT OF THE
FUTURE

IN the attempts which contemporary theologians are making to describe how the future provides scope for the preaching of the Christian message one factor which is somewhat lacking is any concrete evaluation of the 'future' as a phenomenon. Perhaps a theologian should allow his hearers to feel more of the perplexity and embarrassment into which he falls as soon as this word is mentioned. For what is it, this future? I suppose that faced with this question we should immediately emphasise that the future does not consist (or at least that it does not consist exclusively) of that which is foreseen in the concrete and which will actually be in existence by tomorrow, since our concrete plans for it are already laid and the means for accomplishing it are already to hand, so that all that we still need in order to bring it to reality is a little more time. Properly speaking, all this already belongs to our present. One of the characteristics of futurity is that it is mysterious, that for the most part we are unaware of it – indeed that we actually suppress the awareness of it in ourselves. And the concrete future which has already been determined by us as depicted above, only partakes of the nature of true futurity to the extent that it is threatened by uncertainties: the question of whether our plans may not yet be thwarted by some alien factor or another, whether we shall not be prevented from experiencing tomorrow in the same way as we experience today by the factor of our death – for instance through heart-failure. Hence evolutionary ideas cannot be taken as a starting-point either for our understanding of the future. For in that case it would in fact precisely be something which we already possessed in our designs and within our abilities, namely that so-called 'natural order' which simply represents a further actualisation of possibilities which we already possess and of which, in principle, we are already aware, even though we need a little more time in order to bring them to reality: just a little more patience, it is already coming! On this view there is a certain pride in our attitude, for we think that our relationship to the future is such that it is already present to us so long as the 'reality' turns out as we have foreseen in our designs and estimates, whether of a theoretical or practical kind. On this showing the future reality is, properly speaking, formed and determined so as to fit in with the plan as it exists in the present. It serves only to confirm the presence of the all-penetrating spirit and the rightness of its calculations. The only interest it still possesses is that it serves as a proof of the fact that we have not made any mistakes in our estimates or in our plans. I cannot avoid the impression that in the attitudes of enthusiasm with which both Western theorists and Marxists view the future there is a constant temptation to confuse the real future with this 'tomorrow which is already here today', and which is based on evolutionary or technical theory or on a combination of both; a temptation, therefore, to call this combination of plans plus time in the sense of being a pure formal and empty interval the 'future', and thereby distorting the true relationship which man bears to the real future, and suppressing the real meaning of future altogether. I have nothing against planning; nothing against that enthusiasm with which we greet the fact that ultimately speaking man is no longer merely subject to the play of external forces over which he has no control, but is himself the manipulator; that man imposes his own existence no longer merely at the theoretical level but at the practical level as well, and that he possesses a futurology; that man already knows what he wants his future to be, and how he intends to ensure that it shall be this; that man can no longer be surprised; that he can calculate correctly and foresee; that he imposes his own will as formed by him today upon tomorrow and, on the basis of what actually is, knows what this same reality is destined to become tomorrow. It is remarkable that all this is already an accomplished fact; that man, with his cunning and yet tormented by the factor of blind chance, has actually managed to catch the approaching event as his prey in the meshes of his own will; managed already in the present to build those paths by which his children are destined to travel – though admittedly here there is one point precisely that still remains vexing, namely that it is our children and not we ourselves who are to travel by these ways. Nevertheless at the same time we have become extremely well informed on our own account. Yet still even this is precisely not the future.

But in that case what is the future? Precisely that mysterious element in that which we are accustomed to call the future, and which, nevertheless, we have deprived of its true nature and turned into a part of the present by anticipating it through our plans and the abilities we have acquired, though we certainly recognise the rights which belong to him who is far-seeing and able. The future is that to which we ourselves cannot reach out, but which rather comes to us of itself – when it decides to – and with which we have to deal, strangely, precisely on *these* terms. The future is that which does not evolve, that which is not planned, that which is not under our control. It is all this, and it is this precisely in its incomprehensibility and its infinitude. The future is that which silently lies in wait, and which, when it springs out upon us, rips up the nets of all our plans, the false 'future' which we ourselves have constructed, so as to make that which we have planned or foreseen a present fact. The true future is that which is uncontrollable, that which is, and which remains in control calmly and silently, incalculably and yet patiently giving *us* the time we need because it itself needs none, for it never comes too late. It is that which cannot be controlled or calculated, which again and again wells up and breaks through the most precise calculations of the future, makes room for them and yet at the same time always makes them provisional and doubtful of accomplishment. It is that which cannot be calculated or controlled, and which has the effect (this is something of which we are convinced, however strange it may be) that in this human history to which we are subject we are never finished with working out the so-called future, and trying to draw it down into the present. It is that which cannot be controlled or calculated, and that in which we cannot intervene. It does not depend for its life on any power of ours, but rather has power of itself. It can of itself make its own impact in that which we experience – but precisely as future. In relation to it we are able to be that which we have to be in order for it to impose itself. But precisely in virtue of this very necessity it confines us to those limitations in virtue of which we ourselves are precisely *not* it, but of our very nature always have before us the element of the uncontrollable in it as the alien factor in our lives.

We cannot escape from the necessity of having to deal with the future precisely because it is not subject to our control. It can be suppressed and forgotten as the spectre which makes fools of us, which the sensible man looks down upon; as our shadow which we cast before us (admittedly it may be asked why that which is sheer nothingness does not swallow up this shadow too and thereby free us from it). But even so this future is there: as the silent expanse, empty so far as we are concerned, within which alone we can trace out our narrow courses of life. It is there as the mystery which we must always take into our calculations in raising those questions which we answer to ourselves. It is there as that which empowers us freely to exercise the power given to us, for this power of ours can only achieve that which we have determined within the sphere of that which we ourselves have precisely not achieved. For we would not be able to begin to achieve it at all unless it was already open to be achieved by us. When we have made some moment of pleasure for ourselves we can command it to stay with us, and it makes no difference whether it punishes us for this by remaining and 'freezing', or whether it strikes us dead by departing from us. We are always guilty when we command it to remain. For of its nature it exists in order to die, in order that by its coming and its departure from us the future, with its incomprehensibility and uncontrollability, may be there and may manifest itself and conceal itself at the same time in all the instabilities of this present as constituted by that which we have decided for ourselves.

We have constantly to come to terms with the true future, even when we are embittered enough, ill-disposed enough, cynical enough or culpably naive enough to seek to achieve a state in which we are untroubled by it. Its silence becomes so loud that we believe we are deafened when death begins to impinge upon our awareness and our senses, when the glory of our past achievements is suddenly transformed before our eyes into the boundary beyond which we cannot pass, yet without our being able to forget that glory, and when that which we grasp at so greedily escapes from us once more by turning out to be that which is not, after all, what we seek in the depths of our being. Now there is a certain attitude of trust which we may discover within ourselves – discover it not merely because it is there (whether accepted or denied) but because it is manifested in us as part and parcel of our conscious presentation of ourselves. This attitude of which I am speaking is one in which we trust that this incomprehensible and ineffable future is not merely that which was and which remains the eternal that pre-exists us, and which serves to show us the limitations to which we are subject, but is rather intended to be and to become the future precisely as *arriving* for us without ceasing thereby to be in itself the nameless mystery. Now supposing that we did in fact have this attitude of trust, what in that case would properly speaking be taking place in this life? What would be taking place in this event in which the attitude of trust and the future itself considered as arriving for us neither could nor should any longer be distinguished from one another, but where there would be a self-commitment in trust (or trust would be ventured upon) as the still-unfolding event of this future precisely in its aspect of arriving, and in this sense as a hope in the future?

Apparently nothing. The world would continue to go on just as it would in any case. We would make plans and ourselves construct the future which would be the present of today and perhaps of tomorrow –

but always as lost in the infinitude of the true future. But yet at the same time everything would be different. But before we raise the question of the reasons for this difference this 'would be' must be corrected. Perhaps it *is* different, not merely 'would be' different. For in fact, to put it at its lowest, it might be the case that we actually *have* this attitude of trust which consists in hope in the true sense; that we are actually making it real and effective, and that all that we still lack is the courage openly to declare that we have it. It would be perfectly possible for a man to be quite incapable of drawing any clear distinction between one who really has this attitude of trust and one who has not. It could even be the case that it is actually achieved, and yet that we can only become consciously aware of the fact that it has been achieved at that stage at which we no longer need to speak about it. The achievement of trust in its fulness in this sense is especially apparent in death, where the individual himself is silent, and where it is not we but the truth that begins to speak. There where this trust is present and where our hope on behalf of ourselves and others also is of *this* kind, there that which is hoped for actually takes place even when this trust has not yet arrived at the stage of reflecting upon itself and being recognised for what it is. We must no longer ask, therefore, what in fact 'would be the case' *if* such a hope was attained to. Rather we already have this attitude of trust and hope, and with this attitude no longer ask what 'would be the case'. We have already long passed the stage of wishing to ask this question. The assumption involved here includes the supposition that with regard to this attitude of trust we are quite incapable of establishing any way of testing or comparing what is and what might be or perhaps is, in the case of a specific individual. Only with this proviso do we ask what would be or is if someone either has, or could have this trust, that the absolute future is that which is actually breaking in upon him.

What does it mean, therefore, for a man to have this trust in the absolute future considered as that which is radically breaking in upon his own life?

First, the world of the future that we construct for ourselves still remains. It would in fact not exist at all if there were no reference to the absolute future, whether this is present as that which is actually coming to meet us or as that which repels us. This absolute future is present as presiding over us in some way or other in that it is made over to us as the 'material' of the future we construct with all its variations between good and bad fortune. The existence of this – as the presence of the future in the temporal sense – is to this extent precious and indispensable. Admittedly from this aspect it must not be interpreted as a future which can be constructed merely in technical terms. It also includes invariably the event of the love which proceeds from the 'thou' to the 'thou', which constitutes, in a manner quite different from the future which can be constructed at the technical level, that which provides a foothold for the future which cannot be controlled. But at the same time this absolute future gives the future which we construct for ourselves its place in the real and effective openness of true human history. There is no future which can be constructed, no plan which would not open outwards and forwards into that which has not been foreseen and which no system can provide for. Every humanism with a predetermined content is relative. It can become other than it is and contains no promise within itself of any abiding permanence. Man is never aware of himself as the being who is open to the mysterious and absolute future in such a way that he could devise any adequate plans for himself. All ideals which he formulates in the concrete remain, when their true nature is not misunderstood, bounded by the 'ideal' of the question which is kept open. The one who exposes himself to the mystery of the absolute future is the one who knows least of all about himself and who defends this awareness of his non-awareness as the ultimate achievement of life and as the ultimate truth which is proper to himself. There are, then, two attitudes to be considered here: first the attitude in which we take with absolute seriousness the future which we can construct, considering this as the medium of the absolute future, and second the factor in this future which can be constructed which makes its contents relative and conditional. It is this latter factor that distinguishes it from the future that is absolute. Now through both of these factors taken together the man who has this trust calmly and quietly faces the vicissitudes of the future which can be constructed with an attitude of ultimate freedom, without falling into any kind of Stoic apathy. He actively engages himself in his lot, taking this as his absolute duty, and endures with composure any corrections which may be imposed upon him by that which is outside his own personal control. For this too is in its turn the onset of the future that is absolute, provided only it is accepted without reserve.

The true future, the ultimate which itself cannot be constructed, takes place quite simply. It comes to meet us. It is intended to be imparted to us as the incomprehensible mystery. We are those who precisely experience the impact of it as a lightning flash in the hope that our darkness may be the blinding effect of its very brilliance; that it is not striking us dead, but rather imparting to us a healing that is eternal. And if anyone supposes that he has no experience whatever of this, he must say that even so he does experience it and is not aware of it, provided only that he accepts his own life unconditionally. But because he is immersed in human history, man can always keep watch to see whether he finds in his history anyone in relation to whom he can entertain this trust for him and so for himself also, in such a way that he attains to that attitude in all its purity in which he submits to the breaking in upon his own life of the absolute future. It is this precisely that is also a promise for us. This would be the starting-point from which we should have to go on to speak in particular of how Christianity is related to the future. But since this has already been done in another context[1] we can break off this fragmentary consideration at this point.

[1] On this cf. K. Rahner, 'Marxist Utopia and the Christian Future of Man', *Theological Investigations* VI (London and Baltimore 1969), pp. 59–68.

13

ON THE THEOLOGY OF HOPE

WE have no intention here of giving the impression that in the pages which follow we could, in any sense, present *the* theology of hope. The title has been chosen with care because only certain aspects of such a theology are intended to be expressed, and the choice of these has been somewhat arbitrary. Hence we cannot set forth, with all the fulness they deserve, the contributions to this subject of scripture itself, of traditional scholastic theology, or of more recent works which have appeared over the last few years,[1] especially those of P. Lain-Entralgo, G. Marcel, E. Bloch, J. Pieper, O. F. Bollnow, J. Moltmann, W. D. Marsch, J. B. Metz, E. Schillebeeckx, H. Schlier, J. E. Fison, A. Brunner, G. Sauter etc.,[2] though in fact all these have made contributions.[3] Moreover, on even a brief survey of the hypotheses which have been put forward from the aspects of philosophy, existential ontology, psychology, depths psychology, moral theology, exegesis and systematic theology, the impossibility is plainly revealed of claiming in any sense to

[1] cf. the bibliography in *L.T.K.* V (Freiburg, 2nd ed., 1960), 423/424 (P. Engelhardt).

[2] Apart from the more detailed works cited in *L.T.K.* V, 423 f. cf. P. Lain-Entralgo, *L'attente et l'espérance* (Paris 1966); J. Pieper, *Hoffnung und Geschichte* (Munich 1967); J. Moltmann, *Theologie der Hoffnung* (Munich, 4th ed., 1965); W. D. Marsch, *Hoffen worauf?* (Hamburg 1963); G. Sauter, *Zukunft und Verheissung. Das Problem der Zukunft in der gegenwärtigen theologischen und philosophischen Diskussion* (Zürich–Stuttgart 1965); H. Schlier, *Über die Hoffnung: Besinnung auf das Neue Testament. Exegetische Aufsätze und Voträge* (Freiburg 1964), pp. 135–145; P. Engelhardt, 'Der Mensch und seine Zukunft. Zur Frage nach dem Menschen bei Thomas von Aquin', *Die Frage nach dem Menschen. Festschrift für Max Müller*, H. Rombach ed. (Freiburg 1966), pp. 352–374; P. Schütz, *Charisma Hoffnung* (Hamburg 1962); idem, *Parusia – Hoffnung und Prophetie* (Heidelberg 1960); J. B. Metz, *Verantwortung der Hoffnung* (Mainz 1968).

[3] cf. further from the wide field of connected literature, H. Kimmerle, *Die Zukunftsbedeutung der Hoffnung. Auseinandersetzung mit dem Hauptwerk Ernst Blochs* (Bonn 1966); E. Roeder von Diersburg, *Zur Ontologie und Logik offener Systeme. Ernst Bloch vor dem Gesetz der Tradition* (Hamburg 1967).

provide a full examination of all this wealth of literature.[4] By way of preliminary an attempt should by all means be made to set forth the various ideas of what the essence of hope consists in, the means of attaining to it, and the actual place it occupies in contemporary theology. Anyone who casts an eye precisely at the more recent hypotheses put forward by J. Moltmann and J. B. Metz, including the controversy which has arisen in this connection (though of course we cannot pass any judgment upon this here), will be in the best position to understand that the only considerations which can be put forward here with regard to the problem as a whole are only of the most fragmentary kind. Here we shall be confining ourselves to the area of those questions which have been raised *primarily* by scholastic theology. But this should not be taken to imply that we are remaining wholly within the ambience of this theology as initially worked out in those circles, or that we regard this as adequate for a theology of hope for today. But if we begin with the way of setting out the problems that is more familiar to us from scholastic theology, then we have not only the advantage of opening up an approach which is more generally comprehensible, but also the opportunity of uncovering certain essential aspects and dimensions in the nature of hope. It is true that to arrive at a fruitful understanding in contemporary terms these can be adjusted and rearranged in many ways, but it is also true that they conceal within themselves the hidden treasure of prolonged and mature experience, and this may, perhaps, be able to make a contribution which is not inessential by deepening and filling out the hypotheses put forward in contemporary theology, or even serving as a kind of corrective to them.

I

Primarily, therefore, we are taking as axiomatic what is laid down in the classic theology of the scholastics: the existence of three theological virtues in man which are 'divine', which go to make up the concrete content of his justification to the extent that this can be conceived of as the power to produce acts which are directly salvific in faith, hope and love. Scholastic theology is also concerned with the specific quality of these 'divine' virtues to the extent that the theological virtues of their nature

---

[4] This also applies particularly to the works on the history of theology, cf. e.g. L. A. Arand, *St Augustine, Faith, Hope and Charity* (London 1947); M. Lods, *l'espérance chrétienne d'Origène à St. Augustin* (Paris 1952); R. Schwarz, *Fides, spes und caritas beim jungen Luther* (Berlin 1962); L. Ballay, *Der Hoffnungsbegriff bei Augustinus,* = *M.T.S.* 2, 29 (Munich 1964).

signify God himself as he who, in an act of grace which is unmerited, which raises man to a supernatural level and 'divinises' him, directly constitutes himself, in the glory which is proper to his own interior nature, as the salvation and the ultimate goal of the creature endowed with spiritual faculties. Yet a further tenet of scholastic theology is the existence of hope as the second of these three virtues, one which follows upon faith and constitutes a prior condition for love. Again scholastic theology is concerned to define the nature of hope on the one hand inasmuch as it is a quality proper to the will and the exercise of its freedom, causing it to reach out in a spirit of trust in God for God himself as the absolute good and therefore as salvation, and to the extent that on the other hand this good appears as something still to be attained, something difficult of attainment, i.e. not immediately or evidently attainable, yet which is, nevertheless, made possible for us to attain through God's promise and in the light of his omnipotence and his kindness in forgiving us. Again scholastic theology draws a sharp dividing line between presumption on the one hand and despair on the other, and a further point is that all particular and individual goods which are still unattained and which are difficult of attainment, but are nevertheless genuine and possible, are subsumed under the subject-matter of the theological virtue of hope, in so far as these are included in God's purposes, a 'means' of attaining to salvation. In scholastic theology the christological aspect of hope is also dealt with inasmuch as Christ, the risen Lord, constitutes the concrete realisation in history, and the eschatological consummation of the divine promise which is the basis for hope and which makes it possible. It defines the connection between hope and certain related attitudes or individual aspects such as 'expectancy', 'perseverance', 'patience', 'trust', 'assurance of salvation', 'self-interested love', 'selfless love'. And a further point which is defined in scholastic theology is the relationship of theological hope to hope in general considered as a basic 'existential' or essential factor in human living as such. It is concerned with the nature of hope to the extent that this is not merely an individual 'virtue' practised in isolation by one who is pursuing his own private salvation, but rather something that provides a basic framework for the attitude of the people of God as such on their pilgrimage, and one in which each individual does not merely hope for himself alone, but each hopes for all. All this – and certainly in itself it already constitutes a major and difficult task to investigate – must be regarded as given and presupposed.

II

A first attempt to penetrate somewhat more deeply into the nature of hope must now be made, and in order to do this we shall take as our starting-point the classic principle of Catholic theology that hope is a special *theological* virtue which must be assigned a place together with and between faith and love.

At first this statement seems to be readily understandable. A theological virtue is an attitude freely adopted by the subject endowed with intellect and will, yet supported by God's self-bestowal in grace. It is an attitude which is related not, as with the moral virtues, to a particular finite moral value which can be defined in 'this-worldly' categories, but bears upon God himself as he is 'in and for himself', and as such becomes, in a direct sense through this act of self-bestowal in grace, our absolute good. In this way, therefore, God becomes radically and effectively 'God for us'. But hope bears precisely upon God in this sense, God who has promised himself to us in this dimension of his nature and who constitutes our absolute future.[5] This seems to be enough to enable us to understand the fact that hope is one of the three theological virtues and why it should be so. In fact, however, not everything is *ipso facto* clear, especially if we are to understand that hope is not merely a preliminary and provisional form of faith and love, not merely faith and love 'on the way' and before they have attained their goal, not merely, therefore, a form conditioned by that situation in human existence in which we are still making pilgrimage and therefore in danger. On the contrary hope is to be thought of as a unique theological virtue in its own right, and one which cannot be reduced to the other two. This, however, is not clear immediately or without further explanation.

In order to recognise the obscurity here we must consider the following factors. In the doctrine of the Trinity[6] we know of *two* 'processions', in other words two modes of mediation through which God as ungenerated (the Father) utters himself and possesses himself in love, so that three modes of subsistence in the one God are constituted, the 'procession' as Word and also as 'breathing forth love'. In conformity with this, in any Christian interpretation of man, we must hold fast, in spite of many

---

[5] cf. K. Rahner, 'Marxist Utopia. . . .', *Theological Investigations* VI, pp. 59–68, *idem*, 'A Fragmentary Aspect of a Theological Evaluation of the Concept of the Future', in this volume, pp. 235–241.

[6] On this cf. K. Rahner, *Mysterium Salutis II*, J. Feiner, M. Löhrer edd. (Einsiedeln 1967), pp. 317–410.

contrary tendencies of recent times, to the fact that there are two basic modes of human (transcendental) self-realisation: awareness of, and reflection upon the self through knowledge and through free love, corresponding to the two basic transcendentals *Verum* and *bonum*, in which the one (*unum*) being (*ens*) imposes itself. These two basic transcendentals, then, are such that we cannot at will add any others to them on the same plane. Thus it appears that from what we know both of God and of man it is natural to expect two basic attitudes to be involved in man's right realisation of his own nature, two basic virtues which correspond to this original transcendental duality inherent in man. This is all the more true in view of the fact that a 'divine' or theological virtue is sustained precisely by God's self-bestowal, and the response of the creature who has personal status and is endowed with spiritual faculties to this divine self-bestowal is precisely made possible and effective by the divine self-bestowal itself. Now there are only two such modes or – better – aspects in this *one* divine self-bestowal: the first aspect is constituted by the *Logos* and the second by the divine *Pneuma*. It is precisely through these two aspects that God as ungenerated, God the 'Father' (not, therefore, an abstract divinity!), who is incomprehensible and never loses his incomprehensibility even through his act of divine self-bestowal, imparts himself. Because of this we cannot imagine that the Trinity in the modes of subsistence in the one God implies *ipso facto* that there is also a trinity in the response by which we accept this self-bestowal of the Father in *Logos* and in *Pneuma*. The fact that there is only *one* act of self-bestowal in which the 'Father' imparts himself in *Logos* and *Pneuma* implies that in the response, i.e. the 'theological' virtue, of man which is itself upheld by this divine self-bestowal, only a single act is conceivable with *two* modalities: faith and love, to correspond to the Word and the Love of the Father.

It also seems to be in conformity with this that in the theology of the bible the twofold combination of faith and love is earlier than our threefold combination of faith, hope and love, even though in not a few passages in the New Testament itself ἐλπίς has been inserted between πίστις and ἀγάπη. Thus hope is intended to figure primarily as a mere formal aspect of faith and love taken together, the power and the mode in which man, while still in peril, lovingly yearns for God as the absolute essence of truth as apprehended by his faith, and as the absolute essence of all that is good as the goal of his love, reaching out for him under these aspects as a salvation that is still to be attained in the future, but is, nevertheless, promised. Hence it is that hope does not figure so very clearly as a distinct attitude in its own right with an independent status of its own and a nature of its own somewhere between faith and love. Nor can we evade the question arising from this merely by pointing out first that hope is appropriate to the nature of this present life considered as a pilgrimage, as provisional, as lived in *statu viatoris*, seeing that later it is to be left behind, abrogated, once we 'possess' God, and second that this is also proper to faith, which ceases and gives way to the vision which is 'face to face'. For in one passage in which he is dealing with all three of the theological virtues which he mentions in 1 Cor 13 Paul ascribes to them a definitive permanence, a μένειν that is absolute. Thus he does not recognise any total abrogation of πίστις or ἐλπίς. On the other hand, however, and *e converso*: If we follow the traditional interpretation, and regard hope as coming to an end with 'possession', just as faith comes to an end with 'vision', then this 'possession' of God would still be constituted precisely by a vision and a love which unites, and hope would once more appear as the mere mode in which man for the time being, and in his *statu viatoris* strives for this possession of God as truth and love. Hope as such would be abrogated in a far more radical manner than faith, which is raised to the level of vision. In comparison with faith or vision and with love, whether as still in process of development or in its definitive form, we would constantly be in a position where we could not yet ascribe this status to hope as of the same origin as these other virtues and as 'enduring' like them as that in which the basic fulness of human life is achieved in the attainment of God. Thus at this stage it seems as though we can only construct a triad of divine virtues by postulating an interrelationship of initially disparate concepts which is relatively superficial, and only in such a triad can hope be considered one of the three theological virtues. Now despite all appearances to the contrary this problem is not a question of subtle, and ultimately superfluous playing with concepts. On the contrary, the process of finding the answer to it will bring us perforce to a deeper understanding of the nature of hope, and thereby of man and even of God himself. This is why we have dwelt upon this problem in all its acuteness. But what is the solution to it?

III

It would certainly be false for us to seek to find a solution to the problem by contesting the statements which have been made, as for instance by holding that ultimately speaking what is being postulated is a third basic power to which hope would correspond as its appropriate virtue. In fact we do not need to conceive of the triad of the theological virtues as such that it necessarily presents us with three virtues together, unified by a strict principle of distinction which is common to them all in the same sense and at the same level, so that they have precisely the *same* relationship *among themselves*. We do not necessarily need to argue against the correctness of regarding these three virtues as constituting a triad. We do not need to adopt this approach even though 'hope' is regarded as the mid-term and the common factor between the two other virtues. Admittedly in saying this we are assuming that it is not regarded merely as a *transient* modality of the two other virtues and of the 'powers' corresponding to these, but rather as that property which endures in them, and which draws both equally together into one. We must not regard hope merely as standing 'between' the two other virtues. Rather we must think of it as constituting the original and unifying medium between them. If we can show this then we are justified in speaking of a triad, but at the same time we do not have to conclude from its existence that hope must be related to faith and love in precisely the same way as these two are related to each other. Nor is it, ultimately speaking, of decisive importance whether the basic modality of the relationship to God as understood here is that which is called 'hope' in the common parlance of everyday, or whether rather there is something which lies concealed behind this term, but which, nevertheless, this term is used to point to because there is no better one for it.

It is common practice in scholastic theology to replace the vision of this quality of hope which is so obscurely pointed to by the conceptual model according to which hope is dissolved by 'possession', by the 'attainment of the goal'. This conceptual model is drawn from everyday experience, and from the experience of 'hope' at the profane level. Initially, for instance, we 'hope' for a position in life which we have not yet attained to. But once this has been achieved, once we 'have' it, then we no longer need to 'hope', but at most hope to retain that which we have achieved, though in that case we experience or interpret this attitude as something quite different from 'hope'. But what is to be said of precisely *that* basic act in which (it is called theological hope) we reach out towards God? Can we interpret this basic act too as a mere provisional attitude which will be dissolved once we have attained to that state of 'possession' which itself in turn is constituted by 'vision' and unifying 'love'? In that case hope will be abolished as something that belongs to the past, because now there is nothing more that has to be 'hoped for', but rather everything is already in our possession, and we do not even have to fear that we may lose what has been attained to, in other words we do not even have to hope that this will continue permanently. But is this line of thought correct?

In fact, however, it is questionable in the extreme – in other words basically inadequate – to take as our guide the conceptual model of 'possession' in order to understand the definitive consummation of man's life, and on this basis to conceive of hope as that which is merely provisional. This conceptual model in fact distorts the special quality of man's final consummation as consisting in vision and love, and thereby too that basic modality belonging to this final consummation which is both expressed and concealed at the same time in the term 'hope'. This basic modality only constitutes the authentic nature of *that* theological hope in so far as it is present in the life of the pilgrim here below – and here admittedly it has a certain provisional quality. The act of attaining to God as truth in the 'vision' of God in fact allows for the transcendence of this God as the incomprehensible. The event in which this takes place, inasmuch as it is made possible by the divine self-bestowal, is not the act in which the absolute mystery which is God is finally overcome and solved, but rather the act in which this truly unfathomable mystery in all its finality and its overpowering acuteness is no longer able to be suppressed, but must be sustained and endured as it is in itself without any possibility of escape into that which can be comprehended and so controlled and subordinated to the subject and his own nature as it exists prior to any elevation by grace. The act of attaining to love as love is the response to, and acceptance of, a love which, totally independent of any element in ourselves, is rather freedom in its most radically incalculable form. The intelligibility of this love is not to be found in any prior quality in ourselves which makes us 'worthy to be loved' (even though the love itself does confer this). On the contrary, it always depends totally and eternally on this freedom of God which is based on nothing else than itself alone. In this radical sense the love we are speaking of is, and remains eternally, 'grace'.[7] The 'possession' of God – if in spite of what has been said we may still use this term – is that radical transcendence of self and surrender of self which is entailed in the act of reaching out for truth into the unfathomable mystery, and it is also the radical self-surrender and self-transcendence of that love which cannot charm love from the beloved through any act of self-surrender on its part, but lives totally by the love of that which is beloved as based on nothing else than itself. It is pure act of reception and *as such* sustains the mutual interplay or *commercium* of the love involved, but is not itself upheld by this *commercium*.

[7] On the question as a whole cf. also K. Rahner, *Theological Investigations* V (London and Baltimore 1966), 'The "Commandment" of Love in Relation to the Other Commandments', pp. 439–459.

These qualities inherent in the response to and acceptance of God as truth and as love have an interior unity and a common source in the one radical attitude which draws us 'out of ourselves' into that which is utterly beyond our control. This 'letting of one's self go' is certainly the essence of man, rightly understood *in the concrete* as already bearing 'grace' within itself. Once he has discovered this nature of his and freely assented to it, man has attained to freedom in the true sense, which consists in realising himself and fulfilling the meaning of his life. And precisely this fulfilment of his nature is that 'outwards from the self' attitude of the finite subject reaching out into the incomprehensibility and incircum-scribability of God as truth and as love. In the word 'hope' this one unifying 'outwards from the self' attitude into God as the absolutely uncontrollable finds expression. Hope, therefore, represents this unifying medium between faith or vision and love (still on the way and also, even when it has achieved its 'goal'). *'Hence "hope" does not, in this most ultimate sense, express a modality of faith and love so long as these are at the provisional stage. On the contrary, it is a process of constantly eliminating the provisional in order to make room for the radical and pure uncontrollability of God. It is the continuous process of destroying that which appears, in order that the absolute and ultimate truth may be the intelligible as comprehended, and love may be that which is brought about by our love.* We would like to be those who set up God for ourselves through that which we ourselves do, acting (morally) as free and intelligent beings, and thereby having him as ours to dispose of as we will. But hope is the name of an attitude in which we dare to commit ourselves to that which is radically beyond all human control in both of man's basic dimensions, that, therefore, which is attained to precisely at that point at which the controllable is definitively transcended, i.e. in the ultimate consummation of eternal life. Taken in this sense hope is that which 'endures'. And this means that it also shares in this character of 'enduring' which is involved in the definitive finality of the relationship to absolute truth. Hence Paul can say that faith itself 'endures', even when vision has been attained to. A further point also becomes clear in the light of this, namely that the love of eternity can only rightly be understood if it is thought of as carrying the quality of 'hope', so that we can just as truly speak of a *fides* and *caritas spe formata* as of a *fides* and *spes caritate formata*. Hope implies the one basic character which is the common factor in the mutual interplay of truth and love: the enduring attitude of 'outwards from self' into the uncontrollability of God. Conversely we can say: where hope is achieved as the radical self-submission to the absolute uncontrollable, there alone do we truly understand what, or still better *who* God is. He is that which of its very existence empowers us to make this radical self-commitment to the absolute uncontrollable in the act of knowledge and love. One might almost say our radical self-commitment to the 'absurdity' of truth and love, because both derive their true essence – quite otherwise to what we would have thought at first sight – from the incomprehensibility and uncontrollability of truth and love in themselves.

This means that radically speaking hope is not the modality of the historical process by which we pass through time to that state which is definitive and eternal, but rather the basic modality of the very *attitude to the eternal* which precisely as such sets the true advance towards eternity 'in train'. In the light of this both presumption *and* despair are, at basis, the refusal of the subject to allow himself to be grasped by the uncontrollability and to be drawn out of himself by it. Clearly all that has been said with regard to the ultimate nature of hope does not imply any denial of the fact that it itself, in the *status viatoris* it bears certain properties which can no longer be ascribed to it in the eternal life in which it achieves its consummation. But these properties – the striving for the finite *within* that process in which the encounter with the provisional is still taking place – conceal more than they unveil the innermost essence of hope. For this encounter, even when we rise above it in our hope for the future, always gives rise to the impression that that which is definitive and final too will one day be possessed in the same way as now we comprehend, dominate and so dispose of the provisional and temporary benefits available to us.

IV

We must now adopt a second approach, and attempt thereby to penetrate still more deeply into the absolute essence of hope. In this we must once more take as our starting-point certain familiar theological data. In this way it will be sought to clarify still further the unique and original nature of hope which, perhaps, even after our first approach, still continues to be understood as a modality of faith and love in *such a way that* it is not sufficiently made clear how faith and love too themselves only appear rightly in their true nature when they are conceived of in the light of the original and independent status of hope.

In the average Catholic theology hope appears almost as an inevitable consequence of faith. Faith is the assent and apprehension not merely of the theoretical statements in which divine revelation is formulated, but also of God's promises which are proclaimed in this revelation, the promises of grace, of forgiveness and of eternal life. Once these promises are apprehended and are present by *faith* itself, then – so the average theology of hope appears unreflectingly to suppose – everything is clear and simple. These promises which are present and apprehended by faith itself considered as *fides historica et dogmatica* apparently set hope in train of themselves. Hope as a reaction on the part of the free will appears to be the simple consequence of the *assensus intellectualis* of faith considered as the act by which revelation is initially accepted, but it is this only provided that this freedom is not used to block the way in an incomprehensible and nonsensical refusal of these promises as theoretically apprehended, to which faith has already given its assent and which it offers to the free will as a subject on which to exercise its power.

This conception of hope, unreflecting for the most part but nonetheless real, is of course only the reflection of a more general theoretical intellectualism, according to which the 'will' is almost reduced to the status of the executive power for attaining to that good which is the *verum* of the intellect as *ipso facto* attained to, and which, therefore, in its original essence as the final consummation of knowledge as such, also signifies its beatitude. In saying this we have no intention of entering into the questions raised in the traditional controversy between Thomism and Scotism, or of supporting an option in favour of will, freedom and love as against 'intellect', if from both points of view the matter is conceived of as a choice between two 'powers'. Both historically speaking and of their real natures, the factors involved are not so simple. On the contrary, what has just been said is intended to be understood as an indication of a prior and more radical unity of knowledge and will, which the word 'hope' is precisely intended to represent in its status as a prior medium or common factor between faith and love, and therefore between knowledge and will.

But let us notice in greater detail the misunderstanding indicated above, in which hope is interpreted as a simple consequence of faith. On the one hand what does faith offer in the way of promise if it is understood in the traditional sense of *assensus intellectualis* as put forward by the Council of Trent and the First Vatican Council? And what promise is it, on the other hand, that becomes the object of hope as such? We can and must answer this question in the following terms: in both cases it is far from being precisely the same promise, however much the second too, though not in isolation, may be based upon the first and depend upon it. From this a fresh insight can be obtained into the special quality and radical uniqueness of hope. Faith – viewed more in its 'theoretical' nature (including in this the dogmatic and historical specifications) – can only proclaim the 'metaphysical' kindness and holiness of God, the universal and fundamental meaningfulness of existence, God's universal will to save all men as 'prior' to man's response and conditioned by it, the existence of 'sufficient grace' for all and the existence of 'efficacious grace' for 'those in whom its presence cannot be recognised', so that we can never know precisely to whom this efficacious grace is *de facto* to be attributed. Faith in this sense, therefore, can only express a universal 'promise'. *This* faith as such cannot tell me that God has conferred this efficacious grace precisely on *me* in particular and is thus bringing about my salvation in the concrete.

Now if it were sought to object to this point that it is only through some inexcusable *fault* that a given individual can forfeit salvation in general and so *his* salvation, which is set before him as something that is possible and actually offered to him precisely through this faith and the universal promise of freedom which it contains, then we must rejoin that, without prejudice to the fact of the inexcusable fault on the individual's part, the distinction between 'sufficient' and 'efficacious' grace is prior to this as established *by God himself*, so that the presence or otherwise of this efficacious grace does not simply depend upon his fault. Faith in its theoretical aspects, therefore, cannot overcome this difference which is established by the freedom of choice of God's grace, and so not subject to any influence of ours. It cannot remove this difference according to which there is a distinction between the universal promise and the concrete and particular promise which intends and brings about the salvation of me as a concrete individual through this 'efficacious' grace. Certainly grace as formulated in dogmatic terms only realises its authentic nature and attains its true purpose when it is subsumed and transcended, when the theoretical promise which is proper to it is transformed into the specific and particular promise in which it is applied to the individual. But this takes place precisely in virtue of the fact that faith is transformed into hope. The free subject recognises that in spite of his freedom, and precisely *in* it he himself is subject to God's control, even though it still remains true that this cannot diminish his personal responsibility before God. Wherever and whenever he exercises his freedom to receive the salvation that is offered to him, this acceptance is itself in turn the effect of the grace of God which as such is unmerited and '*effective*', not merely 'sufficient'. The will of God is 'prior' to the decision of man in his freedom. And this will of God is as such distinct from God himself and not merely from man, so that it is beyond our powers to discern even so far as theoretical faith is concerned. Does this will of God, even at that level at which it is prior to my free decision, *de facto* represent the ultimate and definitive meaning of existence for me in particular in such a way as to exclude all other possible meanings? This is a question which no-one can answer by turning the fundamental statement of theoretical faith with regard to the general promise of God's will to save all men into an absolute statement. But although such a statement is not possible *theoretically* speaking, and though we cannot achieve any positive knowledge of the meaning of existence or of our salvation in the concrete, nevertheless we must find another way of making this assertion to ourselves, because a positive decision of this kind is necessary for the subject himself who takes the initiative: I must hope.

Hope, then, is an act in which we base ourselves in the concrete upon that which cannot be pointed to in any adequate sense at the theoretical level, that which ultimately speaking is absolutely beyond our power to control, namely upon God who, in himself, can be the God of grace *or* the God of anger, but who in this case is apprehended as the God of grace and under no other aspect. And it is apparent from what has been said that hope in this sense is a basic modality of human existence. Hope, therefore, is not merely a function which follows manifestly from knowledge, including in this the factor of theoretical faith. Certainly it can be demonstrated 'in theory' and 'in principle' that there must be hope. But this does not make hope a secondary function of the insight provided by theoretical faith. For the concrete hope of each individual in particular for *his* salvation is, in a certain sense, authorised even prior to any theoretical judgment precisely by this theoretical insight and by his knowledge of the general promise. But while this is true, still this hope cannot be constituted by these factors alone. They cannot provide the actual *basis* for this concrete hope. This can only be the 'efficacious' will of God to save as applied to the concrete individual case, and it proceeds from God alone and remains hidden in him. This 'basis' is not something that faith provides for hope, but rather something that is grasped solely by hope as such. As providing the basis for hope the will of God to save in the concrete is only present and attained to in hope itself and as such. It is the hope that is not derived from something other than itself, i.e. from faith, unless indeed we are to understand faith – with Luther – as being itself *fides fiducialis* and as such already including hope within itself. But this would be to obliterate the sound and permanent distinction between theoretical and practical awareness.

Hope, therefore, appears as *that* act in which the uncontrollable is made present as that which sanctifies, blesses and constitutes salvation without losing its character as radically beyond our powers to control, precisely because this salvific future is hoped for but not manipulated or controlled. However true it may be that hope has its basis in the special, but uncontrollable promise of God, it still can and must be said without any cheap attempts at paradox, that it is only hope itself that provides its own basis and in this sense creates that basis. For this special and particular promise takes place only *for* the individual who hopes as such, and only in hope itself as such. Hope alone is the *locus* of God as he who cannot be controlled or manipulated, and so of God as such.

This does not mean that the function of hope as the medium of the theological virtues is removed. The *perichoresis*, the mutual interaction between the three theological virtues by which they condition one another and permeate one another (cf. above Sections II–III), is not disrupted. But what we have said does, perhaps make plainer that in hope which is irreducibly unique and underived: we only know who God is and who man is when we hope, i.e. when we take as our basis that which is incalculable and uncontrollable as the blessed which as such, and only in this guise, makes itself present to us in hope. The expression 'the incalculable and uncontrollable as the blessed' here is to be taken as the expression of a closer identification, although one that presents it more as having the nature of an event. For he who commits himself to the absolutely incalculable and uncontrollable is committing himself to the blessed one and to salvation. Presumption *and* despair both entail the same basic refusal to commit oneself and so to abandon oneself to the incalculable and the uncontrollable.

This does not mean that the status of Christ as the fundamental promise of hope is done away with in favour of a hope which, by its sheer racidal quality, is based upon itself. For precisely this radical quality inherent in the 'outwards from self' movement into the absolute incalculability and uncontrollability of God as our absolute future, is based upon that grace of God which finds its unique historical manifestation in Christ precisely as *crucified*, and thereby as surrendering himself in the most radical sense to the disposing hand of God. It is in this historical manifestation that the grace we are considering here definitively establishes itself in the world. But precisely this takes place in the death of Christ as the most radical act of hope ('into *thy* hands I deliver up my life').

Whatever divisions there may be in human powers, in theory and practice, in knowledge and in free love, they are all subsumed alike in respect of what is common to all and what is peculiar to each of these elements, under the single factor of their common creaturehood and their orientation to God who, in his act of self-bestowal, makes himself the absolute future of man. And to this extent the act of hope stands revealed as the acceptance of this orientation towards the incalculability and uncontrollability of God. This act comprehends and unifies all these divisions even though, in order to be realised in the concrete, it has itself to be distinguished into faith and love. For, even allowing for this, this orientation must come from God and find its consummation in attaining to him.

V

In order to allay the suspicion that up to now we have been speaking of hope too much in terms of individual salvation, our considerations must now be supplemented by a third line of approach. Certainly it is not possible to include a full treatment of all that contemporary theology and existential ontology has to say with regard to the cosmic and social dimensions of hope, with regard to hope as exercised by the people of God on pilgrimage as such and in the course of its journey, with regard to the exodus which this people is constantly undertaking afresh, quitting all situations which have become 'frozen' and static in all dimensions of human existence.

Let us concentrate simply upon a single small passage in the Dogmatic Constitution on the Church, *Lumen gentium* (cf. C. IV, No. 35) which has for the most part gone unnoticed. There it is stated with regard to the laity that they should not conceal their eschatological hope in the innermost depths of their hearts (*in interioritate animi*), but should rather give it concrete expression ('exprimant') in the complexities and in the framework (*per structuras*) of secular life (*vitae saecularis*). This admonition is found in the context of the prophetic function of the laity in the Church and in the world. Surely it would be to misunderstand it if we sought to interpret it merely as a moralising conclusion of a secondary kind, following from the nature of that hope which the 'sons' of *the* 'promise' (*ibid.*) could ultimately speaking have lived by even without 'informing' the secular framework of the world with their hope in this way.[8] Contrary to this view, the admonition contains a statement about an element which is essential to hope itself. The process by which this becomes an achieved reality involves a permanent transformation of the framework of secular life. Abstracting for the moment from the fact that 'revolution' is an extremely indeterminate and ambiguous concept, we might go so far as to say that the significance of this admonition is that Christian hope is at

[8] cf. K. Rahner, 'The Theological Problems Entailed in the Idea of the "New Earth" ', in the present volume, pp. 260–272.

basis a continually revolutionary attitude on the part of Christians in the world. If we interpret the significance of Christianity aright, and if Christians themselves have a right understanding of the real significance of their own commitment, then the position is the diametrical opposite of what is generally thought both within and without the Christian body. The hope that is directed towards the absolute future of God, towards that eschatological salvation which is God himself as absolute, is not entertained in order to justify an attitude of conservatism which, from motives of anxiety, prefers a certain present to an unknown future and so petrifies everything. It is not the 'opium of the people' which soothes them in their present circumstances even though these are painful. Rather it is that which commands them, and at the same time empowers them, to have trust enough constantly to undertake anew an exodus out of the present into the future (even within the dimension of this world).

In reality man as physical and as belonging to the historical dimension actually fulfills the ultimately transcendental structures of his own nature not in the abstract 'interiority' of a mere attitude of mind, but in intercourse with the world, the world made up of his own environment and of his fellow men. 'Practice' in the real sense, and as opposed to, and radically different from, theory, is, moreover, not confined solely to the mere execution of what has been planned and so is merely theoretical, but rather consists of an opening of the sphere of action in general and an attitude in which we dare to enter upon that which has not been planned, so that it is only in practice itself that any genuine possibility is given of what we have been bold enough to commit ourselves to. Planning may be necessary and justified in the manipulation of our environment (by technical measures), of the society we live in (by social measures), and of man himself. But all this does not derogate from the element of the unplanned which presses in upon us, and does not reduce it to a mere remnant of the contents of our lives which we have 'not yet' worked out. On the contrary such planning increases the element of that which is unplanned and has the effect of causing it to stand out still more sharply as the outcome of practice itself. Man himself, in the very process of breaking down the factor of the incalculable already present *beforehand* in his life, actually builds up those incalculable factors which are produced by *himself*.[9] Now the effect of these two elements is that in the very act of venturing upon the future which is unforeseen and incalculable in 'this worldly terms' in his practical life as understood here, man realises, and necessarily must

---

[9] On the problems involved here cf. K. Rahner, 'The Experiment with Man: Theological Observations on Man's Self-Manipulation' in volume IX.

realise, his eschatological hope as a commitment 'outwards from self' to that which is incalculable and uncontrollable in an absolute sense. The Christian must, therefore, impress the form of his hope upon the framework of the world he lives in. Of course this does not mean for one moment that certain specific and firm structures of the secular world he lives in could ever be such that they could constitute the enduring objective realisation of his eschatological hope (in the sense of being established as this once and for all). On the contrary, every structure of secular life, whether present *or still to come* in the future, is called in question by hope as that in which we grasp at the incalculable and uncontrollable, and in this process of being called in question, the act of hope is made real in historical and social terms. Admittedly this is not the only way in which this is achieved. The Christian also accepts in the 'form of the world' as it passes over him those factors for which he himself is not responsible, and which he merely has to endure. He accepts these as part of the individual lot of his own personal life in death and in the renunciations which prepare for this, and it is no less true that he makes his hope real and living in this process too. A wildly revolutionary attitude, taken by itself, can be one of two things: either it implies that an absolute value is accorded to the form which the world is about to assume in the immediate future, in which case it is the opposite of hope, namely a form of presumption which only recognises that which can be controlled and manipulated, or which treats that which is not subject to our control or calculations as though it were so. Alternatively this attitude signifies despair, a state in which nothing more is hoped for, and therefore everything is absolutely negated because there is nothing final or definitive, or because nothing of this kind exists at all. But to subject the structures of this world too to constant reappraisal and criticism is *one* of the concrete forms of Christian hope which, as the courage of self-commitment to the incalculable and uncontrollable, must never hold fast to anything in this worldly life in such a way that it is as though without it man would be cast headlong into an absolute void. Hope commands man in the very moment in which, far more clearly than hitherto, he actually becomes the fashioner of his world, not only to let go of that which is taken away from him, but more than this actively to renounce that which, in the light of the limitless future which hope opens up to him, he recognises as provisional, and which, because of this, he can also understand to be dispensable already in this present time.

It is strange that we Christians, who have to achieve the radical commitment of hope in which we venture upon that which is incalculable and uncontrollable in the absolute future, have incurred the suspicion both in the minds of others and in our own that so far as we are concerned the will to guard and preserve is the basic virtue of life. In reality, however, the sole 'tradition' which Christianity precisely as the people of God *on pilgrimage* has acquired on the way is the command to hope in the absolute promise and – in order that thereby this task may not remain at the level merely of a facile ideology of ideas – to set out ever anew from the social structures which have become petrified, old and empty. Precisely *in what* this hope is to be brought to its fulness in the concrete in an exodus which is constantly renewed in this way, precisely *what* the Christian is to hold firm to (for this too is in fact possible) – because his hope also divests the future, even within the temporal dimension, of any false appearance of being the absolute future – this is something which 'theoretic' faith cannot answer as a simple deduction following from its own tenets. This concrete imperative is not merely the result of applying the theory of faith in practice. It would be just as wrong to hold this as to say that faith as such, and by itself, transforms the general promise into that special and particular one which is only realised in the original and underivable act of hope. But this hope summons the Christian and Christianity to venture upon this imperative, underivable in each case, in which they have constantly to decide anew between whether they are to defend the present which they already possess, or to embark upon the exodus into the unforeseeable future. This is something which hope can do, for hope itself has in fact already all along achieved something which is even greater. In it man has surrendered himself to that which is absolutely and eternally uncontrollable and incalculable by any powers of his. In the power of this greater hope he also possesses the lesser hope, namely the courage to transform the 'framework of secular life', as the Council puts it, and the converse too is no less true. In this lesser hope the greater one is made real.

There remain, therefore, faith, hope and love – these three. But the greatest of these is love. So says Paul. But we could also translate this: 'Faith, hope and love constitute that which is definitive and final.' Perhaps it has been shown that hope is not simply the attitude of one who is weak and at the same time hungering for a fulfilment that has yet to be achieved, but rather the courage to commit oneself in thought and deed to the incomprehensible and the uncontrollable which permeates our existence, and, as the future to which it is open, sustains it. Perhaps it has also been shown that such courage has the power to dare more than what can be arrived at merely by planning and calculations. Perhaps it has been shown that in the final and definitive consummation hope still prevails and endures, because this definitive consummation is God.

14

THE THEOLOGICAL PROBLEMS ENTAILED
IN THE IDEA OF THE 'NEW EARTH'

I

THE basic imperative which permeates the whole of the 'Pastoral Constitution on the Church in the World of Today' of the Second Vatican Council is the demand that the individuals in the Church shall collaborate in those forms of contemporary human existence which are more worthy of human beings at all of its levels. And in fact – this is the decisive point – this is achieved on the basis of their ultimate Christian interpretation of existence, because their status as men is not something over and above their status as Christians, but rather they act as men precisely because they are Christians. The task which they have in common with all men of good will (even atheists are not excluded from this) is therefore one that they must accomplish on the basis of their specifically Christian faith, their eschatological hope and their love for God and men, that love which has been bestowed upon them *by God himself*. The Constitution interprets this point (at least so it appears in many passages which we shall be considering in greater detail at a later stage) not in the sense that this basic Christian attitude represents merely a certain motivation for fulfilling this task, an ideological 'motive force' or merely a new supplementary, but only formal, duty, presented by the Church in such a way that the *material* content of this task remains unaffected by this motivation and by these new duties. For in that case the content itself would be determined on the basis of a knowledge purely belonging to this world, purely at the level of philosophy and natural law, and existing purely at the concrete and practical level. On this showing the most that revelation would have to do would be to guard this knowledge from any error, and there would be a certain moral necessity in this in the sense implied in the First Vatican Council. What is said rather is, for instance – and even at this stage we are already coming to grips with more precise indications – that Christians must impress the framework of *secular* life with the stamp of their *eschatological hope*. Surely this means that the specifically *Christian* determination of the worldwide task which has actively to be engaged in consists not merely in the fact that the Christian must so fashion the world according to principles of merely natural law that in it Christianity is afforded sufficient room for developing the specifically religious and 'supraworldly' mission which is proper to itself, for in fact this would also be possible even on the basis of tolerance and freedom for an 'ideological' pluralism in society.

But in that case how can this task of creating a world more worthy of men be the common task of all men of good will? How, furthermore, can any 'understanding' be aimed at between all men, if the Christians and members of the Church have basically speaking, after all, a conception of this task which is precisely Christian in its *material content*. Of course the precise nature of what Christianity has to undertake at this level of material content in the task of renewing the world remains at this stage wholly indeterminate and unclear. Can it be then, alternatively, that the conciliar Constitution is taking back what has been said with regard to this task when it emphasises the 'secularity' of the world, the autonomy of the intellectual and cultural areas of human life, and when, still more clearly than in the social encyclicals of the popes from Leo XIII to Pius XII, it lays down that the Church cannot offer any readymade 'blue-prints' for the concrete formation of the world and history, explaining rather that to apply such 'blueprints' and imperatives in the concrete is the common task of all men who are conscious of their human responsibilities? Does a certain veiled inconsistency appear at this point in the Constitution, which has still not clearly been resolved? Or is it simply the case that in concrete practice there are still so many tasks to be performed in *common*, so many *preparatory* stages to be gone through for Christians and non-Christians together in order to achieve a 'better world' even though there is a material difference between Christians and non-Christians in their interpretations and deeds even at the purely secular level, the way they interpret their goal and their (relatively speaking) completed task? Can we, therefore, allow this difference to go unreconciled for the present, to await our attention as *cura posterior*?

The difficulty, which must first itself be made clearer, consists not so much in the mere fact that a task to be performed in common with *non*-Christians as such has been postulated, for it would in fact be quite possible to hold that even with these there may perhaps be some common ground in that even in the case of non-Christians the ultimate motive force behind their acts and decisions as a part of human history is still, even in their case, precisely *grace*, even though they do not recognise it. It could further be said that in every pluralistic society (and this is recognised by all as the situation in which we have to act in common) the common ground has to be established from *different* currents in human history coming together in a freely achieved harmony. It must not, therefore, be considered in any way surprising that Christians invest this situation of open dialogue and collaboration with their own conception of the future.

II

The difficulty lies, rather, in the nature of the case itself. Have we, or can we have at all, precisely *as* Christians a peculiarly *Christian* ideology of the future applicable to the secular world? To the extent that the question bears not upon general *principles* whether of 'natural law' or of 'Christianity itself' (though such principles do exist), but rather on a *programme in the concrete*, upon certain unambiguously concrete imperatives (for today and tomorrow, even though they always remain open to the more distant future) it is certainly clear that the official Church *cannot* include any such absolute programme in the concrete in her preaching.[1] This is no part of her commission. She is not capable of it, nor does she claim the right to perform any such function. But this is not merely *ipso facto* to decide the question that has been raised in the negative. For it is still at least conceivable[2] that the Church, as the concrete people of God, does in fact find and choose such a programme in the concrete in a concrete, and in a certain sense 'political' decision even though this is precisely not a mere 'deduction' from the principles of natural law and of Christianity itself. In this connection the question can here remain open of what any such act on the Church's part signifies for the individual Christian in her, i.e. whether as an individual he is *ipso facto* committed to being 'for' it. A further question which must remain open is *how* in the concrete any such historical and 'political' decision on the part of the Church considered as the people of God is arrived at, and *how* she succeeds in putting it into effect in forming the will of secular society *as a whole*, whether this takes

[1] On this cf. K. Rahner, 'Grenzen der Amtskirche', *Schriften zur Theologie* VI (Einsiedeln 1965), pp. 499–520.

[2] On the distinction which follows cf. the Pastoral Constitution *On the Church in the World of Today*, Nos. 43, 74, 75, 76. In the pages which follow the title of this Conciliar Document will not be included in references to it. Instead the relevant numbers will be given, e.g. No. 43 etc. Other conciliar decrees will be cited by their respective titles.

the form of a state, an association of nations etc., or alternatively how she strives in vain to do this. It would also be possible to imagine that the official Church, having arrived almost instinctively at such a decision in principle, and having formulated it to herself almost unreflectingly, might then go on to articulate it more plainly in its application to a concrete earthly future for mankind, and to proclaim it in the form of a 'proposal for guidance', something which is clearly to be distinguished from doctrine and commandment. Now if we regard some such measure as possible in principle,[3] i.e. if we recognise an intermediate position which is neither that of the Church in her role as authoritative and as speaking with an official voice, nor yet that of Christians merely as individuals who then act merely as individual members of secular society albeit under Christian 'inspiration', then this in itself would provide us with the material for working out a specifically Christian programme for the future of this present world of this kind, and for arriving at a decision about the present world in this way irrespective of how far *de facto* the Church succeeded in carrying through her ideas.

Is there a future of this kind for the material world, such that it can be mapped out from the point of view of Christianity itself? When the Pastoral Constitution lays down[4] that the future and the world it brings must be 'more humane', 'more just' and 'more peaceable' than the present, that it must be permeated by a justice and love which make possible the free unfolding of each individual man, which cause the unity of mankind as a family of brothers to develop, which wage war more effectively upon the destructive spirit of egoism and other kinds of sinfulness etc., when it further goes on to apply these basic principles in detail to the concrete realities in the form of demands for a just policy, upholding the status of the family and so guarding the dignity of man, working out an economic system that is just, working for peace etc., then certainly this does set the goal which Christianity, i.e. the Christian faith and the command of God, demands. But still, in all this there is nothing specifically Christian in what is here proclaimed as the content of the future which is to be striven for. Again the same is also true of the statement that the future shaping of society must be permeated by a Christian spirit. Nor is it any

[3] For a more developed treatment of this cf. K. Rahner, 'Zur theologischen Problematik einer Pastoralkonstitution' in *Volk Gottes. Zum Kirchenverständnis der katholischen, evangelischen und anglikanischen Theologie*, R. Bäumer and H. Dolch edd. (Festgabe für J. Höfer) (Freiburg 1967), pp. 683–703, in the present volume, pp. 293–317.

[4] On the following points cf. the Pastoral Constitution Nos. 11, 15, 21, 23, 24, 26, 37, 38, 40, 41, 43, 55, 57, 58, 61, 63, 76.

clearer that anything more has been added when emphasis is laid upon the fact that love of God and love of neighbour are one, or when the importance of revelation is extolled as contributing to the effective recognition of man's dignity. Indeed it would be possible to think not only that the emphasis on the fact that all Christians have this earthly task in common with all men of good will (e.g. No. 21 etc.) is rather an indication that the answer to our question is negative, but also that this is made even more probable by the fact that a distinction is drawn between man's 'total' (other worldly) vocation and his earthly task (No. 11). This is shown from such statements as that the 'building up of the world' 'contributes to the total vocation of man' (No. 35), that the growth of the kingdom of God on the one hand, and earthly progress on the other, are distinguished as two different entities (Nos. 36, 38, 39, 42, 43), and also from the fact that emphasis is laid upon the relative autonomy of the order of creation (Nos. 34, 36, 39, 41, 59, 67). But even though the connections are also emphasised a distinction is drawn between responsibility for the world order and the duty of striving to attain to our homeland in heaven. Emphasis is also laid upon the fact that the two orders of knowledge are distinct (No. 59) etc.

III

But we must now consider the other side. What does it mean to say that there is a unity of mankind such that on the one hand it is based on *Christ* (No. 32) and must *grow* until the time of consummation is reached (No. 32), while on the other hand it still seems not simply to be in all respects identical with the Church as such seeing that in fact the whole of mankind must be brought into the unity of the family of God?[5] What does it mean to say that the kerygma of the gospel is, to a certain extent, already latent in the human situation even before it is brought to light, for instance through art and theology (No. 62)? What is the significance of emphasising that humanity strives for a future in which mankind itself will become an offering pleasing to God (No. 38), in which it is also mentioned that the earthly service of mankind makes ready the 'material of the celestial realm' (No. 38)? At several points in the deliberations of the Council

---

[5] cf. Nos. 40, 43; *Lumen gentium* No. 28. What is being referred to here, however, is surely not that controversial question, the process of incorporating the whole of humanity into the Church and so *this particular* sense of the phrase *unitas familiae Dei*, especially in view of the fact that the 'growing body of the new family of mankind' is not to be thought of merely as a quantitative entity and is not identical with the Church, and yet does represent an *adumbratio* of the world to come (cf. No. 39).

mention is made of the 'new earth' and the 'new heaven'. This 'new earth' is, in fact, certainly presented as the eschatological gift of God himself, and is, therefore, not simply the outcome of the *progressus terrenus* (No. 39). But at the same time it is also not simply something which replaces what has gone before, in that it merely suppresses and does away with this, but rather a transformation of the world as it has existed hitherto (*transformatio mundi*, No. 38; *universi transformandi*, No. 39). But this world which is so to be transformed still appears to be not simply that which God himself has fashioned (in other words the substantial continuance of this simply as such). For it is said (No. 39) that not only love endures but also the *work* (*opus*) of this, and that we will also 'rediscover' the *industriae nostrae fructus*, in other words, surely, the fruits of human activity itself (since these are, in fact, thought of as 'purified'). Surely what is being thought of, therefore, as the world which has to be transformed, is that which man himself has shaped in 'projecting further the work of creation' (Nos. 34, 57). For this 'further projection of the creation' of God is often mentioned even when it is regarded as the carrying out precisely of the will of God as *Creator*, and so as distinct in a certain respect from the supernatural will of God to save. The divine love is also the law of the *transformatio mundi* (No. 38), and an intrinsic element in this is a *fraternitas universalis* which manifestly consists in something more than simply the Church as such (*ibid.*). The eschatological hope has itself to impose its own stamp upon the framework of the *vita saecularis* (*Lumen gentium* No. 35). While, therefore, the *renovatio mundi* is already an irrevocably established fact and is already to be anticipated in a real manner even *in hoc saeculo* (*Lumen gentium* No. 48), still this presence by anticipation of the eschatological *renovatio mundi* is surely given not merely in the Church in her *kerygma* and cult *exclusively*, but also precisely in the framework of the *vita saecularis*. Only so can mankind as it exists in the present give some idea in basic outline of what the future world is to be (No. 39). The indications supplied by the Constitution must certainly not be pressed too far in our interpretation. Certainly in the Constitution there is no clear attempt to work out how the 'formation of the future at the secular level and in a purely earthly and transient sense by the Christian spirit' on the one hand, and the 'Christian formation of the future brought about by man himself and having a final and definitive significance' on the other are alternatives. Nor is it really made clear precisely *how* we should react to these alternatives. But for all this the Constitution does lead us, albeit itself hesitating and feeling its way, to the point where we have to face up to these questions.

IV

Perhaps as a result of what has been said the real problem now becomes clear with which we are here concerned: is the world which man himself fashions only the 'material' in which he has morally to prove himself, and which in itself remains indifferent? And when the final consummation of the kingdom of God comes, will the world simply be done away with? The problem expressed in this question has in fact become more acute of itself in view of the fact that this world is no longer *merely* the 'situation' brought about by God himself in which man has to act in a morally right way. A further and more pressing reason is that it is a world which has reached a second stage in realising its potential: man himself takes it upon himself as a task with which he has been commissioned to fashion it and so to complete, in a process of historical evolution, the creative work of God himself. Can we nevertheless compare the world as understood here with the rush-baskets which the ancient monks of the Scythian desert wove by day and unravelled once more in the evening in order that they might fill up without sinning the interval of waiting for the eternity of this future which still lay wholly before them? Or does this second world, itself pass, albeit inconceivably 'transformed', into the *eschaton* properly so called? Does the 'new earth' come down from heaven (even though, as it were, on the 'neutral ground' which God once fashioned and which is constituted by the fact that the body remains substantially one and the same even after it is glorified, and by the material world only in so far as it is entailed by *this*)? Or alternatively will this world be constructed here in time by man himself? Are we to read the relevant phrase as 'new earth' or 'renewed earth' (admittedly taking this as applying to the final consummation of God who is eternally new)?

Formerly the question could not be put in so plain a manner. For precisely *this* world did not exist before. Man lived in a world of 'nature', which he simply had to accept as something already given. In so far as he himself produced anything it was only small and frail, from the body which died to the relatively minor products which were the material outcome of the exercise of his skills. All this seemed merely to be the fuel for the future conflagration of the world, which could only leave ashes behind it. It was from the outset impossible for man to think that the real eschatological outcome of history would consist, properly speaking, in anything else than the moral element in the immortal 'soul' which is to be taken with us into the 'life beyond'. Certainly a 'resurrection of the body' was expected. Man could even picture to himself how the marks of the wounds

in Christ's glorified body lasted on as signs of the victory he had won in
his personal history. In some way, therefore, the question we have raised
here was already present on the very periphery of man's awareness then –
but no more than this. As the Pastoral Constitution shows, no clear
working out of it as a question has been achieved even today. Nevertheless it is no mere scholastic subtlety, as for instance when the hair-
splitters break their heads over the question of whether those who have
risen again can still eat. For the question is – albeit in a particularly
refined form as presented here – the question of the more precise relationship between the hope of Christian eschatology and the present-day
ideology of the future or of the future Utopia (in a neutral sense of the
term). Are we ourselves those who achieve the final consummation when
we respond to the creative task which God lays upon us even in this world
in a spirit of justice, love and obedience, and so become the completers of
his creation? What we are speaking of here is a final consummation to be
wrought out in the substance of man and of matter merely as these have
been fashioned by God himself.[6] Are we then to become the completers
of God's creation in this sense in *such a way that* this final consummation
is to be constituted by a morality of human history which, in its ultimate
basis, remains at the meta-empirical level?[7] Or alternatively, is human
history at the material and physical level itself to become a part of this
definitive consummation, albeit through a process of death and radical
transformation?

This question has, after all, an important bearing on the relationship
of Marxism and Christianity, for the Christian interpretation of human
history and for much else besides in the Christian interpretation of existence. As Christians we have in fact to fight not against a naive form of
Marxism which simply uses the individual as the material for a future
society and history. This would be to postulate a Marxist act of faith in
which man believed either that he himself could build the 'kingdom of
God' simply of his own resources, or alternatively viewed the future as
being, after all, simply the mirage of history forever unobtainable, forever
leading on into infinitude, and never to be possessed by anyone as a
rounded whole. We Christians have to allow Marxism to put the question
to us (though in doing so we always have to maintain the proviso that by

---

[6] From the Christian point of view this applies *sensu positivo* to every case and is
something of which Christianity has always been clearly aware.

[7] The ultimately ethical quality of history as it exists in the sight of God is something that cannot in fact be deduced from history itself by our judgment with any
unequivocal certainty.

the mere fact of taking something in the world too seriously it would be possible precisely to corrupt it) of how in any real sense we Christians take with due seriousness the world which we have been commanded to achieve. Does this world, so far as we are concerned, constitute merely the material, ultimately speaking indifferent, upon which we exercise our own virtues? Is this of itself taking it seriously enough? On this showing is not the world itself a matter of indifference, since in fact it would be possible to exercise these same virtues in a world that was held fast in the grip of reactionary forces? In such a world we might practise above all the virtue of patience with a world that was mean, agonising and unjust. If we Christians were to answer this question we could not simply concentrate on those aspects of the world which make it a situation of testing and proving for those who seek the kingdom of heaven. We would have to recognise that we have to prove these heavenly virtues of ours which alone 'endure' precisely in the 'material' which is presented to us in the here and now by the world itself in its course. And if this world were to change, *then* we would have to face up to the further question of *why* this should be so, seeing that, in spite of the change, it would be the same virtues which alone endure that would have to be perfected even though the 'material' in which they were exercised and the 'objective' outcome which they achieved would merely recede into the past and absolutely cease to exist. In putting this question we have no intention of pressing it to lengths that are artificial. For in any case it remains true that concrete human history, with all its physical aspects, is the dimension in which the final consummation and the absolute future are made real. All that the Council has said remains in any case valid with regard to the responsibility which Christians have for the world, and with regard to the falsity of any artificial opposition between the integral vocation of the Christian (including, therefore, the 'other worldly' aspects of this also) on the one hand, and his task in the world on the other. But for all this perhaps it can be understood that the question we have raised is not unimportant either in view of the current intellectual climate in which Christianity has to make its message comprehensible.

v

But *can* this question be answered at all, and *how* is it to be answered?

First the following is clearly true: the kingdom of God, the final consummation which brings history to an end and 'raises' it is that which is coming of itself. It is not merely the mirage towards which history constantly reaches out, or its final goal, utterly different in kind from history itself. If it were this then it would only have the function of maintaining history in movement. This definitive finality will not exist simply as a final and definitive stage and the final outcome of the history planned and accomplished by man himself. Rather it will the deed of God which, admittedly, is to be thought of here, as elsewhere also in the history of nature and of the world, as the *self*-transcendence of history (divine, free and something which is totally beyond all our calculations if we take as our starting-point the movement which we ourselves initiate). History and its consummated finality are always different and distinguished from one another by that which is experienced in the personal history of the individual as death, and which signifies a radical 'transformation'. This transformation applies just as much to universal history as death does to the history of the individual. 'We do not know the time for the consummation of the earth and of humanity. Nor do we know how all things will be transformed' (No. 39). Therefore the statement that history will endure not only in the meta-empirical morality realised in it but also in its historical outcome cannot simply be set aside as mistaken in view of that other statement about the radical transformation of history into that which is unknown and into an openness to the absolute future which is God himself. The actual *conception* of history as it will exist in its enduring finality is impossible. Any attempt at depicting it (and in a real sense we are actually warned against this in Mt 22:30) would be pseudo-Christian apocalyptic and no true Christian eschatology. The very attempt to *depict* to ourselves a glorified body as it exists in itself leads into contradiction. How much more this would be true if we sought to make the same attempt with regard to the body of humanity which it gradually forms for itself in its one and continuous history! On the other hand it cannot be objected from the opposite point of view either, against what has been said, that it is not merely the final and definitive stage of human history precisely as such that can have the opportunity of acquiring an eschatological validity and lastingness, since on this showing nothing that belongs to *any* concrete reality of history whatsoever would be assumed into this final and definitive stage. For the same objection could be raised with regard to the physical aspects of the personal history of the individual. No one stage in a man's life can be *the definitive* model for the definitive and final state of the body, and nevertheless the Christian tradition thinks of this final and definitive stage as such that it brings what it has become in the concrete throughout its entire concrete history to a state of glorification.

So far as we are concerned in the here and now there is a basic dialectical tension between the two statements, on the one hand that human history will finally endure, and on the other that it will be radically transformed. This tension maintains us in an openness to the future while still according a radical importance to the present. Both statements are hermeneutic principles and at the same time statements of fact. Bearing these points in mind as provisos we can positively say: history itself constructs its own final and definitive state. That which endures is the *work* of love as expressed in the concrete in human history. It remains itself as something achieved by man, and not merely a moral distillation of this, something which history leaves behind it as though it were the 'grapes' from which the wine had been pressed. History itself passes into the definitive consummation of God, and not merely man who has once influenced the course of history and then, after he has played his 'part' (as in Hugo von Hofmannstahl's 'Everyman') leaves this behind him as something which has become inessential.

Why should we say this? Because the Logos of God has himself wrought upon and endured history. If our thesis were altogether false, then he would have had *totally* to lay aside his 'role'. But he remains for all eternity the God-man. And his humanity is not merely that which has received the reward of glory, but rather remains above all his *own*, something which, if this thesis is not accepted, would strictly speaking have become superfluous. The opposed thesis would lead, ultimately speaking, to an intolerable division between 'soul' and 'body' and between the noumenal and the phenomenal. 'History' in the true and proper sense, and as worked out by the exercise of personal freedom, demands of its very nature to be brought to a definitive consummation and does not receive any such consummation merely as a reward. Consummation is not something that is located 'beyond' history, as it were, seeing that it is in history that that takes place for which we are responsible even though it may not appear on the surface of any reality that we know and cannot be judged by us. And the correctness of our thesis is made even more probable by the positive answer which we must surely give to the question of whether the moral element (without prejudice to the fact that it is something that must be performed as a work of freedom) does not, after all, precisely *consist in* that which takes place in history as concrete, and the question of whether it does not achieve its meaning in history and from history. This means, therefore, that history itself must have a final and definitive significance if the moral is to have any such significance.

VI

The outcome of what we have said is that a history that is constructed by man himself as event and as the end product of his activities has a final and definitive significance. And if this is true, then it also becomes apparent what is the basis and the necessary presupposition for this, namely that precisely this 'world in its worldliness', which as such retains all its secularity, nevertheless, still in itself and as such, at basis exhibits a secret Christianity. The task of completing the creation and the fulfilling of it appear as an intrinsic element in the one total redemptive and divinising will of God for a world in which his self-bestowal is achieved, and this task and the fulfilling of it derive from this totality their ultimate meaning and a concrete form. In virtue of this, task and fulfilment alike, precisely in the specific worldliness, are orientated towards their consummation. Admittedly in all this nothing has yet been said of *that precisely in which* in the concrete this Christianity of the task of achieving the 'this-worldly' future consists. It should not be supposed that because the answer to this question is extremely difficult that there is precisely no such thing as this Christian element. Moreover, as has already been said, the actions in human history of non-Christians too, which are designed to shape the future, fall under the impulse of grace. And because of this it is by no means the case that in seeking a more precise answer to this question we must necessarily fall into the dilemma of simply having to choose between the two following alternatives: either of having to point out some Christian element in this future such that it can be attributed exclusively to those who are 'explicit' Christians, or to recognise what is being striven for as *merely* 'human'. Therefore (and over and above this) the situation can be such that the Christian 'meaning' and the ultimate Christian roots of a reality which is in process of being brought about in history (whether in the social, political or some other sphere) only reveal themselves for what they are when they are already present and so able to be reflected upon and interpreted as an explicit subject for investigation. This appears, for instance, in the case of the growing unity of mankind so often referred to in the Pastoral Constitution, which is at the same time the necessary prior condition for a world Church that is relevant to the contemporary situation. The same could perhaps apply to the openness of the future which is becoming clearer, and the plans for this, the dialectical interplay in which the element of planning and the factor of the unplanned and unforeseeable develop side by side, a development which is explicitly and formally anticipated as such. It may be that in this dialectical interplay, the elements in which cannot be separated from one another by any power of ours, the absolute future of God appears as a silent presence. This Christian mould imprinted upon the 'this-worldly' future towards which mankind is being impelled does not, therefore, depend, in the last analysis on whether or not Christians as a body have certain special demands of their own to raise in the concrete affecting communal, political, social and other aspects of human living, which could not otherwise be raised by anyone else. But the point that is sought to be made clear in this thesis is that in the deepest sense the Christian has not two tasks which are held together merely by a 'moral' bond, namely precisely the fact that he has a duty to perform both. In other words they are united by something more than the fact that the Christian's task for this world has an abstract moral significance for all eternity.[8]

[8] In order to throw further light upon the questions treated of here the author may refer to the following studies in which he discusses the problems involved: 'Marxist Utopia and the Christian Future of Man', *Theological Investigations* VI (London and Baltimore 1969), pp. 59–68; 'The Experiment with Man. Theological Observations on Man's Self-Manipulation', 'Christian Humanism', *Theological Investigations* IX, (London and Baltimore 1972), pp. 187–224.

15

IMMANENT AND TRANSCENDENT CONSUMMATION OF THE WORLD

THE very nature of the subject of this brief study is such as to entail noteworthy difficulties of methodology. The approach to the actual *reality* to be considered, and as pointed to by the title 'Immanent and Transcendent Consummation of the World', is made difficult by unsolved problems in the philosophical and theological fields. Obviously it is not possible here to examine with sufficient clarity the conceptual areas defined by the terms 'immanence', 'transcendence' and 'consummation', important though this is in itself from the point of view of the history both of the concepts concerned and of the previous discussion of the problem. We cannot introduce our study by providing any systematic discussion of the actual terms in themselves. The origin and original meaning of these concepts are in fact insufficiently explained even at the level of historical fact. For this reason it may be permitted to contribute a study which unashamedly refuses to observe with too much exactitude the difference between philosophy and theology, but which, on the contrary, freely employs the methods and basic principles of both disciplines. The attentive and understanding reader will therefore constantly be aware of what the background is to certain of the ideas presented here.

I

The word 'consummation' can be applied:

1. to a particular material event as such of a purely physical or biological kind.

2. to the sum total of all such particular events, in other words to the material world considered as a whole.

3. to the spiritual and personal history of an individual.

4. to all such spiritual and personal histories considered as constituting a unity, and accepting as axiomatic that in spite of the particular subjects

of these each being individual spirits in their own right, this unity and totality of all their individual histories is something more than a final amalgam in which they are all summed up.

5. to the real unity (here presupposed) of the material world together with the history of the spirit at both the individual and the collective levels, in other words to the real unity and totality of the temporal creation, of the 'world' in the widest sense.

It is obvious that the concept of consummation assumes a different meaning according to which of the five entities mentioned above it is applied to. This of itself implies that when we ask whether we should speak of an immanent *or* transcendent consummation, or of an immanent *and* transcendent consummation the question itself likewise assumes a different meaning in each particular case, that the shifts in meaning of the question correspond to the shifts in meaning in the actual use of the term 'consummation'.

Before we can even begin to raise the question of the relationship between immanent and transcendent consummation at all, we have to ask whether the concept of 'consummation' has any meaning when it is applied to the two first-named entities, in other words to the material world merely as such and taken by itself, and to a particular physical or biological event within it to the extent that this can rightly and meaningfully be regarded in isolation from the development of the physical world as a whole to which it belongs. In connection with this we shall formulate the following thesis:

The concept of consummation is totally inapplicable in any meaningful sense to the world as signified here, or to an event taking place in it as such and in isolation; the physical world as such is in itself radically incapable of 'consummation'. It has, if we may so formulate it, no will to achieve its own consummation, but rather tends to continue as that which is abidingly unconsummated. For 'consummation' is (if the word is to have any meaning at all) applied to a *temporal* event regardless of whether the temporality entailed in it is simply experienced by us ourselves or whether some other kind of temporality can be conceived of, e.g. that of the angels.

As applied therefore to such a temporal event and to that which takes place in it the concept of consummation implies:

1. that this event has an end, still regardless of whether the cause of this is inherent in the event itself or brought about by some cause which is different from it.

2. that this event not only has an end, not only 'ceases', but in time

produces a result, something definitive which is different from the event itself, independently of how this abiding result in its validity and 'lasting-ness' is to be conceived of more precisely as compared with 'time'.

3. that this result which has been produced in time is that for which the event considered precisely in its temporal development as event took place, that which it 'sought' and in which the event itself finds its meaning and its justification.

In this connection the question may for the moment be left undecided of whether such a 'consummation' considered as the final product of a temporal event, e.g. in the free personal history of an individual spirit, is only present when this personal history achieves its final consummation – we call it 'salvation' – in a manner that is *positively* moral and religious, or whether alternatively it is still justified and meaningful to use the concept of 'consummation' even when such a history of the free individual 'consummates itself' negatively in final perdition. In any case this concept of 'consummation' which, as the very term implies, has been presented as the opposite of a mere end, cannot have any meaningful application to a mere material event as such. The material event 'runs out'. It remains radically and constantly open to a further future so long as it is not thought of simply as having been terminated. Whether it is conceived of as having *entropeia* or not it does not of itself produce a result different from it. Of itself in any case it does not exhibit any 'will' to achieve a final and consummated state, for in its temporal development it does not show any qualitative difference between elements such that *one* element as compared with another appears to be preferable. Even when we think of and accept such a total and undifferentiated process of development as a state of being directed uniformly, so that it is irreversible, still any given later stage in it is basically of the same quality as the earlier ones, and open to a further stage, or else to that stage at which this movement is brought to a halt, in which case we cannot attribute any higher value to this final stage than to the event itself as such. Now if we regard the material event as having, of its very nature, an intrinsic reference from the outset to the spirit – however we may conceive of this unity of spirit and matter[1] – then certainly we can think of a 'consummation' of the material world. But in that case there has already been a shift in the question itself, so that it is now concerned with the problem of the consummation of the 'personal'

---

[1] For a more developed treatment of this point cf. K. Rahner, 'The Unity of Spirit and Matter in the Christian Understanding of Faith', *Theological Investigations* VI (London and Baltimore 1969), pp. 153–177; K. Rahner (with P. Overhage), *Das Problem der Hominisation* (Freiburg ³1963), pp. 44 ff.

history, although it is true that a special problem arises in turn precisely in *this*.

The thesis formulated above also applies to the special case of biological life as such. Certainly here we can speak in some sense of a 'consummation', namely when the due and proper temporal development of some biological entity in its course of life is not distorted or destroyed by external causes, and so has attained to the full unfolding that is due to it. But even in this case this 'consummation' is nothing else than this due process of temporal development as such and in itself, and it is not a result different from the actual outcome of the temporal process which has run its course. But this is precisely what 'consummation' means. Nor does it make any difference to this when and to what extent such a due process of temporal development initiates a new process of temporal development of exactly the same kind through generation etc., or even itself prolongs its existence indefinitely without being subject to temporal change, as in the case of the 'immortal' primitive organisms. The case here is the same as with other kinds of physical event.

'Consummation', therefore, is a concept which can meaningfully be applied only in that kind of history which is worked out in personal freedom, though admittedly in this it acquires a special property, because this history worked out in personal freedom fastens onto the material event as an intrinsic or extrinsic element of itself, and so from this *among other factors* (and not *solely* from this) can be and is the *single* history of a person in the individual or the collective sense as endowed with spiritual faculties.

It is not possible here to enlarge upon the nature of the personal spirit, its freedom and, arising from this, the special kind of historicity and history that belongs to it, and so to arrive at a satisfactory concept of its consummation based on full and precise arguments. This would be possible *only* by adopting an approach of this kind, of an ontology of the free and personal spirit and the historicity that belongs to it. Here it must be sufficient for us by way of preliminary simply to formulate the following thesis in itself: *the nature of the personal spirit as acting in freedom and as having a personal history implies that there takes place a free and definitive final state of the spirit worked out in time which we call its 'consummation', and which carries within itself those three elements which we have set forth above as constitutive for the concept of consummation.*

Here once more a question arises which we have already touched upon, namely whether the concept of 'consummation' can or cannot be applied also to the *negative* or *wrongly* worked out definitive state of freedom considered as the self-determination of the personal being to perdition. The question involves something more than a mere terminological difficulty. In any genuine ontology of freedom the good or bad exercises of freedom are not ontologically equal as possible uses of it. It is true that in God's sight freedom can achieve its final outcome as a consummation of the self in final and definitive evil. But still the nature of being, of good and therefore of freedom too, is such that this is not a possibility open to the free being which is ontologically on the same level. Such an outcome of the history of the free person as intrinsically involved in the definitive state he has reached is, on the contrary, to be understood as the final and definitive state of *non*-consummation. There is the same dialectic of being and non-being in this as in the evil actions in the concrete of the personal agent in general.

I

This in itself is enough to establish the fact that we have to begin with the problem of the relationship between, or alternatively the mutual exclusion of, immanent and transcendent 'consummation', and indeed of the very meaning of these two concepts as applied to the consummation of the spiritual person in freedom. Only on the basis of this (if indeed at all) can this problem be applied to the world, its course and the human history it contains.

If we take the terms 'immanent' and 'transcendent' consummation primarily in the sense which is suggested by the very nature of the terms themselves, we shall say that an *immanent* consummation is that which arises from the 'immanent' essential composition of the being which is in process of achieving its consummation, i.e. from the resources proper to it and through the intrinsic tendency of what is taking place towards a future goal. Immanent consummation, therefore, is considered precisely as the final outcome which has been worked out in time purely from within the event itself: the definitive finality of the freely posited event in itself. We have attempted to describe the concept of consummation above in these or similar terms. By contrast with this, *transcendent* consummation would in that case be a consummation which comes *ab externo*, being conferred upon the agent independently of the action he himself posits. And this means that it would be that which is given rather than the final and definitive state arrived at by the being itself in its process of reaching maturity. On this showing, therefore, a consummation of this kind would precisely *not*, properly speaking, be something that could be discerned simply from the process itself and nothing more; it would be something, therefore, that went beyond it, 'transcended it' in *this* sense. We would have to think of such a consummation, on this showing, as something already existing in its own right prior to the actual process by which it was arrived at, something towards which this was impelled (if indeed the temporal process has any active part to play at all), something which it only attains to but does not, properly speaking, bring about. It would, therefore, be that which is 'transcendent' in this sense also.

Now let us apply the two concepts of immanent and transcendent consummation as interpreted above to that particular case to which they originally belong, namely to the definitive finality of the free person working out his own destiny in time. When we do this, then immediately the whole range of problems involved becomes apparent. These problems themselves in turn are due to the most divers causes.

The nature of the person endowed with spiritual faculties, including in this his freedom and so his human history too, in other words his 'immanence' *is*, precisely, transcendence. For transcendence establishes a reference to the absolute being, to that which cannot be constructed, cannot be developed into something beyond itself. Transcendence imparts an orientation to the beginning, which is not simply left behind as that which has never been achieved and never been conceived of. It imparts an orientation towards the 'absolute future'.[2] This, as constituting for every specific outcome of human action, a boundless horizon which lays open vistas which are unimaginably remote, always includes every kind of consummation which can be conceived of in 'this-worldly' categories. Ultimately speaking it is orientated towards the absolute mystery, incalculable, uncontrollable and inconceivable, which permeates every material project for achieving a consummation, and calls it in question.

This of itself is enough to make it questionable whether we should postulate any contrast between 'immanent' and 'transcendent' consummation. The following formulation could just as well be adopted: *the immanent consummation of a history worked out in freedom by a being endowed with spiritual faculties is its transcendent consummation* because the immanence is the transcendence; or: *a spiritual being, acting of its knowledge and freedom, has of its very nature no immanent consummation* because the immanent transcendentality rises up to that which is truly transcen-

---

[2] On this cf. K. Rahner, 'Marxist Utopia and the Christian Future of Man', *Theological Investigations* VI (London and Baltimore 1969), pp. 59–68. On the phenomenological aspects of the concept cf. K. Rahner, 'A Fragmentary Aspect of a Theological Evaluation of the Concept of the Future', in this volume, pp. 235–241.

dent, and this (however we understand it) must precisely not be conceived of as the goal of a relationship of transcendentality in the sense of the German idealism. On the same basis it would be possible to formulate it as follows: *The transcendent consummation of a personal freedom is the only true immanent consummation.* If spirit really does *constitute*, in the sense indicated, a transcendence opening up to the mystery, to the absolute being, to the incalculable and uncontrollable future, and if it is precisely this that constitutes its very essence, then the terms 'immanent' and 'transcendent' consummation are deprived of any unambiguously definable distinction. The reason why such a distinction appears to be possible is merely the fact that the free personal being is conceived of after the pattern of a being to which a quite specific function has been assigned, a being thought of purely at the biological level, or a machine which develops its 'goal' from within itself by an 'evolutionary' process. In this sense, therefore, it can have a certain determinate immanent consummation, to which another can be thought of as being added, this time a consummation of the transcendent type, coming from without. Though in that case it still remains somewhat obscure how the nature of this can be conceived of in such a way that it really 'comes' and really is itself a consummation of the being already consummated. But this conceptual model is precisely false. The very definition of man is his indefinability, i.e. precisely his transcendence as absolute openness to being in the absolute. This transcendence of his, therefore, is such that it is radically incapable of being limited to any given future whatsoever, such as might be determined for it in 'this-worldly' categories, or to any given mode of consummation determined for it in this sense. For the limits of such a consummation would already be predetermined, and would be immanent in it from the very nature that was proper to it.

III

What has been stated up to now in very formal terms with regard to the problems involved in the contrast between immanent and transcendent consummation will be made plainer, and at the same time given added precision, if we introduce certain data of the theological anthropology of Christianity into our question.

If we sought to do this in very precise terms then undoubtedly questions would have to be touched upon which are matters of controversy between the Christian confessions, and to some extent even within the circle of Catholic theologians. These relate primarily to the relationship between nature and grace, and ultimately speaking to the relationship between God and man considered in his sheer creaturehood. For instance in the classic Protestant doctrine of justification the justification of man is only 'juridical'. It consists in the gracious will with which God regards the sinner, but ultimately speaking leaves him in his sinful condition. Now certainly another conception is involved in this with regard to the possibility of an 'immanent' consummation than in the Catholic doctrine of justification, in which grace pervades the essence of man from his very roots with divine influence, and thereby gives him the possibility of acting positively for his own salvation, and so implants in him a free and active tendency towards his own consummation. In other words in this Catholic doctrine the tendency towards consummation is much 'more immanent' than according to the Protestant conception. Similar differences might be developed if we were to present in more precise terms the different conceptions with regard to the exact relationship between nature and grace which Catholic theologians have put forward, and the logical outcome of which is that they make the consummation of man appear either 'more immanent' or 'more transcendent' according to the particular position of the theologian involved. But we cannot enter, in any explicit sense into all these questions here. We shall simply be taking as our starting-point a specific conception of grace which we regard as tenable within the framework of Catholic theology, and which appears to us correct.[3] From this we shall go on to ask what conclusions may be drawn in the light of this for the problem of 'immanent' and 'transcendent' consummation. God is not only the Creator of a world different from himself. Of his own initiative, and in that act of immediate self-bestowal which we call grace, he has made himself an intrinsic principle of this world in that creature belonging to it which is endowed with spiritual faculties and which is one element in this one world. This grace can be conceived of in such a way that the power which God has to create out of nothing is seen to be one element in the more sublime and more comprehensive power of God as he who is able to bestow himself in a free exercise

[3] For a more developed treatment and justification of this cf. K. Rahner, 'Concerning the Relationship between Nature and Grace', *Theological Investigations* I (London and Baltimore 1961), pp. 297–317; *idem*, 'Nature and Grace', *Theological Investigations* IV (London and Baltimore 1966), pp. 165–188; *idem*, *Handbuch der Pastoraltheologie* II/2 (Freiburg 1966), pp. 208–239 (bibliography pp. 203–207). In addition to these works of more recent date by the following authors should, of course, also be mentioned: B. Stoeckle, H. Bouillard, I. Willig, M. Seckler. J. Ratzinger etc. But the work which we should particularly notice is H. de Lubac, *Augustinisme et Théologie Moderne* = *Théologie* 63 (Paris 1965); *idem*, *Le Mystère du Surnaturel* = *Théologie* 64 (Paris 1965).

of love. It can also be conceived of in such a way that we see that God has *de facto* willed the creation (even though he might have willed it even without his act of self-bestowal) precisely *because* he willed, as an act of free love, to surrender himself, to empty himself, *himself* to come out of himself. 'Nature', therefore, is in the real order willed from the outset for the sake of 'grace', and 'creation' for the sake of the covenant of personal love. In this self-bestowal as an act of free love God remains on the one hand he who is absolutely free and in no sense in need of his creatures, and he who is infinitely raised above all his creatures considered as the subjects to whom such a free and possible self-bestowal is extended. He creates the world and the creature endowed with spiritual faculties precisely *as* the subjects to which such free and possible self-bestowal is addressed in uncreated grace, but in this self-bestowal God, while remaining the absolute transcendent, nevertheless becomes the innermost principle, the innermost basis, and in the truest sense the goal of 'spiritual' creation. God is not only *causa efficiens* but also *causa quasi formalis* of that which the creature is in the truest and most concrete sense. The nature of the spiritual creature consists in the fact that that which is 'innermost' to it, that whence, to which and through which it is, is precisely *not* an element of this essence and this nature which belongs to it. Rather its nature is based upon the fact that that which is supra-essential, that which transcends it, is that which gives it its support, its meaning, its future and its most basic impulse, though admittedly it does so in such a way that the nature of this spiritual creature, that which belongs to it as such, is not thereby taken away from it but rather obtains from this its ultimate validity and consistency and achieves growth and development because of it. The closeness of God's self-bestowal and the unique personality of the creature grow in equal, and not in converse measure. This self-bestowal of God, in which God bestows himself precisely *as* the absolute transcendent, is the most immanent factor in the creature. The fact that it is given its own nature to possess, the 'immanence of essence' in this sense, is the prior condition, and at the same time the consequence, of the still more radical immanence of the transcendence of God in the spiritual creature, this creature being considered as that which has been endowed with grace through the uncreated grace of God. The conceptual models which are constructed on the basis of the difference between 'inner and outer' break down at this point. The orientation towards the self-bestowal of God as most radically different from the creature is the innermost element of all in it, and it is precisely this that makes the immanence of that which is most external of all to it possible.

IV

What has been said must now be applied still more explicitly to the concept of 'consummation'. In the movement of the creature endowed with spiritual faculties towards its consummation God is not only the ultimate asymptotic point of reference, not only the goal of this movement in all his immediacy. Rather God himself has, through his grace – and not merely through an impulse formed by him as something different from himself – become its ultimate and innermost principle. The point which we must not lose sight of in this is the unity which exists between uncreated grace considered as *causa quasiformalis* and created grace as the necessary prior condition and at the same time the consequence of the uncreated grace.[4] God in his absolute immediacy is, in the concrete order of reality, not only the consummation, the goal (*beatitudo objectiva*) of the spiritual creature, but the principle in the movement which is most proper and necessary to it, the sole really connatural principle by which it is impelled towards the consummation of this goal. The truly ultimate movement towards consummation, towards the goal, is achieved 'in the goal itself'. In the deepest sense, therefore, the present is sustained by the future itself. Our perfection (as prelude) is the 'consummation of that consummation' which already exists and, in spite of being future, is already making its impact (*quoad nos*). All this does not remove the openness of this true future in which our consummation consists. In fact it is God the absolutely incomprehensible who constitutes this future and maintains the movement towards it. He is this future because he is that love that is absolutely free, which has no law outside itself by which it could be measured or judged. Even if we can say that because of it we are what we must be in order that it can be what it is, namely that love which is prodigal of itself, even *so* precisely this love, in virtue of the necessity which it has in itself, imposes upon us those limits which ensure that we ourselves are precisely *not* it, but of our very nature constantly have before us that element in it which we have never possessed or prevailed over, and which is foreign to us, so that we receive it as free and unmerited love. *The 'immanent' and 'transcendent' consummation of the spiritual creature is the same. It is one consummation in which the one aspect demands the other.*

[4] On this cf. K. Rahner, 'Some Implications of the Scholastic Concept of Uncreated Grace', *Theological Investigations* I (London and Baltimore 1961), pp.319–346; I. Willig, *Geschaffene und ungeschaffene Gnade = Münsterliche Beiträge zur Theologie* 27 (Munster 1964).

Two further points are to be noticed. The first is that Thomas, no matter how much he makes plain that the one goal (the *visio beata*) is also the principle of the movement towards it in its aspect as 'supra-natural' and 'unmerited', and so transcending the nature of the creature, in fact does not recognise the concept of a *finis naturalis* for the creature endowed with spiritual faculties. The second point is that any such concept of a 'natural' and, in this sense, *merely* 'immanent' consummation is *de facto* devoid of any ultimate meaning. We have only to rid ourselves of the prejudiced view that at least some kind of 'consummation' which merits this name must be 'due' to the creature, in order to see this point. The very term consummation (German *Vollendung*) precisely implies full completion (German '*Voll-* endung'). But when the *potentia oboedientialis* for grace and for the *visio* is identical with the nature of the spiritual creature, then this nature precisely achieves its true and full consummation only when it has discovered the state of absolute proximity to God through grace and in the *visio*.[5] If this nature is precisely the nature of openness to the *free* love of God, such that it could not be blessed at all if it were not for the freedom and unmeritedness of this love, then there is no need to construct any consummation or any *finis* for such a creature such that it would be merited by him. Only the quality of unmeritedness in love can really bring this creature to its consummation.

If this quality of being unmerited inherent in the one and unique consummation implies that it could also be 'refused', then we may ask straightforwardly with Rom 9:14–18; 11:33–36; 'Why not?' It must be pointed out that even in respect of predestination to salvation and of the efficacious grace that comes from God, Catholic theology teaches that these are unmerited in the same way, even though it is impossible to conceive of even a 'natural consummation' without these factors. It is true that we can construct a positive finality and completion of the decision taken in freedom at the 'natural' level as a reality which is conceivable in itself and as providing a basic conceptual framework. And within this we can imagine the supernatural elevation of man being refused. We can do this in order to clarify the unmerited nature of the love with which God bestows himself upon us. But in that case we should not call this positive and final moral state 'consummation'. It is from this that the idea of a merely immanent consummation can also be developed in the

[5] In this connection one conciliar text has a not inessential bearing. It lays great emphasis on the point that 'in truth there is only *one* ultimate vocation of man, the divine' (Pastoral Constitution on the Church in the World of Today', No. 22).

sense that this, taken by itself, might be the definitive state which man arrived at solely through the resources of his own nature.

In what we have said so far we have had in mind the individual being which exists at the spiritual level. But this can also be applied to mankind as such. For mankind is not the final summing up, at the conceptual level, of all the particular persons endowed with spiritual faculties and of their personal histories as free individuals. On the contrary, in respect of its origin, its existence and its determination mankind constitutes a unity, a fact which is clearly brought out in the theological concepts of 'people of God', 'covenant', 'communion of saints', 'kingdom of God', and in the doctrines of 'original sin', 'redemption' etc. Even though the precise nature of this unity cannot be set forth here,[6] still we can say this much: even the course of the one history of mankind as in this sense constituting a unity, as it moves towards its consummation in the kingdom of God, transcends that alternative which seeks to assign history to *either* an 'immanent' *or* a 'transcendent' consummation. On the basis of the self-bestowal of God this opposition is radically overcome. But this self-bestowal in turn is intended for the individual nature endowed with freedom, *and at the same time* for the community of all such natures. And because of this all that has so far been said concerning consummation as 'immanent' *and at the same time* 'transcendent' applies also to the consummation of mankind as such.

V

The primary question which now remains to be asked is what the implications are of all that has been explained if our investigation of the concept of 'consummation' is extended to the question of the consummation of *the world as a whole* (i.e. including the basic element of the material in it). We have in fact already said that the concept of 'consummation' cannot meaningfully be applied to the material world *purely as such*. For this as such and taken in isolation is radically incapable of being consummated. But the problem is not solved merely by saying this. For the world is a unity of spirit and matter, and in this unity matter is an essential element. The answer given above, namely that the material world is radically incapable of being consummated, therefore, presupposes an abstraction,

---

[6] On this cf. K. Rahner, 'One Mediator and Many Mediations' in volume IX pp. 169–184; in addition see 'Evolution and Original Sin', *Quaestiones Disputatae* (Freiburg 1968), for the problem of the unity of mankind; cf. his earlier observations in *Theological Investigations* I, pp. 274 ff.

and it is not in terms of this that we can come to grips with the real problem.

Any effective attempt at answering the question now to be treated of must depend on how we conceive, in more precise terms, of two further factors: first of the relationship between spirit and matter in general, and then of the metaphysical nature of the development of the material world. Here too only a few theses can be formulated here.

It is justifiable to postulate a real unity and mutual interrelationship between spirit and matter as these exist in creatures.[7] The physical world is not merely the outward stage upon which the history of the spirit, to which matter is basically alien, is played out, such that it tends as its outcome to quit this stage as swiftly as possible in order really to achieve full and complete spirituality in a world beyond that of matter. In a metaphysical interpretation matter is considered rather as that other factor which is necessary, in which and upon which alone *a finite and creaturely* spirituality can be *precisely that which* it is of its nature, and can bring this to its fulness. And this is constituted by the attributes of self-awareness, transcendence and freedom. Without that materiality which is the expression and medium of the self-fulfilment of the finite spirit, spiritual creaturehood at the finite level is totally inconceivable.

We do not need to allow ourselves to be held back from this basic conception by any neo-Platonist or dualistic interpretations of the Christian teaching on angels, or by the interpretation of human death as the 'dividing' of the spiritual soul from matter. Quite apart from metaphysical considerations, this basic conception is made more probable by the Christian dogmas of the substantial unity of spirit and matter in man, by the doctrine of the divine *Logos* becoming *flesh* (without this undergoing any angelic transformation), by the fact that man's personal history as spiritual being is identical with his material and biological life (it does not pre-exist this, nor is the soul 'sojourning' in an alien setting, nor does it have any further and separate history of its own after death). Again it is made more probable by the 'simultaneous' creation of spirit and matter, by the 'resurrection of the flesh', and by the consummation of the world in the new heaven and in the new *earth*.[8] We can only avoid attributing to

[7] In addition to the studies referred to on p. 275, n. 1 cf. also K. Rahner, 'The Secret of Life', *Theological Investigations* VI (London and Baltimore 1969), pp. 141–152.

[8] The question of the theological significance of the making of plans for the future at the 'this worldly' level, and therefore too the question of the significance of the 'new earth', are rendered more difficult in view of modern man's planning for and control

all these dogmas an overtone of anthropomorphism and mythology if we take *a priori* as our starting-point the essential mutual interrelationship of spirit and matter in the creature.

It is precisely in the light of these factors that the essential difference between spirit and matter becomes clear, without us having constantly to trouble ourselves (and that in vain) to point to a creaturely spirit in its concrete existence and as a complete entity in its own right such that it would no longer also be 'material' at the same time. Spirituality and materiality are essentially different *precisely in that* they constitute the metaphysical principles of the *one single* spiritual-material being. Nor is this conception invalidated by the consideration that there was matter and material development 'before' spirit entered 'into' the world. This objection could in fact be met first by pointing out that according to Christian doctrine God '*simul ab initio temporis utramque de nihilo condidit creaturam, spiritualem et corporalem, angelicam videlicet et mundanam*' (DS 800, the IVth Lateran Council of 1215); in other words the material world has always been the counterpart of the 'principalities and powers' with their personal and spiritual mode of being, and these have had to fulfil their natures, once they have been created, in and through the material world, albeit not in a corporal mode such as that of man himself. But even abstracting from this: in the case of a being which is essentially subject to time, the essential unity of the metaphysical principles which constitute its being do not need to be denied on the pretext that the 'potential' principle has some kind of temporal priority over the other, provided only that it is totally ordered to achieve its proper fulfilment in being actualised through the other principle. Now in our case this can be assumed unhesitatingly in spite of the essential difference between spirituality and materiality. For we can make the following statement without any difficulty: the dynamic tendency and development of the material world is ordered to the spirit, and that too in a development which – provided the term is rightly understood – we can even designate as 'immanent'.

For the concept of an 'immanent development' rightly understood implies the idea of a 'self-transcendence' and a 'projection beyond the self'.[9] It does not imply for one moment that in such an 'immanent

---

over the earth. On the question as a whole cf. my brief study of the problems involved, 'The Theological Problems Entailed in the Idea of the "New Earth" ', in this volume, pp. 260–272.

[9] On this concept cf. the bibliography provided on p. 275, n. 1 and p. 285, n. 7, esp. *Das Problem der Hominisation*, pp. 55–78, 84–90.

development' all that takes place in every case is merely that an essence which remains the same is made to run its course, or that we have to think of the development as, in a certain sense, a machine-like process whereby a structure is set in motion and made to repeat its appropriate action again and again. There is this also, but 'development' (and precisely as such it is an *immanent* development) in its true nature consists in 'self-transcendence', in a projection into that which is new, that which essentially goes beyond what has hitherto been achieved. The idea of becoming, taken in its full significance, is radically thrown into relief by another mental picture. Such self-transcendence implies an ultimate common bond between the point of departure and the final outcome of a development. Otherwise it would merely be a question of one factor simply being replaced by another and totally different one. In that case there could be no question of one and the same object undergoing a process of becoming and development.

Now there really is in fact an ultimate common bond of this kind between spirit and matter, for matter too is an element in the creation (which participates in God) wrought by God who is absolute and simple spirit. And God cannot make anything which is opposed to him and to his nature as absolutely disparate from it and alien to it. Matter exhibits its 'spirituality' in that it appears as an intrinsic co-principle in a spiritual and personal being, and shares in the destiny of this being. Unless the roots of being are to be considered as nothingness, the concept of a self-transcendence also implies at the same time that this process of rising beyond the self is made possible and sustained by the absolute being of God. But this power of bringing about transcendence, which belongs to God as Creator, does not have the effect of adding the higher principle to the lower *ab externo*, but rather precisely gives to that lower the capability of rising beyond itself. The new element is then that which is really and essentially higher (in a real 'qualitative change'), and yet at the same time the outcome and goal towards which the 'lower' is orientated. This creative impulse implanted by God is in this case too the 'supraessential' factor in a (material) being, in other words that which transcends it and precisely as such that which is most immanent in it, through which *it* itself alone is a being in process of becoming, and therefore one that rises beyond itself.

VI

Taking these considerations as our premises, we can now come directly to grips with the question of the 'immanent' or alternatively 'transcendent' consummation as this applies to the material world as well. What has been said earlier remains in force here. The material world as such, so long as it remains confined to itself, has no consummation, just as a prelude as such cannot have any finale. But it is perfectly possible to accept that the material world, by reason of its essential orientation to the spirit, is sustained from the outset by that creative impetus, implanted by God, by which it tends towards the spirit as the goal of the self-transcendence of the material element. This impetus can be conceived of from the outset as the impetus of the divine *self*-bestowal which of itself implies, as a necessary factor, the impetus to create a material and spiritual world as the subject to which this self-bestowal is addressed. A further thought which may arise from this is that this impetus of the divine self-bestowal upon the material and spiritual world implies the manifestation in terms of material history of the absoluteness and victorious power of this self-bestowal upon a material and spiritual world *precisely as this is subject to the process of history*, and from this we can recognise that there is present in this creative impetus, as its goal and climax, that which we are accustomed to call in Christian terms the incarnation of the divine *Logos*.[10] In this impetus of the divine self-bestowal upon the material world in order that it may achieve its self-transcendence in the spirit a point that we must always bear in mind is that this self-transcendence of the material world in spirit and freedom takes place in history, in a contest, therefore, in which sin is also possible and which can lead to a radical refusal of God. This self-transcendence is achieved in such a way that it leads to an absolutely open future, for this is what human history in the true sense involves. It is precisely the *self*-transcendence of the material world that is being treated of here. And precisely because of this two further factors should be borne in mind. First the history of the personal spirit in freedom, in redemption and divinisation, must not be thought of simply and exclusively according to the pattern of mechanical or evolutionary processes in material events as such. Second, it is, after all, the real history in which the *material* world itself arrives at its goal and the fulness of its consummation.

Finally the following point must be noticed, as it were as a supplement to what has been said above. On metaphysical grounds (matter as the complement to the creaturely spirit as such), and also on theological grounds, matter (the 'materiality' of the spirit which always and in all cases constitutes an 'environment' for the spirit) must be thought of not as a condition for the spirit, or as something necessary for it to be brought

[10] On this cf. K. Rahner, 'Christology within an Evolutionary View of the World', *Theological Investigations* V (London and Baltimore 1966), pp. 157–192.

to its fulness such that once its consummation has been achieved it is simply cast aside as a means which has become superfluous or as a transitory stage through which it has passed. It endures as an intrinsic element of the spirit and of its history even in its consummation.[11] This is not to dispute the fact that we are totally incapable of forming any conception whatever of the mode of existence of matter in the consummation of the free history of the spirit (cf. 1 Cor 15:35–56). But surely we can hardly form any better idea of the consummation of the creaturely spirit. In as much as the material world as such is carried beyond itself in an act of self-transcendence it achieves in the consummation of this its own consummation. This, therefore, likewise transcends the dilemma which, formulated in these terms, is insoluble, of 'immanent' and 'transcendent' consummation. Its movement towards its consummation is, right from the outset, sustained by divine power, which consists in the love which bestows itself absolutely in freedom. In that this is and remains that which transcends all that is finite, it is the most immanent element in every creature.

It is no mere pious lyricism when Dante regards even the sun and the other planets as being moved by that love which is God himself as he who bestows himself. The innermost principle of this self-movement of the sun and the other planets towards their consummation which lies concealed in the incomprehensibility of God as the absolute future is God himself. He is the 'transcendent' consummation, and therefore can and will, precisely as *God*, himself be the 'immanent' consummation and the 'immanent' principle of the movement towards this single real and uniquely fulfilling consummation that is the *fulness* of finality: God – all in all.

[11] For a more detailed development of this statement cf. provisionally *Theological Investigations* VI (London and Baltimore 1969), pp. 151 f., 154 f., 161 f.; cf. also 'Der Einzelne in der Kirche', *Schriften zur Theologie* VI (Einsiedeln 1965), pp. 499–544; cf. also *Theological Investigations* II (London and Baltimore 1963), pp. 203–216.

PART FOUR

Church and World

16

ON THE THEOLOGICAL PROBLEMS ENTAILED IN A 'PASTORAL CONSTITUTION'

THE distinctive characteristics of the Pastoral Constitution on the 'Church in the World of Today' are already apparent even from the very title, as well as from the preface. These in themselves are enough to show that what is in question here is a conciliar declaration of a kind that is absolutely new and unique at least in intention. Earlier conciliar decrees were either expressions of the official teaching of the Church, and therefore doctrinal in character, declarations, in other words, which embodied some revealed truth which had a permanent validity, or else they were regulations and prescriptions of the Church's law. And while it is true that these latter were consciously promulgated as subject to temporal conditions and therefore capable of alteration, and only in so far as they corresponded to the concrete circumstances of a particular epoch, nevertheless they still constituted something quite different from what this Pastoral Constitution of the Second Vatican Council is intended to be. At the same time it is not easy to say what a Pastoral Constitution really is. In fact the terms of the title itself are still not enough to make this clear. The preface too describes this idea primarily in negative terms: it states that while it is true that in the *first* part the Constitution is primarily doctrinal in character and so is to be interpreted according to the *hermeneutic* principles applicable to the doctrinal statements of the Church in general, still in the *second* part it is primarily intended to correspond to the concrete conditions of the age and therefore, so far as these declarations are concerned, actually undergoes the same risk of being changed which applies to the conditions which it is intended to define and to assist in overcoming. Even this, however, is properly speaking only a negative expression of the fact that the Constitution, in virtue of being bound up with the particular epoch, its attachment to this being at least partly conscious and intended, precisely does *not* have that 'supratemporal' validity and universal binding force which belongs, albeit in varying degrees, to a declaration of the Church's official teachings.

I

But over and above this, what does the term 'Pastoral Constitution' signify *positively*? The word 'Constitution' (as distinct from 'decree' or 'declaration') certainly implies first that the Council intended to attribute a very high degree of importance to this document, and therefore gave it the same designation as those on the liturgy, on the Church and on divine revelation. But what does this special importance of this document consist in?

The word 'Pastoral' does not, initially speaking, throw very much light upon this question. For when we say that 'pastoral' signifies 'that which belongs to care of the flock', 'that which arises from the exercise of the office of shepherd', 'pursuing aims directly concerned with the cure of souls', 'intended to promote the eternal salvation of mankind', then certainly 'pastoral' does acquire a meaning which corresponds to the term itself, and also one which is in harmony with this Constitution. But on this approach we have still not gained very much insight into the special quality of this document, because if this is all that we can say of the meaning of the term, then all the Constitutions, Decrees and Declarations of the Council can and must be called 'pastoral' in some sense or other. For all of them are expressions of the Church in her one and unique function: to promote the salvation of man, to be the mediatrix of salvation.

Now it might be said that the term 'pastoral' is intended to designate this Constitution as an act of the 'shepherd' function in the Church as distinct from an act of the purely doctrinal function as such. But even this, taken by itself, does not advance us very much further in our understanding of the meaning we are seeking for. It is in fact immediately clear that the Church's specifically juridical activity in promulgating laws is in itself also an act of her 'shepherd' function, and of the supreme power of the Church. Yet it is certainly not this that is being treated of in the Pastoral Constitution. This document is manifestly not concerned with lawgiving, obligatory prescriptions, or the promulgation of fresh directives. In view of this, therefore, it still needs to be made clearer what further function can be covered by the concept of the Church's pastoral office (as distinct from her teaching office). We can put this question in a still more developed form if, instead of the Council's distinction between three distinct functions belonging to Christ and the Church (*munus sanctificandi, munus docendi, munus regendi*) we take into consideration the more basic classical distinction between the *potestas ordinis* and the *potestas jurisdictionis*.[1]

---

[1] On this cf. the Constitution on the Church, *Lumen gentium*, and the author's commentary, especially on Chapter III, Nos. 18, 21 etc. of this, *Das Zweite Vati-*

Manifestly the pastoral office must be seen as falling under the concept of the *potestas jurisdictionis*. Yet this concept covers so many factors which are irrelevant to the meaning which we are seeking for that it becomes still more obscure what really can be meant by speaking of a constitution as the act of the pastoral office of the Church (for the Church's teaching function and her authority to make laws are also assigned to the *potestas jurisdictionis*).

But supposing we say that this document is manifestly concerned to throw light upon the concrete contemporary situation in which the world, the Church and the individual Christians live and have to accomplish their tasks, and, over and above this, with the instructions, recommendations, admonitions, warnings and encouragements which the Church of herself addresses to Christians and to all mankind in order that they may all shape their lives aright in this situation which they have to endure; and supposing that such instructions on the one hand do not have the character of a mere 'doctrine' (with eternal validity) or of binding laws in the strict sense of the term, while on the other hand instructions and explanations of the situation of this kind do nevertheless belong to the tasks, powers and duties of the pastoral office, then certainly we have succeeded in describing a meaning contained in the term 'pastoral' which is surely intended here. But at the same time we have brought to light a fresh question, and one to which we must now give our attention.

II

Certainly the first point to be recognised about such *'instructions'* (we are using this term to cover all the aims latent in a specifically pastoral constitution as set forth above) is that in principle it has a doctrinal basis. For what could be the starting-point for such instructions, from which they could derive their standards and the authority which they do ultimately claim to have, if not the message of the gospel, the doctrine of the faith which the Church upholds and proclaims in virtue of her teaching authority? Manifestly instructions contained in a pastoral constitution also have to be supported by those principles *de rebus fidei et morum* which are proclaimed and authoritatively interpreted by the official teaching of the Church. This fact is, indeed, explicitly brought out in the preface to the

---

kanische Konzil. Konstitutionen, Dekrete und Erklärungen. Kommentare, Vol I (Freiburg-im-Breisgau 1966), pp. 211–221; cf. also *ibid.*, p. 221, n. 2, the studies quoted by K. Mörsdorf.

Constitution, when emphasis is laid upon the fact that this Constitution too is not devoid of a doctrinal character. Now it is manifest that there is no intention in this Constitution of drawing any absolutely binding conclusions from these principles, such as would then themselves ultimately have the force of sheer doctrinal norms in their own right.[2] And in view of this fact it is manifest that a fresh question now arises: why is it *only* or primarily 'instructions' that are derived from these principles,[3] why do these principles not give rise simply to '*norms*', *each with its own distinctive message, certainly with an application to the concrete situation, but at the same time with an unambiguously binding force*, such that these norms can be presented as belonging integrally to the official teaching of the Church?

Now one answer to this question might be: 'Because the concrete situation to which these principles have been applied is such as to make it impossible any longer for instructions *bound up with a particular epoch and a particular set of circumstances* to have this force.' But such an answer, which manifestly approximates to the argument presented in the preface, still merely gives rise to yet another question. For a specific situation can indeed be contingent and transient, and yet nevertheless, as a result of applying universal principles to it, it can give rise to a distinctive norm which has absolute binding force in its own right for the circumstances here and now prevailing. And under certain circumstances this norm can be promulgated by the Church as part of her authoritative teaching: as a distinctive *principle* which has an immediate and strictly binding application to the here and now, which, in other words, is something more than a mere instruction. Why, therefore, is the Constitution characterised as pastoral, seeing that this implies that at least part of it consists in a presentation of mere instructions? In view of this, what is such an instruction in more precise terms, seeing that it must be clearly distinguished from a distinctive norm carrying binding force, and yet at the same time is intended to be something more than simply a non-binding expression of opinion with regard to a concrete situation, or a reaction, likewise non-binding, to the situation – a statement, therefore, such as a Council

---

[2] Such have in fact actually been put forward, for instance in many of the encyclicals of the past hundred years even though they were intended to be wholly doctrinal, and not 'merely' pastoral in character. In the present context it makes no difference to the point at issue whether these encyclicals always succeeded in their purpose or not.

[3] Here we may for the moment set aside the fact that in several, or even in many cases something more than 'instructions' does nevertheless *de facto* appear as a result of the document concerned having this character. Here we are concerned simply with the question of what gives such a pronouncement its specifically pastoral force.

manifestly could and should omit? What sort of awareness of the situation does the Church have, that it leads her to try to respond to it with an instruction precisely of this kind, or – to consider it more precisely – that from the knowledge thus acquired she deduces not a distinctive principle but precisely an instruction? Clearly there are questions here which draw our attention to the special quality of a pastoral constitution.

In all these questions the only way in which we can really make progress is to take as our starting-point a thesis which has a basically existential and ontological force. This *thesis* could perhaps be formulated as follows: *While recognising to the full the validity of the universal, we must say that any free decision, as a concrete individual act, and therefore as an act of the person endowed with spiritual faculties in the concrete, is never merely one instance among many sharing a common nature. And for this reason it can never, in the last analysis, be fully deduced from universal principles.* Even if we abstract from the well-known general problems of the ontology of the individual, still this thesis must apply at least to the concrete free decision of the person endowed with spiritual faculties.[4] This thesis can be upheld at least in its application to this free decision, and its practical value appears precisely in its application to the questions we have raised here, and its power to throw light upon these (this in turn serves to confirm the basic correctness of it).

The individual decision in the concrete, therefore, is, in respect of its reality and its moral necessity or non-necessity, not capable of being totally reduced to the universal as expressed in a principle. But in saying this we must overlook the fact that even the 'most concrete' of individual principles still always is, and continues to be, a universal principle. The concrete decision is always *at the same time* the realisation of the universal. For this reason it certainly falls under universal principles, however, we may interpret the universal and its relation to the concrete individual in more precise ontological terms. On this showing any radical 'situation ethics' is false. Like the gospel itself the Church can define even a material ethics as binding. But the free individual decision, in its nature as a unique act in the concrete, is something more than merely a particular instance of this universal, even though this 'something more' is not directly comprehended as such by any exercise of the abstract

---

[4] For a concrete exposition of the problems involved here the author may refer to the following studies of his own: *Das Dynamische in der Kirche* (Freiburg-im-Breisgau ³1965); 'On the Question of a Formal Existential Ethics', *Theological Investigations* II (London and Baltimore 1963), pp. 217–234; Section entitled 'Der Einzelne in der Kirche', *Theological Investigations* VI (Einsiedeln 1965), pp. 499–544.

intelligence reflecting upon and objectifying it, and always having to refer back to universal concepts. On the contrary, the most we can do is to describe it ideographically by means of a thousand approximations. On the other hand in itself it is experienced as such through the concrete act of the individual subject, who carries out and consciously possesses within himself this decision without reflecting upon its nature from the ultimate standpoint of himself as subject endowed with the spiritual faculties inherent in human nature. At the same time it must be remembered that any such individual decision, in common with all intellectual acts on the part of a physical person, has an intrinsic structure of its own. This is because there is a unity, and at the same time an inalienable duality, between subject and object. In other words even in the most basic act there is already an element of objectivation which is the outcome of the universal and the reflexive elements,[5] and for this very reason, even though the individual decision cannot be resolved into the universal, still it is to a certain extent able to be reflected upon, albeit always merely at the asymptotic level. In terms of human intercommunication this decision is also as such able to be summoned up by an *imperative*[6] in the form of counsel, concrete example to be imitated etc.

III

We have now arrived at a point at which we can give a possible and reasonable explanation of what is meant by 'instruction'. *Instruction is the counsel to take a concrete decision which, while it is intended to give reality to a universal nature and to a universal principle in a specific situation* (because of the value and binding force of this universal), *is nevertheless incapable of being derived from this universal in any full or compelling sense, either in respect of its content or in respect of its binding force, but remains, both in its uniqueness and its factuality, that which belongs to history, and something which, in the last analysis, can be completely understood only in its actual realisation.* Now if what we have said is rightly understood, then it is immediately evident that instruction too, by the very fact of being the act of the instructor, is a decision. For even as the act of the instructor it cannot be deduced solely from the universal (considered as its genus and its principle). It cannot be so deduced even when, both in the instruction

---

[5] For an understanding of how freedom and the spiritual are to be objectified cf. the author's observations in *Über die Freiheit*, M. Horkheimer, K. Rahner, C. F. v. Weizsäcker edd. (Stuttgart ²1965), pp. 35 ff.

[6] On this cf. K. Rahner, *Das Dynamische in der Kirche . . .*, pp. 14 ff.

itself and in the decision corresponding to it the situation in which it is taken is actually included in the consideration. For one thing the situation, at least as constituted in part by free decisions taken at an earlier stage in the unfolding process of human living, is itself incapable of being fully or exhaustively thought out in all its aspects. A further point is that every analysis of a situation on the part of a concrete individual subject must be something more than merely material for the speculative intellect to theorise about in an absolutely neutral manner. In all cases and inevitably it must also be the spontaneous act of the practical intellect. In other words it must *ipso facto* itself be a decision. Even if we neglect these aspects which belong to any analysis of a situation (this is something which for the most part we are right in doing in the practical activities of everyday life), still even then the fact remains unaltered that in a specific situation – at least in principle, even though perhaps not in practice in every individual case – there are *several* possibilities for taking a decision, and moreover for taking it in such a way that several further decisions still remain open as, from the aspect of the *universal* norms, *morally* permissible. This remains true even though for the most part the range of what is morally permissible as a result of combining universal norms with a concrete situation will be extremely limited. Instruction, counsel, recommendation etc., therefore, constitute a free decision taken in the developing process of human living with the aim of using the intercommunication which exists between one human subject and another in order to make that other choose one specific decision among several possible ones (possible, that is to say, even in the sense of being permitted by the general norms of morality). In this process of causing him to choose one particular decision, therefore, what is aimed at is neither to impart to a given course of action the force of a duty by the application of universal norms, nor yet to impose any compulsion. For any 'response' of this sort does, of course, still leave the decisive question open: whence does instruction derive its unique character as having the force of a demand, since this force is manifestly attributed to it (albeit in a different way than in the case of a universal norm, which is binding as a matter of moral duty)? For evidently the instruction is not intended to sink to the level of a mere expression of opinion or of the sort of wish on behalf of the other which imposes no obligation on him whatever.

In order to obtain a deeper insight with regard to the nature of the instruction and the concrete decision taken in the unfolding course of human life, the first point for consideration is that even the individual decision as such can have a certain binding force although, or even to the extent that, this force is not something that can be deduced from the relevant moral norm with its universal application. From the theological point of view this binding force is, to the extent that it is a genuinely moral element that is in question here, to be interpreted on the basis of the *summons uttered by God in the concrete* to the individual, and directing him to take a *specific* decision. This summons is precisely not identical with the binding force of universal norms considered as divine commandments. In the individual case this summons is always conveyed through the medium of the concrete situation in which a moral decision has to be arrived at. However, this situation, objectifiable though it is to human thought, is not of itself *ipso facto* sufficient to supply all that is necessary for such a decision to be arrived at in all its fulness. Whether the course we decide upon among several morally permissible ones *always* has a binding force of this kind as a result of God's specific summons to us in the individual case, or whether it has this only in many cases, is a question which, for our present purposes, we may leave on one side. But what is certain is that this character of moral obligation can be attached to a specific position in the concrete as one of these morally permissible courses. Now when an instruction, while continuing to have this force, is presented as an act of the instructor in the awareness of being authorised and endowed with moral obligation in virtue of such a divine summons (of course this need not necessarily be explicitly defined precisely in these terms) what is constituted thereby is that which can be called, in the stricter and more proper sense, a *theological* instruction. Even an instruction of this kind is directed to the standards freely adopted by the other in taking his own individual decision. This is true not merely because the authenticity and compelling power of the instruction as such can never be established by appealing to principles which can be objectively defined and in this sense recognised, not merely because the individual instance of the divine summons conveyed by the instructor to the other cannot comprehensively be grasped in those modes of objectifiable knowledge which are open to us in other cases, for because what is implied in this divine summons is a quite unique mode of knowledge and testing on the part of the 'addressee' or 'recipient'.[7] On the contrary, instruction as understood here also appeals (though without thereby losing its character as demand) to the free and open decision of the other to the extent that we cannot *a priori* exclude, or pronounce meaningless, that case in which someone, prompted to a

---

[7] In traditional language this mode of knowledge and examination is called the 'discernment of spirits'. On this cf. K. Rahner, *op. cit.*, pp. 100 ff. (bibliography in n. 35).

decision by the summons of God, gives an instruction, without the binding force of the divine summons to the individual also applying immediately and *ipso facto* to (any) one *specific* addressee in the concrete, to whom the instructor directs his instruction. For the instruction can, e.g., perfectly well have meaning and validity in the Church as such, can be designed to be put into practice in a spirit of obedience by specific individuals, without the instructor himself knowing precisely *who* this instruction is ultimately addressed to in the intention of the divine summons which the instructor himself responds to in obedience. The result is that the instructor must, properly speaking, direct his instruction to individuals who are 'anonymous'.

IV

It will now be relevant to apply what has been said about the nature of instruction in general to the action of the Church. The Church is not merely the upholder and interpreter of the truth of revelation, or the dispenser of the sacraments. As subject she is constituted as a society, and as such she is also the upholder of her own concrete resolutions and actions, which, of course, have to be realised by physical subjects in the concrete. Moreover, over and above the function of proclaiming the truth of faith and dispensing the sacraments, the Church has also, as is made clear by the very fact that she has a pastoral function, a task of guiding and an authority to guide the Christian actions of her individual members, who have to respond to this authoritative guidance by their own individual decisions and actions in the concrete. So far as the question goes with which we are here concerned, it makes no difference, ultimately speaking, in this second case, what the nature of this authoritative guidance consists in more precisely, as applied to the individual members of the Church. In other words it makes no difference whether the Church has any such power to guide only to the extent that the individual Christian must contribute to a common life of the Church as such (something which undoubtedly belongs necessarily to the nature of the Church), or whether the Church's authority to guide can extend beyond this and beyond the preaching of faith and dispensing of the sacraments so as also to bear upon the Christian life of the individual Christian in his 'private dimension' as such. In any case a power to guide does exist in the Church, and this power bears upon the concrete decisions and actions of the individual Christian. Now it cannot be contested that under certain circumstances the Church's power to guide in this sense *can* apply to the action of a

Christian in the concrete to some extent with an imperative force, in other words as claiming to be morally binding in the same sense as a commandment or prescription (this is true at least of the individual Christian's 'exterior' activities, and we may leave aside the question of whether the Church as such can directly command an 'interior act'). But what is certain is that general commandments or prescriptions of this kind are not the only way in which the Church's power to guide can take effect. The very fact that many factors have to exist, and many things have to be done in the Church (and, moreover, in directions and ways which, while they are quite specific, are nevertheless open to change) for the carrying out of which the Church can appeal to specific individuals without necessarily exercising her power of command over them. The *Caritas* movement in the Church, her work in the missions, ecclesiastical education, ecclesiastical learning, and much else besides, are factors which must be present. They are tasks which are obligatory upon the Church, and yet she is not able to impose these duties of her own volition as binding upon certain specific individual Christians. The realisation of her own fulness is something that is necessary and a duty for the Church, something, moreover, in which there is always an element of contingency, since it belongs to the dimension of concrete history, and since *de facto* it can be achieved only through the free decision and the free act of individual Christians. And yet the Church cannot, of herself, make this a duty in the strict sense for specific individuals as a matter of law or concrete commandment which they can be compelled to carry out.[8]

Now there is no doubt that it is to this area that the 'instruction' (counsel, exhortation to perform something which is incapable of being the subject of an order etc.) belongs. If it were not that the Church had the power and the authority to issue such instructions, it would be quite inconceivable how she could apply her pastoral function in the concrete. Laws and commandments taken by themselves would never achieve what has to be achieved and done in the Church.

V

We have already said above that the very fact that the instruction is an

---

[8] Here it is apparent that we can only conceive of the nature of the Church if we include within our purview the controlling force of the Church's Spirit who by his grace causes the individual to decide of his own freedom to obey this impulse which moves him in his freedom and so to do that which the Church cannot command and yet which must be done because it is necessary to the Church.

act of the instructor *ipso facto* implies that a decision is involved which cannot wholly be deduced from general laws and norms applicable to the class of action involved. Now there is no doubt that this also applies to the Church. When she causes an exhortation to be issued in the sense of an 'instruction' as understood here, when she emphasises some special point in these recommendations, exhortations, desires etc., when she recommends one course of action with special urgency today and another tomorrow, then in such instructions she herself makes decisions which cannot be compellingly deduced *solely and exclusively* from her understanding of the faith *de rebus fidei et morum*. Moreover these decisions (at least in very many cases) do not derive unambiguously and in the concrete from this understanding of the faith which she has, even when we take into consideration as one of the relevant factors the situation of the Church herself, of the world and of the individual, in which such instructions are issued. For even for the Church the basic principle applies that even in a concrete situation several morally justifiable decisions can be arrived at in so far as these are measured merely by the general principles of whether they are morally permissible. Now in the case of such instructions how does the Church come to recognise which specific ones she *should* promulgate and which others she can or should leave undefined even though, from the moral and Christian point of view, they are possible?

It has already been said above that a moral decision in the concrete becomes recognisable as something that ought to be done not solely or exclusively because of the normative power of the general material and formal principles to which it is related, in other words that the concrete decision, precisely as concrete and individual, can come to be recognised as something that ought to be done in virtue of a divine summons. This also applies to the instructions of the Church to the extent that they constitute concrete decisions of the Church who instructs. The Church cannot issue any instructions she likes, only restricting herself in this to the extent of ensuring that any instruction she does issue does not come into conflict with her general principles. Nor is the individual obligation involved in a concrete instruction removed in virtue of the fact that he to whom it is addressed can, without violating any general moral norms, act upon the instruction or not as he wills. For even the instruction as such constitutes an alteration in the sphere of freedom open to the other[9] to whom it is directed, and therefore entails certain moral demands. Hence in

---

[9] cf. the study referred to in n. 5, pp. 41 ff., and the author's brief study on what is needed for a right understanding of religious freedom in the small volume entitled *Religionsfreiheit*, M. Schmaus and E. Gössmann edd. (Munich 1966), pp. 7–23.

effect the question must be raised of whence, in that case, the Church knows how her concrete instruction has to be issued, what brings her to recognise that individual summons of God which imparts to a decision (in this case the instruction) its specific character as something that ought to be promulgated in the particular circumstances. Now certainly it can be said that the Church (in her official representatives) gives, and should give, such an instruction 'according to the highest dictates of her one conscience'. In other words in such an instruction she should command what seems, in the light of the concrete situation, most probably to be the 'better' course, what is most calculated to serve the interests and aims of the Church and of the realization of Christian living in a concrete situation. A further point wholeheartedly to be conceded is that in her practice the Church must act in this way, just as an individual man also, in a concrete situation, follows the 'dictates of his conscience' in selecting one of various possibilities even when his theoretic intelligence is incapable of recognising any one of these possibilities as absolutely and certainly the only one which can be entertained.

VI

Manifestly, however, this alone is not enough to explain how the Church recognises that any one specific instruction is such as to express something that ought to be done in a particular set of circumstances, and thereby becomes aware that she herself is authorised and empowered to issue this particular and specific instruction. For simply in virtue of the fact of issuing instructions alone, decisions are arrived at which are, all things considered, of such great importance for the Church herself, for the individual Christians and for the world, that it is hardly possible to conceive, merely on the basis of our understanding of the Church, that the manner in which they are arrived at is no different from the manner in which those resolves are arrived at by which an individual man, acting upon 'the highest dictates of his conscience' makes experiments in his life because nothing more is possible for him. But then one point which the Christian is aware of with regard to the Church is this: the Church is constantly being guided by the Holy Spirit.

We must develop this statement. It is certain that this Spirit is bestowed upon her primarily in order that she may not depart from the truth of Christ in any *definitive* doctrine, and in order that in her that hope and that love may always remain alive and may also be manifested in history in adequate ways (cf. D 1794), without which the Church would not be what she must be, and, moreover, must always remain, through the eschatologically victorious grace of Christ.[10] Certainly the fact that she has the assistance of the Holy Spirit does not exclude the fact that there are sins in the Church, and, moreover, even in the official representatives of the Church as such, and therefore, that there are wrong decisions, wrong developments, denials of the Church as such. The Church is not only a Church of sinners but also a sinful Church, an *Ecclesia semper reformanda*.[11] But the fact that the Church abides in the truth of Christ, in his hope and love, is in fact not simply a static condition established once and for all, but must always be made actual afresh through specific individual acts and decisions in history on the part of those officials and human individuals in the Church who are commissioned to uphold her official functions in the concrete. This essential state of the Church abiding in the truth, hope and love of Christ, therefore, is necessarily achieved through the assistance of the Holy Spirit, and there is no other way whatever in which it can be achieved, because the institutional Church is totally incapable of guaranteeing that she will abide in them in this way. But from this it follows that this assistance of the Spirit extends precisely to the whole range of those decisions, acts, omissions and mutual influences in all their variations, in which the abiding of the Church in Christ is realised in the concrete.

A further point is that in the Constitution on the Church of the Second Vatican Council the Church explicitly teaches that what belongs to her intrinsic nature is not merely the institutional factors of universal doctrine, sacraments and law, but the charismatic factor as well. There is no need to provide a detailed exposition at this point of what this means.[12] What we must emphasise here, however, is one of the implications of the statement that even the *laymen* are the bearers of such charismatic gifts belonging to the Church. In no sense does this truth have to be bound up with the idea that *the holders of official positions* in the Church are not the bearers of such charismatic gifts, or not recipients of such charismatic

[10] For a fuller treatment of this cf. *Theological Investigations* VI (London and Baltimore 1969), pp. 295–312, especially pp. 301 ff., 305 ff.

[11] For an understanding of this cf. the author's study, 'The Sinful Church in the Decrees of Vatican II', *Theological Investigations* VI (London and Baltimore 1969), pp. 270–294.

[12] cf. K. Rahner, *Das Dynamische in der Kirche* . . ., pp. 38–73; *L.T.K.* II (Freiburg ²1958), pp. 1027–1030 (with bibliography); *Handbuch der Pastoraltheologie* I (Freiburg-im-Breisgau 1964), pp. 154–160; Vol II/1 (Freiburg-im-Breisgau 1966), pp. 76 ff. (Bibliography). cf. also below n. 14.

influences on the part of the Spirit of God.[13] It is perfectly possible, therefore, to conceive of these officials in the Church as the bearers of charismatic gifts and as receiving the assistance of the Holy Spirit, which is never totally withdrawn from the Church. With regard to such charismatic gifts the Constitution on the Church emphasises that we should not, at any rate not always and not in the normal instances of them, think of them as extremely miraculous or spectacular phenomena. In other words they may be manifested in forms which seem to belong to life at an extremely down-to-earth, everyday and sober level. Now this point which is so much emphasised naturally applies also to the Church's officials and to their acts to the extent that the charisms play an essential part in determining the nature of these, charisms which are to be thought of as bestowed with the assistance of the Holy Spirit (at least in principle) as extended to the generality of the Church's official functionaries. The fact that we have to think of the effects of the assistance of the Spirit and of his charisms as taking place in unspectacular ways should not obscure the conviction of faith that this influence of the Spirit and of his charisms is present in the Church's officials even though sometimes the concrete image of the Church may seem disappointing and may lead us to wish that this power of the Spirit could be manifested more clearly and in ways which transcend all merely institutional levels.[14]

This provides us with a starting-point from which to answer the question posed above, that namely of what enables the Church to recognise in formulating her instructions (these being considered as decisions on the part of her official functionaries) which of these instructions in the concrete do in fact express what ought to be done, seeing that this cannot be deduced in any adequate sense either from the general principles of the Church or merely from an analysis of the situation, or even from a combination of both of these. We are now in a position to formulate the following principle: *The instructions of the Church considered as decisions on the part of her official functionaries are (at least amongst other things, or at least in specific instances) charismatic instructions formulated with the assistance of the Spirit in the Church.* It is from this that that unique character

[13] On this cf. *Handbuch der Pastoraltheologie* I, pp. 154 ff.; *Theological Investigations* VI, pp. 305 f. Even in the concept of the sacrament of order we already find an ultimate unity being pointed to between a power that is official and institutional and a grace which is personal and consecrating, and as such capable of having charismatic effects.

[14] On this cf., in addition to those works by the author mentioned in nn. 12 and 22, especially 'Do not Stifle the Spirit', *Theological Investigations* VII (London and Baltimore 1971), pp. 72–87.

of such instructions derives, namely of expressing what ought to be done (this is inherent in the instruction and for those who are the recipients of the instruction). This unique character is such that it belongs neither to a law, a norm or a commandment, nor can the instruction itself be reduced to the level of a mere expression of some opinion which the promulgators happen to favour, or of a wish which imposes no obligation whatever upon those others to whom it is addressed.

VII

On the basis of this point which we have now recognised as correct we can attempt to think out in more precise terms the true nature of a pastoral constitution. But before we do this there remains to be investigated yet another aspect of a charismatic instruction of this kind. Certainly this 'instruction' which we intend to recognise as the distinctive element in a pastoral constitution ultimately constitutes the charismatic decision through which the Spirit guides the life of the Church in the concrete, and leads her to adopt ever fresh modes of self-realisation and ever fresh forms in which to express herself in concrete history. though these can never be worked out solely or totally at the theoretical level. But this does not exclude the simple fact, which is readily observable at all times, that such decisions and instructions emerge in all cases only in the context of a concrete encounter with a specific situation in which the Church finds herself. Inspiration from above is always made real in and through the 'material' which is supplied from below, even though it is equally true that this inspiration can never be established totally and exclusively, as it were, by a process of synthesis from below. Here, however, we are considering how this situation comes to be recognised. And while according all due importance to the factor of the guidance and assistance of the Spirit of God (precisely in this process of recognition as well), we must say that this recognition is a *human* recognition, with all the necessary prior conditions, developments and systems of thought which belong to a human process of recognition, and above all to the recognition of a particular individual factor in history. It must be remembered, however, that *the Church has something more to do* than merely to preach the enduring truth of the gospel, something more than merely to ensure that the abiding essence of the sacraments shall be realised again and again in innumerable particular concrete instances. Over and above this she must *act in and upon history, and the necessity of such concrete action in history also belongs to her own intrinsic nature. Now if all this is true then the necessity and the power of recognizing the situation in which she has so to act and so to realise herself likewise belongs to her own intrinsic nature, or to the full realisation of this.*

Now in saying this we are expressing something which is a truism, and yet at the same time astonishing. We say so easily and so unreflectingly that the Church draws her life *solely* from the revelation of God in Jesus Christ, from the gospel which *always remains the same*; and that this revelation (for all the possibilities it offers of historical development and explicitation, and for all the necessity that exists for progressively unfolding it) was *closed* with the death of the apostles and is not susceptible of any further additions. Yet through this very truism which we have just expressed it becomes manifest that it is quite impossible for the Church to draw her life *solely* from the revelation of God (the progressive unfolding and right interpretation of this). In order to be able to act at all, and in fact to act in a way such that without it she would not be what she must be at all, she needs a knowledge of the situation in which she lives. Certainly this knowledge of the situation can likewise be achieved with the assistance of the Spirit and, as a knowledge belonging to the Church, may bear, in some respects, a charismatic character. In other words it may be something different from knowledge of a historical situation at the merely secular level considered as a secular analysis of the age, of society etc.[15] And a further point which may be conceded as perfectly correct is that the occasion of acquiring such knowledge, in which a theoretical analysis of the situation (despite the fact that it is always incomplete) is concluded and made the basis for decision and action in the concrete, also includes, as it were, that point in this concluding of the analytical stage and in this transition to decision and action to which the working of the Spirit is primarily to be assigned. But all this does nothing to alter the fact that the Church has need of a non-revelatory kind of knowledge, a knowledge which does not belong to the *depositum fidei*, in order to be herself and to be able to act.

VIII

This fact only seems not to make much difference therefore. It has been able to remain more or less unremarked, and has not given rise to any particular theological reflection, because in earlier ages this knowledge

---

[15] The author has carried out an analysis of the present of this kind (partly in collaboration with N. Greinacher) in *Handbuch der Pastoraltheologie* II/1, pp. 178–276; the basis in scientific theory, pp. 180–188. cf. also 'Theologische Deutung der Position des Christen in der modernen Welt', *Sendung und Gnade* (Innsbruck ⁴1966), pp. 13–47.

of the situation was an extremely simple and uncomplicated factor which could be presupposed as already present to an adequate extent in everyone endowed with practical wisdom so long as they had a little personal experience of life, and could therefore also willingly be attributed – at least by presumption – to the individual leaders of the Church. But in this respect too the situation has altered. Knowledge of the situation in which the 'world' and the Church have to live, act and make decisions today is so multidimensional, complex and confused that it can no longer be attained to solely through the simple experience of life in the concrete which prudent and mature people achieve. Today it has to be made the subject of the fullest consideration, of a learning which is both manifold and far-reaching in the methods it uses which include several auxiliary sciences (in certain circumstances computers etc. may be employed) in order really to achieve what has to be achieved: to impart to a society, a state, the community of nations and to the Church as well[16] that knowledge of the situation which is the necessary prior condition for any course of action which measures up to the realities involved. This being the state of affairs, the problem of precisely *how* the Church can acquire knowledge of the situation in which she has to act, since she cannot create this knowledge for herself from revelation, suddenly becomes extremely awe-inspiring. The Church cannot give her decisions, even when these are merely 'instructions' issued to her members, without achieving a confrontation with the situation in which instructions need to be given, and in acquiring knowledge of this in the world of today she is perforce put in a position by men themselves in which she is dependent upon sources of knowledge and methods of gaining it which are artificially controlled,[17] and which she is, in effect, quite incapable of controlling for herself in any adequate way. And yet her own action depends at least in part upon this knowledge, as also do the achievements of the *ex professo* scholarly element within her ranks, as distinct from the charismatic impulses of her spirit.

The fact that there is a problem here which has been insufficiently worked out in terms of any theory of the Church's knowledge (if we may so express it) appears from a single small fact, in itself insignificant, but

---

[16] Hence in the sphere of the Church too a livelier awareness is needed of the necessity for planning, for prognostication, and for analyses based on scientific theory. cf. on this *Handbuch der Pastoraltheologie* II/1, pp. 214 ff., 258 ff., 274 ff., II/2, pp. 19 ff., 76 ff.

[17] cf. K. Rahner, 'The Experiment with Man', *Theological Investigations* IX (London and Baltimore 1972), pp. 205–224.

in this context rich in implications. At the Council there were certain
conservative theologians who expressed their opposition in very strong
terms to any attempt on the part of the Council at providing an official
analysis of the contemporary situation – just such an analysis, in fact, as
was, in the end and in spite of these objections, set down in the *expositio
introductiva* of the Pastoral Constitution. But what these conservative
theologians said was: *Whence* is the Church to know precisely *what* must
be said in this Constitution if after all she cannot draw this knowledge
from the sources of knowledge bestowed upon herself? How is she to be in
a position to make some binding pronouncement on the subject? *How* can
she avoid the danger in such discussions either of putting forward mere
platitudes which can be found better expressed elsewhere or of hazarding
assertions which rightly meet with rejection on the part of those who are
specialists in analysing the contemporary situation and in estimating what
the future will hold? In this latter case the Church cannot even defend
herself by putting forward the proposition that in the last analysis she is,
in fact, more competent in these matters than the specialists themselves.
Such objections are certainly to be taken seriously, and in so far as they
are answered at all by the terms of the Pastoral Constitution they are
answered only *via facti*, without any explicit or conscious reflection upon
them, somewhat as follows: The Church has dared to attempt such an
analysis of the contemporary situation because she absolutely needs such
an analysis. Moreover, given that she has to undertake an analysis of this
kind, it is only fair that she should also be allowed to state freely to her
members and to the world the findings which she has drawn from it.[18]

The question we are treating of here is concerned with a theory of the
Church's teaching office as this bears upon the nature of that knowledge
which is necessary to the Church, yet which cannot be acquired directly
or exclusively from the sources of revelation. Now in the last analysis the
problem this involves can only be solved if we take into consideration
among other factors the charismatic assistance of the Holy Spirit available
to the Church in this process of reflecting upon her own situation which
is necessary for the conduct of her life and her activities. Moreover, as
understood here, this assistance does not exclude the process of reflecting
upon the contemporary situation at the human level, which today is extremely complex and involves the use of all those methods which human

---

[18] In this connection it is, of course, almost self-evident that inasmuch as this
analysis of the present was relegated to the *Expositio Introductiva* it is not adequate
and, furthermore, that it makes no claim to be so; in other words that the Church
certainly knows more upon this subject than it expresses in this Constitution.

science has made available. On the contrary it includes this and becomes effective precisely in and through such humanly acquired knowledge. Nor does the assistance of the Spirit as understood here exclude the fact that the Church may fall short in her analysis of the situation through human limitations and human failures, or even through culpable obstinacy and narrow-mindedness, the refusal to recognise her own faults, a lack of charity in recognising the value of those outside her etc. In all these ways the Church may fall short of what can be achieved and what should be striven for in such an analysis. Obviously in acquiring such knowledge the Church too has to recognise certain limitations at the existential and ontological levels to which all men are subject. It is true of all men, when they embark upon an analysis of their situation as a prelude to 'estimating' what the future holds for them, that however advanced their 'futurology' may be, their true and actual future always remains to a large extent unknown, and so not subject to their control. And this applies to the Church also. But this should not for one moment obscure the basic insight of faith by which we recognise that even when the Church undertakes an analysis of the contemporary situation of this sort – something which is vitally necessary to her – she is still acting under the charismatic influence of the Spirit. It is quite unnecessary to regard this influence as consisting primarily, or indeed at all, in the fact that in the course of this analysis the Church discovers factors which have not been, or could not have been discovered equally well by secular and uncommitted bodies undertaking a similar analysis of the contemporary situation. On the contrary, this influence of the Spirit is manifested primarily in the following two facts: first that the Church actually does venture upon an analysis of this sort, not attempting to suppress the factors adverse to herself which she may, under certain circumstances have to recognise in doing so, but rather facing up to them in all openness and humility; second, that the Church is able to select from the incalculable number of individual facts and findings to which such an analysis gives rise those in particular to which the charismatic summons of the Spirit directs her when it is mediated to her in the process of arriving at her own decisions and instructions. What has been said so far is not intended to give the impression that the problem of the theory of the Church's knowledge raised here has now been solved in a satisfactory manner. But if we have to speak of the nature of a Pastoral Constitution issued by a Council, this problem too should at least be touched upon.

We are now in a position to make the following statement:

The essence of a Pastoral Constitution consists in instructions issued by the

Church primarily for her own members, and to some extent over and above this for all men who are ready to pay attention to the Church. These instructions are issued in view of the contemporary situation as evaluated under the charismatic influence of the Spirit and in response to the charismatic summons of God.

In this description the terms 'instruction', 'summons' and 'charismatic knowledge' are, of course, to be regarded as involving that content which we have attempted at least to indicate in the preceding sections. Admittedly too, in order that this description may be valid, a further qualifying clause must immediately be added to it as follows: '. . . *if* and to the extent that a Pastoral Constitution really is intended to be, and is capable of being, something more than a mere amalgam of principles put forward in a doctrinaire manner, these general principles being developed into particular principles with as precise an application as possible to a specific situation.' Obviously, however, this taken by itself would not entail anything that went beyond a doctrinal pronouncement of the Church based solely on her sources of revelation.

IX

The very moment we have arrived at this mode of describing what a Pastoral Constitution of the Church essentially means we find ourselves inevitably and spontaneously brought up short by the question: Is there really any such thing? But the question which will occur to us first and foremost is: Can we really claim precisely *this* Constitution of the Second Vatican Council as a Constitution in the sense which we have now defined?

With regard to the *first* question, what has already been said needs only to be supplemented by the following further observation: In the history of the Church there undoubtedly have been, and still are men and women who are charismatically endowed. These have made statements which have subsequently become 'instructions' of the Church of precisely this kind, instructions which are not derivable merely from the principles of revelation alone. Moreover these utterances of theirs have commanded attention and have thereby contributed very notably to the concrete history in which the Church is in process of achieving her own fulness.[19]

[19] From this point of view Church history would have to be rewritten *precisely in its pastoral aspect as understood here*. We may think, for instance, of such definitive breaks with the past as were brought about by the acts of individual Christians such as Catherine of Siena or Joan of Arc, or even of still greater achievements on the part of whole groups such as the work of missionaries in China (Ricci), the experiment of the worker priests etc.

A further consideration to be borne in mind in this connection is that when such instructions, deriving as they do from those favoured with charismatic impulses, have emerged in the Church's life, they have invariably been dependent for their success upon a certain acceptance on the part of the Church's official representatives, although this acceptance may perhaps have been at a quite inexplicit and unofficial level. In view of this, and even apart from what has been said above, we can see no compelling grounds for excluding the official Church too as such radically and *a priori* from the possibility of itself giving utterance to 'instructions' of the same kind in the Church as a whole. Moreover we who recognise the Church (differing in this from the Old Covenant) as an indissoluble eschatological unity of institution and Spirit, must not conceive of the abiding distinction in her between the 'institutional' and 'charismatic' elements in so primitive a manner.[20]

The *second* question, it must be conceded, is more difficult to answer. Does this Constitution in its actual and existing form really possess the character of a 'pastoral constitution' precisely as *we* have attempted to define this? The first point we have to make with regard to this question must in all honesty be that it is not easy to supply any assured answer to it. The point of departure for our description of the essential nature of the Constitution is to be found in the preface to it. And it must be conceded that here it is neither as ample in scope nor as well substantiated as we could wish. For it can be asked whether the reference in the Constitution to its own 'pastoral' character, that is to that 'something more' which it contains over and above the assured and abiding doctrinal statements, is such that our explanation of it is wholly compelling or in fact the only possible one. It can legitimately be asked whether after all this preface is not intended to say merely that from the *general* principles of Christian revelation the Constitution draws particular *principles* with a narrower application in view of the nature of the present situation as it exists in the concrete and as subject to change. On this latter showing, however, the composers of the Constitution would have had in mind the implicit proviso that they would not vouch for the correctness of these particular principles in every case or with their *ultimate* authority, and that obviously *a fortiori* if the situation itself changed principles different from those actually expressed would then acquire greater relevance and force. A further point that has to be conceded is that, apart perhaps from a few quite minor and timid statements, there is a lack in this Constitution of any radical consideration of the nature of a 'pastoral constitution' and,

[20] cf. pp. 305, 306, nn. 12 and 13.

over and above this, of the nature of the pastoral office, its possibilities and its limitations and also the ways in which it can be exercised (precisely as including the authority to instruct) as distinct from the teaching office, even though, in view of the content of this Constitution a consideration of this kind could properly have, and perhaps even actually should have, provided the subject matter of one of its basic themes. At the same time however, we must still be careful to avoid any denial of the fact that it does have the character of a Pastoral Constitution in the sense which we have worked out here. Here we must confine ourselves merely to pointing out certain further indications of why this should be so.

A point which can be established fairly clearly as a matter of historical fact is that not only in respect of its subject matter, but also in its whole inspiration and attitude this Constitution follows in the footsteps of the great encyclicals of John XXIII.[21] It is true that in these encyclicals too there is a similar lack of any radical consideration of the real significance of what is there being enacted. But even so the specialists, accustomed as they were to the 'doctrinalism' (using this term in no pejorative sense) of Pius XII, were sometimes extremely startled at what they found in these encyclicals. For here statements were made and demands put forward which can no longer be shown to follow compellingly as conclusions drawn from the general principles of Christianity. Even when due attention is paid to the contemporary situation in the concrete, and even if it is sought to find principles with a more particular and more concrete application to this, still even these do not follow solely or with full certainty from the general principles referred to. Now does this mean that John XXIII exceeded his own competence in doctrinal matters; or has he achieved, and moreover quite rightly achieved, something quite different (at least in part and with regard to the ultimate point and significance of his statements) than to explicitate further in doctrinal terms the content of the *depositum fidei* as such? Has he perhaps achieved precisely that which we have here called 'instruction' in a quite specific sense? In these encyclicals has he perhaps acted as an 'issuer of instructions' in precisely the same way as in the convocation of the Council, seeing that here too he was convinced

---

[21] Admittedly here we can only recognise the need for a historical study of these connections without ourselves carrying it out. Nor do we intend, in the thesis we have stated, to maintain that Paul VI has abandoned this course which his predecessors had embarked upon (this is especially true of his encyclical, *Ecclesiam suam*). Rather he has supplied different and fresh emphases to what had gone before. But it remains the achievement of John XXIII, with his bold and charismatic directness, to have initiated these difficult undertakings. As always this initiative has to be further developed and guided in *different* ways.

of the fact that no compelling ground for this decision could be drawn either from the nature of a Council as such or simply from the relevant factors in the contemporary situation and in the Church, but rather that in convoking the Council in this way he was acting under an inspiration from above?

X

Now if we are inclined to reply to these questions in the sense indicated here, then we shall be still more justified in arriving at the same conclusion with regard to the Pastoral Constitution of the Second Vatican Council, and, despite all its undeniable and striking deficiencies, we shall be able to regard it as a Pastoral Constitution in the sense described here. Of course this does not imply (in fact the introduction itself already makes this clear) that there is no doctrinal element in this Constitution. Actually it is quite obvious that from the purely quantitative viewpoint this doctrinal element far outweighs all other elements. This is in fact inherent in the very nature of the subject matter. An 'instruction' always constitutes a summons to some act. And this act must also realise in the concrete some necessary value the force of which is abiding and immutable. (Here, for example the dignity of man or the values of justice, love, the unity of mankind etc.) And every instruction, even in the secular sphere and whatever the form in which *de facto* it emerges in history, is issued as pertaining to the proclamation of principles which are constant and immutable in their validity. It is these, and not the nature of the instruction itself, that those issuing it have consciously in mind, even though, outwardly speaking, the instruction is something more than a mere application to the present of these permanent and immutable principles. Again in the light of this it is not surprising that even a Pastoral Constitution in our sense can give the impression to its readers almost of being a collection of particular principles drawn from the spheres of moral theology and social politics, and that any explicit reflections upon its real nature are either totally absent or at any rate extremely imprecise. The ultimately concrete element in this which constitutes the true essence of an instruction is in fact wholly incapable of being the subject of speculation. And quite evidently the process of reflecting at the *theoretical* level upon an essence of this kind in the manner presented here cannot bring any particular *concrete* actualisation of this essence under our microscope. In other words so far as any one specific 'instruction' is concerned such theoretical speculation can only have a very secondary importance. At the same time the theologians, sociologists, futurologists and other specialists must subject this Constitution to the closest possible scrutiny and, in a certain sense, test its various elements to see where and how the Constitution goes beyond the limits of a purely doctrinal presentation, and achieves the status of what we have called 'instruction' as issued under the charismatic summons of God to the Church. When we say, however, that this is demanded by the very nature of the case, we precisely do not mean that the boundaries between the two can be made absolutely clearcut and unambiguous. We have only to achieve an understanding which is correct in a genuinely ontological sense of the relationship between the universal and the particular, and between the knowledge we can have of the former and of the latter, in order *ipso facto* to see too that it is quite impossible for human knowledge, radically bound up as it is with history, to draw the boundaries between 'doctrine' and 'instruction' as sharply as this would imply, the more so since every act of human cognition, even at its most theoretical, invariably and of its very nature has itself in turn the essential status of an act and decision on the part of the practical intellect also as realised in the concrete.

This does not mean, however, that it is unnecessary and meaningless to look for such possible boundaries between doctrine and instruction. In those cases in which the theologian believes that he is no longer able to see at the theoretical level how a given statement in the Constitution follows from the sources of revelation alone, he should not straightway start talking about the possibility of error or of the composers exceeding their competence etc. (though admittedly even in a conciliar constitution which is precisely *not* intended to be a definition this is possible). The theologian should ask himself whether a statement of this kind at the theoretical level, yet not fully supported by arguments, is not precisely an 'instruction' justifiably issued to summon the Christians of today to a specific decision in history. It may be too that the character of 'instruction' is to be ascribed to this 'Pastoral Constitution' in virtue of the selection which it arrives at between those statements and demands which it actually makes and those which – from the theoretical point of view – it could just as well have made but in fact does not. Here too we should not be too hasty in speaking of the finite nature and the limitations of even the Church's pronouncements, or of the element of chance or even the effects of fashionable mental attitudes, even though it may be admitted as an obvious factor that the fathers of the Council too are not immune to these. But there is something more in the reasons prompting a selection of this kind than can be accounted for purely at the theoretical level. It may be that behind it lies the summons of the Spirit in history, that Spirit whose will it is to have *both* enacted in the Church of today, demands as well as doctrinal statements. And if this is so, then it is something that despite whatever 'one-sidedness' there may be, the Church both can and should do in all trust,[22] without having to be anxious as to whether in taking this course she is betraying the inexhaustible resources of her own nature. For this always contains something 'more' than merely those elements which are traditional and customary or the obvious lines laid down for the development of her teaching and practice.

[22] On this cf. *Handbuch der Pastoraltheologie* II/1, the work mentioned in n. 14, p. 626 and also K. Rahner, *Im Heute glauben* (Einsiedeln [1]1966), pp. 24 ff., 32 ff.

17

THEOLOGICAL REFLECTIONS ON THE PROBLEM OF SECULARISATION

I

THE aim we shall be setting ourselves in what follows is to conduct a *theological* consideration of the reality and the idea of that which the term 'secularisation' is intended to convey or that which we have to understand it to signify in order to obtain a correct view of this reality.[1] Now the first point to be established for this is that the concept of 'secularisation', both historically and in terms of its actual meaning, imports primarily and essentially a relationship to the *Church* considered as a social entity, and not, in the first instance, to God, his salvific grace or the historical realisation of this in the world. In German it is perfectly legitimate to distinguish between *Säkularisation* (secularisation), *Säkularisierung* (secularising considered as a process) and *Säkularismus* (secularism),[2] taking this last term to signify – though it in turn has many different levels and shades of meaning – the phenomenon of the 'world as it has been rendered worldly and profane', the world as self-authenticating *without* having, either in theory or (above all) in practice, any particular reference to God. In view of the history of the term 'secularisation', however, and also for reasons connected with its actual content, it is more accurate and more in conformity with the facts to take the term 'secularisation' as our starting-point, using this to signify the growing influence of 'world' (as the outcome of human ingenuity) and the process by which it becomes increasingly autonomous and separates itself more and more from the Church considered as a social entity in the world. A point that may be readily conceded from the outset in this connection is

[1] On the concept cf. H. Lübbe's work, *Säkularisation* (Freiburg 1965); this includes a section explicitly devoted to the historical development of the concept which is strongly recommended.
[2] On these key words cf. E. Hegel, 'Säkularisation', *L.T.K.* IX (Freiburg ²1964), 248 ff.; A. Auer, 'Säkularisierung', *L.T.K.* IX, 253 ff.

that for the purposes of a truly theological consideration (as distinct from one in which considerations of canon law are included) it makes little difference whether such a 'secularisation' has been achieved by compulsory measures taken by the state appropriating the material resources of the Church or by the state abolishing or frustrating the Church's organisations (such as orders, confraternities etc.). The element in this concept which is of decisive importance for us is the fact that the 'world' in this sense separates itself from the 'Church', and that there is an increasing separation between *sacerdotium* and *regnum*, an increasing profanisation of the world by comparison with ages in which religion as an institution on the one hand, and the life of society on the other – in other words 'Church' and 'world' – constituted a homogeneous unity.

This 'secularisation' or worldliness in relation to the Church must not simply be identified with an a-theistic profanisation of the world.[3] For one thing there is such a phenomenon as a 'religious attitude'[4] which does not find expression in the sociological group or the Church. But more than this, and even if we view the matter from the point of view of the Church, the world even as secularised still falls under God's universal will to save. It is permeated by his grace, and in virtue of this is far from being in any position to be atheistic in any absolute sense, even though it may sometimes interpret its own position in this sense at the level of explicit and conscious reflection. This means that the world is actually playing a positive role in the history of salvation and revelation, whether it consciously realises and accepts this or not. The most radical illustration of this truth is the fact that even one who is in all good faith an atheist properly so called at the level of conscious and explicit thought can still attain to salvation and can therefore still be in possession of grace and faith.[5]

Of course in spite of this distinction between 'secularisation' considered as the removal of the Church's influence and 'secularisation' considered as an attempt at atheistic profanisation, these two realities are closely interconnected. In its scope and the manner in which it is brought about, the process of ridding the world of the Church's influence can acquire a

[3] On this cf. K. Rahner, 'Science as a "Confession"?', *Theological Investigations* III (London and Baltimore 1967), pp. 385–400; *idem*, 'The Man of Today and Religion', *Theological Investigations* IV (London and Baltimore 1969), pp. 3–20; *idem*, 'Universal Salvific Will', *Sacramentum Mundi* V (Freiburg/London 1970), pp. 405–409.
[4] cf. *Handbuch der Pastoraltheologie* II/1 (Freiburg 1966), pp. 228 ff., 253 ff.
[1] cf. 'Atheism and Implicit Christianity', *Theological Investigations* IX, pp. 145–164.

specific form, one which gives it a tendency towards an atheistic profanisation. It can proceed from such a tendency or alternatively give rise to it or demand it.

At this point[6] we would wish deliberately to impose certain restrictions upon ourselves by confining ourselves to the concept of 'secularisation' considered as ridding the world of the Church's influence in so far as this is possible in view of the connection between the two concepts we have mentioned. In doing so we are conscious of the fact that this means that we are passing over the more ultimate aspects of the matter. We shall not, therefore, be speaking directly of the atheistic interpretation of the world in all its manifold forms as the 'world without religion' (Barth, Bonhoeffer), the 'death of God' movement (Altizer, Hamilton, van Buren etc.), the 'non-religious interpretation of biblical concepts' (Bonhoeffer, Ebeling), the 'worldly world' as such (Metz), the 'world as attaining to its majority' to the extent that this in itself already presupposes a certain separation between world and Church etc. Even when we have restricted our aims to this extent it is still possible to treat only of *some* but not all the specific aspects which are necessarily raised even when the subject-matter is as limited as this. We shall present our considerations in five brief theses, each of which will be followed by its own particular interpretation. As the final section of the whole study we may be permitted to draw certain conclusions from the rest of the theses which will have the effect of removing the restrictions which we shall meanwhile have imposed upon the subject-matter, broadening our viewpoint once more so as to relate our findings to the profanisation of the world in general and to the manner in which the Christian can live in it (cp. Thesis V, Section VI).

In our considerations we shall be taking as read certain aspects upon which much has already been written in recent years, and some of which are vitally relevant to the question of secularism and secularisation. In this study, therefore, we do not have to speak of the biblical and theological concept of 'world', with all the discussion it involves concerning that which is merely 'creaturely', that which must not be invested with 'numinous' quality, that which as created reality is good and is intended to be 'permeated with human influence' and by man as the 'environment' which is orientated to him. Similarly we shall not be returning to the question of the sinfulness of the 'world' considered as 'the present aeon' from which we have to detach ourselves in order to be ready for the 'aeon

[6] cf. The author's studies in *Sendung und Gnade* (Innsbruck [4]1966), pp. 13–47; *Handbuch der Pastoraltheologie* II/1, pp. 222ff., 234 ff., 242 ff., 267 ff., II/2, 35 ff., 40 ff., 42 ff., 208 ff., 228 ff., 269 ff.; cf. also J. B. Metz, *ibid.*, pp. 239–267.

that is to come' of the 'kingdom of God'. We are presupposing as a point that is already familiar the idea that the dynamism inherent in Christianity itself gives rise to a justifiable process slowly working itself out in history by which the world becomes worldly, even though in the concrete the representatives of Christianity and the Churches have often been so misled in their understanding of the world, due to their ideas being ossified at particular epochs, that they have actually sought to hold back this process. In saying this, therefore, we are conceding not only the radical difference between 'world' (society, state) and 'Church' which 'in itself' is always valid and which is to be taken in the sense formulated by Leo XIII, but we are also asserting that this difference itself and in its own turn has a history of its own worked out in theory and practice which tends towards a growing clarification of the difference involved and so too to a growing awareness on the part of the two entities in themselves of what they really are and what the mutual relationship between them consists in.[7] We cannot treat of the basic relationship between Christian hope for the 'kingdom of God' which is God himself in his act of self-bestowal upon us as the absolute future and the future towards which the 'this-worldly' hope of man is orientated and which he sets up before him as his aim in his struggle against all alienation from the self.[8]

II

Our first thesis runs as follows:

A phenomenon frequently apparent in the history of the Church is a false integralism. By comparison with this the process of secularisation is, judged by genuinely Christian standards, right and just.

It is true that this statement expresses much that properly speaking belongs to the content of those principles which we have designated above as presupposed to our present considerations. Here, however, we must investigate with particular care the idea and the true nature of 'integralism', because even today the unreflecting attitude and mentality which this implies have not altogether died out in the Church. In view of this we can take an objective evaluation of this concept and of the reality it signifies as

[7] For a bibliography on this topic cf. *Handbuch der Pastoraltheologie* II/2, pp. 203–207.

[8] Also K. Rahner, 'Marxist Utopia and the Christian Future of Man', *Theological Investigations* VI (London and Baltimore 1969), pp. 59–68; in this volume cf. 'A Fragmentary Aspect of a Theological Evaluation of the Concept of the Future', pp. 235–241; 'On the Theology of Hope', pp. 260–272; 'The Theological Problems Entailed in the Idea of the "New Earth" ', pp. 242–259.

a starting-point for arriving at a clearer conception of a kind of 'secularisation' which is, of its nature, legitimate, and also of the wholly practical consequences arising from this. What we are concerned with in the idea of 'integralism' is not that historical phenomenon consisting in the part played in the Church's history in the closing years of Pius X by the anti-modernist group under the leadership of Mgr. U. Benigni. Nor are we thinking of similar movements in the concrete which took place after the Second World War (*intégrisme* as the counter-tendency to *progressisme* in France, 'right-wing Catholics' as opposed to 'left-wing Catholics' in Germany etc.). What we shall be concerned with here is simply the essential nature of a reality which can be called 'integralism' (though there are other names for it also) because it signifies a specific interpretation of the relationship of the Church to the world (in the humanities, in science, in society and in politics), an interpretation in which every kind of 'secularisation' is rejected. Integralism in the sense intended here is that attitude, whether at the theoretical or at the practical (though unreflecting) level, according to which human life can be unambiguously mapped out and manipulated in conformity with certain universal principles proclaimed by the Church and watched over by her in the manner in which they are developed and applied.

Integralism in this sense implicitly presupposes that in his acts man simply puts his theory into practice, and that the world and its history, considered as the material field in which these acts of his are posited, is sufficiently predictable, malleable and submissive to his will, to make such a procedure possible. Integralism in this sense, therefore, entails a failure to recognise that the 'practical intellect' has an element of the autonomous in it. Its acts of apprehension can be achieved only within the context of the free decision as actually posited in hope. An integralism of this kind presupposes that the Church is already in possession – at least to a sufficient extent for all important purposes – of these principles which are needful, and thereby denies the existence of any genuine historical development of dogma and theology at least for the sphere of practical action and the principles covering this. Furthermore integralism tacitly implies the opinion that in those cases in which it cannot be shown by just and valid argument that a given course of action is in direct contradiction to the universal principles of the gospel and of 'natural law', it follows *ipso facto* that this course of action is of itself and of its very nature so 'secular' in character that from the point of view of morality it is simply and absolutely irrelevant, so that *ipso facto* there cannot be any question of evaluating it as an act leading to salvation or alternatively to perdition. In virtue of the fact that the Church is the proclaimer, and also the interpreter, of these principles as understood precisely in *this* sense the exponents of integralism regard her wholly and unreservedly as the guide of the world, at least *de jure* and in view of what she claims herself to be.

Nor is it sufficient in itself to overcome this attitude of integralism to emphasise that point initially made by Leo XIII and still upheld by Pius XII, namely that the Church recognises the relative autonomy of the world, the state and the departments of secular learning, and that in these dimensions of human living she ascribes to herself only a limited authority *ratione peccati*. For there are[9] two questions with regard to the doctrine of any such *potestas indirecta* or *directiva* belonging to the Church in relation to the world which we have to answer rightly in order that integralism may really and effectively be accounted as overthrown:

First: Given that the Church has the right to draw the dividing line between that which is morally permissible and that which is unethical, in other words to apply the criterion of the *ratio peccati*, does this give her the power to determine in the concrete what the 'world' should do in the here and now? Or alternatively does the establishing of this dividing line leave, at least in principle, the way open to various possibilities so that the world acts autonomously and on its own responsibility in making its choice between them? (Though this does not mean that the content of the decision as taken in the concrete is *ipso facto* of no 'human' significance, or that morally speaking it is simply irrelevant). The question is to be answered in the second sense, though the reasons for this need not be given in any greater detail at this point,[10] and this is despite the fact that integralism, for all that it verbally upholds the doctrine of the *potestas indirecta* or *directiva* of the Church, tacitly answers the question in the first sense and so, for all its outward professions, can still 'indirectly' assert that the Church has, or at least claims to have, a kind of dominion over the world which enables it positively and effectively to shape its course. There is a further point, which we need only mention in passing, with regard to that element in a course of action freely entered upon which, unlike the other elements, cannot be determined in the light of universal

---

[9] In this connection we must for the moment abstract from the fact that on this theory the importance attached to the Church's role is in reality too little. This is a point which we shall shortly have to demonstrate.

[10] On this cf. K. Rahner, 'Grenzen der Amtskirche', *Schriften zur Theologie* VI (Einsiedeln 1965), pp. 499–520. On the problems entailed in the use of the term 'ecclesiastical' in this connection cf. *Handbuch der Pastoraltheologie* II/2, pp. 211–214; on the actual subject itself cf. also in the present volume 'Practical Theology and the Social Work of the Church', pp. 349–370.

principles. It would be wrong and prejudiced to suppose on this account that this element is *ipso facto* morally irrelevant, or to put it another way, that the *only* way in which we can recognise the morality of an action as such is by applying universal principles to it, as though there were no 'logical' way of working out the ethics of human action at the individual level.[11]

Second: the correctness of a further idea tacitly presupposed by integralism has also to be called in question, the idea, namely, that we know what ought to be done once we know (precisely through the Church and her pronouncements *ratione peccati*) what we ought *not* to do. The fact that it is possible and justifiable for the Church to prohibit certain courses of action must not be doubted. Yet in reality such a prohibition does not *eo ipso* or of its very nature supply us with any positive idea in the concrete of what course of action we can and should adopt.

There may be many simple and unremarkable instances in the morality we practise in our everyday lives in which this may be the case. But it is not so as a matter of principle, and still less is it so in the sphere of 'political' ethics as applied to major social and historical events. In spite of the *ratio peccati* as defined and applied by the Church, the sort of responsibility which the 'world' has to take with regard to these is quite different from that which integralism imagines it to be. In this context the insoluble *casus perplexus*, from being the subject of the subtleties of moral theology, can become a matter of deadly earnest such that moral theology at the theoretical level, with its abstract concepts and *quaestiones disputatae*, is of no avail to solve it. In these circumstances once more the world has to be left to itself by the Church. To give an example: no pope and no Council has been able to say *in the concrete* how we can effectively, and in the actual situation as it exists, escape from the vicious circle of the balance of fear created by the atom bomb, or how we are to face up to the worldwide population explosion. Absolutely speaking we have to respect all principles of abiding validity in arriving at those solutions which we have to find in the here and now. But these abidingly valid principles do not yield any solution in the concrete. Ultimately speaking the question that remains constantly present is concerned with those goals defined by

[11] On this cf. K. Rahner, *Das Dynamische in der Kirche* (Freiburg ³1965); 'On the Question of a Formal Existential Ethics', *Theological Investigations* II (London and Baltimore 1963), pp. 217–234; *Schriften zur Theologie* VI (Einsiedeln 1965), pp. 521–544. 'Do not Stifle the Spirit', *Theological Investigations* VII (London and Baltimore 1971), pp. 72–87; 'On the Theological Problems Entailed in a "Pastoral Constitution" ' in this volume, pp. 293–317.

principles laid down by the Church and, in an asymptotic sense (i.e. as never quite attainable), binding 'in themselves' and 'in principle' to be striven for in an historical development (both at the individual and the collective levels). Do these aims *ipso facto* actually have to be capable of realisation at every moment of history? Or alternatively is it possible for man, under certain circumstances, to fall short of them even consciously, and in doing so to incur 'material' sin indeed but not formal sin, and precisely in that very act to attain to the best possible course in the here and now?[12]

Whatever answer we may arrive at to this question, the raising of it represents the first serious attempt to take into account the historical conditions to which man is subject as a factor essentially affecting the moral demands which are required of him. Whatever answer to it we may arrive at it does appear from the considerations which we have set forth above that the Church is in no position whatever to determine unambiguously the 'human' factor, or even what constitutes moral behaviour in the world, seeing that this can vary according to the circumstances prevailing at any given time. For this reason too the Church is in no position to claim such determining power when she emphasises the binding force of the principles she upholds, principles which, ultimately speaking, always have the force of defining boundaries which must not be overstepped. The Church is never, and never intends for one moment to be, the total and exclusive force determining and administering human conduct and morality in the world. She is not the sum total of this, but rather an element in this sum total made up of many factors, for at basis and of its very nature the sum total of all that determines human morality is essentially 'pluralist' and derives from numerous elements: from the concrete historical situation, which can never be thought out completely in all its aspects; from the principles of the gospel and also of the 'natural law' as rightly understood, *and at the same time* from the decision taken in a concrete set of circumstances which is unique in each particular case, and yet which, even as such, is still subject to the claims of morality. Man has the task of unifying all these heterogeneous factors and, once more, it is not for the Church, but rather for God alone to say how this is successfully to be achieved in the concrete. Why else, for instance, does the Church avoid making any moral judgment on the Vietnam politics of the USA? If she could make such a judgment *ipso facto* she would also be under an obligation to do so.

It is not merely that integralism in the Church has never been able to be

12 On the principle here being enunciated cf. provisionally *Handbuch der Pastoraltheologie* II/1, pp. 152 ff. (with references).

achieved in practice. It is actually false in principle too. Now all this taken together has the following significance: Of her very nature the Church constantly leaves the world free to be itself in its 'worldliness' and to have its own responsibility (and this not only in the execution of its decisions but in the actual process of arriving at the imperative underlying these also) even though this worldly element as such still precisely does *not* cease to have a 'moral' relevance and to have a *significance for salvation*. This worldly element is not merely the secular 'material', in itself indifferent, 'in which' Christian action is to be made real, but also includes (though it is not co-extensive with) Christian activity itself, since not every aspect of this can be controlled by the Church. In this process of 'secularisation' of the world which she herself promotes, the Church supplies the grace of God, the principles of the process and its ultimate boundaries. But the human and Christian conduct desired is something that is achieved by the world itself on its own ground and its own responsibility.[13]

III

The second thesis runs as follows:

The secularisation of the world in the good sense implies that the Church has a quite new task, namely to create a new ecclesiastical integration between the faithful themselves within herself taken as a whole and in the individual communities.

This second statement is intended to draw a conclusion which, though it represents but a short step, is in itself not unimportant in view of a new task which the Church has to perform in her own sphere. The Churches as the sum total of the faithful and the human groups which assemble at particular places of worship are intended to be communities. But they are this not merely in virtue of the juridical structure of the Church in the purely formal sense, together with the confession of a common faith and the celebration of a common liturgy. These are not the sole factors even if this liturgy as realised in the mystery of the Eucharist is aimed at the emergence of the community in sacramental power.[14] In earlier times the Church and the communities of local Churches were able to achieve an

[13] For a treatment of the principles governing the relationship of the Church and the world cf. K. Rahner, 'Kirche und Welt', *Zehn Jahre Katholische Akademie in Bayern*, ed. by the *Katholischen Akademie in Bayern* (Würzburg 1967), pp. 9–27.

[14] On this cf. 'The New Image of the Church' in the present volume, pp. 3–29; 'The Presence of the Lord in the Christian Community at Worship', pp. 71–83, 'On the Presence of Christ in the Diaspora Community according to the Teaching of the Second Vatican Council', pp. 84–102 (with the bibliography attached to each article).

integrated community life of this kind even at the sociological level, relatively speaking without any special efforts on their part, in virtue of the fact that the Christian community (together with the specifically ecclesiastical elements in its formation as a community: a juridical structure, creed and cult) could presuppose as already in existence in the secular sphere a socially integrated group characterised by the following elements: a cultural life which made equal demands upon all, a society which, at the civic level, was homogeneous rather than pluralistic, an ethical system which was immediately and manifestly common to all, and which went beyond abstract moral principles. In other words (to put it briefly) it could presuppose all that which lies at the roots of a stable and homogenous society integrating the individual into itself, defining for him the boundaries beyond which he could not pass, and relieving him of his burden by offering him security.

This situation also had its effects upon the specifically ecclesiastical elements in the ecclesiastical community: the common creed was also a manifest factor at the social level. This meant that those vested with official authority in the Church were relieved of certain burdens. The cult was also experienced as a sacral sublimation of the unity of the secular community. Today it is quite otherwise. Earlier the 'world' introduced *ipso facto* and of its very nature certain vital basic factors into the 'Church'. Today the society which penetrates into the Church, and which has to form a community there from the outset, is the world as 'secularised' even in the sense that it no longer immediately and of its very nature supplies the necessary substrate for the formation of the Church's community, as was formerly the case. It is pluralistic in the patterns of life in the world which it offers. It is made up of men of whom no one individual any longer has command of the whole of knowledge, of culture, or of the trends towards the future which are present throughout the whole of society. In spite of the fact that there has been a great increase in universal education, that masses of information in various fields are now available, and that the media of communication have multiplied so rapidly, society as a whole has become less possible to evaluate with regard to its condition, more difficult to guide and more incalculable with regard to the future towards which it is tending. In brief: society is less integrated, with all the consequences which this has for the individual and for society itself. Now this gives rise to quite a new task for the Church in working for the fulfilment of her own true vocation. She must herself create what she could formerly presuppose as the social or 'natural' substrate for the formation of her own community.

Admittedly this precisely does *not* mean that the Church has to transform this world as secularised and pluralist in this sense back into that former state of being a homogeneous society which of its very nature brought its own integration with it into the Church. The Church does not have to do this even to the extent that this present world as secularised and pluralist has to be absorbed ever anew into the Church herself. Indeed if the Church were to attempt such a thing – and the temptation to do so is always present and always great – she would be building herself a ghetto and, in terms of the sociology of religion, the very tendency of her own efforts would be such as soon to turn her into a 'sect'. But *even within* the boundaries of the Church herself she must herself remain an 'open society'. Indeed she must become this far more than formerly. She cannot practise any kind of 'negative selection' in the sense that unconsciously, but nonetheless really, she seeks to address herself to, to reach and to win over only individuals of a particular social or cultural stamp. She must have a place for conformists *and* non-conformists, for men of the most diverse political tendencies, for philosophers with the most diverse ideas, for *catholiques de droite* and *de gauche* etc. She must cope with this state of pluralism in an anti-integralist way. In fact she must learn to view and to experience this as something positive.

But this in turn precisely does not mean that the Church has no task of integration at the higher level with regard to this abiding intellectual and social pluralism within her. If this task were not recognised and fulfilled, then the Church would be a 'sect' designed for the satisfying of merely individualistic religious needs, and still more would once again become a mere 'official Church' of clerics;[15] these alone would, in fact, satisfy such religious needs, and the believers could, as an unintegrated multitude, be nothing more than the recipients of the Church's salvific acts despite all ideological ptotestations to the effect that they are something more than this: to a large extent the really constitutive element of the Church. The Church would not be in a position to fulfil any responsibility to the *world* or any task for the *world* precisely as a *Church*.

But what is this 'integration' of the Church considered as a community, and how is it to be presented, seeing that it cannot be the act by which the pluralist world is rendered homogeneous after the pattern of an integralism interior to the Church herself, nor yet a restoration of that earlier degree of integration which the society of the Church enjoyed, nor even a mere

[15] On this cf. the article already cited on p. 323, n, 10. 'Grenzen der Amtskirche' and in addition to this cf. especially K. Rahner, *Vom Sinn des kirchlichen Amtes* (Freiburg 1966).

ideological superstructure of devotionalism ('We *are* already the Body of Christ')? It is difficult to find an answer to this question. The following alternative answers might be considered possible:

First, in answer to this question concerning a task for the Church which is still hardly recognised we might point to all the social work for the 'new' integration of society which the Church is performing, should perform and could perform in common with secular society which undertakes the same work with similar aims.[16] It might be said that the Church must undertake precisely this work, even though it seems to be wholly secular in character, primarily in relation to her own baptised members. Thus for example her children, adults, the old etc., who have, each in their own way, to be integrated into the society and to find a place in it and security for themselves.

Second, a plea must be entered in this connection for a genuine process of democratisation in the Church. Rightly understood this term as applied to secular society stands not so much for a 'liberation' from all kinds of compulsion, but is rather the key word for institutions, standards of conduct, models, rules etc. which have to be formulated in order that a society which is pluralist in character and has to survive as such may be a *society*, and not a radically disintegrated accumulation of individuals and groups, each with their own special interests. In accordance with this, 'democratisation' in the Church does not in the least need to be understood as a battle-cry against the authority of the official hierarchy of the Church, but rather should be taken as the key word standing for the integration of that secular and pluralist society in the Church which today constitutes her enduring substrate, which the formation of the Church has to presuppose.[17]

Third, we might refer to a factor (as something that also has validity in this connection), which will have to be spoken of further in our third thesis, with regard to a quite new function of the Church as a whole in relation to secular society.

However, as we have said, we shall have to devote a fresh section in our considerations to the discussion of this. What we have said up to this point on the subject of the second statement is, of necessity, very abstract, first because the task indicated here, which the secularised state of society makes necessary for the interior life of the Church, has still scarcely been

---

[16] In fuller detail in my study, 'Practical Theology and Social Work in the Church' in this volume, pp. 349–370.

[17] For a concrete treatment of this cf. 'Dialogue in the Church' in this volume, pp. 103–121.

recognised, and second because, for want of space and also of competence in the field, we have not been able to make any practical proposals at the level of 'pastoral theology'.

IV

The *third thesis* may be formulated as follows:

In its situation of pluralism and secularism the Church leaves society to develop along its own lines. Now precisely because she is incapable of shaping the course of society in its concrete decisions in an integralist, doctrinal or juridical sense, the Church herself has a quite new task in relation to this society, a task which might perhaps be characterised as 'prophetic'.

But what this presupposes is that new formation of the people of the Church in terms of ecclesiastical and social organisation which has already been referred to in the second thesis. This statement is obscure and must be clarified.

The process of secularisation on which we sought to cast light from the theological aspect in the first thesis appears initially and at first view to imply that the Church lacks influence in many departments of life in the world. Certainly the Church can set herself to establish certain boundaries *ratione peccati*. She can lay down certain universal norms. But against any tendency towards an integralism beneath the surface she cannot control the history of the secularised world in the concrete either by means of her – admittedly valid – doctrine or by means of her pastoral commission (considered as *potestas jurisdictionis*). Are these negative determinations now sufficient fully to determine the true relationship between the Church and the secularised world? Is it the case that the only way in which the Church can achieve any further influence on the formation of the secular-ised world is simply as a 'grace' and through the individual Christians as such, through the power of grace and the 'mental attitude' of the gospel as inculcated into these Christians?

I believe that no clear answer has been given to this question even in the Second Vatican Council. Such an answer is to be found neither in the Constitution on the Church *Lumen gentium*, nor in the Decree on the Apostolate of the Laity, *Apostolican actuositatem* nor in *Gaudium et spes*. The reason is that the activity of the Church, in those contexts in which it is not to be identified with the activity of the individual Christians, is still viewed too much as an assistance in *doctrinal* terms, in other words as a 'communication of principles'. And this despite the fact that that idea which is so often invoked of 'collaboration' on the Church's part with all men of good will and with their social institutions points in a different direction.[18]

Our third statement is intended to provide an answer to the question which we have just presented: the Church as Church can achieve something more than a mere counselling of the world by the preaching of her own principles, something more too than mere 'collaboration' which in practice could only be achieved through the work of the individual Christians in the secular institutions, allowing for certain exceptions of no great importance.

In order to see what is positively intended we must begin by considering the following point. In a democratic and pluralist society which is functioning well each of its informal and formal groups has the purpose and the right to exercise its influence in the general decisions which still inevitably have constantly to be taken by the society as a whole. The groups concerned can use all justifiable means in doing this, beginning with discussion and extending to propaganda and the use of their own power in legitimate ways. But what is constantly presupposed is that such a group has an 'opinion' as to what ought to be done in the here and now with reference to such decisions taken by society as a whole and with a view to the actual taking of them. A concrete 'programme of action' of the kind envisaged is itself an extremely complex entity, and yet in the practical 'will' of the group concerned it constitutes a unity. It contains within its own nature elements of rational and conscious calculation measured by the reality itself with regard to the particular matter involved, and it is by means of these that an attempt is made to win over the rest through *instruction*. Such 'rational' elements are present both with regard to the goal to be aimed at and also with regard to the objective means by which it is to be attained. But a 'programme of action' of this kind, belonging to a particular group, always contains a further element over and above that which can be justified on purely rational grounds which have consciously been thought out. This is an element of creative imagination. It is 'creativity' which makes the 'utopian' a possibility. It is a decision taken from the freedom inherent in human living which, from many possible or conceivable courses of action, chooses – perhaps all unreflectingly – one in particular, resolves upon this and seeks to carry it out. It actually creates, and does not merely endure, the process of human history.

---

[18] For a fuller treatment of this theme cf. 'The Theological Problems Entailed in the Idea of the New Earth' in this volume, pp. 260–272; 'On the Theological Problems Entailed in a "Pastoral Constitution" ', pp. 293–317, and 'Practical Theology and the Social Work of the Church', below, pp. 349–370.

All this takes place at that level of practical living which cannot be deduced from mere speculation, which carries its own conviction, and does not, in any full or comprehensive sense, derive this from the sphere of speculative thought.

The Church too can, should and must be a group of this kind within the secular and pluralist society. The pluralist society itself cannot prohibit the Church from having such an aim. For only a society which is absolutely totalitarian in structure can have the intention of allowing social groups to exist only as subdivisions and subordinate functionaries of a society which is set up and controlled in a totalitarian and authoritarian manner from a single central point. A pluralist and 'open' society, which, unlike a 'closed system', does not merely make room, legally speaking, for a single point of control for all its powers, cannot *a priori* have anything against a community of believers freely and constantly forming itself anew with such an aim, provided only – and this *is* presupposed – that it keeps the 'rules of the game' belonging to such a society and to the interpositions of its decisions and its 'practice'.[19]

But the Church should have an aim of this kind. Whether she is in any position to achieve this, whether she can be equipped for it, what degree of social unity she has to have and the manner in which she can form such a unity within herself in order to be the 'subject' of such an aim at all – these are questions which at this present and initial stage cannot yet be discussed. Nor shall we yet at this point be raising the question of how far she can in practice be successful in bringing this aim to fruition in the secular society, namely of making *her own* 'programme of action' either wholly or in part a principle of action for the secular society. We have no intention either of implying that such a programme of action could from the outset and in its first inception *only* be that of the 'explicit Christians'. God's grace can also inspire others to adopt the same programme. On theological grounds the Church can and must have such a name, such a programme of action if she can manage it. She has a task to perform for the world. She is there not for herself, but is rather the basic sacrament of salvation for the *world*.[20] She must be the leaven of the world. The worldly

[19] On the process by which the common will is formed in contemporary society cf. K. Rahner, 'Reflections on Dialogue within a Pluralistic Society', *Theological Investigations* VI (London and Baltimore 1969), pp. 31–42.

[20] For a treatment of the basic principles involved here cf. K. Rahner, *Kirche und Sakramente* (Freiburg ²1963), pp. 11–22; 'Konziliare Lehre der Kirche und künftige Wirklichkeit christlichen Lebens', *Schriften zur Theologie* VI (Einsiedeln 1965), pp. 479–498; 'The New Image of the Church' in this volume, pp. 3–29, esp. pp. 12 ff.; *Handbuch der Pastoraltheologie* I (Freiburg 1964), pp. 118–142.

activity of Christians and the working out of their salvation are not two areas of her activity which are materially speaking completely distinct, but – at least in part – two aspects of one and the same process by which the lives of Christians are brought to their fulness. Now this fulness is achieved essentially in intercommunication and in social living as realised in the concrete 'space-time' dimension of history. As 'visible' the Church is a concrete historical and social entity which, even if she did not wish it, necessarily influences society as a whole in various ways and, indeed, in ways which proceed not merely from her nature as 'eternal' but also from the form she inevitably assumes of her own free will and in the concrete. These are effects for which the Church has to answer. The Church as such has *de facto* willed to have such an effect – one which goes beyond her doctrine and the activites of the individual Christian – and has exercised an influence of this kind upon the world. And in view of this state of affairs there can be no serious question of the Church in principle having to renounce this influence and to withdraw into the 'sacristy'. The question rather is precisely *how* the Church is to be able to direct this legitimate influence in relation to the secular world today.

These indications must suffice at this point as a basis for our thesis concerning the legitimacy and the need for the Church to have such an influence upon the world, over and above the statement of her doctrine in principles and the specific activities of the individual Christians. The points that are of more immediate concern to us here are as follows:

First, the attempt to determine to some extent the precise nature of this influence, and this not merely in negative terms as formerly, and

Second, the question of what form the Church herself ought to assume in her concrete structure and in the minds of her members in order that she may in fact be able to exercise such an influence upon secular society.

In order to make some contribution to the answering of the first question it is advisable initially to devote some consideration to the character of many of the encyclicals of John XXIII (*Mater et magistra*, *Pacem in terris*), as also of the encyclicals of Paul VI, *Populorum progressio* and above all the pastoral constitution *Gaudium et spes* of the Second Vatican Council. In what does the special quality of these documents consist? While they rightly and necessarily contain much that is fundamental and of permanent validity in the way of 'doctrine', the true focal point of their significance, that in them which is so striking and which actually 'shocks' those who expect them to remain at the purely theoretical level, consists in their underlying purpose which, following the language of the Second Vatican Council, we can characterise primarily as 'pastoral'. But it would be to undervalue this 'pastoral' element, and to deny its true nature, if we sought to understand by it merely those 'practical' consequences which – at least in view of the world situation as it actually exists – could certainly and compellingly be drawn from the universal principles. The climactic significance of these documents plainly lies in certain 'imperatives', in certain assignments of emphasis, in the unfolding of an historical programme which summons the world to certain decisions. Indeed this is also shown from the fact that the actual analysis of the contemporary situation which in part provides the basis for this 'pastoral' element is neither something given in revelation nor so simply capable of being established that it could present the 'situation' as a 'brute fact' which no-one is in a position to doubt. On the contrary it belongs inseparably to that sphere of practical activity in which knowledge of the situation and the reaction to it in terms of human decision and action constitute a unity and *mutually* condition one another.[21] The demand, for instance, for a 'super-UNO'[22] or the formation of a world fund for aid to the under-developed peoples in *Populorum progressio* are certainly demands representing lofty aims and ones which, even in material terms are wholly justifiable. But undoubtedly they represent something which cannot compellingly be deduced as a *conclusio theologica* from revelation for each individual, such that every Christian is *obliged* to accept this demand. On the contrary, they constitute programmes of action, having the character of a decision, assertions of the practical intellect, precisely as this cannot be deduced from pure *intellectus principiorum*. They constitute decisions in which the Church does something more than merely to conceive of putting her principles into practice; something in which she actually *wills* to realise these principles in the concrete in a specific form and one which cannot be deduced from those principles, and in which the Church exercises an influence upon secular society as a concrete group within that pluralist society in virtue of this will of hers.

The discovery of this imperative directed towards society can, in view of the nature of the Church, only be characterised as 'prophetic' although this does not exclude, but rather includes all the other elements in such a discovery such as are found in other contexts in any decision of social and

[21] On the theological difficulties involved in an analysis of the contemporary situation cf. *Handbuch der Pastoraltheologie* II/1, pp. 181–187; 'On the Theological Problems Entailed in a "Pastoral Constitution" ', in this volume, pp. 293–317; 'Practical Theology within the Totality of Theological Disciplines', *Theological Investigations* IX, pp. 101–117.

[22] On this cf. *Gaudium et spes*, No. 84.

political relevance. This means that a pastoral 'instruction' is, at that point at which it fully realises its ultimate nature, the *prophetic* instruction of the Church considered as a decision taken in terms of concrete human living and ultimately not derivable from theory, and in fact directed to the secular world.[23] Of course this applies only to that which the Church can demand of this secular world precisely for its *salvation*. But this is not in dispute.

But the question which we have now to consider – this is the second of the two questions we have just raised – is whether the Church as actually constituted in the concrete is the sort of subject which, as one of the groups within the secular and pluralist world, can address the world with a programme of this kind with even a little prospect of success. This hope can indeed not be based (merely) upon the fact that the programme of action is in some respect enlightening in itself or that other groups are raising the same cry. The difficulty entailed in this hope and the prospect of the Church having any effective influence on the secular world is two-fold: on the one hand we have the official Church, which in this respect cannot, of its very nature as Church, be anything much more (though at the same time it must be this) than the *herald* of a prophetic impulse which is present elsewhere in the Church, or at most *one* of the possible points of entry for the Church's own Spirit with its power to influence history. This official Church has, in relation to the world, only as much 'authority' and influence to move it as belongs in a thousand ways to the 'Church' considered as a social group. On the other hand the official Church cannot lay it upon the believers belonging to her in virtue of her formal teaching authority or jurisdictional power to follow this prophetic imperative which the official Church sends forth.[24] The Church as people of God must 'go along with' the official Church in these prophetic imperatives if they are to have any real effect on secular society. Now the truth that stands revealed at this point is that the Church is fundamentally something different from, and, for practical purposes must henceforward become something different from, the institution of truth merely at the level of the speculative reason, supplemented by the necessary conse-

---

[23] On the concept of the prophetic 'instruction' cf. 'On the Theological Problems Entailed in a "Pastoral Constitution" ', pp. 293–317, esp. 295 ff., 298 ff., 302 ff.

[24] Even within the Church phenomena analogous to this are to be found: e.g. the Church can for instance recommend the gaining of indulgences, but what real meaning would the Council of Trent's dogma on indulgences have if an overwhelming majority of the faithful used their *Sancta et iusta libertas filiorum Dei* (Thus Paul VI in the Apostolic Constitution 'Indulgentiarum Doctrina' of 1.1.1967, No. 11) so as to decide not to gain any indulgences?

quences that correspond to this in terms of the administration of the sacraments and the apparatus of ecclesiastical government. Rather she must be the institution of the truth of the practical reason, the 'vision' and activity of which also belong to that institution which the revelation of God has created for itself. She is the people of God on pilgrimage, which is intended to, and wills to, imprint its eschatological hope upon the structures of worldly life through the orientation of this pilgrimage in the concrete, which is not fixed and determined *ipso facto* and from the outset by the maps which revelation at the theoretical level provides. It must and will also achieve harmony with the secular world in its course, without being able to determine this course in any doctrinal or even integralist sense.

But how much there still is to be done in the Church in order that this task can be fulfilled with all the effectiveness that is necessary! A 'political theology' of a fundamental kind would have to be developed. That is theology (considered as content) in general and ecclesiology in particular would have to be developed in their significance for social politics and the shaping of history, and thereby the exaggeratedly narrow and individualist view of revelation as pertaining to the salvation of the individual in isolation would have to be overcome. A 'mental attitude' would have to be developed in believers in which they no longer confronted the official Church with the dilemma, either to make pronouncements that are doctrinally binding or else to be 'uninteresting'. Instead believers with this mental attitude would be ready seriously to respond to 'prophetic' impulses, to make their own attitudes worked out in the freedom of human living, to share in the formation not merely of opinions but of resolves too. In the official representatives of the Church a readiness would have to be developed (and that too not merely with regard to specifically religious matters such as e.g. new devotions etc.) to take up *prophetic* impulses in the Church. For however true it may be that for the most part these become really effective only when they are extended beyond the official representatives of the Church to the Church as a whole, and thereby to the world, still they do not necessarily emerge in this way, but in a few cases they actually appear for the first time precisely in the holders of office in the Church. That process of social integration within the Church would be required of which we have already spoken from a different aspect in the second thesis, and which can be of assistance to the Church in achieving her effect only when it is applied at the social and political levels.

V

Our *fourth thesis* runs as follows:

The relationship of the Church to the secular world as it exists today demands, within the framework of 'practical theology' that a special theological discipline shall be worked out and shall have a constitution of its own.

This constitution we shall call, provisionally and for want of any better term, a *'practical ecclesiological cosmology'*.

What is meant by this? First a word must be said with regard to 'practical theology', which is commonly – and even in the Second Vatican Council – called 'pastoral theology',[25] since this 'cosmology' of which we speak is to be understood from the outset as a discipline which is part of 'practical theology'.[26] 'Practical theology is not a mere amalgam of 'practical' maxims which emerge necessarily and of their very nature from dogmatic and moral theology and from canon law. Much less does it consist merely of such guidelines as are of importance for the 'pastoral' work of the priest engaged in the cure of souls. 'Practical theology', so far from being this, is a discipline in its own right because its subject matter and its methods cannot be deduced simply from the 'systematic disciplines' of theology. It enquires in a properly worked out and methodical manner into the ways in which the Church as a whole can achieve her due fulness according to the demands made upon her and the possibilities open to her at any given time in *all* her dimensions, and not merely in the clerical sphere and through the activities of clerics. It differs, therefore, from other disciplines in which ecclesiological questions are raised in that these can enquire merely into the abiding nature of the Church's self-realisation, and the essential forms in which this can be achieved as determined by revelation or – as in the case of canon law – into the *jus conditum* and its history. But they cannot consider in any adequate manner the *'jus condendum'*. Now in order to realise what is entailed in this self-achievement of the Church as something to be realised at a particular point in time, and which extends far beyond the mere putting into practice of abiding principles and of the Church's *jus humanum*, we need to make a theological analysis and an interpretation of the contemporary situation

---

[25] cf. my study, 'Practical Theology within the Totality of Theological Disciplines', *Theological Investigations* IX, pp. 101–114 (together with the references to further studies there provided).

[26] On this concept of a 'practical cosmology' cf. further the study entitled 'Practical Theology and Social Work in the Church', and especially below, pp. 339 ff., 350 ff.

of the Church both in its internal and external aspects. Now this analysis cannot be worked out in terms of any other theological discipline. Moreover what we are faced with here is a quite distinct subject for theological investigation in its own right – it is not 'revealed'! – so that it also entails a distinct theological method, one which cannot merely be that which is applied in secular sociology, history, the study and evaluation of cultures etc. And precisely for *this* reason 'practical theology' is a theological discipline which is, in a genuine sense, original and unique in character even though it does presuppose all other theological disciplines. This must suffice for our present purposes as a description of the nature of 'practical theology'.

Now within this self-achievement of the Church as she exists at any given time the relationship of the Church to the secular world is something that has to be discovered not merely in its permanent and immutable nature, but also, and no less essentially, as it has to be realised in the circumstances actually prevailing in the here and now. And to this extent this relationship assumes not indeed the only place, but still a place of such significance that it has to be the subject of a special consideration in its own right and one that is worked out by precise and correct methods in practical theology. The general grounds for regarding practical theology as an autonomous discipline in its own right are in themselves sufficient to show that this relationship cannot be treated of in other theological disciplines, for this relationship is changed by the changes which take place in the secular world considered precisely *as* the situation of the Church. But this situation itself cannot be the subject of the disciplines of systematic theology. Moreover the recognition of this relationship, in view of the complexity of this situation, can precisely *not* any longer be deduced from the mere pre-scientific experience of individuals. A further point is that this relationship entails, as one of its characteristics, an element of prophetic decision. In other words it is totally incapable of being interpreted as a mere combination of two elements alone, namely a theoretical ecclesiology and a recognition of the situation.

Now this doctrine concerning the relationship of the Church to the world as it exists at any given time, even though it is a part of practical theology, has no name. And hence it comes about that this task for theology for which there is no name is in fact far from being recognised sufficiently clearly or evaluated sufficiently clearly in its urgency or its importance. This task is not identical with the 'social science' of Christianity, for this latter discipline is concerned with the basic forms of secular society (in economics, law, civic constitution etc.) and with what these *ought* to be according to Christian principles.[27] Nor is this discipline simply a department of dogmatic ecclesiology, for this can at most treat – if only it did so! – of the permanent forms assumed by the relationship of the Church to the world. Nor is this discipline identical with 'political theology' as so urgently demanded today by J. B. Metz,[28] for this is concerned with the social implications and the social relevance which are universally and abidingly immanent in the revelation, the doctrine and the hope of Christendom, and is not concerned with what ought to be the relationship of the Church, in the actual circumstances prevailing, to the world in its worldliness as it actually exists in the here and now. This discipline which we have postulated really has no name. And for this reason it would almost be true to say that it has hardly any existence yet either in the Church and in theology. We recognise it immediately when we think of *Gaudium et spes* and in doing so resist the temptation to reduce what is said there to mere 'dogma', 'moral theology' and 'social science', and when, on the contrary, we try to recognise the element of the 'prophetic' in it and *then* ask ourselves precisely what theological discipline this Pastoral Constitution considered as a whole and in its distinctive character is properly speaking intended to assume. We cannot point to any one because the theological discipline which we have postulated has no name and so has not yet been constituted at all in any explicit sense as a discipline in its own right. For want of a better name we may call this subdivision of the science of practical theology which we have attempted to define 'practical ecclesiological cosmology', but in doing so we hope that the term 'cosmology' as used here will retain the biblical connotation of 'cosmos', and that no-one will confuse this kind of cosmology with the discipline belonging to 'natural philosophy' which bears the same name.

Today the task which awaits a 'cosmology' of this kind is an almost immeasurable one. In our naiveté we constantly suppose that we know the world in which we live; that we are familiar with its forms, its diversity, its ideologies, its hopes and impulses, the co-existence of the various levels of human living within it, which are present in it simultaneously right from the origins. We find no difficulty in believing that we know what manner of men they are to whom the Church addresses herself in her specifically religious mission, but also, over and above this, in the message

---

[27] On this cf. W. Weber, 'Kirchliche Soziallehre', *Was ist Theologie?*, E. Neuhäusler, E. Gössmann edd. (Munich 1966), pp. 244–265 (Bibliography).

[28] On this cf. the summing up of J. B. Metz in his study, *Verantwortung der Hoffnung* (Mainz 1968).

she has to give with regard to the wellbeing and prosperity of society and its future even within this present world. We do not know these men. Or at most we know only a particular group of them, separated from the rest by our own mental attitudes, conditioned as these are by our membership of the Church and the bourgeois outlook of our own times. We need only to notice the emphasis, the perspectives and the choices of subject-matter which are made in the official pronouncements of the Church, and to ask ourselves precisely which *men* can pay heed to these pronouncements, to see that in spite of all her good will the Church does not really know, in any adequate sense, man as he exists today.[29]

In this cosmology innumerable aspects of the relationship which the Church is required to bear to the secular world today would have to be considered. The directly religious mission of the Church certainly does not belong to *this* part of practical theology. Nevertheless this cosmology would have quite sufficient material to consider with regard to the relationship between the Church and the world. Certainly there are many particular subjects belonging to this complex of questions within the theological discussion – all those which are treated of in the second part of *Gaudium et spes* and which in fact also constantly point by implication to a function which the Church has in relation to the world. But is this enough to include all the particular subjects? Are there not others which, as we can foresee, will become urgent in the immediate future? Are there not many such particular subjects, in relation to which the Church *de facto* merely adopts a theoretical and detached attitude, a dialectical approach characterised by the phrases 'on the one hand . . . on the other' without venturing upon any *concrete* imperative as a prophetic instruction? Or are there not certain subjects to which the Church responds only with an imperative so timid and so hedged about with provisos that it is inevitably ignored? Indeed – for this is how it sometimes seems – are such imperatives actually formulated with the secret hope precisely *that* they will be ignored? In other words they will be there as an alibi and yet create no offence anywhere.

Certainly a scientific cosmology of the kind we are thinking of cannot of itself formulate such imperatives. But it could pave the way for them and provide the scientifically and critically informed conscience leading to them, and at the same time the encouragement necessary for concrete action. It could serve to keep alive in the Church the awareness that she

---

[29] How otherwise, for instance, would it be possible to speak with so little embarrassment even today, e.g. of the 'fire' of purgatory, as Paul VI still does in his most recent Apostolic Constitution, '*Indulgentiarum Doctrina*'?

herself is far from being a mere organisation for satisfying the religious needs of the salvation of the individual merely because she is not, and cannot be, that which controls the world in an integralist sense. Rather she must recognise, in the particular area which we here have in mind, that the secular world is a *free* partner in an open dialogue. Indeed she must recognise that she herself is a genuine *part* of this secular world which collaborates as an element within history in the history of the world of which God alone is the autonomous controller. And in this history she herself is not simply *the* representative of God.

VI

Up to this point we have sought to consider and to concentrate methodically upon that process of 'secularisation' in which *the Church and the world* become involved in a greater diastasis, one which is conditioned by the relevant epoch, and are thereby compelled to strive afresh to achieve a positive relationship to one another, one which consists neither in 'integralism' nor yet in a mere negative withdrawal and the exercise of a critical function towards the world on the part of the Church. In conclusion, however, we may permit ourselves to extend our theme of investigation somewhat, so as to include in it the distinction between the 'secular world' and the 'grace' of which the Church is only the effective sign without thereby *ipso facto* being identical with it. This means that we are regarding the 'world' as worldly no longer in virtue of its distinction from and relationship to the Church and vice versa, but as it is in itself. We do not intend, however, to take up once more those questions with regard to the 'worldliness' of the world which we have already established as in principle answered at the beginning. Rather we shall attempt to make a somewhat deeper and more far-reaching theological assessment with regard to this worldly world, which is at once abiding and changing from age to age. This assessment which we shall attempt to make will bring into play certain findings of early theology which seem to have become uninteresting and uninspiring to the scholastic theologians, but which in the context with which we are concerned, once more acquire their original significance and weight.

On this basis we may formulate our fifth thesis as follows:

The situation entailed by the secular world is one of pluralism and 'concupiscence'. Now the process by which man unreflectingly allows himself to become involved in this situation is not ipso facto *or 'of itself' sinful. What this situation signifies, rather, at all levels in which man strives to achieve the*

*fulness of his own existence, including those levels characterised by 'gnoseology',
is the necessary prior condition and the existential context in which the mode
of human living in which the Christian is involved is one of contest and struggle,
and one threatened by sin (the sin namely of forgetfulness of God). This
situation must be accepted and realistically endured by the Christian as something that is permanent, and in doing this he must not fall into any ideologisa-
tion of this world in an integralist sense.*

In order to understand what is meant by this statement a few words
must first be said with regard to the 'concupiscence' of man in the theological sense of the term.[30] 'Concupiscence', rightly understood, implies
an interior pluralism within man at all levels of his being and in all his
impulses, and that too a pluralism of such a kind that it can never be
totally or radically integrated into the *single* decision of freedom (either
for or against God) by man as a personal and consciously reflecting being
endowed with freedom. This inalienable state of 'disintegration' appears
at all levels of human self-fulfilment, not merely in moral acts in the
narrower sense but also in the dimension of knowledge, which as such is
always at the same time a 'practical' activity. It appears at its bitterest and
starkest in the 'disintegration' of death and of life considered as a *prolixitas
mortis*. Now it would be to deny this interior 'fleshly' state of disintegration and the impossibility of ever overcoming it[31] if we sought to conceive of it as consisting of 'interior' conditions terminating, so to say, at
that point at which the subject of them makes contact with the external
world. Man is an open 'system', constantly in communication with the
world. Right from the first he is orientated outwards to the world. The
world is in him and he in it, and what we call the 'environment' of man is
man himself in his state of radical outward orientation in space and time.
In this state he is at once himself in possession of himself and yet sharing
this otherness of his in his identity with others. The constitution of man as
'concupiscent' and as having an 'interior' life of his own, and at the same
time the constitution of the world he lives in, necessarily correspond to
one another. Thus it is easier to deduce what 'concupiscence' properly

---

[30] On this concept of concupiscence cf. especially K. Rahner, 'The Theological
Concept of Concupiscentia', *Theological Investigations* I (London and Baltimore
1961), pp. 347–382; 'Justified and Sinner at the Same Time', *Theological Investigations*
VI (London and Baltimore 1969), pp. 218–230; J. B. Metz, 'Konkupiszenz', *H.T.G.* I
(Munich 1962), 843–851.

[31] Of course this does not exclude, but rather takes into account the point that the
control we exercise over our human living in history must always be actively directed
towards a state of total integration, even though this is a goal which is only asymptotically attainable in this world.

speaking consists in from the world than to do so by a process of 'psychological' introspection into man as he is in himself. This concupiscence has an unfolding process of its own, the process precisely in which man endures and in which he constantly, but only imperfectly, overcomes this state of disintegration to which he is subject. The statements of traditional theology with regard to 'concupiscence', therefore, can with perfect justice be interpreted as statements of theology with regard to the secular world which, considered as the area of human living in space and time and as a prolongation of the physical side of man, display exactly the same basic qualities, subject to change from age to age, as does that 'interior' element of concupiscence which is in man himself: a plurality of the objective factors involved and of the various dimensions at which they exist, their state of disintegration, the abiding impossibility for man, even though asymptotically speaking it is something which man must constantly strive to overcome, of ever achieving a point of unity from which man himself can control all these diverse factors and so overcome this pluralism; the fact that this pluralism as it exists in the concrete, together with the attempts at achieving integration in it by subsuming all the factors involved (under a single idea, a single representative body vested with power etc.) is finite and subject to the vicissitudes of history.

Thus we can see that the statements of theology with regard to concupiscence are *ipso facto* statements of a theological interpretation of the world. The interpretation of the world by Christians, and thereby of their own relationship to it, can therefore be deduced from the theological statements with regard to the interpretation of concupiscence. We shall therefore concentrate particularly upon the three basic statements of the Council of Trent with regard to 'concupiscence', and interpret them as statements about the secular world.

First: the non-integrated pluralism of the human reality which is called 'concupiscence', and therefore too of the secular world, is not *ipso facto* and 'of itself' sin, but rather an element in saving history, a stage which is 'open' to further development and which leads to an integration which can only be attained to in the consummation of man and of the 'kingdom of God'. This 'declaration of innocence' is not so immediately obvious or so insignificant as might appear at first sight. In order to see this we do not even need to remind ourselves of the heterodox interpretations of the world such as those of Gnosticism, Manichaeism etc., though in fact even in Christianity as it actually exists these continue to have an underground existence, albeit not at the level of conscious theory, at least with regard to specific and particular levels of human existence which are subject to change from age to age. There is no need whatever for these denials of the 'innocence' of the 'concupiscence' of the secular world to be set forth dramatically. They are actually *lived* in the unreflecting modes in which human existence is fulfilled. Cases arise in which one particular milieu and mode of life is from the outset preferred before all others as *the* truly 'Christian' one, for instance the 'simple and modest way of life', the life which refrains from any 'dangerous' erudition or a 'puritan' life character-ised by a mistrust of the factor of sex and of any happiness taken in the 'enjoyment of life'. Cases arise in which certain specific ways of life which are open to man are from the outset regarded as suspicious and not 'suitable' in any any true sense for the Christian. 'The soldiers' calling' (in earlier times!), the life of the politician and involvement in politics (as a 'dirty business'), the callings of the actor or artist in general etc. And wherever this is the case there we have the underground influence of the sort of denial we are speaking of, of the innocent and unblameworthy pluralism of the world, even though it is not stated in so many words. Efforts are made to escape from the non-integrated pluralism of the world by excluding from the outset certain dimensions as not 'relevant' to human or Christian life. There is an effort to simplify life, to reduce it to a unity (German *ver-ein-fachen*) in order not to have to endure and sustain the burden of the non-integrated and 'concupiscent' pluralism. But the only way of achieving a simplification of this kind is to regard that which one has excluded from one's life and so the complexity of the world with all the heterogeneous forces in it, as a world that is rightly to be rejected and pronounced 'guilty'. The Pastoral Constitution *Gaudium et spes* (No. 25) clearly recognises the difference which exists between the disturbances (*perturbationes*) involved in the inevitable 'tension' (*tensio*) of economic, political and social factors on the one hand, *and* on the other the distur-bances which arise from sin. In those cases in which we pronounce the first kind of 'disturbances' and tensions as *ipso facto* and of themselves 'sinful' we are undertaking a secret manoeuvre to rid ourselves of a bur-den, because in that case we are in fact simply producing objectivations of our *own* guilt which add nothing whatever either new or different to this sinful world.

Second: Concupiscence is imposed upon man *ad agonem*. We can trans-late as follows: the world as pluralist, secular and non-integrated is no abode of 'peace' in which man can enjoy a world that is integrated and in which the various elements are 'reconciled' and brought into harmony with one another, and one that, provided 'good will' is present, can quickly be set up. Rather it is the sphere in which man's life is one of *agon*, contest and struggle.[32] Certainly this *agon* is directed towards a goal, namely the integration of all realities in the final fulness of the love of God as encountered 'face to face'. But this is a goal which can never fully be attained to in this age. Always it lies before us and because of this it constantly leads us into areas of fresh opportunity. But the primary demand which this *agon* makes upon us is that it shall be readily accepted – *viriliter*, as the Council of Trent expresses it. Now it is not accepted so long as man's ultimate attitude is one in which he refuses to accept and endure the pluralism of his life as non-integrated and the forces present in this life to which he is constantly exposed from the very outset. For instance he is failing to accept the situation in which he has to live as conditioned by 'gnoseology' and also by concupiscence so long as he sacrifices the open and unresolved conflict between its many heterogeneous 'sources' of experience and knowledge, which cannot be subsumed under one another, in favour of a system in which one particular 'science' – whether it be theology or metaphysics – is made simply to dominate over the rest without allowing itself to be called in question by them in any 'open dialogue', or modified in any way in the unfolding processes of human living. This would give it the status of a universal science which sought to extract and to integrate within itself all knowledge from all the schools, so that its practitioners would be afraid to allow that there was anything that they did not know. They would be unwilling to be surprised by anything that they really had not 'heard before', any alien piece of knowledge such that they would have to change their own system in order to admit of it, not having previously provided any place for it in that system. The truth is, however, that even the *areopagus* of the spirit constitutes an 'open society' in which a constantly shifting balance is maintained between the various forces.

Such an attitude represents a failure to accept the *agon* present in human life through the medium of the world as pluralist and subject to the forces of concupiscence, and not already reconciled and brought into harmony so long as we believe that we are not empowered to entertain 'interests', joys, initial options and preferences which have not yet fully been subjected to a process of criticism and choice by the standards of explicitly religious and 'supernatural' motives. The *agon* as it exists in the secular world is not accepted (though it does, of course, remain even while it is denied and suppressed, and precisely as such becomes more dangerous) when, in an attitude of hostility towards the incalculable

[32] On this concept of peace cf. my study, 'The Peace of God and the Peace of the World' below pp. 371–388 (and also the fuller bibliography supplied there).

factors in life because of the 'disintegration' which they introduce into it, we seek, in a spirit of harsh obstinacy to reconstruct it through and through in a 'Christian 'sense, as though its confused cacophony had to be brought into harmony here and now by us ourselves in a process of integralism guided now not by the Church but by the Christian himself of his own power and by his own right.

Third: 'Concupiscence' implies an impulse to sin (*ad peccatum inclinat* DS 1515). This is not the place to consider concupiscence, and so too the world as pluralist and non-integrated, in all its bearings from the point of view of its origin ('original sin') and its consequences (personal sin and the objectivations of this in the world both at the individual and collective levels). We may confine ourselves to drawing attention to one point, because it belongs directly to the subject of the 'world'. We do not need to derive our knowledge of what that sin is which threatens us in the concupiscent world from any other source. This knowledge is already present in the worldly and concupiscent situation itself. Sin is precisely the failure to sustain and the failure to endure this situation in the private or public departments of human life. It causes man anxiety not to have any absolute fixed point at his disposal within the integrated instability of the open system of human life. He does not dare to abandon himslf to the uncontrollable factor inherent in that unique unity which is to be found in this totality of the pluralist at its still unintegrated stage. This uncontrollable factor is open in all directions. It leads backwards into the hidden origins, forwards into the unplanned future, upwards into the limitlessness of transcendence, downwards into the darkness and sheer impenetrable factualness of the material. From the basis of this 'mortal fear' (Heb 2:15) one particular element in the non-integrated and pluralist world is, whether in theory or (perhaps also) in practice, accorded an absolute value. In other words man in his self-will and fear elevates it, as it were, to the single and all-dominating point of reference for the integration of the world which, it is claimed, will be autonomously achieved. This is what takes place at the theoretical level in that which constitutes a (bad) 'ideology', and at the practical level in that which in simple terms is called sin. Now to the extent that man's theoretical and practical activities themselves in turn constitute an element in the world, and to the extent that man's original decision taken in freedom necessarily achieves its fulness beyond himself in the physical and social objectivations which this freedom achieves (although this freedom does not absolutely speaking enter into the objectivations concerned and therefore the objectivations of it remain ambiguous), it follows that through any 'integration' precisely of *this* kind the world itself is altered. It becomes the 'world of sin', 'this present age' in the biblical sense of the phrase. The objective relationships are affected by the various ways in which sin works itself out.[33]

So long as the integration given by God has not been achieved in the world there are always some ways, albeit *essentially* different ones, in which man, even though 'free', yields to the pressures of the non-integrated world.[34] Moreover there is a division between the non-sinful pluralism of the forces of concupiscence in the world on the one hand and the disintegration imprinted upon it through sin on the other (for sin as a pseudo-integration is really a strengthening of disintegration). Now if this division is asserted to constitute an unambiguous criterion of 'judgment', then it in turn becomes a way of attempting to achieve an alleged integration through one's own power. For if this were indeed the case then we would know 'what we have to hold firm to' as that which, as reconciled within itself, constituted our own good. But this is not the case. Now because of all these factors the secular world constitutes a unity of many heterogenous realities which is not for us to shape or control, and which are invisibly involved with one another: the world as made up of manifold created goods; the world as made up of many different, though justifiable human activities; the world as the objectivation of man's guilt in his will autonomously to reduce the world 'to order' in an integralist sense.

The secular and pluralist world is the 'world' as envisaged in scripture. The pluralist world can be precisely this because it is *history* and not a mere static 'system'. At the same time, however, this secular world is also precisely that world which the Christian expects, acts upon and endures from his own innermost Christian understanding of himself. For in this he does not regard the world as alien by reason of some ideological or integralist attitude, but rather views it as it actually is. Here, then, at the end of these theological considerations on the problem of secularisation, we have returned to a truth which is quite simple and, for Christians, never to be forgotten. In spite, therefore, of the differences which sometimes seem to threaten our lives to their very roots, it is the same 'world'

[33] On this cf. also *Gaudium et spes*, No. 25.

[34] This takes place in a twofold manner: first through an exercise of basic freedom amounting to pseudo-integralism in that it accords an absolute value to some element in the world ('mortal sin'). The second way bears upon that dynamic impulse towards a genuine integration of the world which is constantly striving towards, and in *process* of attaining to its goal but asymptotically, never wholly reaching it. In this second way the act of the will delays and holds back this process ('venial sin'). Of course as a matter of concrete practice neither way can, with complete certainty, be distinguished from the other.

which God loved so much that he took it upon himself and laid down his life for it. If the Christian takes this central point of his faith as the centre of his life too, then he can endure even the secular world and, in the right sense, be of service to it.

[35] This would provide a suitable starting-point for presenting more fully the necessity and the concrete function of the evangelical counsels. cf. K. Rahner, 'Kirche und Welt', *Zehn Jahre Katholische Akademie in Bayern* (Würzburg 1967), esp. pp. 22–24; 'On the Evangelical Counsels', *Theological Investigations* VIII (London and Baltimore 1971), pp. 133–167.

18

PRACTICAL THEOLOGY AND SOCIAL WORK
IN THE CHURCH

IN order to speak upon this topic as I have been commissioned to,[1] I can only imagine myself, even on the most favourable showing, as being like Balaam's ass who uttered prophetic speech and yet remained an ass. Certainly I am no expert in the social sciences, and no specialist in practical theology either. Still less have I any practical experience in social work, whether in the ecclesiastical or the secular sphere. It may perhaps be true that the dogmatic theologian should have a certain minimal understanding of these matters, seeing that he has to think out, from his central watchtower of theology, the significance of the Christian and the Church, among other things in their relationship to the world and to the circumstances of human living in this present world. But if this is true then the dogmatic theologian of today as he exists in the concrete will in turn have to make a report which is either very deficient or almost wholly negative: the much vaunted 'theology of earthly realities' is, despite the Pastoral Constitution 'On the Church in the World of Today', still barely in its initial stages. I cannot conceal this situation, and therefore what *I personally* can say will be said with the courage of despair.[2] If I

---

[1] For the occasion on which this lecture was delivered cf. the detailed list of sources appended at the end of this volume.

[2] For this reason the author is compelled to refer to a wide range of preliminary studies of his own. cf. especially the expositions in *Handbuch der Pastoraltheologie*, F. X. Arnold, K. Rahner, V. Schurr, L. M. Weber edd., Vols I–II/1–2 (Freiburg 1964–1966) concerning the connections between Church and world, the situation of the Church today etc. For an explicit statement of the principles involved, therefore, reference must be made to this work in particular (and also the comprehensive bibliographies there provided). On the present subject cf. also especially the expositions of R. Völkl, I, pp. 385–412; II/2, pp. 403–423; another approach which the considerations which follow presuppose, but which was undertaken with different aims in view, is offered by K. Rahner and K. Lehmann in II/2, pp. 389–402 (bibliography). cf. also A. Ziegler, *Thesen zum Verhältnis von Sozialarbeit und Theologie* (Caritas-Verlag, Lucerne, special edition); A. Hunziker, 'Geistige und berufsethische Aspekte der Sozialarbeit', *Caritas* 45 (1967) (Supplement to Section 3), pp. 102–116.

altogether fail or achieve far too little of importance then I can only appeal to the forebearance and forgiveness of my readers, and can only hope that at least the contradictions which my remarks will occasion may perhaps lead to other insights which are better than those offered here. We shall attempt to present our considerations in four key statements and lines of argument.

I

The first is that principle which belongs to 'scientific theory' to the effect that the teaching with regard to the Church's works of charity and social work is an intrinsic element in pastoral theology which should better be called 'practical theology'. 'Pastoral theology' so called can in fact no longer be understood today as teaching and direction relating, for instance, to the world of the cleric charged with the cure of souls in his particular field. Today, rather, it consists in theological reflection upon the *entire* process by which the Church as a whole brings her own nature to its fulness in the light both of her own nature *and also* of the contemporary situation of the world and the Church today thought out from a theological point of view. Now those actively involved in this task of bringing the Church as a whole to its fulness include *all* degrees in the Church's hierarchy and *also* the laity, as well as everything which is included in the concept of this self-fulfilment of the Church: not only cult, doctrine and pastoral work in the narrower sense as immediately concerned with the mediation of salvation to the individual, but also, and no less essentially, the charitable work of the Church and the whole of her impact in all its aspects upon that which we call the 'world'. This means that the social work of the Church too belongs to this inasmuch as there is a special way of carrying out this social work, of defining its aims and limits, which pertains precisely to the Church as such. The situation of the Church in

---

For a brief presentation of changes in social work and work to raise standards of living, and also of the role of the Church today, attention must particularly be drawn to these studies. cf. also K. Rahner, 'On the Theological Problems Entailed in a "Pastoral Constitution" '; 'Christian Humanism'; 'The Presence of the Lord in the Christian Community at Worship'; 'On the Presence of Christ in the Diaspora Community According to the Teaching of the Second Vatican Council'; 'Theological Reflections on the Problem of Secularisation', in the present volume pp. 293–317; 71–83; 84–102; 318–348; and Vol. IX, pp. 187–204. On the range of subject-matter involved in the study which follows cf. also a further study by K. Rahner, 'The Christian in his World', *Theological Investigations* VII (London and Baltimore 1971), pp. 88–99.

the world and in the unfolding process of salvation history is constantly changing, and not everything that an individual Christian does is to be included in this self-fulfilment of hers at any given time, for there is certainly a 'private' sphere of Christian living too. But on the other hand this self-fulfilment is not to be identified with the activity of the officials of the Church either, or even, it may be, of the laity to the extent that they are carrying out some commission for the official Church. The Church (which, however, is not identical with the hierarchy) achieves this self-fulfilment of hers in the most manifold forms of activity and in widely varying degrees. But all these, which characterise her and in which she is involved, belong to this process of self-consummation. Certainly there is such a thing as a 'private' level of Christian living as well, a process, therefore, of intercommunication between individuals which is private, Christian and sustained by the grace of Christ, and which therefore constitutes a love, a charity in the theological sense of the term, in which the Church as such is not involved. At the same time, however, charity and social work are integral elements in the self-fulfilment of the Church as such, and therefore also constitute a subject for practical theology, however difficult it may be in the concrete to discriminate between *caritas* at the level of the Church and the *caritas* of the individual in his private Christian life.

This first principle, which we have only been able to explain very briefly above, is no mere theological subtlety, a play with words at the level of scientific theory. First the theological consideration of the Church's charity and social work precisely at the ecclesiastical level has, without prejudice to the fact that the work of charity is the subject of a distinct scientific discipline in its own right, its own essential place in practical theology, and is not a mere floating or arbitrary theory about something which is now actually to be found within the sphere of the Church, in her sanctuary and before her walls. Second, practical theology does not merely draw the more concrete conclusions for the Church's activity which follow from a mere 'essential' ecclesiology, but rather constitutes an original and autonomous science, because it alone can say, on the basis of an analysis of the present worked out in theological terms, what the Church should do at the particular time concerned (not therefore at all times); and also because it actually has to say this with the force of a certain prophetic imperative. Thus it comes about that the science of *caritas* need not confine itself to describing what constitutes the *caritas* of the Church *at all times* and from the very nature of the Church herself. Rather this science has to define what the *caritas* of the Church must be precisely today, in the particular circumstances prevailing now, rather than always, but in these circumstances, once more, as interpreted in terms of a theological critique. The science of *caritas* has a critical, almost a prophetic, function with regard to the *caritas* which the Church *de facto* performs, and must to some extent employ the creative imagination which springs from hope to project the ever-fresh forms which the *caritas* and the attitude of the Church towards the world have to assume. It can be concluded from the nature of practical theology as rightly understood that the science of *caritas* is an original theological science, and also a critical and normative one, which must at basis include sociology, futurology and similar sciences as its aids, if it is to recognise what form the *caritas* of the Church has to assume today. It is not a mere collection of practical counsels deriving from the nature of Christian charity, nor merely an appendix to moral theology.

There is, however, straightaway something further to be said – at least in the form of a question – once we have recognised the necessity for such a change in the form of charitable works on the basis of a scientifically thought our charity of this kind: there is a Pastoral Constitution 'On the Church in the World of Today'. There is a Secretariate providing for the Church and Christians to enter into dialogue and (perhaps) collaboration also with 'unbelievers' (better with non-religious humanism). There is much more besides in terms of thought and action which leads in the same direction. Yet so far as theological consideration goes there is still no name whatever for all phenomena of this kind which are slowly coming to the surface in the form of questions, teachings and action. And yet something is 'there' palpably and unforgettably only when it has a name. Certainly this nameless phenomenon belongs to the sphere of practical theology, but it is not identical with the whole of practical theology since in fact this also has to take into consideration the cure of souls in the narrower sense. Nor is this nameless phenomenon a department of dogmatic ecclesiology for the area which this has to investigate is the enduring relationship to the Church, and not that which arises adventitiously at a particular time. Nor yet can this nameless phenomenon be identified with Christian social sciences, even though it is related to these. For these sciences are concerned with social and economic factors etc. in so far as these, while retaining their own secular status, still fall under the norms of the natural law and the gospel. But what the sciences do not consider is the mutual interrelationship of the Church and the world as such, both in its active and its passive aspects. Nor is the designation 'theology of earthly realities' correct, because in fact what is being treated of here is the relationship of the *Church* to the world, and that too to the world considered as a social entity, as a work of man and not as the immediate outcome of the creative work of God. J. B. Metz has once more seized upon the term 'political theology', but even this does not signify what is being pointed to here, because 'political theology' includes within its purview the social relevance of faith and the entire reality which it envisages. The Americans call this phenomenon simply 'Church and world', but mean by this a special theological discipline in its own right. We should perhaps provisionally call this phenomenon 'theological and ecclesiological cosmology', if this name cosmology had not already, and, at least in a still provisional sense, been appropriated for a philosophical discipline which admittedly is gradually being eliminated in favour of a transcendental ontology and anthropology on the one hand and a scientific study of nature and history on the other.

Whatever course we adopt in order to fulfil the urgent and important need to find a name for this anonymous reality, one question may be posed: always given that the science of the works of charity is understood as a department of, and an intrinsic element in practical theology, should it not, in these times, be expanded and reorganised on the basis of this 'ecclesiological cosmology'? Would this not be reasonable in view of the following two factors: *first*, that it is probably inevitable that the work of charity as practised today should be caught up in the process of changing its forms and modes of expression even though its essence endures. Even the charitable works organised on an ecclesiastical basis cannot any longer simply be identified with 'welfare', and the borderline between charity properly so called and the whole range of works performed by the Church for the world in general and in the field of social work in particular is, both in theory and in practice, extremely difficult to establish – *if* indeed there is any such; *second*, that theological and ecclesiological cosmology is still seeking for a foothold and a home, still seeking, therefore, for some real possibility of being systematically studied. Charity would not be being false to itself if it were to extend its scientific aspects so as to include a 'cosmology' of this kind. It would be combined with that 'hope' which is so very neglected and isolated,[3] and together with it would form a cosmology made up of futurology and ecclesiology of this kind as a part of practical theology, and so construct a framework within which these two theological virtues would find a place proper to themselves in speculative theology alongside that assigned to faith. It is clear, therefore, that the

[3] On this cf. K. Rahner, 'On the Theology of Hope', in the present volume, pp. 242–259, esp. pp. 256 ff.

science of *caritas* and the theology of the social task and work of the Church would thereby achieve a closer and more comprehensible relationship. All this, however, has been put forward merely as a *question*.

II

Now let us come at last to those factors which the actual terms *caritas* and 'the social work of the Church' are intended to stand for, in order to approach one stage nearer to our real subject. In accordance with this the *second* principle runs as follows: the difference between the Church and grace on the one hand, and 'the world as it has become worldly' on the other, which contemporary theologians are beginning to recognise and to understand as a difference imposed by Christianity itself, determines also and in turn a further relationship. The two terms of this relationship are on the one hand grace as *caritas* and the Church as the historical and social manifestation of this ecclesiastical *caritas*, and on the other that *caritas* the forms of which have been secularised (considering this both as an 'attitude of mind' and in the forms in which it is objectified in society).

Let us first consider not *caritas* and the social work of the Church together with the counterparts to these in the secular and worldly sphere, but rather the factors of grace or Church and world in general and as a whole. 'World' exists not merely as a creation of God, as 'nature' but as a task to be performed, an activity to be entered upon and the objective realisation of these on the part of man himself. It exists as the subject of man's own projects for the future, the world that he has made and has still to make, that to which he himself belongs as one whose course is shaped and directed by himself. World in this sense is to be distinguished not merely from grace and Church in the same way that 'nature' is to be distinguished from grace, for in this latter case nature is that which grace presupposes and to which it is addressed, that in relation to which grace represents the opening up of a new and distinct modality, that which makes it possible for grace to be imparted as the self-bestowal of God. The world is also to be distinguished from grace and Church *from age to age*. As the history of grace progresses this world is, to an increasing extent, made responsible for itself in its autonomy, its maturity, its secularity and its realisation of its own nature. This 'worldliness' of the world which increases from age to age is, despite the distortions and damage due to sin always present in the process, in the last analysis not a disastrous fate which blindly runs counter to grace and the Church, but the mode in which grace itself enters more and more fully into creation: as a liberation and authentication of the world as it is in itself. In this connection it must be recognised once again that a state of pluralistic – indeed of 'concupiscent' disintegration is proper to this world as it is in itself, and must be accepted and endured by man *as such*. In other words in the world as such and as it exists in itself there is no controlling power, whether already in existence or capable of being set up, which could, in any adequate sense, integrate it into a comprehensible and controllable system. It would, therefore, be utterly unchristian to seek univocally to inform and to control the world in its reality and its history in terms of its positive content. And faith and the Church make no claim of this kind. Rather they seek to accord due responsibility to the world itself, to man as mature and free, to his decision and responsibility in the forms which he imposes upon his world. Now for the moment nothing further need be said with regard to what further positive significance faith, grace and the Church still have as contributing to the liberation of the world in its worldliness. For this question will soon be raised again in the course of our present investigation.

For the present, however, it must be recognised that all communication between men at all levels and in all its dimensions belongs essentially to man. Now in accordance with what has just been said, this has the following significance: intercourse between men has its appropriate place 'also' in the world which is liberated in this way by grace and the Church in its worldliness. Certainly there is also a form of intercourse between men which is constituted by grace as such and only by it. This is precisely *caritas* in the theological sense, that unity between men which is constituted by the divine self-bestowal. This specific form of communication between men is manifested in the Church in that special and unique form in which it has the basically sacramental significance of being a sign and effective within the dimension of history. It is this that in principle distinguishes the Church from the world.

But in accordance with the relationship between the Church and the world in general, and also as subject to variations from age to age, this grace-given human intercourse which is made manifest in the Church in *caritas* also releases, as its necessary prior condition, and appropriates to itself, a human intercourse at the worldly level which grows from age to age. The Church renounces any claim personally to exercise control in an 'integralist' sense over this human intercourse at the worldly level, and sends the Christian – and precisely as such – into this context of human intercourse, still at the worldly level, as the appropriate field for him to fulfil in maturity his human *and* his Christian task. At the same time the Church herself imposes upon him as his lot and his burden that human intercourse at the worldly level which is pluralistic, unintegrated and subject to the forces of concupiscence together with the modes in which it is developed to the full and objectified. Grace and the Church leave the world unimpeded in its autonomous reality and its own responsibility with regard to the future in which it seeks fulfilment and the task which confronts it in the present. And precisely because of this the Church avoids the danger of becoming a mere accomplice of the world ('throne and altar') in its social institutions, often petrified and even affected by sin as these are, and achieves that detachment which she needs in order to fulfil her ministry of providing a critique of the world and of opening it to its own future by 'imprinting' her own eschatological hope upon the structures of 'worldly' life, as the Council itself lays down (*Lumen gentium*, No. 35).

From this the following conclusions arise: the element of the worldly, social activities while remaining at the worldly level and the worldly forms in which these are institutionalised cannot, either in themselves or in the manner in which they develop from age to age, be regarded by the Christian or the Church as something which should properly speaking and better be achieved merely by the Church and the Christian as such by their own dispositions and explicitly ecclesiastical guidance. In principle no greater value is to be attributed to the specifically Christian or ecclesiastical element in the field of social work than in any other spheres of activity of the world in its worldliness, of culture or of society. Hence too the theology of the Church cannot of itself alone arrive at any theoretical or adequate judgment with regard to the necessity, urgency, concrete forms or lines of development for such work in order that man may attain to a higher and more fruitful level of socialisation, however much Christians too, considered as individuals, may be called upon by their faith and their *caritas* to collaborate in open dialogue and in competition within the context of human living with all other men as fellow citizens of one and the same world in the unfolding process of this social reality, and however much too the Church may be justified and authorised in offering to the world in its freedom and responsibility a word of prophetic 'instruction' over and above the abiding principles of the gospel.

III

We pass on to a *third* principle. The Church (in all the complexity of this concept) has the task of bringing to bear upon the world the work of charity and social welfare. This work cannot *a priori* and in all cases materially be distinguished from the same work and the institutions catering for this that belong to the world. Any lines of demarcation or any possible overlappings or 'two-way traffic' situations between the ecclesiastical and secular spheres of charitable work can only be laid down for a particular place and time. And, as has been said, there is neither any one *a priori* plan to regulate all that pertains to this nor yet any autonomous body with authority to draw such lines of demarcation. All that we have is an 'open' system, and at most this can never strike more than a precarious balance between the two.

The Church has the task, and also the right belonging to her of her very nature, to make an impact upon the world through her activities in the fields of charitable and social work. We use the simple terms 'charitable' and 'social' work. While for practical purposes it is perhaps possible to draw a certain distinction between charitable and social work, an essential and unequivocal distinction between the two at the theological level is not possible – is indeed actually ruled out. For *caritas* in the theological sense consists in that one love which exists between God and man and between men among themselves and signifies the one all-embracing factor and the one whole which encompasses the whole of man and *so* his salvation. Moreover this love is no mere attitude of mind, but is an action which is made incarnate in all departments of human living (even though perhaps in some cases in forms which appear secular and worldly, and, as it were, concealed). Again it is quite impossible to think of mankind without also thinking of the human intercourse that goes with it and which has to be given objective reality at the social level. Now if all this is true *then* it follows that *all* activities directed to a human intercourse which is right, beneficial and also a part of concrete living in society, can be the 'material', the expression and the event in terms of social living in the concrete precisely of this theological *caritas*, and nothing can be excluded from it *a priori*. Indeed this *caritas*, considered as a factor that comprehends the whole of Christian living, always contains within itself the duty and the impulse constantly to seek out fresh forms in which to realise itself as each particular situation demands and suggests. This also means that all social work, provided only that it is contributing in some way to man himself and to his communal living, is an element in those processes by which *caritas* is brought to its fullness, and that precisely in the circumstances of today it can actually be offered eagerly as something over and above that which is so commonly termed 'charitable' work.

If the very act of feeding the hungry in the simple and biological sense can, and even must be *caritas* and the work of *caritas*, then we can say from the outset that we cannot perceive how anything else pertaining to social service and social work can of itself be excluded from the work of *caritas*. On the contrary, in every age the Christian and the Church must ask themselves afresh what precisely, in view of the circumstances of the time, the seven 'corporal' works of mercy and the seven 'spiritual' works of mercy are to consist in. We should not envisage these according to the old conceptual models of a society and an economy in decline, and so blind ourselves to those forms of activity in which '*caritas*' should be embodied today, even though, perhaps, no-one would call them 'charitable'. It can surely not be the task of the theologian to sketch out a systematic table of the sort of levels of human living in which a *caritas* supported by concrete institutions could become embodied as a factor in the life of society, a '*caritas*' such that its activities would not necessarily be 'charitable' in the usual sense of the term. On the other hand this would be a question which practical theology should not evade. Let us then use the term 'social work' to cover all this field as a whole, together with the achievements, works and institutions belonging to it, and let us also subsume under this head the work of charity (*caritas* as traditionally understood) as a part which is important indeed, but not as the whole of 'social work'.

The Church has the right and the duty to engage in this ministry of social work for, constituted as she is as a social and historical entity, she is not merely the recipient and the witness to the world of the truth in faith and of the future in hope (from both aspects she is the basic sacrament), but also the basic sacrament of unity in the ministry of love.

The subject of social work in this sense is the *Church*. In laying down this principle we must bear in mind that the word 'Church' in it contains many different shades and levels of meaning. Church in the sense envisaged in practical theology and in the nature of the case itself is certainly not *ipso facto* present where the individual Christian, while continuing to act as a 'private' individual in his Christian life, does 'social' work and finds himself compelled to act in the unique place belonging to him within the society of his fellow men, a place which he shapes by his own free and responsible decisions. Nor is the Church yet present in the work of the individual Christian when he discharges this personal task of his as a 'private' individual living in the world, sharing in the communal responsibility for its well-being, or actively co-operating as a member of the community in the social work which it needs at the worldly level, even though in so doing he may be making real at one and the same time the *caritas* which flows from the grace bestowed on him *and* his task in the world.

Despite this, however, the statement that the *Church*, both in her activities and through her institutions, has a social work to perform has several different levels of meaning. One example of the Church's social work in this sense would be those instances in which the pope and bishops play an active part in social measures in the world but precisely as official representatives of the Church as, for instance, has already in fact been the case in the encyclical *Populorum progressio*. This is also true of those cases in which the pope and bishops ensure that their social activities as hierarchically constituted officials of the Church shall be carried out by individual Christians or institutions officially commissioned for the purpose. But a further instance of the social work of the actual *Church* as such is to be found in those cases in which the local communities at the parish level go out from the altar to work actively and to set up institutions (for instance through the *caritas* organisation of the parish etc.) in order to make real the love that exists between the individuals belonging to the community of the faith. In doing this such local communities also make an important contribution to ensuring that the social organisation of secular society shall be sound and healthy.

A further and indispensable instance of the social work of the *Church as such* is that in which Christians as such come together of their own free initiative to set up an institution with the following characteristics: on the one hand it is quite unnecessary that it shall be the outcome of any initiative on the part of the Church's official authorities. It is by no means to be thought of simply as an organ for carrying out the enactments of these ecclesiastical authorities, and properly speaking it does not act as such at all. On the other hand its status as an institution of this kind is due to the free collaboration of Christians and in this sense does have its place within the Church. In other words as an institution of this kind it does recognisably pertain to the Church, and can unreservedly be accounted 'ecclesiastical' at least to the extent that the official authorities of the Church, by their tacit agreement, give free rein to the exercise of the Church's own free charisms. Not everything 'ecclesiastical' is set up by a positive *juridical* authorisation on the part of the Church's official authorities. Of course it is possible in the concrete for institutions to be set up, the forms of which represent a perfectly reasonable mixture of the official on the one hand and the free charismatic on the other, but which are still ecclesiastical institutions. The manner in which these function has to be guaranteed by positive juridical prescriptions of a sensible kind. But in any case 'Church' matters are not identical with 'episcopal' matters in a juridical sense. For even the free charisms are, or can be, integral elements in the Church as such. Of course there are continual transitions and interplay between the two kinds of institutions catering for social work, those which we have mentioned, which are ecclesiastical but inspired by the free charism of the Church on the one hand, and the 'worldly' institutions on the other, which, however, are still either exclusively or principally supported by Christians, and which explicitly appeal to the inspiration of the gospels, even though the Church as such, together with her officially constituted authorities, cannot play any active part in them. This does nothing to alter the basic principle that that which pertains to the 'Church' and that which pertains to the 'official authorities of the Church' are not identical but partially distinct, because the process by which the Church *as such* (even in those areas which are to be distinguished from Christian modes of existence and the life of Christians) realises her own nature implies something more than the activity of the official authorities, and futher because the Church has to become the basic sacrament of the presence of God's grace in the world not merely in virtue of what is done by the official authorities in the Church in the form of teaching, sacraments and official ministries.

It is only at this point, however, that we come to the decisive part of our third statement. Probably it is impossible in principle to draw once and for all any firm, rigid material line of division between the respective areas of social work belonging to the world on the one hand and the Church on the other. Indeed it is probably impossible to devise even a formal principle on the basis of which this borderline can be *deductively* worked out and established with any certainty, in the particular situation prevailing at any given time and on the basis of this, in the sense of a principle as distinct from a prudent and calculated practical decision and as essentially different from theory.[4] To draw a material borderline of this kind, whether directly or in virtue of some formal principle, is impossible and also unnecessary. It is impossible because (sin apart) *every*body can be and should become a medium for fulfilling and manifesting *caritas* as grace – albeit in a process which develops asymptotically, which only attains to its final point in the kingdom of God, and so is continually acting as a sort of counterpoint to the growing worldliness of the world. Thus *all* social work can be the means and the medium for bringing the *caritas* of the Church to its fulness, apart, of course, from those cases in which, whether in principle or in practice, it would tend to do away with the autonomy of the world together with its institutions and the social

[4] cf. K. Rahner, 'Grenzen der Amtskirche', *Schriften zur Theologie* VI (Einsiedeln 1965), pp. 499–520.

work that is proper to it. But even this proviso (already formulated in the second statement) does not yield any principle on which to establish unambiguously the material line of division between secular and ecclesiastical social work. Furthermore, even from the point of view of the world and the state, the drawing of a material line of division of this kind is impracticable. For everywhere where the secular social activities of the community contribute to the abiding dignity of the person, his freedom and his liberation from a state of alienation from himself, where they enable man to be himself and to pursue his earthly and eternal lot in self-responsibility, where they free him from as much as possible of the burden of the pre-personal element in order to lay upon him the heaviest burden of all, himself in his own freedom – in all these areas factors are objectively present in the life of society which are also capable of embodying love, and often actually do so. And in doing so they are capable of belonging to the form in which the Church manifests herself, even though this significance in them is quite unrecognised. Where this is not the case there is no social work or institution either. Whether it remains at so worldly a level as this, so that it is impossible to discern whether it can constitute *caritas* in the theological sense, or whether it really *does* constitute that manifestation of love which proceeds from a heart filled with the Spirit of God – this is something known only to God who alone judges the hearts of men. But this also applies to all social and historical phenomena in which *caritas* is objectively made real through the Church.

In all this it remains true that it is impossible to find any principle on the basis of which to draw a material line of demarcation. Of course in the course of history attempts have been made again and again to make permanent all the lines of division between the Church and the world which have *de facto* arisen: in the field of marriage, education, the special liberties of the clergy, the taxation of Church property etc. The drawing of material lines of demarcation of this kind might be put forward as deduced (whether in a direct and material sense or an indirect and formal one) from principles, and might be attempted by both sides, the Church and secular society, or by only one of these. But in any case such attempts have always constituted an unconscious mixture of two factors; *first* correct (or incorrect) theoretical principles which, however, taken by themselves, and strictly applied, did not yield (even though their exponents thought they did) the desired conclusion of establishing a material line of demarcation, and *second* a resolve and a decision arrived at in concrete history as a freely calculated act and even in circumstances of conflict. But it was supposed that all that was being done was to make effective and real certain immutable principles. In fact, however, this problem of establishing lines of demarcation, however true it may be that we have to respect certain general principles (cf. the second and third statements) is a matter of calculation, of agreement freely entered into on both sides, of historical power in a shifting situation, of creative imagination and even of conflict. It is a matter decided in history precisely as ever unique, ever surprising, which can never be explained in any adequate sense in theory, but is rather 'practice' in a sense which implies something more than the mere execution in time of theoretical principles and plans. Once we realise this, and in doing so accord due importance to the second statement we have enunciated from the point of view of the Church, a significant lightening of the burden is achieved in the difficult decisions which the Church has to take with regard to the question of what particular social work she should engage in in the particular situation prevailing at any given time. This is arrived at from two different aspects. *On the one hand* the Church can freely and to some extent 'without recourse to principles' leave to the world in its growing worldliness much social work which at one time she did perform, for in fact she herself wills the world to develop along these lines. She does not need to be anxious, as it were, lest she should be surrendering something which she is bound to perform for all time. In such cases she is merely giving her assent to a world which, so long as it is rightly performing what is necessary for society, is always in fact creating the objective conditions in which an unrecognised grace can be embodied, conditions, indeed, in which Christians as such can and should collaborate, albeit not precisely as 'Church members', for they should not suppose that the realities signified by the terms 'Christian' and 'ecclesiastical' are co-extensive. *On the other hand* the Church must be equally 'emancipated from principles' in taking over new forms of social work in the sense that she must not suppose that she is faced with the question of whether or not she has a duty and obligation to undertake them arising from her own 'principles' (abstracting from the principle of prodigality in love which is no longer any 'principle' in the true sense). Free from any excessive calculation, she can develop initiatives without check or hindrance, give free rein to creative imagination and to the boldness of love, recognise and seize upon tasks with shining eyes and a ready heart, tasks which no-one else has yet recognised and undertaken. Nor is any such rigid drawing of lines of demarcation based on pre-established principles necessary. For in a society that is free and pluralist in character the state must in fact, of its very nature, will that 'the same' activities shall be performed by the individual groups within it, and shall be incorporated into the society as a unified whole by a process of free competition. For society as a unified whole in this sense is not a closed system directed in a totalitarian way from one single point. Rather it is the 'system' which is maintained by a balance of forces which has constantly to be established afresh. A further factor is that it is precisely *here* that we should apply the principle of the subsidiary role of the state even though it is not suitable to be used as a principle for establishing the lines of demarcation in our present problem. This principle is that the state as such; without actually becoming a 'nightwatchman' of mere legality, must, precisely in the area of social institutions, set in motion on its own initiative only that which the free individual groups within the society cannot perform themselves. This remains true even though the work of the 'social state' or the 'social welfare state' of today must necessarily be great. These are factors that must be borne in mind, and in addition to these it must be remembered, and in fact by both sides, that the free groups, and so the Church too, are becoming more and more suitable as the practitioners of social work. For this is actively pursued not so much in the area of what can be achieved and organised *materially* through *legislation*, and hence compulsorily, but rather in the manner of a help that is given swiftly, spontaneously at the 'personal' level and without complications (though admittedly this does not exclude the institutionalising process). Now the more this is true the more readily it can be perceived that in this question of how the necessary task should be divided in the concrete between the social work of the Church and that of the secular state, there is no need to fear that any insoluble conflicts need arise. The will to arrive at a solution in the concrete can be present on both sides so long as the state for its part has no intention of acting in a totalitarian manner while the Church for its part does not imagine that any development in the worldly world *ipso facto* and of its very nature represents a threat to her own effectiveness. On the contrary she must freely accept the mode of life open to her at the sociological level in a pluralist society and send out her believers into this world as genuine collaborators in order that there they may fulfil their Christian task without any reservations of an integralist kind.

IV

What has been said in the third statement is not intended to deny, and must not obscure, one further point. This is that there can be a form of social assistance which can be fully and legitimately exercised only by the

Church and by the Christian as a member of her. In any case this fourth statement would only contain an implied contradiction of the statement made above if the social work of the Church either could or should be confined merely to that which she can achieve by herself. Obviously it is only on the basis of an adherence to Christian truth that this fourth statement can have any light to throw upon the question, and in order to understand why it should be justified certain further considerations have to be borne in mind.

Human life is subject to a continuous *plurality* in respect of its dimensions, its origins, its awarenesses, impulses and its involvement with society. But in spite of these factors, and in the midst of them, man is essentially *one*, so that there is a constant mutual interplay between each dimension and every other, and so that no one of them is realised in total independence of another and no one of them can be *altogether* sound unless the other too is sound. The *plurality* of the dimensions of human living (whether interior or exterior) in which man exists is such that they can never wholly be controlled from any one point within man's own capabilities. But this also implies that each dimension has laws of its own and a force of its own, and therefore not *every* upset in *one* dimension has an effect of the same magnitude in some other dimension. Nevertheless the effect of the real *unity* which is present in all these manifold dimensions is that, fundamentally speaking, an upset in one dimension can still make itself felt as a factor of disturbance in another dimension. Now the result of this is that it is possible to have disturbances in one dimension such that they can be removed only by the removal of a disturbance in another dimension. This remains true even though, while the difference between the two dimensions still remains, it is justifiable to attempt to remove some upset in one specific dimension (and a certain measure of success may even be achieved in so doing) by means appropriate to itself – as it were as a 'therapy of the symptoms' – without, and prior to, any removal of the true and initial source of the upset concerned, which is to be found in a different dimension. Admittedly this is not to dispute the fact that the same symptom may be the outcome of several causes working together to produce upsets in various dimensions, and that there can be a *mutual* conditioning and intensifying process between the upsets in various dimensions. 'Chain reactions' may be set in motion in the cycle of causes that exists within a system that is, to a certain extent, 'closed' and in which all depends on each among the elements constitutive of the system.

What we have so far stated in abstract terms necessarily arises from the inalienable dialectical unity to be found in the unity and plurality of man and of his world. Now let us apply this to our particular case. Disturbances do exist or are at least in principle conceivable – even at the social level – which can only be removed by the removal or diminishing of disturbances in the dimension of the religious, of faith, hope and love in the strictly theological sense. Because of the 'chain reaction' (and also abstracting from this) 'therapy of the symptoms' is fully justified and also has certain chances of success in exactly the same way as, for instance, a case of insomnia can be removed by soporifics, or at least an attempt can be made to achieve this even though this insomnia derives from a disorder which cannot be controlled. But this does not in the least alter the fact that social conflicts can, and actually do exist – both at the more individual and at the collective levels – which also constitute (though probably they are never merely this) the *consequences* of the upset of the religious relationship between man and God and (because love of God and love of neighbour are one) of the specifically *religious* relationship at the human level and *between man and man*. This basic 'theological' disturbance can be situated in the original and basic relationship between man and God and between a man and his neighbour and also at the ecclesiastical level in the conceptual and so cultic forms in which this basic relationship is socially objectified, a level which is not the same as that of the relationship itself. But disturbances at both levels can have, and in principle actually do have, their further effects in other spheres of human living, and so too precisely in the social dimension, even though not necessarily and not always in a measure which is empirically ('clinically') noteworthy.

In fact: anyone who is not in ultimate harmony with the most ultimate and uncontrollable mystery of existence called God in faith, hope and love cannot accept and endure as he must the human interrelationships and the concrete social conditions in which these are realised either, as these exist with all their hardships and disappointments, the ever-fresh tasks and responsibilities they entail, and the concrete modes in which they are realised in history and society. It is only in the breadth of the freedom of the children of God that man can sustain the narrowness of human intercourse as a whole in all its aspects and in the spatial and temporal conditions to which it is subject in all their length and breadth. It can often be the case that this is attained to by the individual in a Christianity that is 'unacknowledged'. And truly we cannot maintain that it is only those who are *explicit* Christians who are capable of managing their human intercourse in a manner that is 'clinically' adequate. Still less do we maintain that man can manipulate the 'religious' element as a *means* for regulating social conflicts without thereby destroying its true nature. God becomes a genuine help in life precisely and only provided that man sees him as he really is, as holy and worthy of adoration in himself, and provided that man makes him a *goal* and *meaningful* in himself, and not merely a means for achieving something else. But all this does nothing to alter the fact that social conflicts can, and actually do derive from a distorted relationship with God. Hence Christianity and the Church have a special task in social work proper to themselves, one which no-one can take away from the Church. Certainly she cannot herself establish this relationship of man to God, for this is something that every individual has to do for himself in freedom and grace. But she is, nevertheless, the mediatrix of this relationship through the effective sign of her word and sacrament, and also of that love which is made effective and manifest in the community of the believers.

Now this certainly implies that the Church precisely through her specifically religious activities, and as mediating salvation, is also socially effective. But this precisely does not mean that the Church could ever be restricted to this properly religious area of social effectiveness. On the contrary, if we bear in mind what has been said in the third statement, and also precisely with regard to the 'chain reaction' of the various dimensions in human living upon one another, then we must come to the following conclusion: an area of social work is opened up for the Church initially in those situations in which the specifically religious problem is entered upon and so a specifically ecclesiastical and missionary task becomes necessary, and on the other hand such an area is opened up in a situation of specifically social conflict when this represents – at least in part – the consequence and at the same time an intensification of some religious conflict *as well as* simultaneously constituting that situation in, and on the occasion of which the religious problem is, for the most part first borne in upon man and made the subject of his conscious decision. In other words: when there is a specific *work* of love to be performed or expected, a work which, in the long run, can never be performed at all without a love that is reinforced with faith and hope, and when there is a failure to perform such a work, then the situation arises in which the religious question can be explicitly and consciously borne in upon man in the concrete, and this is the place for a kind of social work which is specifically appropriate to the Church. This is to put the matter in terms which are still very abstract and can be no substitute for that creative imagination which is capable of revealing situations of this kind. But still it remains true to say that a pastoral activity that is 'purely' religious in character and expressed in preaching and the sacramental ministry alone is, in a certain sense, too abstract.

Taken by itself this does not make itself felt – or does not do so sufficiently – in those cases in which man is involved in a social conflict having a religious background and religious undercurrents. For these emerge more effectively in the concrete instance of social conflict than in some kind of 'abstract' situation in which action is confined to the 'purely religious' sphere and mediated by the Church. The very fact that a conflict of *this* kind is, in concrete fact, never *purely* religious in origin, and that a justifiable 'therapy of the symptoms' does actually exist, means that it is never possible unambiguously to demarcate it *materially*, dividing it it off from the areas proper to secular social work and aid. Nevertheless in principle it is a 'case' of social work belonging specifically to the Church.

Properly speaking what has been said should in itself be enough to make it clear first that the practitioner of the Church's social aid in precisely *this* sense does not necessarily have to be an ordained priest – indeed that for the most part the earlier formation of priests is, or may be, quite inadequate for this, and second that the lay 'social worker' of the Church acquires, by that very fact, a character and a task which has a specifically religious and ecclesiastical relevance such as has hardly been recognised sufficiently clearly up to the present.

This aspect of the matter could shed fresh light upon the problem of the social worker of the Church as an ordained deacon.[5]

A further point which still remains to be made is this: the social work of the Church upon which we have now focussed our attention certainly has, of its very nature, an extremely 'personal' character. But this does not necessarily exclude a permanent system of organisation and institutionalisation which does justice to its specific nature. If the actual *sacramental* aids to living, e.g. in the sacrament of penance, exhibit an extremely significant element of institutionalism and 'organisation', then this cannot *ipso facto* be impossible in the case we are considering either.

A special sub-species of this specifically ecclesiastical social work, but one which may perhaps be extremely important today, would be the collaboration offered in overcoming those factors of social disintegration which are manifesting themselves at present for the most divers reasons within the local and parish communities of the Christian body itself. This

[5] Of course this must not be taken – and precisely for the reasons adduced in the present explanation – as meaning that the social work of the Church would have to be returned to clerical control. On the problems entailed here with regard to the diaconate cf. K. Rahner, H. Vorgrimler and J. Kramer, 'Zur Erneuerung des Diakonats in Deutschland', *Stimmen der Zeit* 180 (1967), pp. 145–153.

task is certainly the concern of pastoral activity in general, but the social activity we are considering can lend it a support which is quite essential. A first point is that the Christian community must be something more than the embodiment of a parish-dominated ideal, a regionally demarcated human group organised according to essentially pastoral conceptions, or the assembly of many unattached individuals at the same place and the same time to satisfy individual religious needs. A second point is that the community of the Church assembled for divine worship is precisely not now, as it was formerly, *ipso facto* a group that is integrated in terms of secular society. And a third point is that this integration cannot be achieved solely through the actual practice of divine worship as such. And all these reasons are in themselves sufficient to make it necessary for the Church to undertake a kind of social work that is specifically ecclesiastical in character, though probably it is still far from being sufficiently clearly recognised as such.

The Christian community as it exists today (and regardless of whether it is organised on regional or functional lines) is a communal as opposed to a national Church. And because of this it may sometimes be forced to adopt structures which (in terms, for instance, of the sociology of religion) seem almost to be those of a sectarian Church, even though the *only* point of really vital importance is that she shall not allow herself to fall into the *mentality* of the sect, but shall rather be *missionary* in outlook, committing herself boldly and without reserve to share in all aspects of the life of contemporary society, pluralist and secular as it is. But for the most part she has in fact not even the status of a genuine *community* Church, but rather hovers in an undefined no-man's land between the earlier 'national' Church (and she still calls her members from an environment which, sociologically speaking, provided the prior conditions for this) and a community Church in the genuine sense, constituted by individuals who have arrived at a genuine religious decision of their own, an idea which has not yet been realised.

The integration of the community itself in ecclesiastical and social terms, which cannot *solely* be achieved by mere 'preaching' in the normal sense of a theoretical indoctrination, is a specific task for the social work of the Church of today, and one which cannot be performed by the 'spiritual element' alone. This can be expressed in terms of *images*: the diaconal ministry of *caritas* by the deacons and deaconesses as practised today must provide for something more than merely that when the community is already assembled at the 'table' (Acts 6:2) everything shall proceed in a right and orderly fashion. It must also, and primarily see to it that the union of believers whose state of integration is still weak or inadequate shall become a 'com-union' or 'table-fellowship' in fact.

And further – does not something of this also apply in its own way, today being the age of oecumenism, so far as a certain integration of groups which are confessionally divided is concerned, an integration which must come before the unity of the Churches in the strictly theological sense for which we are striving, and which alone will make this possible? Is not something of this kind too a social work of the Church which no-one except the Church or the Churches can perform? Must it not be recognised and performed, seeing that the division between the Churches has arisen precisely from sociological grounds in the broadest sense, and not merely from theological ones?

v

I know that everything which I have been able to say is, and must be, not only liable to criticism and contradiction (which is obvious), but has also remained at so abstract and formal a level that the practical exponent will ask: 'What can this lead to?' I am acutely conscious of the fact that I have only been able to contribute very little by way of an answer to those questions with which we find ourselves confronted in the concrete today, from the very nature of the case. But can the theologian, detached as he is from specialised knowledge and practical experience in these matters, do much more? Perhaps formal considerations of this kind do, after all, provide something approaching a system of co-ordination between the various points within which the real specialists both in theory and practice will be able, given sympathy and good will, to find and to locate a little more easily what they themselves have to search out and discover.

What I have sought to say was properly speaking simply the following:

First: Today the concept of *caritas* as a science and as a part of scientific theology could and should be thought of as an integral element in practical theology, which is itself a theological science in its own right and not simply a 'practical' supplement to the other theological disciplines. This being its status, therefore, '*caritas as a science*', which derives its name from *caritas* as a reality, should be thought out afresh in such a way as to become the most sublime consummation and perfection of all Christian activity, the science of how Christians are to fulfil their responsibilities to the world in the concrete precisely as these arise at any given point, a 'theological cosmology'. In this way it would also be freed from the fatal suspicion that it is merely the theory of that kind of welfare which becomes ever more problematical in a welfare society and in a state which itself is and must be a 'social state' or a state committed to social welfare, because in such a case the welfare services of the Church can at most perform a service of filling in the gaps where secular society unexpectedly fails.

Second: In the second and third statements an attempt has been made to show that the co-existence of ecclesiastical and secular social work is demanded by the very nature of Christianity itself, and that the problem of drawing the line of demarcation between the two is at basis not a problem to be solved by theoretical considerations and *a priori* deductions, but a problem demanding ever fresh decisions as history unfolds. In these decisions the Church can both boldly surrender earlier social functions which she once had, *and at the same time* boldly recognise and engage herself in fresh tasks of social work in the world and secular society. Fundamental considerations, therefore, prompt us to refer the problem of drawing the line of demarcation to the practitioners themselves, even though these may find it unwelcome since it lays upon them a task and decision which they would certainly gladly leave to others. But at the same time it does mean that a greater freedom is achieved for the practice of *caritas* and for its practitioners. They do not need to wait for concrete imperatives from some centre of direction which would be run merely by theorists pursuing principles. The practitioners could themselves decide, by discovering for themselves imperatives which would not merely be the transference of principles into practice, but would constitute historical, indeed charismatic decisions. In these the truth would be made manifest that practice, in contrast to theory, cannot simply be deduced, and that in such cases the practical reason takes priority over the speculative.

Third: Without prejudice to the co-existence of ecclesiastical and secular social work and the mutual influence of the one upon the other, there is a specifically ecclesiastical social work to which quite new tasks accrue today to be performed both in the world and also in the Church herself.

It has not been possible to say more. I would console myself with the ancient saying, *In magnis voluisse sat est,* for it still always remains true that the greatest factor of all is love. If we have attempted to speak of this and to praise this, then we may hope and entreat for pardon.

19

THE PEACE OF GOD AND
THE PEACE OF THE WORLD

I

I T is extraordinary how many different levels of significance can be
found in this subject. For this reason a few preliminary observations
may be permitted in order to indicate the almost incalculable breadth
of the questions and tasks implied by this title, and at the same time to
make clear the limits of what is here being attempted.[1]

1. If we are to speak of peace *theologically*, then we must speak of peace
with God, peace with ourselves, peace in the contacts and relationships
between man and man, and within these relationships peace between the
generations, the classes, the age-groups and the sexes. We should also –
because this too is of concern to theologians – have something to say with
regard to peace in the international sphere and of the old-fashioned idea of
peace. And finally we should give some consideration, precisely as *theologians*, to that *political* peace which is implicit in the current situation, in
which the tendency of world history is towards an ever-increasing and
ultimately total unity.[2] The question of how these various kinds of peace,

---

[1] It has been necessary to keep the actual article concise. For this reason it has been
attempted in the notes to draw attention to certain phenomena and certain problems
in order to make apparent the whole perspective in which the author has intended his
fragmentary observations to be understood.

[2] On this cf. the observations of C. F. v. Weizsäcker, *Bedingungen des Friedens*
(Göttingen [3]1964); *idem, Gedanken über unsere Zukunft* (Göttingen 1966); *idem,*
'Zumutungen der Freiheit', *Über die Freiheit*, M. Horkheimer, K. Rahner, C. F. v.
Weizsäcker edd. (Stuttgart [2]1965), pp. 53–76; *idem,* 'Ethische und politische Prob-
leme des Atomzeitalters', *Integritas. Festschrift für K. Holzamer*, D. Stolte, R. Wisser
edd. (Tübingen 1966), pp. 337–355. cf. also the further studies by Weizsäcker
mentioned in the notes which follow. See also T. Brocher, W. Gerlach, R. Löwen-
thal, N. Sombart, P. G. Walker, R. v. Weizsäcker, *Der Zwang zum Frieden* (Stuttgart
1967). On the concept of peace and the idea of peace in the context of politology and
history cf. the following works: H. J. Morgenthau, *Macht und Frieden* (Gütersloh
1963) and R. Aron, *Frieden und Krieg* (Frankfurt 1963). On the history of the

with God, with one's self, in human relationships, in more private contacts and at the political and international levels, are related to one another
is, of course, in turn, a question in itself for the theologian, for manifestly
he has the impression, even after reading the scriptures, that these various
modes in which peace is realised have an intrinsic relationship and unity
among themselves, and that on a radical view one kind demands the other.
Only the individual who is conscious in some sense of being interiorly at
peace with himself, and who – as we Christians say – lives ultimately
at peace with God, can truly and radically maintain that attitude which
can also contribute to peace among men.

2. In all its dimensions, therefore, this peace – and this is something
that opens up a whole range of further levels in the theology of this concept – has forms which are subject to wide variations. At a later stage we
shall have to see still more clearly that the concept of 'conflict' and 'war'
in a metaphysical sense and in terms of existential ontology, and probably
also in a theological sense, is not so simple or obvious that we could react
to it with a simple refusal in favour of peace as the obviously right attitude
to assume. To that extent there are necessarily genuine forms of peace and
true forms of conflict. And hence even from this point of view the theologian will have to exercise great prudence in his work with regard to the
question of war and conflict on the one hand, and of peace on the other.
Certainly there have already been times at which Christians became, to a
greater or lesser extent, the representatives of the sort of quiet that belongs
to the graveyard, times, moreover, at which a pseudo-*Christian* ideology[3]
was actually invoked in support of the thesis that the primary duty is to
ensure that the citizen shall have quiet. And there is a modern anti-
Christian ideology according to which the sole possible realistic form of
peace consists in an equilibrium of fear.[4] All this shows how widely vary-

---

movements for peace cf. K. v. Raumer, *Ewige Friede. Friedensrufe und Friedenspläne
seit der Renaissance* (Freiburg 1953); H. J. Schlochauer, *Die Idee des ewigen Friedens*
(Bonn 1953); cf. also U. Nerlich (ed.), I. *Krieg und Frieden im industriellen Zeitalter*
and II. *Krieg und Frieden in der modernen Staatenwelt* (Gütersloh 1966).

The comprehensive Catholic literature of recent years bearing on our problem is
not explicitly adduced because it has been reviewed in certain excellent bulletins of
the periodical *Concilium*. cf. R. Coste, 'Pacifism and Legitimate Defence', *Concilium*
5/1 (1965), pp. 45–52; F. Böckle, 'Peace and Modern Warfare; Theological Discussion in West Germany' 5/2, *Concilium* (1966), pp. 69–75; cf. also below, n. 7.

[3] On the erroneousness of this ideological interpretation of the understanding of
peace cf. the radical statements of principle in *Handbuch der Pastoraltheologie* II/2
(Freiburg 1966), pp. 148–180 (with bibliography).

[4] cf. *ibid.*, pp. 142, 184 f.

ing in form that phenomenon can be which is so commonly characterised as peace. From the time of the Fathers of the Church onwards Christianity and the Church have always and actively concerned themselves with the question of the relationship of Christianity to the soldier's calling,[5] to war in the concrete sense, to nationalism,[6] to the question of conscientious objectors,[7] and always in very varying ways and with very varying results. Today the refusal to rely on physical force is certainly on the way or is actually being pressed as a watchword within Christendom itself.[8] This again shows how many theological problems are connected with the question of peace.

[5] For the early period cf. H. v. Campenhausen, 'Der Kriegsdienst der Christen in der Kirche des Altertums', *Tradition und Leben* (Tübingen 1960), pp. 203–215 (bibliography); J. M. Hornus, *Politische Entscheidung in der Alten Kirche* (Munich 1963). On the connected questions cf. also A.A.T. Ehrhardt, *Politische Metaphysik von Solon bis Augustin* I–II (Tübingen 1959).

[6] On this cf. the still always interesting expositions of E. Peterson, *Theologische Traktate* (Munich 1951), pp. 45–147.

[7] cf. the Pastoral Constitution, 'On the Church in the World of Today', No. 79. On peace and co-operation between nations cf. No. 77–90. B. Drees, 'Das Konzil zur Frage des Krieges, des Friedens und der Völkergemeinschaft', *Umkehr und Erneuerung. Kirche nach dem Konzil*, T. Filthaut ed. (Mainz 1966), pp. 393–403. More comprehensive studies on the teaching of the Council are to be found in a symposium of studies on the interpretation of the Pastoral Constitution 'On the Church in the World of Today' published by Paul Brand Verlag (Hilversum), a work which will also be brought out in translation by other publishers: L. J. Lebret O.P. on social and economic life and on the demand for co-operation between nations; J. Y. Calvez S.J. on the life of the political community and D. Dubarle O.P. on the position of the Council with regard to war and peace. cf. e.g. the French edition, *L'église dans le monde de ce temps. Constitution 'Gaudium et Spes'. Commentaires du Schema XIII* (Paris 1967), especially D. Dubarle, 'Le Schema XIII et la guerre', pp. 327–393. Reference must be made in quite general terms to the commentaries on the Pastoral Constitution (cf. *Das Zweite Vatikanische Konzil* I–III [Freiburg 1966–1968]; the commentaries belonging to the series *'Unam Sanctam'* [Paris 1966–1968] etc.); W. Dirks, 'Die Entdeckung des geschichtlichen Risikos und die Folgen. Zum Verhältnis zwischen Politik und kirchlichem Lehramt', *Hochland* 59 (1967), pp. 280–285.

[8] This could be demonstrated for the Catholic side also by pointing to a certain difference in teaching or development in teaching leading up to the acceptance of the Council documents. Apart from the works already mentioned in n. 7 cf. also R. P. Régamey, *Gewaltlosigkeit* (Vienna 1966). On the history of the developments leading up to the conciliar document cf., apart from D. Dubarle, a further work by R. Regout, *La doctrine de la guerre juste de St. Augustin à nos jours* (Paris 1935); R. Coste, *Le problème du droit de guerre dans la pensée de Pie XII* (Paris 1962); idem, *Morale Internationale* (Paris 1964); G. Gundlach, 'Die Lehre Pius' XII vom modernen Krieg', *Die Ordnung der menschlichen Gesellschaft* I (Cologne 1964), pp. 637–651.

3. A more important idea, and one which has a quite direct connection with our understanding of peace, belongs to that which we call 'power'.[9] It is manifest that Christians or theologians are not simply at one with regard to their judgments upon power. Is power something which, on any ultimate view, belongs *ipso facto* from the outset, and necessarily, to the sphere of sin? Does the basis on which power rests consist solely and exclusively in the sinful world and in the fact of its sinfulness, or is there initially a power such that, even though in the concrete conditions of the world it is always, as it were, corrupted by sin, it nevertheless has properly speaking and of its true nature a different function and a real justification for its existence in the world?

In any such question we would first have to explain what is meant by power. Now we may take this concept of 'power' to mean the process in which one man is influenced by another, and the possibility which he has of determining that other's course, this act of determining his course being prior to the free decision of the man so acted upon. For my part I believe that this is more or less correct as a concept of power. Now if this is correct then we may perhaps be forced to say that the presence of some such phenomenon as power in the world is necessary, and that power of this kind belongs to the essential conditions of human living; that although – as the theologians will say – it is true that power is always sinfully misused as well, nevertheless this sinful misuse cannot on that account be totally overcome simply by adopting the attitude of an absolute renunciation of power. On the basis of a conception of power of this kind the question would then have to be raised of the inevitable existence of conflict and – in a metaphyscial and theological sense – of war. On this showing the specifically *Christian* question would be more concerned with the concrete forms and manifestations of power and of conflict in so far as these could, from certain aspects, be considered the responsibility of the Christian alone. The question of how the Christian might gradually attempt to overcome this inescapable 'existential' or condition of human living as defined by power and conflict in history, or at least how he can impart to history a tendency towards such a conquest through that love which, in the last analysis he alone can have who knows that he is loved by God – this is a question the answer to which will only be attempted at a later stage. Here too we shall confine ourselves simply to making clear how the theological

[9] For an initial orientation with regard to the concept of power cf. R. Hauser, 'Macht', *Handbuch theologischer Grundbegriffe* II (Munich 1963), pp. 98–111 (bibliography); *Handbuch der Pastoraltheologie* II/2, pp. 358 ff., 362 ff., 365 ff. (Bibliography, pp. 337–341).

problems involved in peace become lost in a whole range of connected questions which is far broader in its extent.

4. A further question is how to achieve a right approach to peace considered as a theological phenomenon. In this we must not simply postulate some false utopian or romantic image of absolute rest and permanent equilibrium, something which does admittedly represent a lofty ideal in the concrete cirumstances of our life, but which, nevertheless, does not provide us with very much force with which to realise it. And if this is the case, then at the same time we must seek for that concept which, in terms of theological meaning, constitutes the opposite pole to that of peace. The moment, for instance, one formulates the theological concept of concupiscence[10] it carries with it *ipso facto* and in each case the further idea of an interior dissatisfaction on man's part, a state of inward conflict, a plurality of the forces within him of which, ultimately speaking, he is not in control, and which he cannot reduce to any state of definitive integration.[11] What is being spoken of, therefore, is a 'war' and 'conflict' of man within himself, and this involves as its counterpart the opposite idea of peace with himself that comes through God and from God.

5. The theological and Christian problem of peace is further associated with the question of what the idea of 'peace' is really intended to conjure up. What does it mean to conceive of this as 'the order of justice',[12] seeing that 'order' and 'justice' are, and continue to be, in a certain sense extremely obscure concepts? What does such a concept of peace signify when we raise the question of a *dynamism of history* which will certainly not be held at any one specific point in an equilibrium of power, of social relationship

---

[10] This is enough to show, at least by way of indication, why it is inadvisable to present the concept of 'sin' without further distinction (to the extent namely that there is a difference between this and the concept of 'concupiscence'!) as the opposite of 'peace'. On the concept of concupiscence cf. K. Rahner, 'The Theological Concept of Concupiscentia', *Theological Investigations* I (London and Baltimore 1961), pp. 347–382; J. B. Metz, 'Konkupiszenz', *Handbuch theologischer Grundbegriffe* I (Munich 1962), pp. 843–851; cf. also the observations which follow.

[11] Apart from the literature already mentioned cf. *Handbuch der Pastoraltheologie* II/1, pp. 22–24 (with references).

[12] The definition of peace in this sense is essentially connected with our basic understanding of the western concepts of state, justice and order. For a few witnesses to this cf. H. Krüger, *Allgemeine Staatslehre* (Stuttgart 1964), pp. 714 ff.; cf. H. Fuchs, *Augustinus und der Friedensgedanke* (Berlin 1926); F. Wiesenthal, *Die Wandlung des Friedensbegriffs von Augustinus zu Thomas von Aquino* (Diss. jur. Munich 1949); A. Brecht, *Politische Theorie* (Tübingen 1961), pp. 484, 494 ff.; B. de Jouvenel; *Über Souveränität* (Neuwied 1966), pp. 169 ff. Further bibliography in the *Staatslexikon der Görresgesellschaft* III (Freiburg 1959), p. 605.

etc., which is wholly predetermined? What must we say with regard to peace seeing that the question of a theology of revolution can be raised and that the young people precisely are today inclined, even in their Christian representatives, to invoke a Christian watchword to the effect that under certain circumstances revolution may be necessary.[13] This in itself is, of course, enough to indicate the question of how a theology of history on the one hand and the theology of peace on the other are related to one another since they are two factors which can be taken as having a necessary connection with one another and so reveal a further range of theological problems into which the question of peace leads us.

6. Today the peace which we seek in the international sphere is dependent to an extraordinary extent upon the growing unity of the history of the world, upon a situation of secularism in the sphere of culture, of society, of the state and of politics, and also upon the rationalisation and technical manipulation of the world. And in view of this it is obvious that any question of the theology of peace invariably implies also something in the nature of an enquiry into the theology of the worldliness of the world, the unity of contemporary world history in general, a theology which consists in analysing the contemporary situation in world history and the factor of the rational and the technical in human living.[14] This in turn entails a further and almost incalculable range of problems associated with the question of the theology of peace.

7. Properly speaking if the theologian sets himself to consider the question of peace he must also consider his theology of justice and his theology of love, his theology of the mutual relationship between justice and love. He must enter into a problem which, in current theology, is once more becoming very clear: the problem, namely, of how we should conceive of the unity and the distinction between love of God and love

---

[13] The critical attitude of the Christian towards the world as a matter of positive and creative activity is becoming a focal point for the consideration of theologians (cf. e.g. the theologies of hope by J. Moltmann, J. B. Metz, W. D. Marsch), and a point inevitably arising from this is the need for a 'theology of revolution'. The problem appears still more urgent in the recent theologies (chiefly Protestant in character) which can be recognised as just emerging in Asia, Africa and South America. On this subject cf. especially H. Arendt, *Über die Revolution* (Munich 1963); *Guerre révolutionnaire et conscience chrétienne* (published by Pax Christi, rue de l'Abbaye [Paris 1964]); D. Dubarle, *Le Schema XIII et la guerre*, pp. 337 f.; J. B. Metz, 'Religion und Revolution', *Neues Forum* XIV (1967), pp. 460–464; cf. *Ev. Theol.* 27 (1967), Nos. 11–12.

[14] On the problems mentioned above as a whole cf. the comprehensive analysis by the author and others in the *Handbuch der Pastoraltheologie* II/1–2.

of neighbour upon an originally and authentically Christian conception.[15] Undoubtedly the question of peace is not wholly unconnected with the Christian message of love of neighbour, and this love of neighbour has manifestly something to do with that which we call the love of God for us and our love for God. In the biblical concept of *agape* the various aspects of both kinds of love are already indissolubly interconnected.[16] According as each theologian views the love of God and love of neighbour as a unity he will undoubtedly modify also his concept of that peace which is achieved through this single love of God and love of neighbour.

8. In fact a further problem which arises for theology is that of Christian and secular humanism, and this too in turn has connections with a theology of peace. Is there such a thing as a unity between men such that they become one in their humanity and one in their humanism?[17] Is there a material content belonging to a humanism of this kind such that in it Christians and non-Christians could be at one, so that on this basis they could achieve a common concept of what they really understand by peace? These too are problems and questions which are evidently not so easy to solve, and which can serve in turn to throw light upon the whole multidimensional character of a theology of peace.

II

With regard to the biblical concept of peace only a few indications should be given.[18] On any showing 'peace' as presented in the Old and New

---

[15] On this cf. K. Rahner, 'Reflections on the Unity of the Love of Neighbour and the Love of God', *Theological Investigations* VI (London and Baltimore 1969), pp. 231–249.

[16] On this cf. the well known investigations on the New Testament concept of *agape* by C. Spicq, V. Warnach etc.

[17] On this cf. the Council documents 'On the Church in the World of Today', Nos. 21, 85, 88, 90, 'Decree on the Apostolate of the Laity', No. 27, 'Decree on the Missions', No. 41.

[18] On this aspect pertaining to biblical theology cf., apart from the concordances, W. Foerster, G. v. Rad, *T.W.N.T.* II (Stuttgart 1935), pp. 398–418; W. S. van Leeuwen, *Eirene in het Nieuwe Testament* (Wageningen 1940); J. J. Stamm, H. Bietenhard, *Der Weltfriede im Licht der Bibel* (Zürich 1959); J. Comblin, *Theologie des Friedens* I (Graz 1963); H. Gross, *Die Idee des ewigen und allgemeinen Weltfriedens im Alten Orient und im Alten Testament* (Treves 1956); E. Biser, *Der Sinn des Friedens* (Munich 1960); H. H. Schrey, 'Krieg und Frieden im N.T.', *Für Arbeit und Besinnung* 5 (1951), pp. 466–480; S. Herrmann, *Die prophetischen Heilserwartungen im A.T.* = *Beiträge zur Wissenschaft vom A.T. und N.T.* 5th series, No. 5 (85) (Stuttgart 1965); cf. also the relevant treatises in *L.T.K.* V (Freiburg ²1960), 366–369, and in *R.G.G.* II (Tübingen ¹1958), 1133–1135, and in X. Lèon-Dufour ed., *Dictionary of Biblical*

Testaments is one of the most important religious concepts. *Shalom* in the Old Testament signifies, ultimately speaking, a state of wellbeing, of having overcome an evil of some kind. It therefore signifies a state of good fortune, precisely a 'being whole', so that a man can salute his fellow with the greeting *Shalom*, 'Peace be to you'. And even on this basis this state of 'wholeness', precisely in those cases in which it is applied to an area involving human relationships, also acquires the significance of peace, and is therefore translated in the Septuagint as *eirene*. In this connection, however, we must constantly keep clearly before our eyes the fact that this specifically Old Testament concept originally had a far broader, deeper and more comprehensive meaning than that which we attach to the term 'peace' today, thinking of it in a sense that is based on politics or merely on human relationships. This peace in the Old Testament is, of its very nature and right from the outset, something that has to be supplicated from God, because without God there can be no peace. And in the Old Testament prophets Jeremiah and Ezekiel peace in this sense precisely becomes the key word for what is central to the content of salvation in all its aspects, and as such also becomes in the case of Isaiah the key word for messianic expectation. Because of this peace already comes, under certain circumstances – by including, as it were, protology and eschatology within a single conspectus – something approaching the restoration of the paradisal peace which was destroyed by original sin,[19] and on this view the Messiah is the *princeps pacis*, the prince of peace. But even here peace is, once more, interpreted as the all-inclusive content of salvation.

In the New Testament too, therefore, the Christian message (Eph 6:15) can be called the 'gospel of peace', that peace of which God is the author and Jesus Christ the mediator. Peace is, then, that which is mediated by Christ in the Spirit through a new creation as the fruit of the *Pneuma*, so

---

Theology (London 1970), pp. 312–315; also in the Theologies of the Old and New Testaments (W. Eichrodt, L. Koehler, P. v. Imschoot, T. C. Vriezen, M. Meinertz, R. Bultmann etc.). On the concept of peace in the New Testament cf. also P. Mikat in his address on the occasion of the conferring of the peace prize of the German book trade on Augustin, Cardinal Bea and Willem A. Visser't Hooft (Frankfurt am Main 1966), pp. 23–39, esp. 25 ff.; C. Westermann, *Shalom: Der Frieden ist unter uns* (Stuttgart 1967 – Preparatory number for the Conference of the Protestant Church at Hannover 1967), pp. 29–31. H. Bacht, 'Dimensionen des Friedens', *Geist und Leben* 40 (1967), pp. 4–12; 194–203; *Frieden* (Kreuz-Verlag, Stuttgart 1967).

[19] cf. especially the eschatology of the prophets: Hos 2:20; Amos 9:13; Is 9:5; Zech 9:9 f.; Is 9:6; Mic 5:4; Is 2:2, 11:1, 32:15–20, 65:25, 66:12, 48:18. For analyses of these cf. S. Herrmann, *Die prophetischen Heilserwartungen im A.T.* (cf. n. 18).

that *he* is our peace. And this peace is regarded as the peace which exists between God and men (Rom 5:1). Hence peace then ensues between men but in such a way that this peace is also really and effectively the appeasement of that interior conflict which has arisen in man through sin.

On this basis we might pursue the concept of peace through all departments of theology. When we came to consider the doctrine of creation we would have, as it were, to regard the openness of the creature to salvation, the ability to be saved, the possibility of attaining to its own 'union with God' as peace, as well as the counterpart of this from God's side. In Christology, when we speak of the plenitude of grace in Christ then Christ is precisely he who is in his own person this peace between God and the world, and from whom the new order of the world as reconciled with God is initiated. In any presentation of ecclesiology we might wholeheartedly follow the Second Vatican Council in viewing the Church as, so to say, the sacramental sign in history, the historical manifestation, of this self-utterance of God which unites the world with God and in itself, and so gives it peace.[20] In a presentation of ethics peace could be regarded as the goal at which work for the kingdom of God is aimed, and in a presentation of eschatology we could speak of a hope for the eternal rest, and in that case once more this peace would be being regarded as the content of eschatological hope.

III

We must now turn to a further point and attempt to say something on the theology of peace and of the peaceable attitude or state of mind. A thesis might be formulated, however untimely it might sound, which would not give a very Christian impression and yet perhaps would be extremely Christian: the *'conflict' which is a 'war' so long as this world in which we live endures, so long as the 'kingdom of God' is not made present by the act of God himself – is an abiding reality, and insuperable 'existential' of human living*. In spite of this the *Christian* – in precisely the same way as mankind in general – *has an abiding task to create peace*, and so both must constantly be expressing the demand that humanitarian principles shall prevail.

This thesis derives from a realism that is Christian and anti-ideological. As has already been said, any genuine Christian theology can and must recognise the inescapability and the necessity of that which is called and is power. Every individual is, to a certain extent, in virtue of his very existence, and in the very act of his self-fulfilment within the general sphere

[20] cf. the Constitution on the Church of the Second Vatican Council, Nos. 1, 9, 48, 59 etc.

of existence common to all men, one who alters the situation of freedom, the sphere of freedom open to his fellow, restricting it in some measure prior to any agreement on the latter's part.[21] After all this is, more or less, what power means, and a power more or less of this sort is unmistakably present. Of course the Christian will always recognise that this natural 'existential' of human living, which is inevitable and which, therefore, since man is not merely sin, is perfectly legitimate, is *de facto* always conditioned by sin as well, in other words by the sinful uses to which this inevitable power is put. But if such a power is present not merely in the sphere of our private lives, in which we mutually restrict the field of liberty open to one another, but is present also in the dimension of society and of peoples, then it is quite impossible for Christianity, maintaining as it does an anti-ideological realism of this kind, to escape from something like a war in this sense, that is to say conflict or contradiction. For the situation is that many human lives, each of which is multidimensional in itself, are in process of achieving their self-fulfilment in many ways. All of them exist within a single finite sphere of freedom, and therefore necessarily mutually restrict one another within this sphere of freedom. And it is this that constitutes the exercise of such a power, which ultimately speaking cannot be guided or controlled by any earthly authority. The reason for this is that any such central and totalitarian administration, or any division of this single sphere of existence of the kind that this would imply, would in fact represent the greatest exercise of power, in fact the most radical use of force by man.

When applied in an anti-ideological sense, therefore, Christian realism soberly recognises the existence of power and therefore of conflict as one side of human living. It does not raise this power to the status of an ideology or accord it an absolute value. It precisely does not want this power to be administered by an ultimate and central tribunal within this present world.[22] It is, therefore, against any ideological or any practical monopolisation of this power, but at the same time it also recognises that it is

---

[21] On this interpretation of freedom and the scope of freedom cf. K. Rahner, 'Ursprünge der Freiheit', *Über die Freiheit*, M. Horkheimer, K. Rahner, C. F. v. Weizsäcker edd. (Stuttgart [2]1965), esp. pp. 35–44.

[22] On the whole cf. K. Rahner, 'The Theology of Power', *Theological Investigations* IV (London and Baltimore 1966), pp. 391–409. The extent to which modern psychology, sociology and anthropology too regard the state of 'readiness to be unpeaceable', the situation of conflict, 'covetousness' etc. as almost insuperably powerful as factors in human life is made plain in the following studies: J. von Graevenitz, 'Persönliche Voraussetzungen der Friedfertigkeit', *Streit um den Frieden*, W. Beck and R. Schmid edd. (Munich/Mainz 1967), pp. 11–30; T. Brocher, 'Psycho-

inevitable that there shall be something in the nature of conflict, contradiction and war. The Christian, therefore, is sufficiently realistic to take his stand in principle at a point halfway between a total rejection of power, an absolute hostility *towards* it on the one hand, and an attitude on the other in which power is accorded an absolute value raised to an ideology and monopolised.

The Christian is *in principle* opposed to both extremes, for ultimately speaking they come to the same. For the absolute abrogation of power and of the conflict or contradiction ensuing from it, the abrogation of a situation of struggle in general, would be possible only through an absolute monopolisation of power, and this would precisely be absolute tyranny.[23] The Christian cannot agree to any easy compromise, but must maintain a genuinely central position between these two extremes, because precisely in virtue of his awareness of his own creatureliness he must recognise from the outset that he, the individual, *must not* set himself up as the absolute representative of God in the world,[24] since he *cannot* be this. A further reason is that neither the Church or state on the one hand, nor any different body on the other, representing science or some other finite concrete entity in the world, can or should set itself up, as it were, as absolutely acting in God's place, and so as having absolute authority to decide how the sphere of freedom should be divided between men.

The Christian's attitude is that any attempt to develop the ideal of an absolute peace in this present world into an ideology would imply the death, the end of history, a fellahin culture or rather lack of culture, and precisely the state of absolute tyranny.[25] In other words the sober anti-ideological realism of the Christian, who takes due account of conflict, contradiction and war, provides what is precisely the sole genuine possibility of coping with the problem of war and conflict in general in a

---

logische Aspekte des Friedens', T. Brocher *et al.*, *Der Zwang zum Frieden* (Stuttgart 1967), pp. 17–31; T. Brocher, 'Angst und Angriff', *Der Frieden ist unter uns* (Stuttgart 1967), pp. 21–24; K. Lorenz, *Das sogenannte Böse. Zur Naturgeschichte der Aggression* (Vienna ³1964); E. Denker, *Aufklärung über Aggression* (Stuttgart 1966); H. Schoeck, *Der Neid. Eine Theorie der Gesellschaft* (Freiburg 1966); H. R. Lückert, *Der Mensch als konfliktträchtiges Wesen* (Munich 1964); idem, *Konfliktpsychologie* (Munich 1965). In interpreting this situation, which pertains to the nature of man as it *de facto* exists, greater emphasis should be laid upon the factor of 'concupiscence'.
[23] cf. *ibid.*, pp. 497 ff. etc.
[24] In greater detail, *ibid.*, pp. 503 ff. (the temptations of power.)
[25] On this cf. also R. Dahrendorf, *Gesellschaft und Freiheit* (Munich 1961), pp. 85 ff., 237 ff., 321 ff., 363 ff. On this problem cf. also H. Steubing, *Der Kompromiss als ethisches Problem* (Gütersloh 1955).

manner that is fully *human*, because any attempt at radically abolishing conflict and war would precisely imply the ultimate in tyranny, the most extreme concentration of power.

Nevertheless the Christian has the most solemn duty and task, and one which radically and vitally affects his salvation, of restraining this inevitable conflict, of inculcating humanity, and, to the utmost of his power, of avoiding it. Obviously he has also, as one who knows about sins and in fact about his own sins, a critical attitude towards power and authority. He knows that this authority is one of the forces in the world which are indeed created by God, but which, nevertheless, can at the same time constitute the greatest possible temptation to man to put them to a wrong use and perhaps actually to rebel against God by means of them. To that extent he has always the task of bringing humanitarian standards to bear upon the struggle, just as, for instance 'blood feuds' and individual acts of retribution against private enemies have actually been eliminated from our society today.

When, therefore, it is asserted that theology, on the basis of a sober Christian realism which is anti-ideological in character, maintains that power, and therefore conflict too – that is war in the abstract sense – cannot be eliminated this obviously does not mean that the old and seemingly immovable forms in which power has been customarily applied in the past need always remain the same as they were, or even that we can allow them to do so. The opposite is true.[26] Precisely the struggle against these forms of war, forms which are still less than human, must be conducted precisely in the light of the anti-ideological realism of the Christian with its capacity for sober criticism.

IV

Now if we ask as Christian theologians how and in what way this effort or this task to achieve a humanisation of the struggle and of power is to be conducted, then what first comes to mind – at least as far as Catholics are concerned – are the two Christian key words of 'justice' and 'love'. It is in fact stated in a noteworthy manner in the Second Vatican Council that peace is not the outcome of any human dictatorship or a balance of power between opposing forces, but is in a true and proper sense the work of justice.[27] Now obviously we cannot here embark upon an attempt to

[26] cf. the conciliar decrees mentioned in nn. 7, 17.

[27] cf. the Pastoral Constitution 'On the Church in the World of Today', No. 78 (Is 32:17: Peace as a 'work of righteousness'; cf. also p. 375 n. 12.).

present a theology of the nature of what is here meant by justice and love considered as the means by which the conflict is to be humanised.[28] This would go beyond the scope and the limitations of the present consideration. Thus only a few indications may be made at this point.

It could in fact be said that peace exists where 'each individual is accorded his due' in justice. Certainly some kind of description of justice could be given by explaining the phrase *suum cuique*, but in that case what is right and fair for 'each individual'? The question still remains, how can we in this one finite sphere of freedom, attain to that equality in which *no one individual* receives less than his due. Justice is constantly in danger of stopping short at the level of an organised egoism, and thereby, once more, providing the occasion for that conflict and war which has to be overcome and humanised. Whereas justice says, in a certain sense: 'to each according to his due', 'Let me have what is mine and you keep what is yours', Christian love says: 'What is mine is yours.'

Now certainly if we wish to remain realistic as Christians we must always keep clearly before our eyes the abiding fact that justice and love are two distinct entities. In this concrete world in which there is a pluralism even of virtues, justice cannot simply be elevated into that love which never counts the cost to itself, and which is self-forgetful in such a way that all the Christian would have to do for everything to be well would be to practise that prodigality, that self-forgetfulness of love, in which he no longer sought to assert any claims on his own behalf. There remains too a pluralism in our Christian attitudes which itself cannot adequately be integrated or elevated into a higher synthesis – for instance precisely that of love. This is a pluralism which, in a true sense, must be endured by the Christian so long as this present age lasts. This sounds terribly abstract, yet it is an extremely practical matter.

Certainly there is and must be that love in the life of the Christian in which he abandons himself, renounces himself, surrenders his own rights, allows his fellow to have his way with him, achieves the folly of powerlessness, and really rises above the level of organised self-interest to the folly of self-abandonment according to the model which God has set before him in Jesus Christ. But Christian love as applied in the concrete in all that plurality which cannot be controlled by man, and which is to be found even in the virtues belonging to man, also means precisely that under certain circumstances it can be not merely a possibility, not merely morally permissible, but an actual duty for man to establish that kind of

[28] On the basic determining factors in the classical concept of justice or righteousness cf. J. Pieper, *Über die Gerechtigkeit* (Munich ³1960). cf. above p. 375, n. 12.

justice which at some specific point precisely does not put into practice the holy foolishness of love, but rather seeks soberly, intelligently and empirically to create conditions in which rights may be distributed between all concerned. This is what is so fearfully difficult and at the same time once more what is utterly realistic and down to earth in this Christian attitude.[29]

If I may so express it, it cannot reduce love to justice. Love is, from the Christian point of view, really something different from the intelligent organisation of human living such that each receives at least a portion from the cake of worldly prosperity. Love is really something more like the element of madness, of the improbable, of that which does not pay, that through which we continue to be the ones who do the paying and in which we let ourselves be exploited.[30] Love is, therefore, something too in which we are bold enough to make experiments – of the kind, for instance, which our politicians are always so frightened of making.

On the other hand, however, we cannot turn Christian living into some kind of marvellous and blessed paroxysm of love in which we strip ourselves of all power. This task of coming to terms with both aspects *for the sake of peace* is one that is incalculable and that changes according to the changes in the particular situation concerned. It is the task of the Christian, and one for which, ultimately speaking, neither the Churches nor the letter of the gospel can supply any readymade or concrete formula. Admittedly the Christian will again and again have to tell himself – in the spirit and meaning of the Sermon on the Mount – that in a true and ultimate sense it is his duty to keep his eyes fixed upon the folly of God on the Cross, and so in all cases of doubt, whether at the individual or personal level, or at the collective and political one, to opt for the folly of love in that situation in human life in which he is placed in concrete history, which makes demands upon him and yet all the time remains ambiguous. And yet so long as the age of this present world lasts justice, so sober, realistic and hard as it seems, and even when it involves the use of power, whether in private or in public life, can precisely be the earthly form in which an extremely selfless love is embodied, which perhaps even for the sake of another may have to find courage enough to appear as though it were devoid of love.

A further point must be added to this: the experience of man shows

---

[29] On how love is related to the other virtues cf. K. Rahner, 'The "Commandment" of Love in Relation to the Other Commandments', *Theological Investigations* V (London and Baltimore 1966), pp. 439–459.

[30] Here we might recall an interpretation of love in the sense of 1 Cor 13.

again and again that mere justice, however strict it may be in not claiming more than its due, always fails, is always reduced to absurdity and, taken by itself, can never provide a basis for peace.

The sphere of freedom open to us in our mode of living becomes ever more restricted and, from the point of view of sociology, ever more complicated systems of dividing it are required. Because of this it will become, in a certain sense, ever less possible to establish solely as an end in itself an ideology by which to divide this sphere of freedom realistically in order to create peace. The world is a place in which all men are, as it were, justified in living and claiming their own due, and in which they actually seek to assert their own sinful egoism. But this world will become more and more the danger area in which a highly explosive mixture is present. And the more we seek to divide this restricted sphere of living in an equable manner the less peace will prevail. Wherever this sphere of human living is growing ever narrower, and wherever a frenzied will to be just asserts itself as an absolute, there naturally and inevitably an ideology will come into force and will proclaim intolerantly and again and again as a fresh message that there is nothing to wish for, no peace and no justice to achieve, unless it yields power and 'right' to a single absolute autonomous totalitarian centre to determine what is due to each individual, and thereby to achieve a just distribution of the one source of prosperity to be found upon earth.

v

Man after all is not an animal, and even in the empirical world belonging to him there is a vital need for that folly and mystery of love. But when he comes to this point the Christian asks how man can really manage, in a manner that is fully justified, to renounce something to which he has a right or at least supposes that he has a right. I know that regrettably I am forced to speak in very abstract terms, but I believe that thereby we really are attaining to a point of central importance. There is much that an individual can renounce simply because, for instance, he wants to be left in peace; because under certain circumstances he may feel that egoism as practised by a group of two or of many is of greater advantage than being egoistical in a more primitive, solipsist or individualistic sense. But in the human living of the individual and also in political and national life moments will arise again and again in which something should be and has to be renounced such that the renouncing of it no longer benefits the renouncer, where, as it were, he feels himself threatened and injured in the most personal claims which he makes upon existence.[31] Precisely in the Protestant theology of the Reformation period great emphasis was laid upon this, and in the Catholic theology of the natural law perhaps too little attention was paid to the fact that here, in these matters, there is a difference – we cannot examine it in greater detail at this point – between the private sphere and the political and national sphere. But in this case the situation is such that we have to entertain that love which is capable of renouncing that which seems to belong to one as a necessity, a necessity of life, and even a necessity of salvation. And the question is what resources man can find within himself really to achieve this.

Among this world's goods I can only as a last resort renounce that which seems to be a necessity of life if I am conscious of being so radically loved by someone that that which is mine is constituted by the infinite fulness of life that is his. Thus, as it were, in him and in his love is to be found the only place in which I can give way and allow my fellow his due within this present world. And this is precisely the point to which any rationally organised and intelligent egoism no longer extends. On the other hand a man cannot, in any true sense, adopt a position of sheer paradox by taking his fellow more seriously than himself,[32] and ultimately speaking he can only take himself and his fellow seriously, and concede something to him which is truly his, if he is conscious that both he and his fellow are already at rest in, and encompassed by the infinite land, in the infinitude of love and freedom, in peace with God. Only then can there no longer be any question of whether I have this or that, whether I am a little more or a little less fortunate, more or less solitary. Here peace with God, his love bestowed in the event of his self-utterance, becomes that which opens the way to and makes possible that other love which is also precisely that which opens the way to peace among men.

Obviously this is not to provide a formula which, if it were applied in this sense, would bring the world once and for all into a condition of peace, that is of a sheer absence of disagreement. In fact all this takes place in a changing history. All this takes place in a synthesis which is ever new, and which has to be discovered in ever different forms, between a love which commits itself and offers itself and a justice which asserts itself even rightly so that under certain circumstances this love can even initiate

---

[31] cf. also in this sense the Pastoral Constitution 'On the Church in the World of Today', No. 79. (Bibliography cf. p. 373, n. 7.)

[32] The problem of 'love of self' cannot be treated of at this point. On this cf. R. Völkl, 'Selbstliebe', *L.T.K.* IX (Freiburg ²1964), 926/927 (with copious bibliographical references).

the use of force or even revolution and a state of 'non-peace'.[33] Thus it can be a correct view that the first duty of the citizen is unrest. All this is possible if love accords justice its right and proper status, confines it within this proper status, and commands it. If the just man is conscious that he can and should be the man who hazards himself and commits himself, the man who dares to make experiments, then this will only be possible in the hope that in this process which is still unfolding – not through the efforts of men but through the deed of God – the kingdom of God is actually present, and in it that peace which surpasses all understanding,[34] a peace which is no longer built upon a synthesis of the kind of which we have been speaking, always unstable, always to be established afresh, or upon a precarious balance of all the elements which constitute human living in the here and now so long as history is still unfolding.

It is obvious that against this background of theological considerations we ought, as men and Christians, to set ourselves to consider specific problems which are necessary in this world as we experience it in the concrete: as a world of hunger, of illiteracy, of atomic bombs, of ever increasing inter-involvement on the part of nations and the histories belonging to them; the world of the technical mastery and the media of communication of the present, of the present needs of man and of the population explosion. It is necessary to consider these specific problems in order thereby to preserve and to establish something at least which holds out some prospect of a tolerable peace.[35] What, therefore, is the final impression which the Christian as he exists in the concrete will receive precisely from the sort of theological considerations set forth above? He

---

[33] It surely does not need to be explicitly demonstrated that in this context a great number of variations is to be found. On the subject itself cf. also p. 376, n. 13.

[34] On the relationship between the kingdom of God, peace and Christ cf. X. Léon-Dufour, *Dictionary of Biblical Theology* (London 1970), pp. 254–258, 312–315, 364–367. On the deeper christological aspects involved cf. K. Rahner, 'Peace on Earth', *Theological Investigations* VII (London and Baltimore 1971), pp. 132–135.

[35] At this point, and precisely in connection with the Council, a whole series of quite concrete measures for peace might be mentioned. cf. the study by B. Drees mentioned on p. 373 n. 7. On the whole cf. also – apart from the studies already cited by C. F. v. Weizsäcker (cf. p. 371 n. 2) – G. Howe, H. E. Tödt, *Frieden im wissenschaftlich-technischen Zeitalter. Ökumenische Theologie und Zivilization* (Stuttgart 1966) and A. Etzioni, *Der harte Weg zum Frieden. Eine neue Strategie* (Göttingen 1965); W. Dirks, 'Erziehung zum Frieden', *Diakonia* 2 (1967), pp. 65–80; *Ist der Weltfriede unvermeidlich?* (C. F. Freiherr's review of Weizsäcker with a discussion appended) = *Bergedorfer Gesprächskreis zu Fragen der freien industriellen Gesellschaft* No. 24 (Hamburg 1966); J. Kuhn ed., *Frieden. Das Abenteuer des Brückenschlags* (Stuttgart 1967).

may think that he can leave them as they were before. He may think that
precisely because he has to be one who loves and serves selflessly, one who
has to work out his own salvation in the concrete reality of his own existence, he must apply himself to the concrete and contemporary questions
regarding peace. And in that case we agree with him. After such theological
considerations the theologian as such once more returns to the ranks and
leaves to Christians as men with concrete human lives to live[36] their due
place and their task which he of course for his part also recognises as his
own.

[36] For this reason the humanity of the Christian as applied in concrete living mani-
fests his will to achieve peace in very varied forms. cf. e.g. R. Schneider, *Gedanken des
Friedens* (Freiburg [5]1957); J. Lasserre, *Der Krieg und das Evangelium* (Munich 1956);
H. Gollwitzer, *Forderungen der Freiheit* (Munich [2]1964); A. Schweitzer, *Friede oder
Atomkrieg?* (Munich 1958); M. Niemöller, *Reden 1958–1961* (Frankfurt 1961);
E. Gross, *Das Geheimnis des Pazifismus* (Stuttgart 1959); C. F. v. Weizsäcker,
'Zumutungen des Friedens', *Streit um den Frieden*, W. Beck, R. Schmid edd.
(Munich/Mainz 1967), pp. 31–52. We should also recall Martin Luther King, the
strivings for peace on the part of Paul VI, the figure of Dag Hammarskjöld and the
'Oppenheimer case', to mention only a few very different strivers for peace. cf. also
U. Miehe (ed.), *Thema Frieden. Zeitgenössische deutsche Gedichte* (Wuppertal 1967).
For a brief orientation cf. J. Beckmann, 'Friede', *Theologie für Nichttheologen* I
(Stuttgart [3]1955), pp. 111–117.

LIST OF SOURCES

THE NEW IMAGE OF THE CHURCH

Delivered as a lecture on 3 January 1966 at Koblenz (The Academy of Theology), on 8 January 1966 at Mülheim/Ruhr (Wolfsburg), on 11 February 1966 at the invitation of the Faculty of Protestant Theology at the University of Tübingen, on 13 February 1966 at a theological conference of the Catholic Academy of Bavaria in Munich, as an invitation lecture to the Philosophical and Theological College of Paderborn on 19 February 1966, on 26 February 1966 at the Institute for Catholic Culture Emmendingen (Baden), on 21 March 1966 at Brussels, on 27 June 1966 at the Loyola Academy in Chicago (USA), on 22 April 1966 at Pforzheim (Institute for Catholic Culture), on 27 June 1966 at the Technical College at Munich (The Society of Catholic Academies), on 27 July 1966 at the first Study Week at Ottobeuren, as one of several invitation lectures delivered during a study course of the Ecumenical Council at Bossey/Geneva from 12 to 16 October 1966, and on 25 October 1966 at Betzdorf (Institute for Catholic Culture). First published in *Geist und Leben* 39 (1966), pp. 4–24 (also published as a special paper).

CHURCH, CHURCHES, AND RELIGIONS

Delivered as a lecture in the course of a conference on the 'Theological Academy' at Cologne on 6 January 1966, and in the Cathedral of Frankfurt on 9 February 1966. Also on 7 January 1966 in Bielefeld. First published in *Theologische Akademie* III, edited by K. Rahner and O. Semmelroth (Frankfurt 1966), pp. 70–87.

ON THE RELATIONSHIP BETWEEN THE POPE AND THE COLLEGE OF BISHOPS

An essay designed for the Festschrift in honour of Archbishop Pietro

Parente (now Pietro, Cardinal Parente), a special number of the Roman periodical, *Euntes Docete.*

THE PRESENCE OF THE LORD IN THE CHRISTIAN COMMUNITY AT WORSHIP

A Latin version was delivered at the 'Congressus Internationalis de Theologia Concilii Vaticani II' at Rome (from 26 September to 1 October 1966). The Acts of the Congress, together with the report in Latin, are appearing very shortly. First published in German in *Die neue Gemeinde,* edited by A. Exeler, *Festschrift für Th. Filthaus zum 60. Geburtstag* (Mainz 1967), pp. 11–22.

ON THE PRESENCE OF CHRIST IN THE DIASPORA COMMUNITY ACCORDING TO THE TEACHING OF THE SECOND VATICAN COUNCIL

Originally prepared as an article for the periodical *Lebendiges Zeugnis,* October 1966 (Vol 2–4); a special volume published as a *Festschrift für Lorenz Cardinal Jaeger zum 25. Bischofsjubiläum* (Paderborn 1966), pp. 32–45.

DIALOGUE IN THE CHURCH

Lecture given at the Fourth Plenary Conference of the Advisory Council on Culture of the Central Committee of the German Catholics at Munich on 2 December 1966. First published in *Stimmen der Zeit* 179 (1967), pp. 81–95

THE SACRAMENT OF PENANCE AS AN ADDITIONAL ACT OF RECONCILIATION WITH THE CHURCH

Originally written as an article for the Festschrift in honour of Alfredo, Cardinal Ottaviani, entitled *Das Volk Gottes. Sein organischer Aufbau im Alten und Neuen Testament* (Rome 1967/68), it then bore the title 'Das Busssakrament als "Versöhnung mit der Kirche" '.

A BRIEF THEOLOGICAL TREATISE ON INDULGENCE

This essay initially appeared under the title 'Über den Ablass' in *Stimmon der Zeit* 156 (1955), pp. 343–355. It was deliberately left almost unaltered (cf. the author's remarks on p. 150f. of this volume) in order to maintain a clear view of the specific position it occupies in the sequence of the author's works on the problems involved in the doctrine of indulgence. The only part to be completely revised was the introduction. The original essay was supplemented by a longer insertion on p. 349, cf. above pp. 157–158 ("We have spoken above . . . left behind") and again an insertion was made on p. 361 of the earlier article, cf. above p. 160 ("The treasury of the Church . . . is precisely not).

All the remaining alterations affect merely the style and method of subdividing the article as a whole.

THE CURRENT OFFICIAL TEACHING OF THE CHURCH ON THE DOCTRINE OF INDULGENCE

This study was initially composed for a second edition of the volume published in Italian and entitled *La penitenza della chiesa. Saggi teologici e storici* (Rome 1964, 2nd ed. 1968). Here the works by the author on both the history and the systematic theology of the doctrine of penance and indulgence are assembled. Apart from being intended as an 'apologia' for the author's own position, this article is also intended to contribute towards an analysis of the Constitution on Indulgence by Pope Paul VI of 1 January 1967. First published in German in *Catholica* 21 (1967) Vol 4.

MARRIAGE AS A SACRAMENT

A lecture given at the invitation of the advisory committee on education of the Catholic Action Movement of the Archdiocese of Vienna on 7 March 1967 in the Great Hall of Music at Vienna. First published in *Geist und Leben* 40 (1967), pp. 177–193.

THE TEACHING OF THE SECOND VATICAN COUNCIL ON THE DIACONATE

The present brief essay is the outcome of a lecture which the author delivered (as a free version from notes) at the International Conference of Studies, 'The Deacon in the Church and in the World of Today' at Rome (22 to 24 October 1965). All that the author had in mind here was to give a presentation of 'The Teaching of the Second Vatican Council on the

Diaconate'. This explains the restricted subject-matter of the present article. First published in German under the above title in *Der Seelsorger* 36 (1966), pp. 193–199. The account of the conference as a whole has been published under the editorship of P. Winniger and Y. Congar in *Le diacre dans l'église et le monde d'aujourd'hui* = *Unam Sanctam* 59 (Paris 1966). A more comprehensive account in *German* of the conference held by the International Association for the Diaconate (Freiburg in Breisgau) is to be found in Vol II (1966) of *Diakonia* (= *Dokumentation des Internationalen Informationszentrums für Fragen des Diakonates*).

A FRAGMENTARY ASPECT OF A THEOLOGICAL EVALUATION OF THE CONCEPT OF THE FUTURE

The published excerpt constitutes the first part of a paper entitled 'Das Christentum und die Zukunft' which the author read on 11 September 1966 at the *Darmstädter Gespräch 1966*: 'Der Mensch und seine Zukunft', first published in *Darmstädter Gespräch. Der Mensch und seiner Zukunft*, edited by Professor Dr E. Schlechta (Darmstadt 1967), pp. 149–160. The other parts of the lecture delivered at Darmstadt are in substance equivalent to the article already published at an earlier stage under the title 'Marxist Utopia and the Christian Future of Man' in *Theological Investigations VI* (London and Baltimore 1969), pp. 59–68.

ON THE THEOLOGY OF HOPE

An initial version was delivered as a lecture on 6 March 1967 to the Association of Higher Studies at Graz, and on 8 March 1967 to the Association of Higher Studies at Vienna. Besides this an English Version was given in October 1967 at several universities in the course of a journey through the United States. The article appeared in revised and expanded form in the first number of an International Periodical published by Verlag Herder (Freiburg) in 1968 and entitled *Internationale Zeitschrift für das Gespräch zwischen den verschiedenen Humanismen*, edited by Karl Rahner and Herbert Vorgrimler (the latter also being the chief editor).

ON THE THEOLOGICAL PROBLEMS ENTAILED IN THE IDEA OF THE NEW 'EARTH'

Initially composed for a symposium volume, *Knowledge and the Future of the Man*, edited by W. J. Ong (Verlag Holt, Rinehart and Winston,

New York 1968) on the occasion of the 150th anniversary of the St Louis University (USA). Delivered as a lecture several times at American Universities in the course of October 1967. First published in German under the title, 'Mitarbeit an der Neuen Erde', *Neues Forum* 14 (1967), pp. 683–687.

IMMANENT AND TRANSCENDENT CONSUMMATION OF THE WORLD

A lecture delivered at the annual conference of the Institute of the Görres Society for Achieving an Encounter Between Natural Science and Theology held at Feldafing (Starnberger See) on 21 September 1966. At the same time it was designed for publication, together with the ensuing discussion, in the Report of the Conference of the Society (Verlag Alber, Freiburg 1968).

ON THE THEOLOGICAL PROBLEMS ENTAILED IN A 'PASTORAL CONSTITUTION'

Composed for the commentary which appeared in Dutch entitled *Schema dertien. Tekst en commentaar* (in collaboration with J.-Y. Calvez, N. D. Chenu, K. Rahner, E. Schillebeeckx etc.) = *Vaticanum* 2. No. 2: *De kerk in de wereld van deze tijd* (Verlag Paul Brand, Hilversum/Antwerp 1967), pp. 315–336. First published in German in *Volk Gottes. Festgabe für Josef Höfer*, edited by R. Bäumer and H. Dolch (Freiburg 1967), pp. 683–703.

THEOLOGICAL REFLECTIONS ON THE PHENOMENON OF SECULARISATION

Lecture at the Congress on the Theology of the Renewal of the Church (20–25 August 1967) at Toronto (Canada). It was repeated at the invitation of the Institute for Catholic Education at Salzburg on 26 September 1967, and at the Conference of Academics of the Diocese of Hildesheim at Hanover on 22 November 1967. First published in the Acta of the Congress.

PRACTICAL THEOLOGY AND SOCIAL WORK IN THE CHURCH

Delivered as a festival lecture on 13 June 1967 at the General Assembly of the Swiss Caritas Association at Lucerne. First published in *Caritas. Zeitschrift des Schweizerischen Caritasverbances* 45 (1967).

THE PEACE OF GOD AND THE PEACE OF THE WORLD

Lecture at a Conference for the Directors of Colleges of Advanced Engineering held by student chaplains and industrial chaplains of the *Evangelische Landeskirche* at Württemberg in September 1966 in the *Evangelische Akademie Tutzing*. The original lecture was delivered freely from notes and recorded. Subsequently it underwent several revisions and expansions, and was supplemented with notes. First published in the Report of the Conference edited by W. Beck and R. Schmid, and entitled *Streit um den Frieden* (Munich and Mainz 1967), pp. 64–85.

In the list of sources given above no mention has been made of a number of excerpts or special papers which were printed in German. Broadcast talks are mentioned only when the article concerned was specially written for these. Nor has there been any special mention of the numerous translations which have been made. Only the work in which they were initially published is mentioned, whether this was in German or in a foreign language.

INDEX OF PERSONS

SUBJECT INDEX

Absolute Future:
God as our 245 ff., 257 f., 259, 272, 278, 288, 321
Absolution 125, 130, 131, 132, 134, 137, 143 f., 174
Adam:
the marriage of 219
Ad Gentes Divinitus Missa 225, 226
Affectus erga Peccatum 184, 185
Agape 377
Agon in human life 344 f.
Anamnesis 77, 78, 99
Angels 285
Anointing of the sick 68, 178
Anonymous Christianity 16, 17, 20, 21, 22, 83, 204, 205, 262, 271, 319, 365
Anthropology 279
Anthropomorphism 286
Anti-ideological realism of Christianity, the 379 f., 382
Anti-Modernists 322
Apocapyptic 269
Apologetics 96
Apostles 126, 231; see also 'Twelve'
Apostolic Constitution on Indulgence, the 166 ff.:
anonymous commentary upon 169 n. 8
Art, religious 108
Asceticism 156
Assistance 'active' and 'passive' 216 n. 33
Atheism, atheist 48, 49, 204, 205, 260, 319, 320
Atomic bomb 387
Authority 26, 27 f., 29, 31 f., 41, 42, 50 ff., 60, 64, 75, 78, 93 n. 18, 107, 110–112, 114, 118–119, 120, 121, 173, 217 n. 33, 227, 231, 262, 293 ff., 295 ff., 327, 329, 335, 357, 381 f.

Baptism 25, 133, 140, 213, 215:
differing from penance 134 n. 50, 136 n. 55, 147, 155
seal of 137

effects of 154, 155
as conferred by lay persons 217 n. 33
as conferred by deacons 224, 226
Beatific vision 283
Beatitude 252
Biblical theology 87, 88 n. 7, 108, 117, 135 n. 50, 218 f., 242
Binding and loosing, power of 134 n. 50, 135, 138, 139, 142 144 ff., 148, 162, 171 n. 11
Birth control 120 n. 19
Bishops 50 ff.:
functions of 85, 89, 115 f., 117, 120, 224
laying on of hands by 136
regional conferences of 69, 114, 227 ff.
in relation to the pope 50 ff.
threefold function of 224 ff.
Brotherhood of man, universal 264 f.
Burial 225 f.

Canonical form of marriage 217 n. 33
Canonical penance 163
Canon Law 67, 107, 131, 133–134, 203, 213, 337
Caritas:
movement, the 302
as a science 352, 353, 354
as social work 351 ff., 356, 358, 360, 369 f.
as a subject of practical theology 351 ff.
in the theological sense 355, 357
as a theological virtue 206
Catechism 199, 218
Catechists 225 f.
Celibacy 223, 228–229
'Chain reaction' of forces in human living 365–366
Character, sacramental 140 f.
Charism 28, 113, 114, 305 ff., 307, 310, 313, 359:
as extended to the Church's officials 306 ff., 308

399

'New earth':
    concept of 260 ff. *passim*, 285
    as the eschatological gift of God
        265–266
New Testament 135, 206, 246, 378
Nineteenth Century, attitude of the
    Church to the world during 107
Non-Catholic Christians, marriages
    between 216 f. n. 33
Non-Catholic Churches 3, 12, 30 ff., 40,
    41, 42, 44, 45, 101, 112–113, 167:
    attitude of to indulgences 150 f.; see
    also Lutheran theology of indul-
    gence
Non-Christians 3, 12, 14, 38 ff., 45, 46,
    47, 48, 106, 112–113, 205, 260 ff., 271,
    352
Norms, doctrinal, juridical or moral:
    in contrast to 'instructions' 296 ff.,
        303 f., 307
Numinous 320

Oecumenism 87, 197, 216 n. 33, 369
Official Church, the 262 f., 327 f., 335,
    360; see also Officials of the Church
Officials of the Church 27, 50 ff., 66, 67,
    79, 110–112, 113, 114, 119, 121, 135,
    262 ff., 306, 312, 329, 336, 351, 359
Official pronouncements of the Church;
    see teaching, official, of the Church
Old Covenant 312
Old Testament, ethics of, 135, 206, 378
Opportunism 227 f., 229
Opus operantis, operatum 81, 82, 176 n.
    18, 178, 179, 180, 194, 202, 214, 215
Ordained ministers, threefold function
    of 224 f.
Orders, Holy 223, 224 f., 230 f., 306 n. 13
Ordinary Magisterium, the 166, 169 n. 7
Original sin 120 n. 19, 284, 378
Our Father the 162

Pacifism and theology 373
Pacem in terris, encyclical 333
Paenitentia interior 141, 144 ff., 147 n. 96,
    181–182 n. 31
Parousia 40
Pastor, pastoral 26, 27, 50 ff., 85, 89, 100,
    105–106, 110–112, 229, 330, 333 f.,
    337 ff.
Pastoral Constitution on the Church in
    the Modern World 3, 12, 94 n. 21,
    96 n. 23, 112 n. 10, 260, 261, 262 n. 2,

263, 267, 271, 283 n. 5, 293 ff. *passim*,
    295 ff., 310, 313, 315, 316, 330, 333 f.,
    339, 340, 344, 349, 352, 373 n. 7, 382
    n. 27, 386 n. 31
Pastoral constitution, nature of a 293 ff.,
    307, 311 f., 313 ff., 315
Pastoral, meaning of the term, 294, 302,
    313, 366
Pastoral office of the Church, the 295 ff.,
    301, 310 ff., 314:
    three functions included in 294
Pastoral theology 6, 337 ff.
Pastor Hermae 137
Paternalism 117
Paul 10, 18, 19, 88, 96, 218 f., 220, 247,
    250, 259, 283, 289
Pax of reconciliation 125, 127, 133, 136,
    138, 140, 141, 147, 148
Peace 371 ff. *passim*:
    anti-Christian ideology of 372
    the biblical concept of 378 f.
    as 'the order of justice' 375
    in relation to theology 379 f.
    as a theological phenomenon 375 ff.
    various kinds of 371 f.
Penance, the sacrament of 125 ff.
    passim, 367:
    different from baptism 155
    in the early Church 136
    from excommunication 134
    greater union with God achieved in
        189
    judicial power involved in 134 n. 50,
        162, 174
    liturgical and canonical form of 137,
        147, 161, 162
    in the Middle Ages 127, 136, 137,
        141 ff., 147 n. 97
    in Patristic times 127, 137
    penances imposed in 163, 165, 171 n. 11
    tradition of from the Fathers 154
'Perdition history' 36 f., 48, 49, 275,
    276–277, 322
People of God 284; see also Church as
    people of God on pilgrimage
Peter:
    position of in relation to the 'Twelve'
        56 f., 61, 65
    power of the keys of 135
Planning the future 235 ff., 239–240,
    257, 271, 361:
    as completing the work of creation
        265 ff.